DOROTHY DAY
AND THE CHURCH

DOROTHY DAY
and THE CHURCH
Past, Present, & Future

*A conference held at
the University of Saint Francis,
Fort Wayne, Indiana,
May 13–15, 2015*

Edited by **Lance Richey, Ph.D.
& Adam DeVille, Ph.D.**

Publishing Team

University of St. Francis
 co-editor Lance Richey
 co-editor Adam DeVille

Solidarity Hall
 publisher Elias Crim
 production Paul Bowman

To Dorothy

Acknowledgments

These proceedings, and the conference which they record, could not have occurred without the assistance of many persons and multiple organizations. It would be impossible to acknowledge them all individually here. However, justice demands that we mention some individuals whose work was absolutely indispensable.

The University of Saint Francis, under the leadership of Sr. Elise Kriss, OSF, not only agreed to sponsor and host the conference, "Dorothy Day and the Church: Past, Present and Future" in May 2015, but was exceptionally generous in sharing its facilities, resources and personnel to insure that the conference was a success and our attendees were well cared for. In particular, the Conference Planning Task Force, very ably led by Tricia Bugajski, included Lynne McKenna Frazier, Maureen McCon, and Jean Elick. Likewise, Matthew Smith, Trois Hart, and Alexandra Ellis Kreager were especially important for planning key elements of the conference banquet and promoting it both locally and nationally. However, nothing could have occurred without the countless faculty and staff from across the institution who gave of their time and energy over a very long period because they came to understand and share the vision and values of Dorothy Day (which so closely resemble those of Saints Francis and Clare, our patrons). We should also thank the many spouses and significant others who bore with the stresses and enforced absences which the conference entailed for these people.

We are especially grateful to the Our Sunday Visitor Institute, co-sponsor of the conference, for its generous financial support of both the event and this volume. In a particular way we thank Greg Erlandson, publisher of Our Sunday Visitor, for his multifaceted assistance throughout the conception, planning, and realization of the conference.

Elias Crim and the entire staff of Solidarity Hall Press have been tireless in helping bring this volume to completion. Phil Runkel, curator of the Dorothy Day Archives at Marquette University, generously shared photographs and other historical materials which greatly enriched both the conference and the present volume.

We would also like to express our sincere gratitude to the keynote speakers, special guests, and homilists at the conference (not all of whom are represented in this volume for various reasons). These include Bishop Kevin C. Rhoades of Fort Wayne-South Bend, who gave both his blessing and active support to our conference; Archbishop José H. Gomez of Los Angeles; Archbishop Joseph W. Tobin of Indianapolis; Robert Ellsberg; Martha Hennessy; Kathryn Jean Lopez; Brandon Vogt; and Tom and Monica Cornell. In addition, Claudia Larson generously shared her outstanding documentary, *Dorothy Day: Don't Call Me A Saint* (www.dorothydaydoc.com), with the University of Saint Francis community and our conference attendees.

Finally, we wish to thank the attendees of the conference, including those whose work is represented here. Their scholarship, spirit of camaraderie, and living witness to the values and vision of Dorothy Day are a great gift to the Church and world, and a constant reminder of that love to which we are all called by the gospel.

Contents

THE PERSONALISM OF DOROTHY DAY AND
THE CATHOLIC WORKER

DOROTHY DAY
AND THE CHURCH

FRITZ KAESER

Reflections on Dorothy Day

Feast of Saint Matthias, 14 May 2015: Dorothy Day Conference Mass

Bishop Kevin Rhoades

Today we celebrate the feast of Saint Matthias, the apostle chosen to replace Judas, as we heard in the reading from the Acts of the Apostles. Matthias is not mentioned anywhere else in the New Testament, so we know very little about him. We do know that he was suited for apostleship because of his experience of being with Jesus from His baptism to His ascension, as Acts tells us. He must also have been suited personally or he would not have been considered and nominated for so great a responsibility. Perhaps the gospel today can help us to see what made him suitable, indeed, what makes us suitable for discipleship and the apostolate.

First and foremost, discipleship involves remaining in Jesus' love. This is what Jesus said to the disciples in His farewell discourse: *Remain in my love.* Jesus and the apostles shared an intimate friendship. Jesus told them that He no longer calls them *slaves* but He calls them *friends*. As He prepares to take leave from them, Jesus asks the apostles to remain in His love, in His friendship. This entails keeping His commandments: *If you keep my commandments, you will remain in my love.* And Jesus gives them the new commandment: *love one another as I have loved you.*

It's all very simple when we think about it. *Remain in my love.* That's the essence of the Christian life, together with the command: *Love one another as I have loved you.* Dorothy Day understood this. With her conversion, she became a true friend of the Lord who, through a devoted prayer life, learned to remain in His love. She understood, of course, that this love for God could not be separated from love of neighbor, especially the poor and destitute. I think of her powerful and challenging words: *I really only love God as much as I love the person I love the least.*

9

Dorothy Day desired to change the world. She and fellow members of Catholic Worker fought for the rights of workers and the poor. In the midst of this battle for justice, she said, *there is nothing we can do but love, and, dear God, please enlarge our hearts to love each other, to love our neighbor, to love our enemy as our friend.*

We can learn so much from the words and example of Dorothy Day. She challenges us with the radical truth of the gospel. She challenges us to love one another as Christ has loved us. She challenges us, as Pope Francis challenges us, to be a Church of and for the poor. They challenge us with the words of Jesus in the parable about the last judgment: "whatsoever you do the least of my brothers and sisters, you do to me." In her typically incisive way, Dorothy Day wrote that "those who cannot see Christ in the poor are atheists indeed."

Pope Francis is very critical of a Church that is egocentric, that is a "self-referential Church" turned in on itself. He is calling us to go out from our comfort zone in order to reach all the peripheries in need of the light of the gospel. This is what Dorothy Day did. At the same time, Dorothy Day and Pope Francis do not mean that we rush out aimlessly into the world. We go out with a mission, a clear mission, the proclamation of the gospel of Christ, the gospel that invites us to respond to the love of the God who saves us.

Dorothy Day's life was anchored in the Word of God and in the Eucharist. The Word and the Mass strengthened and nourished her. She experienced the Eucharist as the sacrament of love, the mystery of the cross made present, the most amazing encounter we can have with God on this earth.

Dorothy Day teaches us that Christianity isn't about embracing abstractions. It's about living the cross. Dorothy Day would quote the words of Dostoevsky: *Love in action is a harsh and dreadful thing compared with love in dreams.* Think of the saints: they were men and women who embodied the gospel. They didn't just talk about it in lofty language. When they saw the hungry, they gave them food. When they saw the suffering, they helped them. This is our vocation as well. As Dorothy Day wrote, *everything a baptized person does every day should be directly or indirectly related to the corporal and spiritual works of mercy.* We are called to sanctity: the perfection of charity, to love God and neighbor, and to love one another as Christ has loved us. Encountering a multitude of challenges in her life and efforts, Dorothy Day kept this at the center: love of God and neighbor. She wrote that *love and ever more love is the only solution to every problem that comes up.*

When we think of Dorothy Day or of the lives of the saints, we should realize that they were not born perfect and they had their weaknesses. But they lived their lives with passion and purpose. What animated their lives was that *they recognized God's love and they followed it with all their heart without reserve or hypocrisy. They spent their lives serving others, they endured suffering and adversity without hatred and responded to evil with good, spreading joy and peace* (Pope Francis, November 1, 2013). This is our calling too. And here at this altar, we see and we experience the epitome of such love, the sacrifice of Jesus. We hear anew the words of Jesus and the real truth of those words: *No one has greater love than this, to lay down one's life for one's friends.* And yes, we truly are His friends if we do what He commands us, which is really to live the Eucharist we celebrate and receive.

The Most Reverend Kevin C. Rhoades is Bishop of the Roman Catholic Diocese of Fort Wayne–South Bend, Indiana.

A Time for Saints:
Reflections on Dorothy Day,
an Apostle to America

Archbishop José H. Gomez

Introduction and Two Caveats

It's a joy to be with you all. I was honored to be invited to give this address—and I'm happy to see so many of you here tonight who want to talk about the Servant of God Dorothy Day.

Let me begin with a short disclaimer: I don't know if Dorothy Day is a saint. That's for the Church to decide. But what I do know is that she makes *me* want to be a saint. And I know a lot of people feel the same way—including some of you, probably.

There's just something about Dorothy Day. When we read her writings, when we reflect on her life, something stirs in our hearts. She makes us want to be better, she makes us want to be holy. When she tells us that we are all *called to be saints*, we believe we can do it and we want to!

We all know the story of her pilgrimage and the "long loneliness" that led her "from Union Square to Rome," from the sins of her "flaming youth" to the tender mercies of God and what she called "the downward path which leads to salvation."[1] That journey of her life is one of the great conversion stories of modern times. Her life reads like the life of a saint. And it reads that way because Dorothy was one of the most gifted writers in Church history. She wrote her life story not only for herself, but also for us, as she frankly acknowledged in one of her diaries: "Reason for writing: to bring news to others of an inner world."[2] That's what she was doing, day in and day out, year after year, for decades. She

---

1 *House of Hospitality* (Huntington, Indiana: Our Sunday Visitor, 2015), 283.
2 Robert Ellsberg, ed., *The Duty of Delight: The Diaries of Dorothy Day* (New York: Image, 2011), 232, 567.

was writing the interior history of our times, the spiritual diary of the twentieth century.

Now before I go any further, I should clarify something. I'm not a scholar of Dorothy Day. I know many of you in the room tonight are. The program for this conference is impressive, and I have to say it's a little intimidating, too.

I come to Dorothy Day's life from a different angle. I come to her from the perspective of a pastor, a priest—one who is entrusted with the care of souls. What fascinates me is the movement of her soul, the ways we see God's hand at work in her life.

Over the years, people have paid a lot of attention to Dorothy Day's radical witness in the Church, her prophetic critique of capitalism and war, and her vision of creating a new social order within the "shell of the old." These are all important points to consider, but more than any of them what really marks Dorothy Day's life is that she *walked with the saints*. The great saints in Church history—like St. Francis, Thérèse of Lisieux, John of the Cross, Teresa of Avila, Catherine of Sienna and many others—were her constant companions; her friends, teachers and intercessors. In fact, she once said she spent her days in conversation with Jesus and the saints of the Church: "There are days when I've not talked much to anyone who is alive, but I've talked plenty to people who once were alive and now have departed for the sight of God."[3] For Dorothy Day, the saints were the real agents of human history, men and women who truly changed the times they lived in. She often said we should study history through the lives of the saints. "The beauty of holiness shines out through the saints and illumines history," she believed.[4]

So that's what I want to try to do this evening: to offer some pastoral reflections on our times and our country—this moment in the life of the Church in America—as we see it through the eyes of Dorothy Day. As I said, I don't know whether she is a saint or not. Only the Church can decide, only God can tell us. But it's clear to me that Dorothy wanted to "think" like a saint and live like a saint. And I believe that what she has left us—the legacy of her writings and her life—is a saint's vision of our times and our society. So let us talk about her vision this evening, beginning with her conversion story and moving on to consider her vision for how we should disciples in our society.

3   Robert Coles, *Dorothy Day: A Radical Devotion* (Boston: Da Capo, 1989), 143.
4   *Duty of Delight*, 414, 486; Robert Ellsberg, ed., *All the Way to Heaven: The Selected Letters of Dorothy Day* (New York: Image, 2012), 382.

Dorothy Day's Conversion and the Story of the 20th Century

Dorothy Day's conversion story is the story of her soul. But it's also the story of her generation and the story of the last century. Her life spanned the century. She was born almost at the century's dawn, in 1897. And she died at the century's first twilight in 1980.

Let us for a moment reflect on those years before her conversion—all the people she met and worked with, all the various "causes" she was involved in: writing for the nation's largest communist newspaper; doing propaganda work for communist revolutionaries in Latin America; getting arrested in a women's suffrage protest at the White House and being sentenced to solitary confinement. These are just a few of her experiences, as you know.

But consider another one, perhaps even more "scandalous" than the above in the eyes of some people: the oldest surviving letter that we have from Dorothy is from 1923. It's a letter she wrote to Margaret Sanger, the eugenicist and founder of Planned Parenthood. In the letter, Dorothy is trying to get a job with Sanger as a public relations director![5]

In all these years and activities, Dorothy describes herself as a *seeker*, a young woman looking for answers. She said all her life she was always asking *why*. Why are we here? Where are going? What does it all mean?[6] Of course, she knew that these are the great questions of religion and life, the questions we are all born asking ourselves: What am I doing in this world? What happens when I die? How should I live? What path should I follow to find happiness? How can I be certain?

I believe Dorothy wrote her account of these early years so that we could see that her whole life was made to pass through the movements and currents that shaped the culture and society of twentieth-century America. She wrote so we could see how she lost her way—and how many others lost their way in her generation, too.

Many of her contemporaries were taken in by promises of "free love," birth control and abortion for the poor, seeking the world revolution of the proletariat. Dorothy and many others thought they had found the "answers" they were looking for in the "progressive" vision of a society liberated from Christian morality and the capitalist economy. But, of course, we know that following this path caused her great pain, including the tragedy of her abortion in 1919, a de-

5   *All the Way to Heaven,* 23.
6   *A Radical Devotion,* 23, 62–63.

cade before her conversion to Catholicism. [7]

If Dorothy Day is canonized, she will be the only woman in the communion of saints to have ever written about having an abortion. But it's important for us to remember that Dorothy Day's experience of the horror of abortion was *not* what brought her to conversion. It was *not* the experience of violence and death, but rather the experience of love and goodness that brought her to God.

As she described it, the beauty of the created world convinced her that there must be a Creator. The joy of human love helped her to realize the beauty of divine love. Ultimately, it was the experience of giving birth to her daughter that made her understand the transcendent dignity and destiny of the human person. In the glory of childbirth, she came to see that God made every one us in his own image and likeness—to share in his divine nature; to be his friends and partners in the creation of life and the redemption of the world.

This is one of my favorite quotations from Dorothy about the birth of her beloved daughter, Tamar:

> I was supremely happy. If I had written the greatest book, composed the greatest symphony, painted the most beautiful painting or carved the most exquisite figure, I could not have felt more the exalted creator than I did when they placed my child in my arms. To think that this thing of beauty...had come from my flesh, was my own child. Such a great feeling of happiness and joy filled me that I was hungry for Someone to thank, to love, even to worship for so great a good that had been bestowed upon me! [8]

Thus we see that Dorothy Day was a convert to love! She came to see that her life—and all our lives—are a search for love, a search for a love that is God. Through her long, lonely journey, she came to understand that we are all born with hearts that are restless for love, restless for God. She came to understand that God made us to love and to be loved. That we are made to give ourselves to some*thing*, to some*body*. And of course, she came to know that this "Somebody" we are all looking for is God.

Dorothy Day wrote her conversion story to teach us a spiritual lesson about our century. It was a hard lesson that she learned through her own suffering.

---

7   Dorothy Day, *The Eleventh Virgin* (Chicago: Cottager, 2011), 303–317.
8   Dorothy Day, *Therese* (Springfield, Illinois: Templegate, 1979), v–vi.

But through her own example, she wanted to show us the temptations of our secular age—and consequences of trying to live without God, trying to live apart from God's design for human life and creation.

How Can We Live in a Society without God?

Now, I believe Dorothy's insights are significant and relevant to us in the Church. The movements and ideologies that she passed through in her century were the seeds for the culture and society we find ourselves living in today. For example, I think we all recognize that the America we live in today has grown radically "de-Christianized" and secularized. More and more, our society functions as if God does not exist and as if religious faith and morality are irrelevant to the concerns of our life together. From this, I expect that we are going to see more and more hostility toward Christian institutions and the expression of Christian beliefs in the years to come. Already we see pressures on believers to accept ways of thinking and acting that are contrary to Christian faith and moral teaching. Already we see our government trying to dictate how the Church operates in serving the poor, the immigrant and the refugee.

So the question we all face is basic and stark: How do we continue to live as Christians in a society that no longer has any room for Christ or for God? This is the challenge I face every day as a Church leader. And it's a challenge that each one of you faces in your own lives. This question goes to the heart of how you live, how you work, how you raise your families.

What's at stake for all of us is the future of the Church's mission. Jesus called the Church to evangelize the world, to spread the good news of God's mercy and love to the ends of the earth. How are we going to carry out that mission in our time and in our society? What does our mission even mean, in a world without God?

Here is where the witness and writings of Dorothy Day are so important. Dorothy Day gives us a powerful vision for how to live in our secular society. And she believed the only answer was to raise up a new generation of saints. As early as the 1950s she saw where we were headed and advised that "the greatest danger of our age is secularism [and] it would seem that it is a time when we must beg God to raise up for our time men in whom saint and hero meet to solve the problems of the day. And not by war!"[9]

Her vision reminds me a lot of Pope Francis. Like the Pope, she calls us to

9   *Catholic Worker* (January 1953).

be *missionary disciples.* She used different language. She spoke of "saint-revolu-tionists," men and women who practiced what she called "heroic charity." But just like Pope Francis, for her, everything was rooted in the encounter with Jesus Christ.

In other words, we need to remember that Day was not converted by an idea or even the teachings of the Church. Those did not convince her to leave the past behind and change her life. Instead, she was changed by Love, changed by the over-powering awareness of the reality of God's love and mercy. As she recounts in one of my favorite stories, she woke in the middle of the night far from home and ready to weep for the sense that her efforts were futile. And then she had a revelation. She wrote:

> And suddenly the thought came to me of my importance as a daughter of God, daughter of a King, and I felt a sureness of God's love. . . . God so loved me that he gave his only begotten son. "If a mother will forget her children, never will I forget thee." Such tenderness. [10]

For her, that love and tenderness could only come from a personal, living God, as she flatly insists:

> I believe in a personal God. I believe in Jesus Christ, true God and true man. And intimate, oh how most closely intimate we may desire to be, I believe we must render most reverent hom-age to him who created us and stilled the sea and told the winds to be calm, and multiplied the loaves and fishes. He is transcen-dent and he is immanent. He is closer than the air we breathe and just as vital to us. [11]

What a beautiful statement of faith! In order for us to live in this society, we need to strive for this same deep, intimate relationship with Jesus Christ. But we cannot stop there: we have to bring others to this relationship, too. We have a duty to be missionaries—to bring everyone we meet to this encounter with the living God.

And "everyone" means *everyone:* Dorothy said we are here to bear witness to

10 Dorothy Day, *On Pilgrimage* (Grand Rapids, Michigan: Eerdmans), 197.
11 *Catholic Worker* (March 1966).

Jesus and to follow his lead even into the "peripheries"[12] (to use a favorite word of Pope Francis). She sought Christ's face among those living in the margins and dark corners of society—in the poor and discarded, the lonely and forgotten.

But not all of us are called to such a radical witness, to literally live among the poor. Dorothy Day didn't think so, either. But she did teach that all of us *are* called to take personal responsibility to care for the poor and vulnerable. Our faith in Christ means we must see Christ and serve Christ in others.

We need to feel the passion that Dorothy Day had for the Incarnation! We need to ponder the humanity of Christ—how he shared in our hungers, our loneliness, our joys and struggles. Dorothy Day helps us to see that Jesus made the works of mercy the way for every Christian. She told us over and over what Jesus said—that in the evening of our lives, our love for God will be judged by the mercy we have shown to others—especially those who are the most vulnerable, those who cannot defend themselves.

Dorothy Day took those words to heart, and so should we. If we do so, then we will fulfill both the needs of our time—as she did—and also our own vocation to holiness:

> There is room for greater saints now than ever before. Never has the world been so organized—press, radio, education, recreation, to turn minds away from Christ.... We are all called to be saints. God expects something from each one of us that no one else can do. If we don't, it will not be done.[13]

The Most Reverend José H. Gomez is Archbishop of the Roman Catholic Archdiocese of Los Angeles, California.

12 *A Radical Devotion*, 97.

13 William D. Miller, ed. *All Is Grace: The Spirituality of Dorothy Day* (Garden City, New York: Doubleday, 1987), 102.

Spiritual and Liturgical
Influences on Dorothy Day

another to greater sanctity, I chose to focus upon Day as an example of one from our time who, like the sinful Levi, was touched by God's ineffable grace through a heavenly agent and did not vacillate in her commitment to serve the poor, voluntarily living a life of true Christian poverty.[6]

There are numerous examples of conversion in the New Testament (e.g. Jesus' healing of an official's son, Jn. 4:46–54; the conversion of Saul of Tarsus, Acts 9:1–19; and to a lesser extent, Jesus' healing of the centurion's servant, Mt. 8:5–13); however, I have chosen to focus upon the call of Matthew because it represents the *causa prima*, or the first cause, which influences other causes throughout our shared history.[7] With the words, "follow me" (Mt. 9:9), Jesus issues a call for conversion, which Levi/Matthew instantly agrees with, and adheres to, without question.

Day also adhered to the call of Christ without wavering, serving the poor and marginalized for the remainder of her post-conversion life to Catholicism, which occurred on December 29, 1927.[8] Her total commitment to the poor can only be viewed as radical obedience to the Beatitudes, and the Sermon on the Mount, born out of love for God as the human other. Day, however, did not experience conversion as instantaneously as Levi did. Her *metanoia* came from a variety of lived experiences which occurred over an extended period of time, involving a number of saints and saintly agents of change. Day could relate very well to each of Lonergan's methods of conversion.

---

6   In the early 1940s, Day had constant thoughts of removing herself from the daily operations of *The Catholic Worker*, but dismissed these ideas as mere temptations. In September of 1943, Day announced that, as an act of humility, she was taking a one-year's leave of absence from the Worker movement in order to more fully explore the "weapons of the spirit" as part of her involvement as an Oblate of St. Benedict. Day did intend to contribute articles for the newspaper, and finish her biography of Peter Maurin. However, within six months of her sabbatical, Day returned to the helm as the leader of daily operations, as there must have been something about her vow of voluntary poverty that constituted a greater calling. See Dorothy Day, "Day After Day," in *The Catholic Worker* (September 1943): 1, 2, 6.

7   For a greater definition of causality, see Gerald O'Collins and Edward G. Farrugia, *A Concise Dictionary of Theology*, revised and expanded edition (Mahwah, New Jersey: Paulist, 2000), 36–37.

8   To put dates into a broader perspective, Tamar Therese Day was born on March 4, 1926, and baptized in July of 1927. Day made her first confession, and was baptized conditionally into the Roman Catholic Church on December 29, 1927. On December 30, 1927, she received Holy Communion for the first time. Day was confirmed about a year later, although the precise date is unknown.

Lonergan's Methods of Conversion

In his *Method in Theology*, Lonergan defined three modes of conversion (i.e. intellectual, moral, and religious), the impetus of which can be seen in Scripture through the call of Levi,[9] a most sinful man who is immediately moved by the example of Jesus Christ and whose witness would inspire a myriad of others to follow in his footsteps. When questioned by the Pharisees as to the reason for conversing with a man considered both ritually and spiritually unclean, Jesus responded bluntly with "I have come to call not the righteous but sinners" (Mt. 9:13).

Lonergan noted three methods of conversion, which are of an intellectual, moral, and religious nature. He further viewed conversion as the total transcendence of the self, where one's movement into a new realm of consciousness brings forth radical transformation. Conversion under this mindset is a gift of God's grace, which brings about continual growth and change. Such advancement of the person is how Lonergan defined conversion.[10]

Intellectual conversion relates to truth attained by perceived, cognitional self-transcendence. Moral conversion relates to values apprehended, affirmed, and realized by an actual self-transcendence. Religious conversion relates to a radical "being-in-love" which affects all self-transcendence, "whether in the pursuit of truth, or in the realization of human values, or in the orientation man adopts to the universe, its ground, and its goal."[11] Conversion, then, involves change towards an ultimate truth which is absolute, and attainable in one's transformation from one realm to another.

By analogy, Lonergan's notions of conversion can be equated to a sinful human being who enters a room, and experiences a brief encounter with the transcendent reality which is God. The sinful individual is transformed in a certain way (i.e., they experience an intellectual, moral, or religious conversion). Although the individual still remains sinful when leaving the room, he or she inspires others to follow suit, and enter into a deeper encounter with God.

It is important to note that there is no particular order to the three experiences of conversion. They may all occur simultaneously, as in the rare case of

---

9   Matthew is not called "Levi" in Matthew's Gospel, but is so named in the gospels of Mark and Luke. I am also aware of the contention that the historical Levi may not have been the same individual later known as Matthew. The larger point, in this example, is the stark contrast between the sinful tax collector, and the converted Matthew.

10   Bernard Lonergan, *Method in Theology* (1972; repr., New York: Seabury, 1979), 238.

11   Ibid., 241.

the sinful Levi or Saul of Tarsus, or they may occur separately over time. In a typical case, an individual is never fully formed in one instance. To continue the above-mentioned analogy, there may be times of self-doubt when the individual will need to re-enter the room in order to re-experience the grace of God.

In Day's case, her conversion experiences occurred over a ten- to thirty-year time span. Although it is difficult to determine the precise moment when Day experienced each of Lonergan's methods of conversion, she did leave us with a wealth of biographical evidence which may be seen as determinative. Day's *From Union Square to Rome,* published in 1938, details her conversion experiences and also serves as a Catholic apology written in response to her atheistic brother John, and her former communist "friends," who had all but abandoned her upon her turn towards the faith.

The seeds of Day's religious conversion were sown in her childhood years; her moral conversion arose from witnessing her mother's care of the poor and displaced during the San Francisco earthquake of 1906, and extended into her young adulthood.[12] Day's intellectual conversion to Catholicism began to be formed after her baptism in 1927, and became more fully ingrained in her conscience after being indoctrinated by Maurin in late 1932.

Lonergan viewed multiple conversions of the single consciousness not in terms of one superseding or eliminating another, but through the lens of sublation, or the assimilation of one method into another, forming a greater singular reality (in a notion similar to synergism).[13] By further analogy, the three individual methods of conversion can be viewed as separate floors of a building— as each story is added on to the building, the other stories remain, and give the completed structure a greater value. Such were the conversions in the life of Day—when her conscience became more fully formed, she was able to provide a witness which enhanced the greater glory of the human other.

Intellectual Conversion

Lonergan viewed conversion of the intellect as a radical movement toward clarity, which occurs with "the elimination of an exceedingly stubborn and mislead-

---

12 June E. O'Connor affirmed the notion that Day's moral conscience was fully formed by the time of her conversion to Catholicism. She stated that Day "had sought to arouse the conscience of her readers as a radical journalist before she met Maurin as well as during her work with him as a radical Christian." See June E. O'Connor, *The Moral Vision of Dorothy Day: A Feminist Perspective* (New York: Crossroad, 1991), 8.

13 Lonergan, *Method in Theology,* 241.

ing myth concerning reality, objectivity, and human knowledge."[14] He further understood meaning in the world to be influenced not by the experience of a singular individual, but by the internal and external experiences brought about through the cultural community.[15] Lonergan advocated that knowledge "is not just seeing; it is experiencing, understanding, judging, and believing."[16]

There were numerous factors which led Day towards an intellectual conversion to Catholicism. She was, however, predominantly moved by works of literature, such as *The Imitation of Christ*, and Francis Thompson's *The Hound of Heaven*. Day was also intellectually stimulated by the works of Dostoevsky, including *Crime and Punishment*, *The Honest Thief*, and *The Brothers Karamazov*. Dostoevsky's body of work also moved Day spiritually, and she quoted him quite frequently, "because he had a profound influence on my life, on my way of thinking."[17]

After her conversion to Catholicism, Day was further edified in the faith by the saintly Maurin, whom Francis J. Sicius claimed "represented the very order of spirit, intellect, and action that Dorothy had been seeking all her life."[18] Day admitted that after Maurin became her "teacher" in 1932, he began to disturb the content of her knowledge,[19] "by talking about the history of the Church, by going even further back into time and speaking of the prophets of Israel as well as the Fathers of the Church."[20] Although it is evident that Day had the intellectual capacity to grasp the basic tenets of Catholicism, it is Maurin who inculcates the faith to her on a much deeper and personal level.[21]

---

14 Ibid., 238.

15 This notion of internal and external transformation will be important to my argument concerning Day, as she inspired a host of saints and saintly figures to both aid and follow her in her mission to eradicate poverty.

16 Lonergan, *Method in Theology*, 238.

17 Day, *From Union Square to Rome*, 19.

18 Francis J. Sicius, "Introduction: Day and Maurin," in *Peter Maurin: Apostle to the World* (Maryknoll, New York: Orbis, 2004), xxv.

19 Dorothy Day and Francis J. Sicius, "A Fateful Meeting," in *Peter Maurin: Apostle to the World*, 38.

20 Dorothy Day, *The Long Loneliness*, 170.

21 Proof that Day was not fully formed intellectually as a Catholic is evidenced by her prayers to God at the National Shrine of the Immaculate Conception in Washington, DC in December of 1932 (during the Hunger March). Day, who had only been a Catholic for five years, prayed to God to show her the way to use her talents. When Day returned home from the Hunger March, she found Maurin waiting for her on her doorstep. In other words, Day had seen the true light, but she did not then know what to do with that light. See Day, *The Long Loneliness*, 166.

Moral Conversion

Moral conversion occurs, for Lonergan, when we change the criteria of our decisions and choices from satisfactions to values. He believed that as we increase our knowledge of reality, "our responses to human values are strengthened and refined, [and] our mentors ... leave us to ourselves so that our freedom may exercise its ever advancing thrust toward authenticity."[22] If an intellectual conversion increases one's clarity, then a moral conversion increases one's charity towards all of humanity.

In my opening remarks of this paper, I related an incident concerning my antiquated notions of the death penalty. As I grew deeper in my faith, I found that what I had valued twenty-years ago slowly began to ebb from my conscience. I experienced a moral conversion, especially after I had met, and read the works of, Sister Helen Prejean (i.e. *Dead Man Walking*, and *The Death of Innocents: An Eyewitness Account of Wrongful Executions*). I was appalled as I read of the gross injustice regarding the number of innocent men and women who were sent to death row, who had been falsely accused of crimes that they did not commit.

Day's moral conversion was seemingly affected earlier than her intellectual turn toward Catholicism. In her youth, she wrote for *The Call*, a socialist newspaper, wherein she opposed the United States' entry in the Great War and railed at the injustice committed against the rights of industrial laborers. In 1917, ten years before her conversion to Catholicism, Day was arrested in front of the White House for picketing in support of the women's suffragist movement. She later admitted that her concern was more for women's rights in the workplace than in the voting booth.

Day was also morally disturbed by the poverty that she encountered both while attending college in the Chicago area and while living and working in Manhattan. She recalled that "[t]he poverty of New York was appallingly different from that of Chicago. The very odors were different. The sight of homeless and workless men lounging on street corners or sleeping in doorways in broad sunlight appalled me."[23]

Although Day had had an abortion in 1919, one must consider the underlying societal pressures (e.g., public shame and ostracism) that she faced as a po-

---

22 Lonergan, *Method in Theology*, 240.
23 Day, *The Long Loneliness*, 51.

tential single mother. [24] In her largely autobiographical work *The Eleventh Virgin*, Day, writing in the persona of "June," recounted her fears of abandonment, which led to her fateful decision.

> In the first place, Dick would never consent to have [a baby]. He had impressed that on her mind many times. If she insisted on having it, he would leave her—leave her as soon as it began to show. Then, how could she go ahead and have it? [25]

Day also related that sinful pride played a decisive role in her fateful choice, stating that:

> [s]he could not sacrifice her pride and go to a home to have a baby. She could sacrifice every vestige of pride—throw it all into the flames to keep her love burning. Her love for a man. But not her love for the child that was beginning to form in her. [26]

Day's pregnancy out of wedlock would likely have caused further consternation amongst members of her family and social circle, but her abortion, considered a crime in 1919, violated the sanctity of human life. Had the event been revealed at that time, Day would have been shunned by an unforgiving society. As it stood, Day's fateful decision to abort her unborn child would haunt her for the rest of her life. [27] However, the event would strengthen her moral resolve in that the next time she conceived a child she would value that life more intimately, choosing the life of her daughter Tamar Therese over a future with the child's father, Forster Batterham.

In August of 1927, Day became morally outraged by the executions of Sacco and Vanzetti—political anarchists who were falsely tried and convicted for

---

24 Mel Piehl reported that Day's abortion occurred in September of 1919: Id., *Breaking Bread: The Catholic Worker and the Origin of Catholic Radicalism in America* (Philadelphia, Pennsylvania: Temple University Press, 1982), 14.

25 Dorothy Day, *The Eleventh Virgin* (1924; repr., Chicago: Cottager, 2011), 304.

26 Ibid., 305.

27 Day later wished to abort *The Eleventh Virgin*, and many copies were destroyed in her lifetime—leaving her first book as an extremely rare collectible. Although there is not a copy housed in the Marquette University Day-Catholic Worker archives (perhaps respecting Day's wishes), there is one to be found in the Marquette University Raynor Memorial Library collection.

crimes which they did not commit. Before their executions, Day lamented that "the knowledge that these men were soon to pass from this physical earth, were soon to become dust, without consciousness, struck me like a physical blow."[28] Day has thus been shown to be exemplary of Lonergan's method of moral conversion, where one moves from the choice of satisfaction to the choice of values. Although her moral conversion can be likened to a meandering river in her youth, Day ultimately learned to value the sanctity of life. She fought for human rights, alienated many by her pacifist stance during numerous wars, and was willing to be imprisoned on several occasions in support of those rights and beliefs.

Religious Conversion

A religious conversion occurs when one is transformed by a concern for God as the other, which is born by a radical love for all of God's creations. Lonergan described religious conversion as a "total and permanent self-surrender without conditions, qualifications, reservations."[29] Religious conversion may be viewed as a gift of God's grace, which is either operative or cooperative in nature.

Operative grace consists of one's actual religious conversion. Cooperative grace is the effectiveness of one's religious conversion, wherein can be seen "the gradual movement towards a full and complete transformation of the whole of one's living and feeling, one's thoughts, words, deeds, and omissions."[30] Operative grace is an internal movement within the person (i.e. *metanoia*). Cooperative grace is an external manifestation wherein the individual person becomes absorbed into the external community—leading to a greater self-kenosis of living towards a common good.

Evidence of religious conversion is also manifest in Day's childhood, in a myriad of ways. She writes of curiously finding the Bible in her parents' attic during her youth, and developing a fascination with the Psalms, exclaiming that "[t]here was an echoing in my heart. And how can anyone who has known human sorrow and human joy fail to respond to these words?"[31] Day later became enamored with the mother of a Catholic friend, whom she found "on her knees, saying her prayers."[32] At the age of twelve, Day was baptized into the

---

28 Day, *The Long Loneliness*, 146.

29 Lonergan, *Method in Theology*, 240.

30 Ibid., 241.

31 Day, *From Union Square to Rome*, 6.

32 Ibid., 26.

Episcopal Church. Her main attraction to the church was the music, especially the *Te Deum* and *Benedicite*. [33]

Day also had a great longing to experience the joy she witnessed from Catholics, whom she encountered outside of church after Mass. She later admitted that, "daily I saw people coming from Mass. Never did I set foot in a Catholic church but that I saw people there at home with Him." [34] Shortly before her conversion to Catholicism, Day witnessed the Mass from the back of the church, recalling that she "knelt ... not knowing what was going on at the altar, but warmed and comforted by the lights and silence, the kneeling people and the atmosphere of worship." [35]

Day's witness of cooperative grace is the very essence of sainthood. Her post-conversion life as a Catholic is one of radical response to Jesus' commands to love both God and neighbor as one. Although Day's conversion may have seemed to be "a strange and lonely experience," she also exhibited a fascinating attraction to the lives of the saints, especially Thérèse of Lisieux. In fact, it is the call of the Little Flower which represents, for Day, the pinnacle experience in her participation in the saintly chain of causality—and yet this calling was not adhered to instantaneously, as Day initially dismissed the writings of Thérèse as childish whimsy.

Thérèse of Lisieux and the Saintly Chain of Causality

Prior to her conversion, Day had been exposed to the writings of Augustine, and Francis of Assisi. Author William James had also introduced her to the writings of Teresa of Avila, whom Day described as "that well traveled yet cloistered contemplative with her vigorous writing and her sense of humor." [36] Day also encountered such saintly figures as Maurin and, later on in her journey, Daniel Berrigan, César Chávez, Catherine de Hueck Doherty, Thomas Merton (by correspondence, only), and Mother Teresa—if not all of these were not saints in the canonical sense, they certainly represented saintly agents of change. [37]

---

33   Ibid., 33.

34   Ibid., 17.

35   Day, *The Long Loneliness*, 84.

36   Dorothy Day, "Preface," in *Therese: A Life of Therese of Lisieux* (1960; repr., Springfield, Illinois: Templegate, 1991), vi.

37   Irish Jesuit William Johnston affirmed that many mystics, such as Day, Doherty, and Merton, tended to gravitate towards each other. He believed that "[t]hey may find that they are dwelling in one another, sharing a common vision as they move towards a com-

The culmination of Day's conversion experience, and her link in the saintly chain of causality, concerns her indirect contact with Thérèse of Lisieux. One may wonder why the focus of Day's conversion was not centered solely upon the birth of her daughter, Tamar Therese. Although the birth of her daughter did lead Day to desire baptism for both her daughter and herself, she later admitted that "[w]hen I became pregnant I thought it was a *child* I had been seeking, motherhood. But I realized that wasn't the answer [for her conversion] either." [38] While convalescing in a hospital bed after giving birth to her daughter, Day was given a saintly medal of the Little Flower by a fellow patient, a Roman Catholic woman whom Day unfortunately does not name. Day initially balked at the idea of receiving the saintly medallion, "this evidence of superstition and charm-wearing. I wanted no such talisman." [39] She acquiesced, and took the medal, recalling that:

> after hearing of St. Therese as the young novice mistress in her far off convent of Lisieux in Normandy, who had died the year I was born, and whose sisters were still alive, I decided that although I would name my child after the older saint [Teresa of Avila], the new one [Thérèse of Lisieux] would be my own Teresa's novice mistress, to train her in the spiritual life. I knew that I wanted to have the child baptized a Catholic and I wanted both saints to be taking care of her. One was not enough. [40]

While preparing for her confirmation, Day was given a copy of *The Little White Flower, The Story of a Soul* by an Augustinian Father of the Assumption. Day found the writings of Thérèse of Lisieux to be juvenile, complaining that her work was "colorless, monotonous, too small in fact for my notice." [41] A "little" seed, however, was planted in Day, and it can be argued that she later patterned her radical devotion of poverty after Thérèse of Lisieux's Little Way. [42]

mon future." See William Johnston, *Silent Music: The Science of Meditation* (San Francisco: Harper & Row, 1979), 173.

38   Coles, *Dorothy Day: A Radical Devotion*, 62, emphasis original.

39   Day, *Therese: A Life of Therese of Lisieux*, vi.

40   Ibid., vi–vii.

41   Ibid., viii.

42   J. Leon Hooper noted that Day needed to adapt her own social concerns with that of Thérèse of Lisieux, and "in the process, transform the range and strength of Thérèse's

Day's indirect encounter with Thérèse of Lisieux led not only to a lifetime fascination with the Little Flower (e.g., Day spent eight to ten years in the researching and writing of her biography of Lisieux), but also cemented the desire in Day to be baptized as a Roman Catholic shortly after her daughter's reception of the sacrament. Although Day had been propelled toward a conversion experience for a number of years prior to her baptism, one could also point to the influence of the saintly chain of causality where one saint touches the life of another, leading to greater sanctification.

What, then, is the saintly chain of causality? It is the transformation of an individual who has been bestowed with seemingly ineffable grace, by contact with another saint or saintly presence. The saintly chain of causality is derived from Lonergan's notion of cooperative grace wherein a saint or saintly individual affects the religious conversion of another. It is relational to what we do with our lives after experiencing a deeper religious conversion.

The saintly chain of causality is further evidenced in Lonergan's definitions of operative and cooperative grace wherein an individual is transformed. Although Levi/Matthew experienced this transcendence instantaneously, it has been shown that Day experienced her conversion over an extended period of time. Even Day's acceptance of the teachings of Thérèse of Lisieux took a number of years to fully blossom. Day, however, also exemplified cooperative grace, albeit in a radical way by living amongst and serving the poor without vacillation for the remainder of her post-conversion life.

Conclusion

How can humanity draw inspiration from the saints, and experiences of conversion, in order to lead more grace-filled lives? In an era of religious fragmentation and growing spiritual malaise, perhaps we need to be strongly reminded of Jesus' universal call for *metanoia*. We must be mindful that although there will always be "those who are sick," so also will there be individuals who are led to experiences of conversion, which are representative of God's desire for righteousness and change.

The essence of sainthood is found in such hope—hope that all of God's creations one day achieve the kingdom of heaven. Day knew the value of hope in her own journey, and she wished the same for others. Of the young African-Ameri-

own social loving. She had to find a socially active agency even in Thérèse's enclosed living." See J. Leon Hooper, "Dorothy Day's Transposition of Thérèse's 'Little Way,'" *Theological Studies* 63, no. 1 (March 2002): 81.

can woman that she had encountered in prison, Day further believed that

> God's grace is such that we don't know what will happen to her. Do you think she will ever forget this book [autobiography of St. Thérèse]? And as long as they keep trying and keep trying. She may fall another seventy times. But that book she read in jail may be her way to final salvation. [43]

Day's hope for the sanctification of others is itself a saintly quality. Although she did not readily see her own role in the saintly chain of causality, [44] she certainly has led many individuals toward a greater experience of *metanoia*. [45] I can attest to a saintly chain of causality because, beginning with my saintly wife, I have experienced a deeper sense of conversion due to Day's radical response to Jesus' universal call, and her witness to the greater good of humanity.

Robert P. Russo has an MA in systematic theology from Lourdes University in Sylvania, Ohio. Over the past four years, he has lectured and written extensively about Dorothy Day. His article "Paper, People and Work: a Review of the Dorothy Day-Catholic Worker Collection at Marquette University," was published in the March 2014 issue of *Catholic Library World,* and he is currently editing his various papers regarding Day, to be self-published as *A Life Remembered: The Conversion, Radicalism, and Mysticism of Dorothy Day.*

43 McDonald, *Catholics in Conversation*, 111.

44 Day has been famously quoted as stating, "[d]on't call me a saint," and, while her rationale may be equated to the Heavenly Virtue of humility, there is a spiritual blindness of the self which may occur with one's total giving to the poor as Jesus commanded. This notion of spiritual blindness is not meant to be critical of Day—we all experience moments of self-abnegation (i.e. "As seen through a glass darkly").

45 Day was in fact responsible for the conversion of many individuals. Of particular interest is the witness of Tina De Aragon, Day's sister-in-law, who converted to Catholicism as she lay dying of cancer. De Aragon attributed her conversion to Day. See Dorothy Day, *The Duty of Delight: The Diaries of Dorothy Day*, ed. Robert Ellsberg (New York: Image, 2011), 669.

Dorothy Day's Spiritual Sources: a Journey in Faith

Geoffrey Gneuhs

The only great tragedy in life is not to become a saint.

—Leon Bloy

Introduction

In his last public audience on 13 February 2013, Pope Benedict XVI mentioned three examples in the twentieth century of people who searched for God in quite different circumstances—some harrowing—in different cultures, and from different religious backgrounds: a Dutch Jewess who died in Auschwitz, a Russian man who subsequently became an Orthodox monk, and Dorothy Day. Of Dorothy, he said:

> The ability to oppose the ideological blandishments of her time to choose the search for truth and open herself up to the discovery of faith is evidenced by another woman of our time: the American Dorothy Day. In her autobiography, she confesses openly to having given in to the temptation that everything could be solved with politics.... The journey towards faith in such a secularized environment was particularly difficult, but Grace acts nonetheless as she points out, "I slipped into the atmosphere of prayer...."

He goes on to say, "God guided her to a conscious adherence to the Church, in a lifetime spent dedicated to the underprivileged."

For Dorothy, her conversion was a long journey in which she rediscovered Christ. Pope Benedict cites Revelation: "Behold I stand at the door and knock. If anyone hears my voice and opens the door, I will enter his house and dine with him, and he with me." (3:20)

There are two key elements in his observations of her, which could be said of anyone desiring to lead a God-centered life: grace and the acceptance of grace. Grace is offered and abounds. But each individual has free will to act, to accept, or to ignore, to reject.

Some years ago I was on a retreat at Regina Laudis Abbey in Connecticut. The foundress and abbess, Mother Benedict Duss, was a formidable, no-nonsense person. I asked her to pray that I would receive grace, and she bluntly stated: "You will. You just have to act on it!"

I was a bit startled, but knew she was right.

We are here today talking about Dorothy Day, a saint for our time, because she acted on grace and took personal responsibilityas she and Peter Maurin both taught—not only for the corporal and spiritual works of mercy, but especially and primarily for a life of holiness, a life centered on Christ. She was chosen by God, just as each person is, as a creature created in His image and likeness. Thus we also are confronted with the fundamental choice, the ontological act of creatures with a free will: Do I choose the Chooser? Do I accept the gift? Not to do so is to be deceived by the great deceiver, Satan.

In what follows, I consider those influences that led Dorothy Day to accept the gift of life in Christ. Her primary spiritual source was of course the Scriptures. She was particularly fond of the Psalms. In this paper, I shall, however, discuss four major writers whom Dorothy herself mentions in her spiritual autobiography *From Union Square to Rome*, first published in 1938, some ten years after her conversion, and intended as an *apologia* to her skeptic brother John. These four writers are St. Augustine, Thomas à Kempis, St. Teresa of Avila, and St. John of the Cross. I shall also give some consideration to St. Thérése de Lisieux, whom Dorothy came to appreciate later in life.

1. St. Augustine

St. Augustine's *Confessions*, his powerful, eloquent, and moving story of his early life, had a strong impact on Dorothy. [1] She had read *The Confessions* before her conversion and before reading the other four sources. Her own conversion

---

1   Dorothy Day, *From Union Square to Rome*, (Maryknoll, New York: Orbis, 2006), 30.

was Augustinian in proportion. Written around A.D. 400, *The Confessions*, after 1,600 years, remains one of the seminal texts of Western civilization, as well as one of the major texts of Christian theology. *The Confessions* is "a vast hymn of praise to the goodness and grace of God."[2]

Augustine of Hippo was born in Tagaste in North Africa in what is today Tunisia in 354, not far from the port city of Hippo, where he later served as bishop. His family were Berbers, and might be what we call middle class. While his father Patricius was a pagan, his mother Monica was a Christian. At ten years old, Augustine was sent away for studies in grammar, rhetoric, and literature. Later, he studied rhetoric in Carthage and then became a teacher. He lived with a woman who bore him a son, Adeodatus. In 372, Augustine became a Manichaean. Somewhat influenced by Zoroastrianism from Persia, the Manichaeans were materialistic dualists, believing in a god of good and light and a god of evil and darkness, both of whom were corporeal beings. He was initially attracted to this sect, and remained so for nine years because he believed their claims could be explained by reason.

In 383, after a failed stint teaching in Rome, while struggling to find the truth after his departure from Manichaeism, Augustine travelled to Milan. There, through Ambrose, the Catholic bishop, he was introduced to the philosophy of the Neoplatonists. As he explains in books V–VIII, through this discovery he finally came to understand the reality of immaterial beings, the limitations of materialism, and the enslaving constraints of the flesh, leading him to the realization of the love and grace of God. This intellectual conversion laid the groundwork for his famous encounter with the Scriptures in the garden where a voice bid him "Tolle! Lege!" ("Take and read!"). Converted to the Catholic faith through this experience, with his son he was baptized on Holy Saturday 387.

In the contretemps with her brother John in her *apologia*, Dorothy, too, had to confront his objections. She, like Augustine, appealed to her own lived experience in her coming to faith, to a belief in the supernatural, and to the acceptance of grace. These for her were realities; moreover, she recognized like Augustine that it was her experience, her yearnings for sexual intimacy, for love, for companionship, these natural desires—which are good, because they are created by God—led her to God and to a life of grace. Her writing is introspective, self-reflective, analytical, self-critical, and intuitive. Her *apologia*, like Augustine's *Confessions*, ultimately is full of wonder and gratitude.

---

2   Rex Warner, *The Confessions of St. Augustine* (New York: New American Library, 1963), viii.

She writes to her brother:

> For you cannot pace the floor of a barred cell, or lie on your
> back on a hard cot watching a gleam of sunlight travel slowly
> ... across the room, without coming to the realization that
> until the heart and soul of man is changed, there is no happi-
> ness for him. On the other hand you have not felt the ecstasy,
> the thankfulness, the joy, which called the Psalmist to cry out,
> "My heart and my flesh rejoice for the living God. My soul lon-
> geth and fainteth for the courts of the Lord." (Ps. 83:1)[3]

She never convinced her brother. But as Augustine concluded *The Confessions:* "How can one man teach another man to understand this? What angel
will teach an angel? This must be *asked* of you, *sought* in you, *knocked* for at you.
So, so shall it be *received*, so shall it be *found*, so shall it be *opened*. Amen." (Book
XIII, chap. 27)

2. The Imitation of Christ

This fifteenth-century manual, as Dorothy recalled, followed her through her
days.[4] This fact is significant. Reading it reveals the fundamental thrust of her
spirituality, which later was fortified by "The Retreat" of Father John Hugo. I believe that the *Imitation of Christ* is the key source for understanding the interior
life of Dorothy Day.

Written in the fifteenth century, it is divided into four books: "Helpful Counsels of the Spiritual Life," "Directions for the Interior Life," "On Interior Consolation," and "On the Blessed Sacrament."[5] Referencing the stages of
Christ's life with Scripture, it is a manual for daily devotion and living an austere, ascetic life. It is hard and rigorous, not the pablum offered by some of today's popular spiritual writers. Yet it was very much part of Dorothy. As she
wrote to her brother John, I "still ... receive great comfort" from it.[6]

Thomas à Kempis, a German, composed it originally anonymously, imitat-

---

3   *From Union Square to Rome*, 160.

4   Ibid., 9.

5   Thomas à Kempis, *My Imitation of Christ* (New York: Confraternity of the Precious
    Blood, 1982).

6   *From Union Square to Rome*, 36; see also 113 and 136.

ing Christ's humility, between 1418 and 1427. Humility is the virtue of this manual as humility is the basis of faith. Christ humbled himself for our sake to do the work of the Father: our redemption and salvation. Thomas was a member of the Brethren of the Common Life, which developed out of the *Devotio Moderna* movement of Geert Groote. This movement was in reaction to the stultified rigidity of late Scholasticism. It influenced the Beguines, one of several reform movements of that period seeking to live a simple, ascetical life in union with Christ. This devotional classic was part of the spiritual reading, of such disparate persons as St. Thomas More, St. Ignatius of Loyola, John Wesley, St. Therese de Lisieux, and Thomas Merton. After the Bible, it is the most published spiritual text in Western Christianity. The 1441 autograph edition is extant at the Bibliotheque Royale in Brussels.

Despite its status as a Christian classic, it has not escaped criticism over the centuries. Modern-day critics of the *Imitation* include Hans Urs von Balthasar and René Girard, who faulted it for being anti-world, too rigorous and ascetical, and ignoring other aspects of Christ's life, teaching, and ministry. Dorothy Day was well aware of similar criticisms, yet she read the *Imitation* for the rest of her life. Its spirituality was also reflected in the controversial Retreat of Fr. Hugo, and she continued in her later years to wax eloquent about the Retreat. [7]

Dorothy recalled that when she lived in New Orleans, where she worked for a morning newspaper called *The Item*, on nights when she had no assignment, upon hearing the cathedral bells she would go to church:

> It was the first time I had been present at Benediction and it made a profound impression on me. The very physical attitude of those about me made me bow my head. Did I feel the Presence there? I do not know. But I remembered those lines from the *Imitation*:
> "Who, humbly approaching to the fountain of sweetness, doth not carry thence some little sweetness?
> Who, standing by a copious fire, doth not derive therefrom some little heat? (Book 4, chap. 4)" [8]

---

7   The greatest critic of The Retreat was Dorothy's daughter Tamar Hennessy who as a child had to endure it. She had such a visceral abhorrence of it that years later at the time of Dorothy's funeral in December 1980 she insisted that the author celebrate the Mass. She said to the author: "Geoff, if Fr. Hugo says the Mass I will not attend." I celebrated the Mass—and Fr. Hugo did not attend.

8   *From Union Square to Rome*, 112.

That the association came to mind even before her conversion reveals the profound influence of the book on her spiritual life. Thus a closer examination of its contents is worthwhile.

In Book I Thomas' emphasis is on withdrawal: "[W]hoever follows me will not walk in darkness." It calls for patience, solitude, and silence and for the endurance of the vacuities and vicissitudes of earthly existence. Dorothy loved Hugo's Retreat (and retreats in general) because it afforded her days of silence, something not available in the hectic life of the New York Catholic Worker houses. Significantly, the *Imitation* stresses the pilgrim nature of the life of the Christian. Dorothy in later years titled her column in the CW newspaper "On Pilgrimage."

In Book II, chapter 10, Thomas discusses grace and writes: "Grace will always be given to the truly grateful. . . ." Dorothy wrote: "Gratitude brought me into the Church and that gratitude grows, and the first word my heart will utter, when I face God is 'Thanks.'"[9] (Appropriately, on her tombstone at Resurrection Cemetery on Staten Island are the words "Deo Gratias.")

In Book III the author constructs a dialogue between Christ and a faithful soul for interior consolation. Jesus recognizes that few turn to him but that "the man who trusts in Me I will never send away empty" (chap. 56). Dorothy's entire focus was on Christ. Today, following our reductive and decadent, solipsistic culture, the self is the popular mode. This was not so for Dorothy. "I am the way, the truth, and the life" (John 14:6), Jesus said. Throughout the *Imitation* there is a call for self-denial and to embrace the cross of Christ. "Unless you renounce all that you have, you cannot be my disciple." (Book IV, chap. 8)

In Book IV the dialogue continues. The subject is the Eucharist, the Blessed Sacrament, and "with how great reverence Christ is to be received." Throughout her life, Dorothy attended daily Mass, receiving Holy Communion with great humility, reverence, awe, and gratitude. She said, and believed, that "the Mass is the most important thing that we do."[10] The Eucharist (the word means thanksgiving) is the supreme act of worship of the Catholic faith and is the sacrament of unity. All of salvation history in words and deeds is summed up in the Mass: Christ's salvific sacrifice. Dorothy knew that with the Eucharist we are never abandoned. Why would God become incarnate and then leave us on our own?

---

9   Ibid., 173.

10   William Miller, *All is Grace: The Spirituality of Dorothy Day* (Garden City, New York: Doubleday, 1987), 84.

Dorothy has a rather lengthy discourse on the True Presence in her *apologia*. She admits that early on "it took me a long time as a convert to realize the presence of Christ as Man in the Sacrament. He is the same Jesus Who walked on earth, who slept in the boat as the tempest arose, Who hungered in the desert, Who prayed in the garden, Who conversed with the woman at the well. . . . Jesus is there as Man. He is Flesh and Blood, soul and Divinity." She continues:

> We are not, most of us, capable of exalted emotion, save rarely. We are not capable always of feelings of love, awe, gratitude, and repentance. So Christ has taken the form of bread that we may more readily approach Him, and feeding daily, assimilating Christ so that it is not we but Christ working in us, we may be made more capable of understanding and realizing and loving Him. . . . Christ is bread on our altars because bread is the staple of the world, the simplest thing in the world . . . for the life of the soul we need food. So the simplest, most loving, most thorough thing Christ could do before He died, was to institute the Blessed Sacrament. [11]

We do not live in a culture of reverence or humility. We live in a very self-centered culture of I-phones, I-pads, and selfies, and so forth.

Too often, the Mass, following distorted interpretations of the Second Vatican Council—for example, doing away with Latin or having the priest face the people, neither of which is prescribed by the conciliar documents—has become a casual affair centering on the priest and the congregants, not on Christ and the supernatural. Yet Dorothy, as taught by the *Imitation*, approached the Sacrament "with a sincere and undoubting faith and with a humble reverence..." (Book IV, chap. 18).

3. St. Teresa of Avila and St. John of the Cross

Dorothy notes in her *apologia* that she was introduced to St. Teresa (1515–1582) and St. John (1542–1591) by her reading of William James's *The Varieties of Religious Experiences*. They were both reformers of their respective Carmelite congregations during the period of the Counter Reformation. In 1567 St. John met St. Teresa and agreed to join her reform movement. They called for a renewed

---

11   *From Union Square to Rome*, p. 162ff.

conventual life centered on detachment, prayer, fasting, self-denial and works of penance, and contemplation—a much needed reform for many religious communities today.

It is equally important to note that these reforming saints were orthodox and wanted the Church and their congregations to be more holy and more faithful to their calling and mission, just as Peter Maurin and Dorothy Day wanted the Church of her day to be. For this they underwent persecution. Teresa was questioned by the Inquisition, while John was imprisoned and tortured by his confreres. However, Teresa was canonized forty years after her death, and in 1970, along with St. Catherine of Siena, declared a Doctor of the Church. Likewise, John was canonized in 1726 and declared Doctor of the Church in 1926.

According to St. Teresa there are three attributes of the soul: memory, understanding, and the will. Dorothy noted, "It is only by exerting these faculties of the soul that one is enabled to love one's fellow. And this strength comes from God. There can be no brotherhood without the Fatherhood of God." [12] St. Teresa wrote: "Until it [the soul] advances it must, of course, seek the Creator through His creatures.... [T]he entire edifice of prayer must be founded on humility." St. Teresa emphasized the love of God for us. Dorothy wrote we should meditate more on the love of God for us, rather than our love for Him." [13] St. Teresa acknowledged that "[p]erfection cannot be attained quickly...." Similarly, Dorothy lamented, "No one but God knows how long I struggled, how I turned to Him, and turned from Him, again and again." [14]

But she could take comfort and hope in how St. John in his *Dark Night of the Soul* treats this reality of the soul: seeking, knocking, and searching. The acts of the soul "must first be darkened and put to sleep and hushed to rest naturally." One should not fear this, "but rather consider it a great happiness, since God is freeing thee from thyself and taking the matter from the hands." [15]

It must be pointed out that the struggle and journey of a soul is ongoing; there are moments of ecstasy (though for most certainly not in the dramatic form that St. Teresa experienced) and moments of weariness, and near despair ("ups and downs," "storms and trials" to use the words of St. John). The spiritual life that was essential to Dorothy and to understanding her faith is, to use simi-

---

12 Ibid., 14.

13 Ibid., 166.

14 Ibid., 161.

15 St. John of the Cross, *Dark Night of the Soul* (Garden City, New York: Image Books/ Doubleday 1990), 154.

les of St. Teresa and St. John, like watering a garden or climbing a ladder; it is all part of the pilgrimage for one who seeks union with God. For as St. Augustine wrote in *The Confessions:* "Thou hast made us for thyself, O Lord, our heart is restless until it rests in thee."

4. St. Therese de Lisieux

In the introduction to her book *Therese,* Dorothy recounts she first heard of St. Thérèse of the Child Jesus as she lay in the maternity ward of Bellevue Hospital, waiting to give birth to her daughter. Another patient asked her what she was going to name her baby and she said "Tamar Teresa." The woman thought it was after St. Thérèse, who had been canonized the year before (1925) and was popularly known as the Little Flower, but Dorothy said that it was after St. Teresa of Avila, having never heard of St. Thérèse. The woman spoke a little about her and gave Dorothy a medal. Then in 1928 Dorothy's confessor, a Father Zachary, gave her a book titled *The Little White Flower Story of a Soul.* Dorothy read it but wasn't impressed. Years later in her own book *Therese* published in 1960 (the only book she wrote on the life of a saint) that "it took me a longer time to realize the unique position of Therese of Lisieux in the life of the Church today" where in "these days of fear and trembling of what man has wrought on earth in destructiveness and hate, Therese is the saint we need."[16]

Dorothy further explains: "St. Therese is teaching the necessity of loving God first, and 'then all these things shall be added unto you'" and adds "this is blind faith, a naked faith in love."[17] But as Thérèse, Augustine, Teresa of Avila, and John of the Cross, and Dorothy Day herself realized, it was faith in God's love for us. Thérèse's emphasis as that of these earlier masters of spirituality is on the interior life, is on God's grace. Dorothy wrote: "We must be ready to give up everything. We must have already given it up, before God can give it back transfigured and supernaturalized."[18] Dorothy did. She forsook the love of Forster Batterham for the love of God in order to live a life centered on Christ. Like Thérèse she knew she had to die in order to live.

Shortly before her death in 1897, Thérèse told her fellow Carmelite nuns: "I feel my mission is about to begin; my mission of making souls love the good God

---

16 Dorothy Day, *Therese* (Springfield, Illinois: Templegate Publishers, 1960), see Preface.

17 Ibid., 87.

18 Ibid., 88.

as I love Him, to teach my little way to souls."[19] She had earlier written in a letter to her sister Celine, "Few are the souls that aspire to be lonely and unknown." St. Thérèse became *the* saint for Dorothy, a saint who embraced suffering, her own physical suffering with joy. What are we to make of her and of Dorothy's embrace of her?

Even before Thérèse was canonized in 1925 she had acquired a huge following from the people, all by word of mouth. It was, as Dorothy pointed out, the "worker," the common man, who first spread her fame. This was before mass media. There were no miracles in her lifetime: "With governments becoming stronger and more centralized, the common man feels his ineffectiveness ... the message of Therese is a quite different one."[20] Dorothy maintained that Thérèse "speaks to our condition," as odd as that may be when many Catholics see faith as something that must be easy and comforting and believe the Church must follow the politically correct ideology of secularism. Dorothy was inspired by the Little Flower because the Little Flower loved God and accepted suffering as Christ himself suffered. Dorothy concludes her book on this humble soul with Therese's own words: "Few are the souls that aspire to be lonely and unknown."[21] How true!

5. The Mystical Body of Christ

For Dorothy, her incarnational spirituality was best expressed by the doctrine of the mystical body of Christ.[22] Paul in his letter to the Romans exhorts the brethren to be "a living sacrifice, holy and acceptable unto God, which is your reasonable service. And be not conformed to this world.... So we, being many, are one body in Christ, and every one members one of another" (12:2–5).

She often used this Pauline expression.[23] The term emphasizes the communal, organic sacramental notion of the Church in contrast to an institutional, juridical understanding. In the Middle Ages it was expressed as *corpus verum*, the true Body of Christ realized in the Mass, the fullest expression of Catholic belief, doctrine, and spirituality.

19 Ibid., 166.

20 Ibid., 174.

21 Ibid., 176.

22 See William T. Cavanaugh's essay "Dorothy Day and the Mystical Body of Christ in the Second World War," pp. 457–464 in *Dorothy Day and the Catholic Worker Movement: Centenary Essays* (Milwaukee, Wisconsin: Marquette University Press, 2001).

23 Cf. *CW*, October 1934; *CW*, March 1935; *CW*, February 1940; and so forth.

Pope Pius XII issued his encyclical *Mystici Corporis Christi* in June 1943, in the midst of World War II and its horrific killing, destruction, and division. He wrote: "[T]owns and fertile fields are strewn with massive ruins and defiled with the blood of brothers." (par. 4) It was a call to share union and charity: "Our paternal love embraces all peoples, whatever their nationality and race...." The image was to give hope in the midst of the great tempest, the great trial, the great scourging. As Dorothy had written earlier in *From Union Square to Rome*, "We are bowed down... under the weight of not only our own sins but the sins of each other, of the whole world.... We are members of His Mystical Body." [24]

For Dorothy the image reflected her personalist philosophy and approach to social and economic problems. It was a call for solidarity in a Christ-centered society. She wrote: "This work of ours toward a new heaven and a new earth shows a correlation between the material and the spiritual, and of course, recognizes the primacy of the spiritual.... Hence the leaders of the work... must go daily to Mass, to receive food for the soul." [25] It was the union of the natural and the supernatural.

For Dorothy (and Peter Maurin) this doctrine was the antithesis of the modern nation state, which had brought so much war. It is the antidote to the intrusive, oppressive bureaucratic, impersonal government that continues increasingly today in collusion with the elites, nationally and internationally.

Conclusion

In response to an exasperated Communist writer's series of "How can you believe...?" questions concerning Catholic beliefs and dogmas, Dorothy answered forthrightly, without mincing words: "I believe in the Roman Catholic Church and all she teaches. I have accepted her authority with my whole heart." [26] Dorothy never challenged the moral and doctrinal authority of the Church. In the December 1972 issue of the *Catholic Worker* newspaper in a front page article titled "A Letter to Father Daniel Berrigan," she affirmed:

> And so when it comes to divorce, birth control, and abortion, I
> must write in this way. The teaching of Christ, the Word, must
> be upheld. Held up though one would think that it is com-

---

24 *From Union Square to Rome*, 13.

25 *CW*, February 1940.

26 *From Union Square to Rome*, 149.

pletely beyond us—out of our reach, impossible to follow. I believe in the Sacraments. I believe Grace is conferred through the Sacraments. I believe the priest is empowered to forgive sins. Grace is defined as "participation in divine life," so little by little we are putting off the old man and putting on the new.

This is what the faith meant to her: It is a journey in grace. Faith requires humility. She wished "to live in conformity with the will of God."[27] Her spiritual advice to "cradle Catholics" was that they need to go through a second conversion that "binds them with a more mature love and obedience to the Church."[28]

The spiritual writers whom I have discussed were reformers, but their reforms were that the Church be more true to her calling, to the truth entrusted to her by Christ. Neither they nor Dorothy called for doctrinal change, or that the Church conform to the fashions of ideology or political correctness. St. Augustine, Thomas à Kempis, St. Teresa of Avila, St. John of the Cross, and St. Thérèse de Lisieux were centered on Christ, the event, and on the interior life in union with Christ and on the salvation of the soul. So too was Dorothy Day, and as she aged, only more so. They lived in times of war and greed and injustice, of lies, deceit, and corruption—no different from ours. Richard Dawkins mocks truth—the God delusion; well, in fact, his is the progress delusion, the atheist delusion.

In our contemporary culture, notions of the soul, the interior life, the transcendent vision, the supernatural are dismissed as irrelevant, unreal, or delusional, but then our age is an age of solipsism, self-indulgence and gratification; it is the age of narcissism. Dorothy believed that God had become man; the world teaches that man has become god. Dorothy's Catholic faith made her life not just tolerable but allowed her to live in hope and love.

To understand Dorothy's interior life, in other words, to understand her, one must read these writers. It's a challenge, but one which she accepted and lived. She was not an activist as the world understands; she was a soul seeking God. To think of her otherwise is to dismiss her. Many years ago shortly after Dorothy's death I was interviewed by what then might have been called a "new" or modern, liberated nun who asked me what I thought was Dorothy Day's legacy, I readily said, "Her faith." The woman was speechless, and looked at me

27 Dorothy Day, *The Long Loneliness* (San Francisco: Harper and Row, 1952), 256.

28 Dorothy Day, "Reflections during Advent—Part Four: Obedience," *Ave Maria*, December 17, 1966, 20ff.

quizzically, no doubt thinking I would have said: her pacifism, her voluntary poverty, or her work for justice.

Dorothy concludes *From Union Square to Rome* with a challenge to postmodernity: "My will—my free will which God has given me—would hold me rigidly in His presence so that in life, which contains such unbearable and terrible things, as well as in death, I will choose Him and will hold fast to Him. *For who else is there?* Would you have me choose Nothingness?"

Geoffrey Gneuhs served as chaplain to Dorothy Day and the New York Catholic Worker. He was the homilist at Dorothy's funeral. He wrote his thesis at Yale University on Peter Maurin. His most recent book is *Saint Thomas Aquinas: A Biography for Young Readers* (New Priory Press). A representational and figurative artist, he maintains his studio in New York City.

What Blasphemy!
Liturgy and Social Justice: Virgil Michel, Dorothy Day, and the Early Catholic Worker Movement

Bryce A. Wiseman

Upon Dom Virgil Michel's untimely death in 1938, there followed an out-pouring of tributes, including one by Dorothy Day, published in a special issue of *Orate Fratres*, the journal he was instrumental in founding.[1] These testimonies collectively reflect the immense variety of activities that had filled his incredibly productive life. Michel, a Benedictine monk of Saint John's Abbey in Collegeville, Minnesota, was a professor of philosophy and English at Saint John's University; the founder of The Liturgical Press and the aforementioned *Orate Fratres*, which continues as the leading liturgical journal under the title *Worship*; a writer of books, pamphlets and articles on liturgy, social justice, education, economics, and art; a translator; a lecturer; a college administrator; an ecumenist; a violinist in the Saint John's orchestra; and a star of baseball and tennis.[2] All of these he accomplished in forty-eight years.

In surveying the voluminous writings he produced in these few, short, years, there is one overarching theme that may be detected: liturgy and social justice. For Michel, however, and quite uniquely for his time and ours, these were not two distinct elements, nor were they at odds one with the other. Rather, they were intimately connected, especially through the Pauline conception of the "Mystical Body of Christ."[3] It seems that Michel was first introduced to this concept under the tutelage of the renowned monk of Mont César, Dom Lambert Beauduin, then the foremost scholar of liturgy teaching at the Inter-

---

1   *Orate Fratres* 13 (1939).

2   R.W. Franklin and Robert Spaeth, *Virgil Michel: American Catholic* (Collegeville, Minnesota: Liturgical Press, 1988), 20.

3   E.g., 1 Cor. 12:12-27

national Benedictine College of St. Anselm in Rome, where Michel had been sent by his abbot for study in the spring of 1924. Beauduin had this to say about his student: "I knew him well in Rome, and when he discovered that I was concerned with the liturgical movement at Louvain, we became quite friendly ... but liturgy was not for him just a matter of study; it was above all a powerful means of doing apostolic work, by increasing the faith and devotion of the faithful."[4] This description tracks many others of Michel, for although he certainly was a scholar, he never lost sight of the practical implications of his studies.

In this study I will be drawing heavily from from Michel's own work, attempting to link together his disparate corpus to present a cohesive overview of his thoughts on liturgy and social justice. I hope that his influence on the spirit and action of Dorothy Day and the early Catholic Worker movement will become clear through these passages, and so, in conclusion, I will present firsthand accounts from Catholic Workers of their own incorporation of the liturgical life and its effect.[5]

Michel begins by squarely setting the issue before us:

> There is a notable lack of harmony between the liturgical spirit and the temper of very many Catholics of today. But if so, who is in the wrong? Why the lack of harmony and sympathy? One possible answer could be that the liturgy *was* definitely only of a certain age and time. But another answer is, that the Catholic of today has unconsciously become quite unchristian in his outlook and sympathies, and that the fault lies with him rather than with the Church and her liturgy.[6]

Virgil Michel pulled no punches in identifying the problems facing both the liturgy and worshipers in the first half of the twentieth century. While both the liturgical and social gospel movements were making inroads into American Christianity, few were making a connection between the perceived increase in social disconnectedness and the liturgy. However, Michel, with his wide-rang-

---

4 Paul B. Marx, O.S.B., *Virgil Michel and the Liturgical Movement* (Collegeville, Minnesota: Liturgical Press, 1957), 28.

5 For more on Michel's influence on the Catholic Worker movement, see Mark and Louise Zwick, *The Catholic Worker Movement: Intellectual and Spiritual Origins* (Mahwah, New Jersey: Paulist Press, 2005), 58–74.

6 Virgil Michel, "Timely Tracts: Modernism and the Chant," *Orate Fratres* 11 (1937): 464.

ing interests and critical eye, had his finger on the pulse of his contemporary society and diagnosed the illness with which it was inflicted.

Thus, when Michel asks, *"What is the liturgy?"* He responds "I am afraid this word has been much abused in the past. ... We have ordinarily understood the word 'liturgy' to mean these *outward* things, whereas the liturgy is actually the *divine reality behind them."* [7] According to Michel, then, the true liturgical spirit as the

> central expression of the mystical body of Christ, must also be the central expression of the life of the member of Christ. As such, it is not merely something in which the member participates for some minutes of the day or some hours of the week and from which he then separates himself in the daily routine of his life. ... The liturgical worship of the Church moulds the heart and soul for the entire life of the Christian; the Mass is the inspiration for the entire life of the day. [8]

This is accomplished "not by passive bodily presence, but by being present in such a manner that mind and heart are actively joined to the official worship and take intelligent part in the holy action." [9] And what is the purpose of this active participation? Says Michel "participation of the faithful in the liturgy will restore to them their native right to a share in ... theological knowledge and understanding, in place of the relegation of theology to an abstract science for experts, such as it has been until recently." [10]

Culturally, however, Michel recognizes that a perverse participation in a culture of ever-increasing acquisition, propelled by an unchecked capitalist philosophy, [11] presents a serious threat to the true spirit of the liturgy:

---

7   Michel, *The Liturgical Movement* (Collegeville, Minnesota: Liturgical Press, 1930), 6.

8   Michel, *The Christian in the World* (Collegeville, Minnesota: Liturgical Press, 1942), 103.

9   Michel, "The Liturgy the Basis of Social Regeneration," *Orate Fratres* 9 (1935): 540.

10   Michel, "The Scope of the Liturgical Movement," *Orate Fratres* 10 (1936): 488–9.

11   "What blasphemy! As if there were anything really Christian about our modern capitalism": Michel, "What is Capitalism," *The Commonweal* 28 (1938): 6.

> This individualism is in our blood to a rather great extent, since it has been the general atmosphere we have been reared in. It is so much in our blood that it has entered into our very religious life.... It shows itself ... in the fact that many Christians pray only for themselves alone and not for the common brotherhood, and again that they pray almost exclusively in words that ask favors from God for themselves. They think only of what they can get out of God, each for his own satisfaction. [12]

This is all fine and good as a description of the sorry state of liturgical affairs, but what is the prescription that can save us from this malaise? According to Michel, "Today man needs a new liberation, a liberation from the narrow confines of his own self, from the atmosphere of pessimism and despair that pervades his life. Far removed from this atmosphere is the liturgy." [13] "Throughout the liturgy the message is the gospel of faith, hope, and love, under the leadership and example and assistance of a divine love descended upon earth in the service of man." [14]

But upon what grounds can Michel make these arguments? He answers "The very texts of the liturgy, as well as the ancient tradition of the church, call for this active participation in it by the faithful. At the same time the very texts ... likewise give constant inspiration and direction for the carrying over of this spirit from the actual worship into the daily life of the Christian." [15] According to Michel "If the first purpose of the liturgical movement is to lead the faithful into more intimate participation in the liturgy of the Church, then the further objective must also be that of getting the liturgical spirit to radiate forth from the altar of Christ into every aspect of the daily life of the Christian." [16]

We have already heard Michel mention the mystical body, and it is this concept that for Michel forms that link between the liturgy and social justice. The mystical body is, for him "the spiritual reality that is *the supernatural fellowship*

---

12 Michel, "The Cooperative Movement and the Liturgical Movement," *Orate Fratres* 14 (1940): 153.

13 Michel, "The Liturgy and Modern Thought," *Orate Fratres* 13 (1939): 211.

14 Ibid., 212.

15 Michel, "The Scope of the Liturgical Movement," 485.

16 Michel, "The Family and the Liturgy," *Orate* Fratres 11 (1937): 393.

of souls in Christ."[17] But what, more precisely, is the connection that can and should be made between the liturgy and the mystical body? Michel: "The liturgy can truly be called the life of the church. Without the liturgy there would be no Church as Christ has instituted. Without the liturgy there would be no Mystical Body of Christ, in which the divine mission of Christ continues. It is above all in the official liturgical acts of the Church that Christ himself lives and acts."[18] Thus, the liturgy is the instrument, the means, through which Christ in present in the world, through his Church, the mystical body. The *effect* of participation in the liturgy is to be formed into the likeness of Christ, whose present earthly form is the mystical body.

In a sense, however, it is necessary to form one's self individually before the social aspects of the liturgy may be realized. The purpose of the liturgical action, according to Michel, is

> the losing of one's life in order to find it on a higher level. It is an ennobling of self, a sort of divinization of self, in which the best characteristics of the self are not destroyed but transformed into a higher supernatural richness of being. Liturgical action means the oblation of self, it is true, but never the annihilation of self. ... All the members participating in the common action become thus enriched, each becomes a new man in Christ, and all are assimilated to one and the same transcendent Christ. And yet all the members thus ennobled remain ever different among themselves, truer and higher individual personalities than before. [19]

Elsewhere Michel address the issue of incorporation rather than annihilation, saying: "It is this double character, the harmonious fusion of the two elements of human nature, the individual and the social, that we must not only keep in mind, but must again become dominant in all human life. How can it be done?"[20] Michel answers that it is through "a harmonious combination of the two complementary factors of humankind, that is, organic fellowship coupled

---

17 Michel, *Our Life in Christ* (Collegeville, Minnesota: Liturgical Press, 1939), 35.

18 Ibid., 50.

19 Michel, "Religious Experience: Liturgy Depersonalizes Piety?" *Orate Fratres* 13 (1939): 494.

20 Michel, "The Liturgy the Basis of Social Regeneration," 530.

with full respect for human personality and individual responsibility."[21]

Michel adroitly brings together the importance of the individual's responsibility to participate in the liturgy while nevertheless emphasizing the implicit social ends to which the liturgy calls. The liturgy changes everything, Michel argues, affecting all relationships between humans and creation. He says:

> The liturgy has an important part to play since it has preserved intact the supernatural model of human fellowship in full harmony with the complete responsibility of all individual members. Having learned again from the liturgy the harmonious relation of responsible personalities and their voluntary cooperation in the common life of the fellowship we must apply these Christian concepts to all the forms of our social life, the family, the community, the state, and thus build up anew a Christian social order of life. The basic notions of duty and right must be given new vitality by a right understanding of human responsibility, of the human person and not the individual as the basic element of social fellowship.[22]

Perhaps even more succinctly, Michel states that the "liturgy is at once the perfection of the individual and the union of the individual in a common fellowship ... whose liturgy is not the spasmodic exercise of isolated acts of worship but the spiritual source and inspiration of life that is to be lived every moment of the day."[23] All of this discussion can become rather abstract, and so it is important be reminded by Michel that at the core, the liturgy and our discipleship from it takes as its model Jesus Christ, whose

> whole mission was one of service. This is admirably copied in the liturgy, as it must be if the liturgy is to continue His mission. ... The faithful cannot participate in the liturgy without in turn being imbued with the spirit of the sympathy of Christ for all men.[24] For it is instinct with Christ's own love for all mankind, and it teaches the service of man for God's sake. That

21 Ibid., 541.

22 Michel, "The Scope of the Liturgical Movement," 489.

23 Michel, "The Liturgy and Modern Thought," 209.

24 Ibid., 210.

is the true meaning of the solidarity of all men in Christ as achieved through the liturgy. Without that the liturgy would have no meaning, and active participation in the public and solemn worship of the Church would itself remain sterile of good. [25]

Elsewhere the connection between liturgy and social action is made more explicit:

A flourishing of the true Christian spirit will help us to see all material goods as destined for the fulfillment of the purposes of God's creation, as instruments of man in service of God. Thus the possession of material goods will change from a mere means of individual privilege and enjoyment, into one of service of God in his fellowmen, and the social duty of wealth will again function in the society of mankind. [26]

None of this is possible, however, without active liturgical participation, which has a double meaning: participation in the rite itself, and in the world.

Michel elsewhere has made a poignant point reminding of the close connection between liturgy and the formation of the kingdom of God. He says it is "the liturgical mystery which is the making present of the work of Christ's redemption, the kingdom of God, in our very souls. Abundant participation in the liturgy means abundant pursuit and growth of the kingdom of God in our own hearts and in the entire unified fellowship of the mystical body of Christ." [27] It is important to note here Michel's insistence that our own efforts are much more than work done for our personal benefit. Our pursuit of holiness has the spiritual consequence of edifying the entire church.

Michel claims that this bold call to action will have a no less radical impact on those who participate in the liturgy: "a restoration of the liturgy to its proper place in the lives of the faithful should make a great difference not only in their active participation on the services of the altar, but also in their daily life and atmosphere at home." [28] Michel argues this is because

---

25 Ibid., 211.

26 Michel, "The Scope of the Liturgical Movement," 489.

27 Michel, "Back to the Liturgy," *Orate Fratres* 11 (1936): 11.

28 Michel, "The Family and the Liturgy," 396.

> [w]hat the member of Christ does in a concentrated way in the Mass must also be done in a wider way in all his actions, in all his contacts with even his material environment. The manner in which the material goods of earth play a part in the liturgical worship must also be a model for the way in which they play their part in all his daily life. [29]

This connection between liturgy and life is one that, of course, Dorothy Day and the Catholic Worker Movement sought to forge every day. Consider just a few examples of this from the CWM already while Michel was himself still alive. As Dorothy Day reflected in her "On Pilgrimage" column of October 1953 "Fr. Michel and Peter [Maurin] used to talk of liturgy and sociology, liturgy and community, liturgy and work until the early hours of the morning." [30] Also, Stanley Vishnewski writes in his memoir, *Wings of the Dawn:*

> It was Father Virgil Michel, OSB, then dean of St. John's University in Collegeville, Minn., who came to us one afternoon and told us about the relationship of the Mystical Body of Christ to society. Father Virgil told us that the liturgical movement was the primary apostolate.... He emphasized strongly the need for liturgical prayers-the recitation of the Divine Office by laymen so as to bring their minds and thoughts into harmony.... As a result of Father Virgil's visit the custom of reciting Compline was instituted in the Catholic Worker." [31]

The following report of a Catholic Worker gathering, published in *Orate Fratres*, explicitly demonstrates the intimate connection that existed between the liturgical, the pedagogical, and the social:

> The relation between Christian living through the liturgy and Christian social thought and work was vividly illustrated at the Catholic Worker Colloquim held at Detroit.... The first day very appropriately began with a dialog Mass and general Communion, and was devoted entirely to addresses and dis-

---

29 Michel, *The Christian in the World*, 104.

30 Day, "On Pilgrimage: October 1953," *The Catholic Worker* (October 1953): 6.

31 Stanley Vishnewski, *Wings of the Dawn* (New York: The Catholic Worker, 1984), 58.

cussions of the spiritual basis of Catholic social activity: the doctrine of the mystical body put into practice in communal liturgical prayer and Sacrifice.... [T]he primacy of the spiritual solution to the problems was emphatically upheld. ... There are of course others who still can see little relation between, let us say, praying Compline and feeding the poor, but the general religious outlook is strongly liturgical among quite a number of the Catholic Worker groups. [32]

And it was not only among the leaders of the movement that liturgical life flourished; their passion influenced those who came into the Catholic Worker houses and farms as well:

The Catholic Worker unit here has been aware for long of the place and importance of the liturgy in its program. The reading of Compline at the meetings has been part of the regular procedure here for the past two years, just as in the center at New York. Now, however, with the opening of the coffee line over two hundred destitute men appear each morning, who offer a rich field for liturgical practice. [33] One of these men suggested that those in the line who were pious Catholics might attend Mass each morning in a group. The idea has been adopted, and each morning many of these men walk in a body to Mass before allowing themselves to the coffee and rolls. Three or four non-Catholics in the group have asked to accompany us, which fact gives great consolation to all the workers. We were made bold by the excellent spirit in so many of the men to carry the liturgical spirit even more intimately into our lives.... We ourselves have come to realize for perhaps the first time how mysteriously and beautifully the Spirit breathes in the words. It penetrates our day in a peculiar way, and has carried a new kind of life into the shop and among the men of the coffee line. [34]

---

32 "The Apostolate: Liturgical Briefs," *Orate Fratres* 12 (1938): 523.

33 Joseph McDonald, "A Liturgical Apostolate," *Orate Fratres* 12 (1938): 272.

34 Ibid., 273.

And this, in the language of the early twentieth century, is "Helping the Hobo to God" by William Gauchat:

> The Catholic Worker movement as a whole is liturgical-minded. It is interested in the practice, the study and spread of liturgical worship. But if the average Catholic layman is largely indifferent to the meaning of the liturgy, what chance is there with these homeless men? What chance with these hoboes, most of whom have forgotten how to bless themselves? Contrary to expectations, when he does come back to the faith—as gradually most of them do who live in the House of Hospitality—he finds his way back to his religion through the liturgy! He finds the spirit of the liturgy more in keeping with his nature than the sentimental private devotions which he had come to associate with the essence of religion. After three years, I dare say that there are more users of the Sunday missal, and the daily missal too, at our House than can be found in any lay group of the same size. And strange too, every evening a large group, a motley group, young men and old men, their faces and their clothes showing the wear of a hard life, assembles to recite Compline together, with no other compulsion than a desire to do so. I suggest that it is the balance and beauty of liturgical prayer, the virility, ruggedness and sense of unity that pervades it, which appeals universally to all men. The feeling of "togetherness" characteristic of liturgical prayer touches souls that have long been separated from their fellows, their brothers. ... The remarkable thing is not merely their attendance at Sunday Mass and the occasional reception of the sacraments, but the "miracle" of their being transformed into men of prayer conscious of their participation in the life of the mystical body. [35]

Since the deaths of both Day and Michel, and since, moreover, the liturgical reforms after Vatican II, progress has been made in clarifying the inherent connectedness of the liturgical and the social. But while progress has been made, there is still much work to be done by all, laity and clergy alike, to ensure the

35   William Gauchat, "Helping the Hobo to God," *Orate Fratres* 15 (1941): 386–387.

worship due to the Creator of all things occurs in a context where all are able to participate and unite themselves together with the Bride of Christ, the Church. Virgil Michel may be considered the father of the movement for liturgical renewal in the United States, just as Dorothy Day was instrumental in mothering the nascent movement for social justice among Catholics, but both would surely insist and remind us of the great work that yet remains. Virgil Michel, whose supposed blasphemy and heresy were ultimately repudiated,[36] pray for us!

Bryce A. Wiseman was born and raised in rural northwestern Ohio and graduated from Huntington College with a BA in philosophy. The next chapter of his life was spent working with a Korean-based non-governmental organization, living in Pakistani-administered Kashmir, Haiti, and Timor-Leste, aiding in the development of conflict resolution curriculum materials, and training teachers and students living in post-traumatic situations. Since returning to the Midwest he has pursued graduate-level theological training at the University of Saint Francis in Fort Wayne, Indiana.

36 "In 1926 the first article on the body of Christ that appeared in the English language for hundreds of years was in *Orate Fratres*. At the time, the best-known theologian at Catholic University stated publicly that he hoped this heresy would soon be condemned as it deserved." Dawn Gibeau, "Fr. Virgil, St. John's Monks Spread Idea that Liturgy Creates Community," *National Catholic Reporter* (December 10, 1993): 13.

The Three Conversions
of Dorothy Day

Mary Francis

Pope Francis published the apostolic exhortation *Evangelii gaudium* in 2013 with the express intent of encouraging the Church to begin a new chapter of evangelization. In this and other writings, he explores new and creative paths for evangelization and calls each of us to become "missionary disciples." Missionary discipleship, according to Francis, begins in an encounter with the person of Jesus Christ and is nourished by a life-long conversion of heart. Together, encounter and conversion form the impetus for joy-filled proclamation of the good news to all people.

As the Church endeavors to form missionary disciples, the example of Dorothy Day in particular exemplifies Pope Francis's model. Dorothy reveals a way to live Pope Francis's vision in a manner both fresh and meaningful to today's Church. Let us look at Dorothy's faith journey through five periods: pre-conversion, conversion, birth of the Catholic Worker movement, second conversion, and re-commitment to the Catholic Worker.

1. Pre-Conversion

This period stretches from Dorothy's entrance into the University of Illinois at age sixteen through her stay in New Orleans, a period of roughly ten years. Many are familiar with her story and know that her journey through early adulthood was not easy. Yet this period was marked by encounter with and the presence of God. Even from childhood Dorothy remembers experiencing God in her life. Pope Francis's words are apt: "Every human person is the object of God's infinite tenderness, and he himself is present in their lives."[1]

Although true conversion was waiting in the future, certain emergent themes became apparent during this time period and marked the character of her faith journey. These themes are attentiveness, solidarity, and a profound aesthetic sensibility.

Attentiveness: Even at a young age, Dorothy was attentive to both the particular and universal. Dorothy absorbed all that she saw and read: classic literature; radical positions endlessly discussed with her socialist, communist, and intellectual friends; and the sights, smells, and sounds of poverty in New York City. Her powers of observation were honed as she practiced her craft as a journalist. She learned the difference between a balanced story and propaganda.

Solidarity: Dorothy also developed a deep sense of solidarity with humanity in all its brokenness. Her two imprisonments, as a suffragette and for morals charges, had a tremendous effect on her. She states: "The only thoughts that brought comfort to my soul were those lines in the Psalms that expressed the terror and misery of man suddenly stricken and abandoned. . . . I was that drug addict. . . . I was that shoplifter. . . . I was that woman who had killed her children, who had murdered her lover. The blackness of hell was all about me."[2] Through praying the Psalms, Dorothy experienced a profound solidarity with all of sinful humanity. This experience led to the insight that personal conversion must necessarily precede any expectation of successful revolution. Only God could heal the disorder within people's hearts; justice would not be realized until healing and reconciliation occurred. Although her insights regarding these experiences were fleeting at the time, solidarity became a hallmark of her mature spirituality.

Aesthetic Sensibility: According to Braxton, in his work regarding conversion and community, when one pays attention to certain patterns of experience a range of questions may begin to emerge. If adverted to, these questions invariably lead to questions of ultimate meaning, which is fundamentally the question of God.[3] For Dorothy, the aesthetic pattern of experience, where she found beauty, played a particular role in her religious development. She encountered the presence of God in the beauty of the Psalms and scripture.

Dorothy's experience of Catholic liturgy at St. Joseph's Church on Sixth Avenue also had a profound effect on her. She found the Mass especially reverent

1   Pope Francis, *Evangelii gaudium*, no. 274.
2   Dorothy Day, *From Union Square to Rome* (1938; repr. Maryknoll, New York: Orbis, 2006), 7, 8, 89 (page citations are to the reprint edition).
3   Edward K. Braxton, *The Wisdom Community* (New York: Paulist, 1980), 54.

and lovely, and was affected by the devotion of the poor who attended there. Dorothy was stirred by seeing that "these fellow workers and I were performing an act of worship. I felt that it was necessary for man to worship, that he was most truly himself when engaged in that act."[4] Beauty continued to be a source of grace for Dorothy throughout her life.

2. Conversion

The period defined as conversion begins when Dorothy returned to New York from New Orleans and purchased a Staten Island beach cottage. It ends at her baptism when she was thirty years old. For the most part, this three-year period was a very happy time for Dorothy. She entered into a relationship with Forster Batterham and for the first time felt herself loved; she in turn loved Forster. The birth of their daughter Tamar Teresa also occurred during this period. Dorothy's love for Forster and Tamar pointed to a greater transcendent Love.

Dorothy's conversion cannot simply be defined as her entrance into the Catholic Church for conversion is a re-orientation of one's life, a radical transformation that is ontic in nature.[5] Dorothy's faith became truly theistic, Christ centered, and ecclesial in nature. She put her personal "moral house" in order. Intellectually, she rejected a purely materialistic worldview. Dorothy became a new person and in her new life an attitude of joy and gratitude appeared. Dorothy also began to acquire the fortitude necessary to develop her prophetic voice. All are marks of missionary discipleship as articulated by Pope Francis.

Aesthetic Sensibility: Dorothy loved living in her Staten Island cottage. Entries from her diary capture the peace and joy she found there. Braxton notes that the aesthetic pattern of experience often results in contemplation, a contemplation that is not merely observation but "a transforming encounter between the artist, the art, and art lover."[6] Dorothy's participation in the beauty of her surroundings was truly an encounter with God, the artist of all creation.

Joy and Gratitude: Dorothy's aesthetic experience and her love for Forster and Tamar brought about intense feelings of joy and gratitude. In a delightful expression of these emotions, she writes:

---

4   Dorothy Day, *The Long Loneliness* (Harper & Row, 1952; reprint, New York: Harper Collins, 1997), 93 (page citations are to the reprint edition).

5   Bernard Lonergan, S.J., "Theology in Its New Context," in *Conversion, Perspectives on Personal and Social Transformation*, ed. Walter Conn (New York: Alba House, 1978), 13.

6   Braxton, *Wisdom Community*, 61, 56.

> Down the beach the Belgians were working.... They stooped
> as though in prayer, outlined against the brilliant sky, and as I
> watched, the bell from the chapel over at St. Joseph's rang the
> Angelus. I found myself praying, praying with thanksgiving,
> praying with open eyes, while I watched the workers on the
> beach, the sunset, and listened to the sound of the waves and
> the scream of snowy gulls. [7]

In a later life interview she admits:

> I don't think prayer for me has only been connected with sad-
> ness and misery.... But when I have felt joy and fulfillment in
> this world I have always wanted to say thank you. I just can't
> believe there isn't someone to thank.... I felt thankful when I
> met Forster and fell in love with him, and he fell in love with
> me. I wanted to express my thanks. [8]

Joy is a key theme that permeates Pope Francis's writings, second only, perhaps, to his emphasis on God's mercy. According to Francis, joy is inherent in
faith in Jesus Christ and is crucial to missionary discipleship. He states: "All creation shares in the joy of salvation.... This is the joy which we experience daily,
amid the little things of life, as a response to the loving invitation of God our
Father." [9] Dorothy's conversion experience fostered an attitude of joy and gratitude that was ever present in her life.

Solidarity: Dorothy always associated her faith in God with the Catholic
Church. She did not engage in an intellectual quest for the Christian religion
that most closely matched her beliefs, nor did she opt for an individualized religion. Dorothy turned to community and embraced a particular tradition; the
character of her religious conversion was essentially ecclesial:

> I had heard many say that they wanted to worship God in their
> own way and did not need a Church in which to praise Him,
> nor a body of people with whom to associate themselves. But
> I did not agree to this. My very experiences as a radical, my

7   Day, *Union Square*, 120.
8   Dorothy Day, quoted in Robert Coles, *Dorothy Day, A Radical Devotion* (Boston: Da Capo,
     1987), 43.
9   Pope Francis, *Evangelii gaudium*, 4.

whole make-up, led me to want to associate myself with others, with the masses, in loving and praising God. [10]

Dorothy had developed a strong love of the poor and worker and these were the people she found in the Catholic Church. It was into this holy, yet imperfect, community that Dorothy desired she and her daughter be joined. Dorothy could not imagine a solitary faith.

Fortitude: Dorothy was under significant pressure from Forster and her radical friends during this period. Not only was she in danger of losing Forster, her entire social support system was crumbling. Later life interviews with Robert Coles indicate some of her circle thought she ought to see a psychiatrist. [11] Dorothy persevered through it all, including the eventual break with Forster. The fortitude she developed served her well when she later acquired the prophetic voice required as head of the Catholic Worker movement.

3. Birth of the Catholic Worker

The next period spans roughly eleven years, stretching from post-baptism to the late thirties, just prior to Dorothy's public proclamation of the Catholic Worker's pacifist stance (marked by her article "On Use of Force"). The first five years of this period were filled with raising a toddler, freelance writing, and living in multiple locations. Establishment of the Catholic Worker movement occurred in the following six years, beginning with Dorothy's infamous prayer in the national cathedral. Dorothy flowered during this period; she became the leader of a burgeoning lay Catholic movement filled with heady, explosive activity. She became a true missionary disciple.

According to Pope Francis, missionary discipleship is rooted in the movements of encounter and conversion. Conversion, for Dorothy, did not end with her entrance into the Catholic Church. Examination of these two movements within Dorothy indicates how they contributed to her spiritual formation. The themes that emerged during previous periods of her life matured and flowered during the birth of the Catholic Worker movement.

Encounter: Dorothy's prayer life grew with the movement and came to include daily Mass and the rosary, short periods of communal or private prayer throughout the day, religious reading, and confession at least once per week. Al-

---

10   Day, *Loneliness*, 139.
11   Day, quoted in Coles, *Dorothy Day, A Radical Devotion*, 54.

though her new life brought great excitement, it also brought great stress. The greater her exterior activity, the more she recognized the need for prayer.

Dorothy encountered Christ through the person of Peter Maurin as well. Through Peter's instruction, her spirituality became firmly grounded in the gospel of Matthew, in the works of mercy, and in seeing Christ in all she encountered. Implementing Peter's programs was another form of encounter for Dorothy. Round-table discussions, house of hospitality residents and visitors, travel round the country: all were opportunities for encountering Christ and continuing conversion. Dorothy traveled to the outskirts, as Pope Francis challenges the entire Church. Dorothy's stance of attentiveness and openness, begun in previous phases of her life, opened the door to greater awareness, grace, and growth.

Conversion: Dorothy's spiritual growth during this period had strong intellectual and moral overtones. After her rejection of the ideologies espoused by her communist, socialist, and anarchist friends, Peter Maurin provided the new intellectual horizon for which Dorothy was looking. Peter's revolution began not with politics and the collective, like the Communists, but within each individual's heart. The mission of the social order was to facilitate one's journey to God.[12] Peter's vision became Dorothy's as well; her missionary efforts flowed from this foundation. In harmony with the intellectual underpinnings of Maurin's thought, Pope Francis writes, "It follows that Christian conversion demands reviewing especially those areas and aspects of life 'related to the social order and the pursuit of the common good.'"[13]

More than the other three planks of Peter's program, the establishment of houses of hospitality signified Dorothy's moral conversion, both personal and socio-political. The New York house was where Dorothy and Tamar lived; the workers and guests were truly her family. Dorothy knew the poor, not from a distance, but from living with them. Some of the people Dorothy lived with were not nice; many had substance abuse issues and suffered from severe mental illness. All these were, in short, people on the peripheries, people often cast aside by the rest of society. But Dorothy did not cast them aside, but sought them out—precisely as Pope Francis stresses again and again: Christians must live in solidarity with society's rejects and must go to the outskirts, to be a poor Church for the poor. He makes it clear that solidarity is not only our mission

---

12 Marc Ellis, "Peter Maurin: To Bring the Social Order to Christ—Part 1," in *A Revolution of the Heart: Essays on the Catholic Worker*, ed. Patrick Coy (Philadelphia: Temple University Press, 1988), 15–46. Online at: www.catholicworker.org/roundtable/pmlegacytext.cfm?Number=65.

13 Pope Francis, *Evangelii gaudium*, 182.

but is critical for our own conversion and redemption: "Whenever we Christians are enclosed in our groups, in our movements, our parishes, in our little worlds, we remain closed, and the same thing happens to us that happens to anything closed: when a person is closed up in that room, he or she becomes ill!"[14] Attentiveness, openness, and solidarity: these were key to Dorothy's continued spiritual growth and they are essential for all Christians.

Proclamation: As Dorothy began to implement Peter's program, she clearly targeted bringing the Good News to the marginalized. Her inaugural article in the Catholic Worker paper states:

> For those who are sitting on park benches in the warm spring sunlight. For those who are huddling in shelters trying to escape the rain. For those who are walking the streets in the all but futile search for work. For those who think there is no hope for the future, no recognition of their plight—this little paper is addressed. It is printed to call their attention to the fact that the Catholic Church has a social program—to let them know that there are men of God who are working not only for their spiritual, but for their material welfare.[15]

According to Pope Francis, and he states this very forcefully, a missionary disciple must be an instrument for the liberation and promotion of the poor, not only for spiritual growth and personal conversion, not merely out of a sense of justice and human ethics, but because this is what Jesus did. Dorothy took Jesus' teaching very seriously; she became poor as He was poor; she implemented the works of mercy; she lived the Beatitudes.

For those who may think Dorothy was too literal in her interpretation of what discipleship means, one only needs to turn to Pope Francis's words:

> No one must say that they cannot be close to the poor because their own lifestyle demands more attention to other areas. This is an excuse commonly heard in academic, business or professional, and even ecclesial circles.... None of us can think

---

14 Pope Francis, "Address to International Congress on Catechesis," in *The Church of Mercy: a Vision for the Church* (Chicago: Loyola, 2014), 19.

15 Dorothy Day, "To Our Readers," in *A Penny a Copy, Readings from The Catholic Worker*, eds. T. Cornell et al. (Maryknoll, New York: Orbis, 1995), 3.

that we are exempt from concern for the poor and for social justice. [16]

Dorothy clearly understood Christ's call; all Christians are challenged to do so as well, finding creative ways of making this crucial aspect of missionary discipleship part of their lives.

4. Second Conversion

A second period of conversion in Dorothy's life occurred when she was in her early forties. This was a period of both struggle and growth for her. After an initial period of great expansion, the Catholic Worker movement met its first major challenge and setback, stemming from its pacifist stance during the Spanish Civil War and the advent of World War II. Dorothy struggled to live with the criticism this engendered. She also struggled with her role as the de-facto head of the Catholic Worker movement and the demands it placed on her life. To survive and find fresh inspiration, Dorothy continuously sought to deepen her spiritual life. She participated in retreats, bringing these experiences to the Catholic Worker community. In the fall of 1943, Dorothy began a private retreat that lasted six months. She seriously considered leaving her position of leadership within the Catholic Worker movement at this time. The conclusion of the retreat marked a period of tremendous spiritual development for Dorothy.

Two themes apparent in previous periods of spiritual growth in Dorothy's life deepened and flowered during her second conversion. Dorothy's horizon further shifted, solidarity became Christian charity, and fortitude became Christian hope.

Christian Charity: By this time, Dorothy had lived amongst the poor for five years. Any naiveté regarding living in a house of hospitality had long fled. She frequently wrote of the pain and anguish she felt living with those society abandoned: "As I sit I am weeping. I have been torn recently by people, by things that happen. Surely we are, here in our community, made up of poor lost ones, the abandoned ones, the sick, the crazed and the solitary human beings whom Christ so loved and in whom I see, with a terrible anguish, the body of his death." [17] Dorothy's earlier experiences of solidarity were transformed into true Christian charity. Dorothy saw the face of Christ in all she served; her love

---

16   Pope Francis, *Evangelii gaudium*, 201.

17   Dorothy Day, *House of Hospitality* (Huntington, Indiana: Our Sunday Visitor, 2015), 125.

was charged with transcendent purpose. Jack English, Trappist monk and former Catholic Worker, was one of many who clearly saw this quality in Dorothy. He remarks that although she could occasionally talk in abstract terms, she always acted and spoke person to person. Through Dorothy, he learned to appreciate the true uniqueness of each human being he met. [18]

Christian Hope: Dorothy struggled with frustration and discouragement during this period, a very common occurrence to all in ministry. Pope Francis teaches that a lack of deep spirituality can turn into pessimism, fatalism, and mistrust, a constant temptation for all missionary disciples. He calls Christians to "an interior certainty, a conviction that God is able to act in every situation, even amid apparent setbacks.... It involves knowing with certitude that all those who entrust themselves to God in love will bear good fruit." [19] Dorothy's retreat experiences, especially the six months spent in silence, seem to have provided the foundation needed for continued ministry the remainder of her life. The virtue of fortitude became Christian hope.

5. Recommitment to the Catholic Worker

The fifties, sixties, and early seventies were active, vibrant years for Dorothy. She continued to live and serve guests in the New York Catholic Worker house; she worked tirelessly for the causes of social justice and peace. She became a founding member of what is now Pax Christi. She, together with other Catholic peacemakers, influenced the course of the Vatican II and its statements regarding the arms race. Dorothy supported the civil rights movement, and the United Farm Workers Union, and was a witness or participant in many of the most significant social movements of the mid-twentieth century.

As we conclude this study of Dorothy's journey, it is fitting to return to two themes that emerged in previous phases of her life, and emerged anew in this final phase.

Sacramental Imagination: Dorothy's attentiveness to those around her and her ability to paint word pictures to highlight injustice developed over the years as she wrote for the New York Catholic Worker and lived in a house of hospitality. What was previously a profound aesthetic sense became a powerful sacramental imagination. All of creation was charged with the presence of God. This caused Dorothy both joy and pain. One of the most moving examples of

18　Jack English quoted in Jim Forest, *Love is the Measure*, rev. ed., (Maryknoll, New York: Orbis, 1994), 148.

19　Ibid., 279.

Dorothy's sacramental imagination was her Catholic Worker editorial, written shortly after the United States dropped atom bombs on Hiroshima and Nagasaki. She thought of the vaporized "men, women, and babies," she wrote, "scattered to the four winds over the seven seas. Perhaps we will breathe their dust into our nostrils, feel them in our faces in the fog of New York, feel them in the rain on the hills of Easton."[20]

Joy and Gratitude: Dorothy struggled with the same kinds of frustration, depression, and desperation that most of us do. Yet Dorothy found great joy in the simplicity of everyday life. It's important to remember that, for the most part, her life was lived in ordinary ways. She cared for her Catholic Worker guests and her grandchildren; she cooked, cleaned, and paid bills. Her journals are peppered with observations and little anecdotes. People were attracted to her; she had a way of making each person feel special, unique, and loved. She inspired those around her to do great things. It may be this quality, more so than any other, that gives evidence of her missionary discipleship according to Pope Francis's model:

> The work of evangelization enriches the mind and the heart; it opens up spiritual horizons; it makes us more and more sensitive to the workings of the Holy Spirit, and it takes us beyond our spiritual construct. A committed missionary knows the joy of being a spring which spills over and refreshes others.[21]

Would that all Christians were missionary disciples like Dorothy Day!

Mary Francis is a graduate of Sacred Heart Major Seminary in Detroit, where she earned an M.A. in Theology. Her master's thesis focused on Dorothy Day's initial conversion utilizing the categories of Bernard Lonergan. She serves as co-leader of the RCIA process and spiritual advisor for the Evangelization Commission at Holy Name Parish. Her extensive volunteer experience includes service as a Girl Scout leader, adult literacy center advisory board member, and various activities involving liturgy and spirituality. Mary is employed at Ford Motor Company as a degreed mechanical engineer leading project management for the Dearborn Design Studios.

20 Dorothy Day, "We Go On Record," in *A Penny a Copy*, 46.
21 Pope Francis, *Evangelii gaudium*, 272.

What Is It That I Love
When I Love My God?
Dorothy Day and
St. Augustine's *Confessions*

James Johnson

During the long Labor Day weekend of 1940, Dorothy took part in a group spiritual retreat she had organized at the Catholic Worker farm in Easton, Pennsylvania. "Too little attention has been placed on the idea of mass conversion,"[1] she had written in an open invitation published in *The Catholic Worker* newspaper. "All are called to be saints." Representatives from over twenty houses-of-hospitality and farming communes joined her from across the country. As Dorothy would recall years later:

> It was the last great get-together the Catholic Workers had before we were separated by [WWII], our workers dispersed to the far ends of the earth, in the service, in jails and conscientious objector camps, the houses closed.[2]

In many ways, this retreat marked a turning point for the first generation of the Worker movement. Though Dorothy knew the "little flock" that broke bread together in Easton would endure great hardship in the coming years, her retreat notes exude faith in the "supernatural" awakening she was witnessing:

> Supernatural actions bring with them a reward, an increase. Natural actions bring natural reward and end at the grave. We must try to amass more and more God in our hearts. "Our

---

1   Day as quoted in William Miller, *Dorothy Day: A Biography* (San Francisco: Harper & Row, 1982), 337.

2   Dorothy Day, "What Dreams Did They Dream? Utopia or Suffering?" *The Catholic Worker* (July–August 1947).

hearts were made for thee, O Lord, and find no rest until they rest in thee."[3]

In this story, we find Dorothy relying on St. Augustine as a spiritual guide. The quotation from her retreat notes ("Our hearts were made for thee, O Lord …") is taken from the first paragraph of Augustine's *Confessions*. It is not uncommon to find similar references to Augustine (along with Thérèse, Teresa, Catherine, Francis and many other saintly companions) scattered throughout Dorothy's writing. In reading her notes, articles, speeches, letters and diaries, it quickly becomes clear that "saints were as real to Dorothy as her visual friends."[4]

In this small study, I have attempted to collect examples of Dorothy's use of Augustine's thought, mindful of the different contexts in which she references *Confessions*. I believe this is a worthy endeavor, now more than ever, because of Dorothy's cause for sainthood. As we follow her through the lengthy process of being canonized a saint, we must look to Dorothy's own reflections on holiness for guidance.

The connection between Dorothy and Augustine has been highlighted before. Most notably, Cardinal John O'Connor described Dorothy's pre-conversion life as "akin to that of the pre-converted Augustine" when he officially announced her cause in 2000.[5] Because Dorothy had an abortion in her early life, O'Connor claimed she was a "model for all in the third millennium, but especially for women who had had or are considering abortions."[6] Cardinal Timothy Dolan also characterized her early life as "Augustinian" when he addressed the U.S. Conference of Catholic Bishops in 2012:

> She was the first to admit it: sexual immorality, there was a religious search, there was a pregnancy out of wedlock, and an abortion. Like Saul on the way to Damascus, she was radically changed.[7]

---

3 Day as quoted in Miller, *Dorothy Day*, 337.

4 Brigid O'Shea Merriman, O.S.F, *Searching for Christ: The Spirituality of Dorothy Day* (Notre Dame, Indiana: University of Notre Dame Press, 1994), 172.

5 Cardinal John O'Connor, "Dorothy Day's Sainthood Cause Begins," *Catholic New York* (March 16, 2000).

6 O'Connor, "Dorothy Day's Sainthood."

7 Cardinal Timothy Dolan in Mark Pattison, "US Bishops Endorse Sainthood Cause of Catholic Worker's Dorothy Day." *Catholic News Service*, November 13, 2012. Online at http://www.catholicnews.com/data/stories/cns/1204800.htm.

Yet, the connection between Dorothy and Augustine is far deeper than these comments suggest. According to Brigid O'Shea Merriman, OSF, reading Augustine's *Confessions* "encouraged and supported Dorothy's conversion to Catholicism and informed and enriched her spirituality for the rest of her life."[8] Merriman refers to *Confessions* as part of a "trilogy" of Christian literature that was foundational to Dorothy's spiritual thought, along with Scripture and *The Imitation of Christ*. Dorothy first read *Confessions* at age fifteen and still referred to it as her "regular reading"[9] at age seventy-eight. She quoted her favorite passage in her last public address in 1976,[10] and quoted it again in her column in *The Catholic Worker* just four months before she died.[11]

Though Dorothy's relationship with *Confessions* is well established, there is still much to be learned from her use of Augustine's insights in her writing. In particular, I wish to highlight Dorothy's favorite passage, which begins with Augustine's question, "What is it that I love when I love my God?" We can easily track her appropriation of Augustine's insights by examining the contexts in which she uses this passage in her writing. In *Confessions*, Augustine declares that his love for God is "not an uncertain feeling but a matter of conscious certainty,"[12] a feeling he encounters wherever he turns. His words will prove insightful in our search to understand Dorothy's claim that "the saints are those who knew how to love, whose lives were transformed by love."[13]

Augustine's Ascent to God

In books I–IX of *Confessions*, Augustine narrates the first thirty-three years of his life, chronicling both his descent into self-indulgence and his ascent to God. Reflecting on his early life and career, he wrote, "my soul was in rotten health. In an ulcerous condition it thrust itself to outward things, miserably avid to be scratched by contact with the world of the senses."[14] After rediscovering the Christian faith of his childhood, he abandoned his career as a professional

---

8 Merriman, *Searching for Christ*, 34.

9 Dorothy Day to Eunice Shriver, in *All The Way to Heaven: The Selected Letters of Dorothy Day*, ed. Robert Ellsberg (Milwaukee, Wisconsin: Marquette University Press, 2010), 422.

10 Miller, *Dorothy Day*, 513.

11 Dorothy Day, "On Pilgrimage," *The Catholic Worker* (September 1980).

12 St. Augustine, *Confessions*, trans. Henry Chadwick (Oxford and New York: Oxford University Press, 1991), X.vi.8.

13 Day as quoted in Merriman, *Searching for Christ*, 173.

14 St. Augustine, *Confessions*, III.i.1.

teacher of rhetoric, left his mistress of fifteen years, and began a new life. In her seventies, Dorothy recalled reading this section of *Confessions* during her conversion to Catholicism in her late twenties. "The story of his past life and his turning from that life," she wrote, "had struck me and I knew that I had reached a turning point in my own life." [15]

After the autobiographical narrative of Books I–IX of *Confessions*, Augustine shifts to a close study of memory, time, eternity and Creation. As one of his translators, Henry Chadwick, notes, "the last four books (X–XIII) make explicit what is only hinted at in the autobiographical parts," namely that conversion "is also the story of the entire created order." [16] Dorothy's favorite passage appears early in Book X, when Augustine asks, "What is it I love when I love my God?" [17] The sensation of love pierces his heart, yet he struggles to comprehend what it is:

> It is not physical beauty nor temporal glory nor the brightness of light dear to earthly eyes, nor the sweet melodies of all kinds of songs, nor the gentle odour of flowers and ointments and perfumes, nor manna or honey, nor limbs welcoming the embraces of the flesh; it is not these I love when I love my God.

These pleasures do not fully possess what Augustine knows he loves, but they point to something beyond themselves. Augustine describes the love he feels through the qualities of the pleasures he has just negated:

> Yet there is a light I love, and a food, and a kind of embrace when I love my God—a light, voice, odour, food, embrace of my inner man, where my soul is floodlit by light which space cannot contain, where there is sound that time cannot seize, where there is a perfume which no breeze disperses, where there is a taste for food no amount of eating can lessen, and where there is a bond of union that no satiety can part. That is what I love when I love my God.

This second part of Augustine's answer is the passage Dorothy so often quoted.

---

15   Dorothy Day, "All is Grace fragment X," Marquette University Archives, Catholic Worker Papers.

16   Henry Chadwick, introduction to *Confessions*, xxiv.

17   Augustine, *Confessions*, X.vi.8.

In it, she identified her own experience of conversion.

According to theologian Carol Harrison, this passage reflects Augustine's "entire anthropology of the 'inner man' ... who is truly the image of God."[18] Given that humanity bears the form of God, we may find the image of God within ourselves. The passage demonstrates a process of illumination in which Augustine discovers the light of God through his experiences of the material realm. Though we perceive our reality through the senses, it is due to the impression of God on the inner person that we are capable of judging the divine in what we experience. Illumination is possible because we are already a reflection of God.

Harrison adds, "[Augustine] does not think solely in terms of knowledge, or the exercise of the memory and understanding, but more importantly and fundamentally in terms of the will and love which inspires man's search for knowledge."[19] The love Augustine seeks to understand is just as foundational to the inner man as the rational mind. What Augustine loves is not identified by the objects his senses find so beautiful, but by the character of his inner experience. To illustrate the point, he tries and fails to pinpoint an object he can identify as his love. He playfully asks the earth if it is his love, but it responds "It is not I."[20] He asks every created thing around him, but all point beyond themselves, responding to his questions by simply reflecting God's beauty. At last, he turns towards himself, knowing that "what is inward is superior."[21] The mind, formed as an impression of God, must be formed in love if it is capable of recognizing love outside itself. For this reason, Augustine quotes Romans 1:20, "the invisible things of God are understood and seen through the things which are made."[22]

The spirit of Book X of *Confessions* is conveyed in its first line: "May I know you, who know me."[23] To know God requires a disposition of confession which, for Augustine, is to remain unhidden from God. He senses that his refusal to confess leaves him hiding God from himself, though he can never hide himself from God. The act of confession is therefore an act of self-disclosure and self-abandonment. Conversion *(conversio)* represents a turning towards God, whereas aversion *(aversio)* represents a turning away. As Carl Vaught notes in

18 Carol Harrison, *Beauty and Revelation in the Thought of Saint Augustine* (New York: Clarendon, 1992), 150.

19 Harrison, *Beauty and Revelation*, 148.

20 St. Augustine, *Confessions*, X.vi.9.

21 Ibid., X.vi.8.

22 Ibid., X.vi.9.

23 Ibid., X.i.1.

his commentary on *Confessions,* to hide ourselves from God is to "lose our positive orientation toward him."[24] This failure can become "a volitional orientation in the opposite direction,"[25] a deformation of the image of God within us.

Dorothy's "Augustinian" Insights

In Dorothy's archives at Marquette University, there is a single, typed page titled "J.28.2." Though it is clearly written by Dorothy, the date or purpose of this document is unknown. It begins midway through a story in which Dorothy and another woman are speaking to each other in a jail cell. The woman sees Dorothy reading a book of Psalms every morning and evening, and confesses to Dorothy she is a drug addict. Comparing Dorothy's habits to her own, she discloses, "the first thing I think of in the morning and the last thing I think of at night is that as soon as I get out of here, the first thing I'll get me is a fix."[26] Dorothy's response is striking: "I suppose it is the same thing we both want." She tells the woman they are both desperately seeking a sense of wellbeing. Reflecting on her encounter with this woman, Dorothy writes:

> "What is it I love when I love thee," St. Augustine cried out in his confessions. Of course it is love we are looking for here and now, from the time we are born until we die. God is love. How loosely we use the word and yet there is no other word for it. We take ever means to find it and often get lost in labyrinthine means.

Dorothy tells a similar story in another document from her archives. This fragment, probably written around 1970, is part of an unfinished manuscript for a spiritual autobiography titled "All is Grace." Weaving together memories from her early life, including rereading *Confessions* during her conversion to Catholicism, she concludes with the story of a young Catholic Worker:

> A devout young woman, who worked for us years ago, fell in love with first one and then another of the young men she encountered in what young people now call "the [Catholic

---

24 Carl Vaught, *Access to God in Augustine's Confessions: Books X–XIII* (Albany: State University of New York Press, 2005), 31.

25 Ibid., 31.

26 Dorothy Day, "J.28.2," Marquette University Archives, Catholic Worker Papers.

Worker] movement" and felt so deeply humiliated by this that she spoke of this to me continually. It took a priest who was as near to being a mystic as anyone I have ever met, to explain to her that this weakness of hers was an overflowing of her own very real love for God which kept trying to find, blindly, objects for this so strong love which was present in her heart. Her own perceptions of God's love were so keen that it overflowed into her physical life. [27]

This passage, which Merriman calls an "Augustinian insight" concerning a young woman "possibly reminiscent to Dorothy of her younger self," [28] is emblematic of the way Dorothy often spoke of Augustine. The ordering and reconciliation of our love for others begins with our experience of the love of God. Dorothy describes the young Catholic Worker in similar terms as the drug addict from the first fragment, lost in the "labyrinthine means" [29] of her experience of God's love. Like Augustine in Book X, they struggle to find objects that can contain their overflowing love.

These two reflections are clear indicators that Dorothy understood and appropriated Augustine's thought on the inner person. In the same chapter as Dorothy's favorite passage, Augustine urges his readers to compare the created order around them with "the truth within themselves." [30] Human beings can easily become enraptured by the love they find in material things, for "by love of created things they are subdued by them, and being thus made subject become incapable of exercising judgment." [31] According to Harrison, it is the effect of our aversion to God, "a turning away and therefore outwards, a scattering and dispersion of [man's] faculties which are no longer concentrated within, upon God." [32] Though Dorothy recognized that the women in her stories felt trapped by their desires, she encouraged them to examine the source of their affections rather than the objects. If love is a gift from God, even misdirected love is a reflection of the reality within us.

In 1976, Dorothy gave a formal address at the Catholic Eucharistic Congress in Philadelphia. It was one of her final speaking engagements, one that filled her

27 Day, "All is Grace fragment X."
28 Merriman, *Searching for Christ*, 36.
29 Day, "J.28.2"
30 St. Augustine, *Confessions*, X.vi.10.
31 Ibid.
32 Harrison, *Beauty and Revelation*, 163.

with considerable anxiety in the days leading up to the Congress. William Miller describes her speech:

> She spoke of the love of God and of the necessity of taking that love into all creation. She told of her own experience of the awakening of that love. "My conversion began ... at a time when the material world began to speak in my heart of the love of God." It had been as Saint Augustine had written, "What is it that I love when I love Thee?" And he had answered his question by listing all of the beauties of creation that delighted his senses. That had been her experience, she said. [33]

Comparing her experiences to Augustine's, Dorothy describes her conversion as the awakening of God's love.

The date of her speech was August 6th, the anniversary of the bombing of Hiroshima. It was also the day after the Eucharistic Congress had held a ceremony in honor of the U.S. military. Though Dorothy spoke of her gratitude to the Church for teaching her "the crowning love of the life of the Spirit," [34] she made a plea that the Church would commit itself to the cause of peace. She spoke of the many lessons the Church had taught her, chief among them that "before we bring our gifts of service, or gratitude, to the altar—if your brother have anything against us, we must hesitate to approach the alter to receive the Eucharist." [35] For the Eucharist to truly be life-sustaining, she told her audience, we must first do penance for our culture's contempt for life. For the love of God to truly awaken in our hearts, we must allow the love of God to speak through the world around us.

In 1978, *The Catholic Worker* printed a lecture Dorothy had given a decade before at a symposium on "Transcendence." Throughout this lecture, she meditates on the "victim souls" [36] she has encountered throughout her life. In their stories, she seeks to understand how they transcended their dire conditions. Dredging her memories, she reflects on her mother enjoying a cup of tea the day she died, a group of homeless men reading Scripture while standing in a soup line in the rain, the many families living in New York slums that attend store-

---

33 Miller, *Dorothy Day*, 513.

34 Ibid.

35 Ibid.

36 Dorothy Day, "'What Do the Simple Folks Do?'" in *Dorothy Day: Selected Writings*, edited by Robert Ellsberg (Maryknoll, New York: Orbis, 2005), 177.

front churches, a Cuban soldier trying to build a sustainable nation "ninety miles from a Goliath of a capitalist land,"[37] and others. To conclude her reflections, she writes:

> Is suffering and death, and the strength to bear them, all there is in this struggle? This search for God would be a pretty grim affair if this were all, and transcendence too high a goal for simple folk.
>
> Let us remember *other* elements, too.
>
> "What is it that I love when I love my God?" St. Augustine cried out in his *Confessions*. "It is a certain light that I love…"
>
> And Catherine of Siena assures us that "all the way to heaven is heaven, because He said, I am the Way."[38]

The contexts for these two references to Augustine, her lecture at the Eucharistic Congress and the symposium on Transcendence, are helpful for understanding Dorothy's perspectives on confession. She believed that the capacity to transcend difficult conditions is rooted in self-renunciation. According to Harrison, this is in keeping with Augustine's thought. Man "must first purify himself and confess his sin" before he can "be open to perceive, know, and judge the beauty of Creation and God's presence in it."[39] Dorothy urged the Church to demonstrate the humility she observed in the poor and destitute.

Final Thoughts

I was honored to share these reflections at the University of St. Francis' conference on "Dorothy Day and the Church," the proceedings of which are collected in this book. Many who knew Dorothy personally were kind enough to share their memories with me, and offer their own perspectives on her spirituality. Everyone I met and heard shared a tremendous devotion for St. Dorothy (canonized or not). Archbishop José Gomez of Los Angeles was one of the most vocal, declaring Dorothy "one of the most gifted writers in Church history," a woman who strove to awaken a new generation of saints.

Dorothy's insights into Augustine' thought are a small part of her written reflections on the saints, but greatly inform the study of her spiritual formation.

37 Ibid., 176.

38 Ibid., 179.

39 Harrison, *Beauty and Revelation*, 179.

The characterization of her early life and conversion as "Augustinian" rings true; Dorothy reread *Confessions* during her conversion to Catholicism and related Augustine's experiences with her own. Yet, as Augustine would be the first to note, conversion is not a single moment, but a continual turning towards God. The clearest evidence that Dorothy's conversion was "Augustinian" is the fact that she gleaned wisdom from *Confessions* from the age of fifteen till her death at eighty-three. Augustine was one of her many spiritual companions, a constant reminder that "we must try to mass more and more God in our hearts." [40]

James Johnson is a Catholic Worker, activist and scholar. Formerly a member of the Winona Catholic Worker community in Minnesota, he is now studying Theology and Education at Loyola University Chicago. He lives in Wilmette, Illinois with his wonderful wife Molly.

40   Day as quoted in Miller, *Dorothy Day*, 337.

Detachment as a Hallmark
of Dorothy Day's Spirituality

James K. Hanna

Dorothy acknowledged the significance of detachment in 1953 when she wrote, "The fundamental means of the Catholic Worker are voluntary poverty and manual labor, a spirit of detachment from all things, a sense of the primacy of the spiritual, which makes the rest easy."[1]

Her words associate detachment and spirituality; but what did she mean by "a spirit of detachment"? And when she says this spirit of detachment "makes the rest easy", what is the rest that was made easy? The bulk of this paper will address the former, but first to identify the rest that was made easy.

Dorothy became an oblate of St. Procopius Abbey in 1955. The rest that was made easy seems perfectly condensed in what is essentially a threefold *munera* found in the prayer for her canonization used by the abbey.

The prayer reads:

> *O God, may the Church recognize the holiness of Dorothy Day, Servant of God and Benedictine Oblate of St. Procopius Abbey, especially in her dedication to the liturgy, her desire for the justice of God's kingdom, and her devotion to the poor as persons in whom Christ is welcomed. Amen.*[2]

In this paper I will illustrate how a spirit of detachment animated her devotion to the poor and her pursuit of justice, nourished by the liturgy.

At the national shrine in Washington, on December 8, 1932, the Feast of

---

1   Dorothy Day, *The Catholic Worker*, July–August 1953. 1, 7.
2   *The Clerestory*, St. Procopius Abbey, Fall 2013, Vol. 8, No. 3, inside cover.

the Immaculate Conception, Dorothy knelt and prayed for a revelation in finding her vocation. "I offered up a special prayer," she wrote, "a prayer which came with tears and with anguish, that some way would open up for me to use what talents I possessed for my fellow workers, for the poor." [3]

From that very moment it seems she tried to live in a near constant state of what Henry J. Koren called "evangelical availability."

Koren (1912–2002) was a Spiritan priest, a member of the Congregation of the Holy Spirit, formerly known as the Holy Ghost Fathers, who wrote at length on the Spiritan charism. Evangelical availability, he proposed, "remains attentive to the Holy Spirit manifesting himself in the concrete situation of life." [4]

Koren maintains that

> this availability contains two aspects. First, availability before Our Lord: we place ourselves before God, desirous of being fully available for Him. This is our personal holiness, which simply says to God: 'Here I am, Lord.' Secondly, availability before our fellow man, which makes us add to 'Here I am' the words 'send me.' This is our apostolic life, based on our availability before God. The two aspects are facets of one and the same availability in the same way as love for God and love for (neighbor) are one. [5]

Here I am, Lord; send me. (cf. Is. 6:80)

Evangelical availability therefore is a double availability, and this double availability suggests two elements. According to Koren, the first element is "an interior life of union with God, that is to say, a life of prayer. Our continuous presence before God in an attitude of availability is the very essence of a life that is really devoted to the evangelical service of our (neighbor)." [6] The second element of evangelical availability is evangelical poverty, which also involves two components: material poverty and spiritual poverty.

Material poverty, Koren explains,

---

3   Dorothy Day, *The Long Loneliness* (New York: Harper and Row, 1952), 166.

4   Henry J. Koren, *Essays on the Spiritan Charism and on Spiritan History* (Bethel Park, Pennsylvania: Spiritan, 1990), 15.

5   Ibid., 16.

6   Ibid.

can be expressed by the words: a moderate attitude with respect to the so-called necessities of life on the material level.
We cannot have a truly evangelical availability before God and
man if we are rich in material goods or desires for riches. In
such a case one will do what the young man did in the Gospel when he heard Christ's answer to his question: 'What
else should I do?' He ended up by leaving Christ's company;
sadly, it is true, but, in the final analysis, attached to his many
possessions.

On the spiritual level, evangelical poverty demands constant openness to the experience of life in its ever-changing
evolution, openness to the world. One wishes to remain always
open to the true needs of our (neighbor) in the historical and
concrete situation of life. [7]

This explanation of evangelical availability sounds very much like a convergence of the teachings of St. John of the Cross and the social message of the Gospel. And sounds very much like Dorothy Day.

If we connect the dots between the life of Christ, the theology of John of the
Cross, and the Catholic Worker retreats, or "the famous retreats" as Dorothy
called them, we will see how she came to understand detachment as a spring-
board to how she lived. Her embrace of detachment has theological underpinnings. It's not simply about austerity or an uncluttered life; it's about Christian
spirituality and the Christian life.

The terms spirituality, spiritual life, and detachment are words whose
meaning seems clear when we casually use them in conversation, but become
less distinct when we stop to consider their essential significance. It is important
to establish working definitions before proceeding, so a brief detour through a
lexicon is necessary.

I once heard someone answer the question of why there is so much violence
in the Old Testament by responding, "You should have lived in those times!",
thereby indicating the need for some fusion of horizons. A somewhat similar
synthesis is called for here as well; although Dorothy's lifetime was not many
centuries ago, her life in the Catholic Worker movement consumed the middle
of the last century. It's been a while. There is some need for a fusion of horizons,
to define the terms—spirituality, spiritual life, and detachment—in a way ger-

---

7   Ibid.

mane to those times, in accord with her Roman Catholic tradition.

This is not to say that the definitions I propose are not appropriate for our times: they are, but it is to save us from a potential error of applying more contemporary nontraditional understandings. I am thinking of a recent *America* magazine cover announcing "Selfie Spirituality" and its feature article titled "Whom Do You Follow? Christian Life in the Age of Facebook and Twitter."[8]

And while there has been no shortage of scholars who have written about the history, measure, scope and meaning of spirituality and the spiritual life, in keeping with a mid-20th century horizon, I will reference the 1965 *Maryknoll Catholic Dictionary* for definitions. I do so with the caveat that the dictionary is not intended to present a logical outline of Catholic faith and doctrine, but does provide functional, clear and accurate explanations.

Spirituality is defined as "the quality of a person who, opposed to materialism and secularism, seeks to live within the circumstances of God's providence according to His will."

There is that connection between spirituality and the spiritual life, as in two sides of the same coin. Drawn from the Latin *spiritus*, spirituality, for Christians involves an understanding of being led, and led daily by the Holy Spirit; led to discern the presence of God in a transformative way, and in a way that leads one to defining his or her spiritual life.

What did the Maryknoll Fathers have to say about the spiritual life? Interestingly, for spiritual life they direct us to the entry for "state of perfection," which reads:

> God has given us not only a natural life but also a share in His spiritual life. All life must be perfected. Perfection is of two kinds: 1) *Absolute*, in which the end of perfection is attained only in heaven; 2) *Relative*, which is the perfection we can reach here on earth, namely union with God. This perfection is reached by the three stages: the purgative way, the illuminative way and the unitive way.

Again, the theology of John of the Cross seems to surface.

The purgative stage is understood as the beginning or first stage of the spiritual life. The aim of this stage is to purify the soul in order to attain union with God.

---

8   Jeffrey J. Maciejewski, "Whom Do You Follow?" *America*, February 9, 2015, 16–18.

The second stage, the illuminative, is so named because the desire of the soul is the following of Christ by the exercise of Christian virtue. Jesus said, "I am the light of the world. He who follows Me does not walk in the darkness, but will have the light of life" (Jn. 8–12).

In the unitive or third stage, the goal is a habitual and intimate union with God thorough Jesus Christ. As St. Paul writes in Galatians, "I live, now not I; but Christ liveth in me" (Gal. 2:20).

In this definition we recognize a fundamental principle of the theology of John of the Cross: that God is all and the creature is nothing, and that to arrive at union an intense purification is necessary. His writings, *Ascent of Mount Carmel*, *Dark Night*, *Living Flame of Love*, and *Spiritual Canticle*, all

> describe the perfection of the spiritual life in the transforming union. The entire path to the union is "night" because the soul travels by faith. John of the Cross presents his teaching in a systematic manner, with the result that it is spiritual theology in the best sense of the word; not because it is systematic, but because it uses as its sources Sacred Scripture, theology, and personal experience. [9]

This helps explain Dorothy's attraction to John of the Cross and her grasp of two sides of the same coin—spirituality and spiritual life—where spirituality finds praxis in the spiritual life. In Bridget O'Shea Merriman's extensively researched *Searching for Christ* Merriman emphasizes that "prayer, work, political and social activity comprised the arena of her spirituality."

Merriman rightly lists prayer as first in this list. As Dorothy said, "We need all the gifts of the Holy Spirit; we need all the help of our guardian angels." [10]

The balance is neatly summarized by Dorothy in her 1945 essay, "Room for Christ", where she wrote,

> I am sure that the shepherds did not adore and then go away to leave Mary and her Child in the stable, but somehow found them room, even though what they had to offer might have

---

9   Jordan Aumann, *Christian Spirituality in the Catholic Tradition* (San Francisco: Ignatius, 1985), 196.

10   Robert Ellsberg, ed., *Dorothy Day, Selected Writings* (Maryknoll, New York: Orbis, 2009), 164.

been primitive enough. All that the friends of Christ did for Him in His lifetime, we can do. [11]

Finally, we arrive at detachment. Detachment is

in the ascetical sense, the result of the ability to have control over the use of material things and over one's own will. It is usually spoken of as a state of preference for the things which pertain to the spirit over the things which pertain to the flesh. The thought of man's eternal union with God motivates man to strive to subordinate all lesser things to this ultimate end, and not rejecting things that are good, but not being dominated by anything that might interfere with man's union with God. [12]

Around the year 1940 Dorothy came to discover the retreat movement which included a message of detachment corresponding with this definition. This was the "Lacouture movement", named for its founder the French-Canadian Jesuit Onesimus Lacouture (1881–1951). The retreat's message of detachment was so strong that its followers were labelled as "the Detachers." [13]

Dorothy's first of many Lacouture-inspired retreats came in 1941. The retreat preached that "the lover of Christ would seek to imitate him in his poverty, in flight from the world and social events, in obedience and crucifixion and death and the heroic Christian was to love and aid the poor and lowly...." [14] By this time, the Catholic Worker was nearly a decade old and Dorothy had already been living in voluntary poverty among and in service to the poor.

As Merriman explains,

The message preached by the Lacouture retreat had not been heard in isolation but in the setting of Dorothy's own experiences. Before she knew of Lacouture, she and Peter (Maurin) had lived from the first days of the Catholic Worker in the midst of the poor and ministered to them. Both had em-

---

11   Ibid., 94.

12   Ibid.

13   Peter Occhiogrosso, *Once A Catholic* (New York: Ballantine, 1987), 309.

14   Brigid O'Shea Merriman, *Searching for Christ* (Notre Dame, Indiana: Notre Dame Press, 1994), 134.

braced voluntary poverty in order that they might serve others in need. For Dorothy, the retreat confirmed their insight and provided her with a larger theological vocabulary with which to express it. [15]

Indeed, a word search of the archives on the Catholic Worker website returns "detachment" in her writings only after her first Lacouture-inspired retreat and none during the many years prior. [16]

Dorothy may have added to her vocabulary but was probably not exposed to very much new printed material in the retreat. She was a lifetime voracious reader and much of what was presented—Scripture, the *Imitation of Christ*, the writings of John of the Cross, Teresa of Avila, and others—she would have previously consumed in mass quantity; but it was the context and quality of the delivery.

Suffice to note that the retreat became controversial; the detachers had detractors, and much is written on that elsewhere. My emphasis is on the message of the retreat and its attraction for Dorothy, and not only the message, but the messenger, the retreat master. One of those messengers was a Pittsburgh diocesan priest by the name of John Hugo (1911–1985), who Dorothy referred to as "a brilliant teacher." [17] And what was it that he taught?

"If you really listened to Father Hugo," Dorothy said, "he was talking about the cross. It was John of the Cross. That's who he was following." [18]

And of course he was following Jesus. She often quoted Hugo, and said that hearing him preach a retreat was like "hearing the Gospel for the first time."[19]

His message and delivery certainly resonated with Dorothy, for although she had written a few years earlier that she preferred to take spiritual direction directly from the New Testament and the lives of the saints [20] she came to call Fr. Hugo her spiritual director. [21]

The preaching of detachment in the eight-day silent retreat was often mis-

15 Ibid., 145.

16 As of date accessed: March 15, 2015, http://dorothyday.catholicworker.org.

17 Dorothy Day, *The Catholic Worker*, June 1956, 2.

18 David Scott and Mike Aquilina, ed., *Weapons of the Spirit, Selected Writings of Father John Hugo* (Huntington, Indiana: Our Sunday Visitor, 1997), 22.

19 Ibid., 16.

20 Merriman, *Searching for Christ*, 140.

21 Scott and Aquilina, ed., *Weapons of the Spirit*, 11.

characterized by critics as too rigorous or even as a hatred of creation.[22] This criticism of John of the Cross was not new. The teaching of the Carmelite was explained and defended in a 1936 book by Fr. Gabriel of Mary Magdalen. His defense squares nicely with our earlier definitions.

Fr. Gabriel writes:

> Our Saint seems hard, yet he is not so. He is guided by the spirit of love, and love knows naught of the narrowness which goes with hardness. The spirit of John of the Cross is uncompromising and all-embracing... but he is not inhuman. While proposing to us the absolute Nothing as the end to be reached, he reminds us that in aiming at it we must proceed "with order and discretion."[23]

He continues:

> We think it well to emphasize this advice of the Saint, for it shows how mistaken is the accusation which stigmatizes his doctrine as absolute and rigid. The principle of necessity of complete detachment is absolute, but in its application the individual must take account of human weaknesses and needs. The man who would banish from his life every alleviation and recreation would soon fall into a physical and moral weariness which would be detrimental to the spiritual life itself. Moreover the pleasures of the senses are not always evil; there are pleasures which are perfectly innocent; but it is a question of not letting ourselves become attached to them. Otherwise we shall seek them in order to satisfy our own self-love, instead of using them for the benefit of our spiritual life and for the glory of God. Hence it is clear that the total mortification of the life of the senses proposed by St. John is not a suppression of the sensitive life, but only its perfect subjection to the spiritual life.[24]

---

22 Ibid., 17.

23 Father Gabriel of St. Mary Magdalen, *St. John of the Cross* (Westminster, Maryland: The Newman Bookshop, 1946), 29–30.

24 Ibid., 30.

Thanks to author David Scott and his website we can listen to a recording of Fr. Hugo preaching a retreat. In Conference 4, titled "The Rule of Love", Hugo speaks of detachment as a virtue. He says,

> Loving God does not mean that we love God above what is evil, but loving God is loving Him above what is good, above every good thing, even the best. This is what we mean by the virtue of detachment. To really love God we must choose to love God above anything and everything. Here is where detachment comes into the spiritual life. Detachment is really the freedom to love. Detachment is an ugly word. It sounds very ugly in the ears. People don't like to hear it. A few years ago we were told that detachment was disappearing from Catholic spirituality, but it isn't. It is the other side of love. [25]

To illustrate, he uses the example of a couple coming for pre-Cana instruction. The priest needs to find out certain things about the couple, but the most important thing is to be sure there is no other marriage; there being no other marriage, the person is free to love.

He continues with a commentary on Luke, chapter 14, to illustrate the conditions of love Jesus demands, that the distance between creature and creator is great, and that our preference for the creator should be greater than any love we have for any creature no matter how beautiful or attractive that creature is in our eyes. [26]

"None of you can be my disciple unless he renounces all that he possesses. Now he is not just talking to Carmelites," Hugo emphasizes,

> [H]e is talking to these ordinary people in the streets; he is talking to you, and to me and to everyone. None of you can be my disciple unless you renounce all that you possess. That is detachment. We have to choose God above every other thing.
>
> This is what we have to do as Christians. This is the absolute detachment that is required. Interior renunciation, interior choice of God above every creature must be made in our

---

25 David Scott, "David Scott Writings", accessed April 21, 2015, http://davidscottwritings. com/encounter-with-silence-a-retreat-for-saints/.

26 Ibid.

hearts. Give up the things of the world. What is an attachment? It is clinging to something not really needed, unnecessary, that rivals God and guides us in a way from what is important.

Hugo does concede that there are certain habits of voluntary imperfection which are never completely conquered, saying that they not only prevent the attainment of divine union, but also prevent progress in perfection. [27]

In summary, the retreat preached that one must avoid attachment; that love begins in preference and ends in union. The essential message was a mortification of desires, not of things themselves.

Without using the word "detachment" Dorothy had cited John of the Cross often in the 1930s, perhaps most notably in *From Union Square to Rome*, her conversion narrative, where she wrote:

> St. John of the Cross ... tells about the different stages of prayer and how the first state is the purgative state. He explains how though we feel this joy and this longing of God, a joy which is so sweet that even the remembrance of it is a constant spur to us, still our own imperfections give us constant suffering and unease, and the struggle for the spiritual life is a wearisome one, and that we must not expect to find ease in prayer. He makes us understand this distaste, this recoil from religion. This lethargy comes from a consciousness of the imminence of the struggle, the fact that it is unceasing and will go on to death, and we often think that sheer thoughtless paganism would be a relief.

Given that assessment, it is important to note that the retreats were not totally about renunciation. As Mark and Louise Zwick have noted in their book, *The Catholic Worker Movement*, the retreat

> was filled with the revelation of God's love—and also good food and beautiful surroundings. When some wondered why there were nice meals at some of the retreats, held in beautiful surroundings, Dorothy answered in the November 1957 *Catholic Worker* that in light of the demands of the retreat, it was

---

27   Ibid.

very helpful to have them: "We needed the comfort of those meals, the beauty of those surroundings, because in that great silence which descended upon us, many of us faced the life of the spirit for the first time, (and) in the resulting conversion of heart were terrified at the prospect of what God might demand of us." [28]

Dorothy's own struggles to give up her attachment to cigarettes, as well as caffeine, are well documented. In a 1971 interview with Robert Coles she addressed her cigarette use, among other comforts:

> The Bible helps me get through the painful times of this life, reminds me of what I am doing here. There are days when I am not feeling too well, and I dream of having a small Greenwich Village apartment, one of those top-floor ones, with the sun shining in, and a good view of the sky, and lots of plants and books and a cat, maybe, and comfortable chairs and my own kitchen, where I could cook up a storm sometimes, just for myself! I picture myself sipping coffee and reading, yes, and smoking cigarettes. Dear God, I was a terrible smoker. It's amazing my lungs are still here. I stopped, eventually, just before becoming a burnt-out case. [29]

She never eliminated caffeine and never travelled anywhere without a jar of instant coffee in her purse.[30] "A cup of coffee," she once said, "never tastes so good as when coming out of a cold room into a warm kitchen."[31] Coffee was not a comfort she kept to herself; she once wrote, "Nothing but the best, and the best is none too good for God's poor. What a delightful thing it is to be boldly profligate, to ignore the price of coffee and go on serving good coffee ... to the long line of destitute who come to us." [32]

---

28   Mark and Louise Zwick, *The Catholic Worker Movement* (New York: Paulist Press, 2005), 243.

29   Robert Coles, *Dorothy Day* (Reading, Massachusetts: Addison-Wesley, 1987), 129.

30   Margaret Quigley and Michael Garvey, *The Dorothy Day Book* (Springfield, Illinois: Templegate, 1982), 3.

31   Ibid., 124.

32   Jim Forrest, *All is Grace*, (Maryknoll, New York: Orbis, 2011), 133.

In the ascetical sense one might say detachment is what is seen in a person one calls austere, self-denying, and subsisting with nominal material comforts. One may choose this as a personal discipline or in Dorothy's case, as both a personal and religious discipline where detachment becomes a characteristic, or hallmark, of a life of evangelical availability, a life of "traveling light through the dark night."[33]

Detachment for her was *a result:* the result of focusing on controlling the use of material things and the result of fostering a state of preference of that of the spiritual over those of the flesh.

For her, the religious discipline was superimposed on the personal; that is, the discipline was motivated by desire for eternal union with God. Her appreciation of this world as a penultimate reality was a motivation to subordinate the lesser things to the ultimate end, lest these lesser things interfere with her progress to this ultimate end.

But subordination need not mean elimination. Detachment was not understood as rejecting things that are good, but as not allowing herself to be dominated by anything that might interfere with her availability for God and neighbor.

Her prayer life and dedication to the liturgy, her desire for justice, and her devotion to the poor are all well documented, but she summed this herself when she wrote, "This work of ours toward a new heaven and a new earth shows a correlation between the material and the spiritual, and, of course, recognizes the primacy of the spiritual. Food for the body is not enough. There must be food for the soul. Hence the leaders of the work, and as many as we can induce to join us, must go daily to Mass, to receive food for the soul. And as our perceptions are quickened, and as we pray that our faith be increased, we will see Christ in each other, and we will not lose faith in those around us, no matter how stumbling their progress is."[34]

In 2002 Cardinal John O'Connor formally asked the Congregation for the Causes of Saints to consider her canonization. Heroic virtue must be proved for beatification and canonization. What is heroic virtue?

Heroic virtue is virtue practiced to an extraordinary degree in motive and perseverance.

Benedict XIV in his 1738 *Treatise on Beatification and Canonization of the Servants of God* defined heroic virtue, in part, as the performance of "virtuous

---

33   Robert Ellsberg, ed., *Dorothy Day, Selected Writings*, 208.

34   Dorothy Day, *The Catholic Worker*, February 1940, 7.

actions with uncommon promptitude, ease and pleasure, from supernatural motives...with self-abnegation and full control of natural inclinations."

This understanding of heroic virtue corresponds with Dorothy's spirit of detachment and all that it animated. It is a correspondence which makes it effortless for many to pray, *O God, may the Church recognize the holiness of Dorothy Day, Servant of God. Amen.*

James K. Hanna holds a degree in theology from Duquesne University. He is an online instructor for the University of Notre Dame's Satellite Theological Education Program (STEP) and a freelance writer whose articles have appeared in *OSV Newsweekly.*

WILLIAM CARTER

Dorothy Day and Distributism

Business Management
for Catholic Workers

David W. Lutz

The Catholic Worker movement belongs to a tradition in economic thought that has been given the name "distributism":

> Dorothy Day and Peter Maurin, the founders of the Catholic Worker movement, believed there had to be a better system than one run by robber barons, in which the majority of workers did not earn enough to support their families and the conditions under which they worked violated the dignity of the person. They advocated instead the economics of distributism—an economics the Catholic Workers considered worthy of the human person made in the image and likeness of God, an economics which allowed each person the ownership of a piece of land or participation in the ownership of the means of production of an enterprise.[1]

Distributism was founded primarily by G. K. Chesterton, Hilaire Belloc, and Vincent McNabb. Chesterton wrote in 1926: "About fifteen years ago a few of us began to preach ... a policy of small distributed property (which has since assumed the awkward but accurate name of Distributism), as we should have said then, against the two extremes of Capitalism and Communism."[2] Peter Maurin

---

1   Mark Zwick and Louise Zwick, "Dorothy Day, Peter Maurin, and Distributism," in *The Hound of Distributism*, ed. Richard Aleman (Minneapolis, Minnesota: American Chesterton Society, 2012), 77.

2   G. K. Chesterton, *The Outline of Sanity*, in *The Collected Works of G. K. Chesterton*, ed. G. J. Marlin et al (San Francisco: Ignatius, 1987), V: 45.

explained that the Catholic Worker movement is also opposed to both capitalism and socialism: "The Catholic Worker stands for co-operativism against capitalism. The Catholic Worker stands for personalism against Socialism."[3]

While Chesterton's identification of capitalism and communism as "two extremes" might suggest that distributism is some sort of golden mean between them, that is not the case. Belloc understood that "Socialism and Capitalism are twin successive products of the same false philosophy."[4] While capitalism and socialism or communism are often considered to be polar opposites, their points of agreement are more significant than their disagreements. Both are materialistic and, consequently, opposed to the Catholic intellectual tradition, which recognizes that the highest goods are not material goods.

One feature of our materialistic culture is binary thinking in political economy: If socialism is unacceptable, we should embrace capitalism. If capitalism is unacceptable, we should embrace socialism. And if both are unacceptable, we need to carve out some compromise between them. Thus, American "conservatives" (capitalism is, in fact, a species of liberalism) read Pope Francis' criticisms of capitalism and then conclude that he is a Marxist. But distributism and the Catholic Worker tradition are neither capitalist, nor socialist, nor an intermediate position on a continuum between capitalism and socialism. They represent a radically distinct alternative.

The central idea of distributism is that the means of production (land and capital) should be widely distributed. Belloc explains that the "proprietary or distributive state" is characterized by "the wider distribution of property until that institution shall become the mark of the whole State, and until free citizens are normally found to be possessors of capital or land, or both."[5]

The Catholic Worker movement looks at the economy from the perspective of labor: "Dorothy wrote about the economic system from the point of view of the Catholic Workers, those who knew the poor."[6] Consistently with this approach, the Catholic Worker movement recognizes the need for a philosophy of labor or work: "The great job that The Catholic Worker has to do is to try to reach the workers, bring to them a philosophy of labor, speak to them of Chris-

---

3   Peter Maurin, *Catholic Radicalism: Phrased Essays for the Green Revolution* (New York: Catholic Worker Books, 1949), 155.

4   Hilaire Belloc, *An Essay on the Restoration of Property* (Norfolk, Virginia: IHS Press, 2009), 9.

5   Hilaire Belloc, *The Servile State*, (Indianapolis: Liberty Fund, 1977), 125.

6   Mark Zwick and Louise Zwick, *The Catholic Worker Movement: Intellectual and Spiritual Origins* (New York: Paulist Press, 2005), 148.

tian solidarity, and point out the need of a long-range program."[7] Dorothy Day wrote of Peter Maurin: "Peter was no dreamer but knew men as they were. That is why he spoke so much of the need for a philosophy of work."[8] And she provides a synopsis of this philosophy:

> Peter's Christian philosophy of work was this. God is our creator. God made us in His image and likeness. Therefore we are creators. He gave us a garden to till and cultivate. We become co-creators by our responsible acts, whether in bringing forth children, or producing food, furniture or clothing. The joy of creativeness should be ours.
>
> But because of the Fall the curse is laid on us of having to earn our bread by the sweat of our brows, in labor. St. Paul said that since the Fall, nature itself travaileth and groaneth. So man has to contend with fallen nature in the beasts and in the earth as well as in himself. But when he overcomes the obstacles, he attains again the joy of creativity. Work is not then all pain and drudgery.[9]

While affirming the necessity of a philosophy of labor, this essay maintains that the Catholic Worker tradition also needs a philosophy of management. Rather than regarding managers as adversaries, Catholic Workers should recognize them as essential to the project of serving the common good through virtuous work.

Bad Jobs

The Catholic Worker movement's founders identified certain industries as deserving of criticism. Peter Maurin focused on banking:

> When the banker has the power
> the technician has to supervise
> the making of profits.
> When the banker has the power

---

7 Dorothy Day, "Day After Day—January 1939," *The Catholic Worker* (January 1939).

8 Dorothy Day, *The Long Loneliness: The Autobiography of Dorothy Day* (New York: Harper & Brothers, 1952), 226.

9 Day, *Long Loneliness*, 227.

the politician
has to assure law and order
in the profit-making system.
When the banker has the power
the educator trains students
in the technique of profit making.
When the banker has the power
the clergyman is expected
to bless the profit-making system
or to join the unemployed.
When the banker has the power
the Sermon on the Mount
is declared unpractical.
When the banker has the power
we have an acquisitive,
not a functional society. [10]

Dorothy Day wrote that we should accept the poverty that results from giving up jobs that do not contribute to the common good:

> This would exclude jobs in advertising, which only increases people's useless desires. In insurance companies and banks, which are known to exploit the poor of the country and of others. Banks and insurance companies have taken over land, built up farms, ranches, plantations, of 30,000, 100,000 acres, and have dispossessed the poor. Loan and finance companies have further defrauded him. Movies, radio have further enslaved him. So that he has no time nor thought to give to his life, either of soul or body. Whatever has contributed to his misery and degradation may be considered a bad job. [11]

If banking, insurance, advertising, and the media are necessarily evil, then we certainly should avoid those lines of work. But are they, in fact, necessarily evil?

It is true that our current fractional-reserve, profit-maximizing banking

10 Maurin, *Catholic Radicalism*, 46–47.
11 Dorothy Day, "Poverty and Pacifism," *The Catholic Worker* (December 1944).

system is unethical. It is also true that credit unions can perform many of the functions of banks. One of the differences between credit unions and banks is that the purpose of a credit union is to serve its members, not to make a profit. But credit unions cannot perform all of the functions of banks. And treating customers as means to the end of financial objectives is an accidental property, not an essential property of the banking industry. It is a consequence of decisions that could have been and can be made differently. But a decision on the part of banks to serve clients rather than mammon is not one that can be made by tellers alone; decisions about the strategic objectives of banks are made at the level of directors and executives.

Although insurance companies often exploit people, they can also reduce the risk of a family's financial ruin in the event of a calamity. Although decisions concerning who receives what healthcare are often motivated more by the pursuit of profit than by the welfare of patients, insurance sometimes enables patients to receive healthcare that they otherwise could not afford. The problem is not that insurance companies are necessarily bad, but that many of the people who manage them have objectives other than the common good.

It is certainly true that much of the advertising by which we are bombarded is immoral. It attempts to create desires for things that are not good for us, to motivate us to pay for things we do not need, and to persuade us to strive for happiness in ways that cannot lead to that end. But is advertising necessarily immoral? The Pontifical Council for Social Communications understands that advertising produces both harms and benefits. Without minimizing the harms, it concludes that it is possible for advertising to be ethical:

> We call upon advertising professionals and upon all those involved in the process of commissioning and disseminating advertising to eliminate its socially harmful aspects and observe high ethical standards in regard to truthfulness, human dignity and social responsibility. In this way, they will make a special and significant contribution to human progress and to the common good. [12]

The cases of radio, television and the film industry are similar to those of banking, insurance, and advertising. Although they are often motivated by the love of money and contribute more to the degradation than the improvement

---

12 Pontifical Council for Social Communications, *Ethics in Advertising*, February 22, 1997.

of society, this is true contingently, not necessarily. The proof that it is possible to produce morally-uplifting films is that some such films do exist. These industries can serve the common good, but only if their leaders decide that they should do so.

If banking, insurance, advertising, and the media are not intrinsically vicious, the most effective means of ensuring that they remain extrinsically vicious is for virtuous persons to shun them. These industries will promote the common good only if persons with the goals of the Catholic Worker movement contribute to changing their characters. And such persons are needed within these industries at all levels, including top-level management, where strategic decisions about purposes and objectives are made.

Bad Shops

The ideal of distributism and the Catholic Worker movement is an economy of small farms and small firms: "We propose to re-establish the peasant, the craftsman and the small (and secure) retail tradesman."[13] Small is beautiful; large is ugly.

Decades before today's mega-corporations, some of which are larger economically than most countries, Chesterton noted the trend towards large firms: "The practical tendency of all trade and business today is towards big commercial combinations, often more imperial, more impersonal, more international than many a communist commonwealth."[14] To use the categories of contemporary economics, he believed that large corporations are both positively and normatively bad: "I think the big shop is a bad shop. I think it bad not only in a moral but a mercantile sense; that is, I think shopping there is not only a bad action but a bad bargain."[15] Belloc was a critic of Wal-Mart before its time: "The chain shop, as we now know it, has, by the way, not only the evil of destroying the small distributor, but the further evil of controlling wholesale distribution and even production."[16] The founders of the Catholic Worker movement criticized large corporations similarly: "Dorothy and Peter objected strongly to the materialistic lifestyle dominating American culture, the consumerism fomented by large corporations with incessant advertising."[17]

13 Belloc, *Restoration of Property*, 35.
14 Chesterton, *Outline of Sanity*, 41–42.
15 Ibid., 85.
16 Belloc, *Restoration of Property*, 36.
17 Zwick & Zwick, *Catholic Worker Movement*, 148.

Although Belloc did allow that some economic functions can be performed only by large firms, he believed that few industries belong to this category: "The necessarily large unit covers a far smaller field than is generally imagined. There is the railway; there is the Post Office, including telephones and telegraphs; there is the road system of the country. But the great mass of production, distribution and transport does not fall under this category."[18] But the class of economic activities requiring something larger than a family business is greater than Belloc acknowledges. "Economies of scale" play positive roles in some cases. Small firms cannot manufacture large ships. Pharmaceutical companies require large research and development departments. Many industrial goods, some of which are actually good for us, would be prohibitively expensive if not manufactured in large factories. Many beneficial commercial projects, in addition to those identified by Belloc, can be better accomplished on a large scale than on a small scale.

Though it is true that many large business corporations are vicious, it is not the case that all large firms are necessarily vicious. But large corporations cannot become virtuous without virtuous managers, capable of directing the activities of workers toward the common good. Furthermore, even a small community of workers, such as a family-owned business, must be managed. Different people have different areas of strength and weakness. One problem with an economy of small farms and small firms is that not everyone possesses the skills necessary to manage them. The failure rate of small businesses in the United States is far above fifty percent. Some workers can better serve society, with less risk of financial ruin for their families, by working under the direction of a virtuous manager than by managing their own work. We cannot achieve the economic system that distributists and Catholic Workers desire without managers of small, medium and large commercial enterprises, who need to have a clear view of the purpose or *telos* of business.

Labor and Capital

The feature of capitalism that primarily distinguishes it from a virtuous economic system is not concentration of ownership of corporations, but the *telos* of the capitalist corporation. Maximization of a financial variable is the end and all else, including "human resource management," is a means. How should workers be treated? In whatever way will result in the highest long-term shareholder

18   Belloc, *Restoration of Property*, 48–49.

value. According to Mark and Louise Zwick, Dorothy Day and Peter Maurin "knew that many business executives did not treat persons, the workers, with the dignity with which God had endowed them."[19] That is no less true today. If our economy were rightly ordered, promoting the common good, including both the good of the corporation itself and the good of the larger communities to which it belongs, would be the end and financial management would be understood as a means to that end. In other words, despite the much wider distribution of the means of production, capital still has priority over labor today. This is contrary to the Catholic tradition, which affirms that labor "is superior to the other elements of economic life."[20]

Aristotle distinguishes two ways of acquiring wealth. Natural wealth-acquisition is limited; its aim is to secure the supply of material goods needed to live a good life. Unnatural wealth-acquisition, however, sees "no limit to wealth and possessions."[21] Aristotle's natural way of acquiring wealth is consistent with distributism and the Catholic Worker movement. His unnatural way has been adopted by contemporary American capitalism.

Understanding the essence of capitalism as making capital the end and regarding all else, including labor, as means is consistent with Amintore Fanfani's understanding of "capitalism:" "The primary characteristic of the capitalist spirit is the unlimited use of all means of acquiring wealth that are held to be morally lawful and economically useful."[22] Understanding capitalism in terms of a disordered labor-capital relationship is also consistent with the thought of Peter Maurin: "Capitalists succeed in accumulating labor, by treating labor, not as a gift, but as a commodity, buying it as any other commodity at the lowest possible price."[23]

Management and Labor

It is significant that, in naming their opponents, distributist and Catholic Worker authors often treat the owners and managers of business corporations as a single group, even though American capitalism is characterized by the sep-

---

19 Zwick & Zwick, *Catholic Worker Movement,* 148.

20 *Gaudium et Spes* no. 67.

21 Aristotle, *The Politics,* trans. Carnes Lord (Chicago & London: University of Chicago Press, 1984), 1257a1.

22 Amintore Fanfani, *Catholicism, Protestantism and Capitalism* (Notre Dame, Indiana: University of Notre Dame Press). 25.

23 Maurin, *Catholic Radicalism,* 27–28.

aration of ownership and control. Chesterton writes about "the hopeless block of concentrated capital and management."[24] And, according to Mark and Louise Zwick, the founders of distributism "insisted that people should not be treated like cogs in a machine or made to work twelve hours a day in backbreaking work in coal mines or factories while the directors and stockholders of the corporations became fabulously wealthy."[25] While it is true that most managers and directors are also stockholders, most stockholders are not managers or directors. In thinking about what is wrong with our economy, we should observe the distinction between the labor-capital relationship and the labor-management relationship. Even if capitalism were eliminated, management would still be required. (Even Catholic Worker houses need to be managed.) Although labor should have priority over capital, labor and management should work together toward common goals.

The idea that workers and managers are adversaries is itself a feature of capitalism. According to Milton Friedman, perhaps the most persuasive twentieth-century apologist for American capitalism, workers and managers should pursue their mutually-conflicting interests:

> In [a free] economy, there is one and only one social responsibility of business—to use its resources and engage in activities designed to increase its profits so long as it stays within the rules of the game, which is to say, engages in open and free competition, without deception and fraud. Similarly, the "social responsibility" of labor leaders is to serve the interests of the members of their unions.[26]

Peter Maurin was in agreement with Friedman that labor and management have conflicting interests, but proposed solving the problem by sacking the managers:

> The C. I. O. and the A. F. of L. help the worker fight the boss. But the worker must have a boss before the C. I. O. and the A. F. of L. can be of help to the worker in fighting a boss. If it is a good thing to be a boss, it is a good thing to help the worker to

24 Chesterton, *Outline of Sanity*, 205.

25 Zwick & Zwick, *Catholic Worker Movement*, 160.

26 Milton Friedman, *Capitalism and Freedom* (Chicago: University of Chicago Press, 1962), 133.

be his own boss. If it is a bad thing to exploit the worker, it is a good thing to help the worker exploit himself. 'Fire the boss and be your own boss' is a good slogan for the worker."[27]

Some bosses, no doubt, deserve to be fired. But every community of workers needs someone to accept the responsibility of directing its efforts toward appropriate objectives. Instead of firing the bosses, we should provide them with a philosophy of management according to which they can become virtuous and promote the common good as managers. One of the reasons there are so many bad managers is that becoming a good manager is not easy.

Catholic Management

Although distributism and the Catholic Worker movement do not provide us with a philosophy of management, they, along with the larger Catholic intellectual tradition to which they belong, provide many ideas that can be used in formulating such a theory. Peter Maurin tells us, "Our business managers don't know how to manage the things they try to manage because they don't understand the things they try to manage."[28] Contemporary capitalism, rooted in the individualistic social-contract tradition, understands the business corporation as a collection of individuals. There is no common good; shareholders, directors, managers and workers all promote their conflicting interests. We should understand the corporation, not as collections of individuals, but as a community of persons. Within such a community, promoting the common good is good for oneself.

Once the ontology of the business firm is correctly understood, the next step is to consider the teleology of business management. Peter Maurin tells us that "corporations are organized to promote wealth for the few."[29] American corporations today are organized to promote the wealth of shareholders, who are few in some cases and many in other cases. But this is not some immutable law of economics; it is a human decision that can and should be made differently. Maurin also tells us, "A private enterprise must be carried out for the common good."[30] To be consistent with the Catholic intellectual tradition and the common nature of humanity, there can be no other objective.

27 Peter Maurin, *Catholic Radicalism*, 136.
28 Ibid., 68.
29 Ibid., 80.
30 Ibid., 186.

The next step is to consider a few of the virtues needed by managers of Catholic workers. Chesterton notes that large corporations lack competence: "The big commercial concerns of today are quite exceptionally incompetent. They will be even more incompetent when they are omnipotent. Indeed, that is, and always has been, the whole point of a monopoly; the old and sound argument against a monopoly. It is only because it is incompetent that it has to be omnipotent."[31]

If large corporations are necessary in some industries, they cannot become competent without competent managers. And becoming a competent manager means acquiring the cardinal virtue of prudence, which enables its possessor to make good decisions in complex situations, where no rule, textbook or calculation can supply the solution. Managerial competence is not learned in MBA programs, but is acquired through years of experience in making better and better decisions. Although no financial objective is the proper end of business management, prudent management, including prudent financial management, is required to achieve the firm's proper end.

Prudence chooses the appropriate means to good ends; other virtues determine which ends are good. Catholic managers also need the virtue of justice. And there is more to justice than distributive justice. In their pastoral letter "Economic Justice for All," the U.S. Catholic Bishops distinguish three dimensions of justice: commutative, distributive, and social justice, where the latter is what Aristotle and St. Thomas Aquinas called legal or general justice. Distributism has much to say about distributive justice. Commutative justice is important in virtuous business; products and services should be exchanged at a just price, which may or may not be the profit-maximizing price. But the third species of justice also has an important role to play. The Bishops comment: "This form of justice can also be called 'contributive,' for it stresses the duty of all who are able to help create the goods, services, and other nonmaterial or spiritual values necessary for the welfare of the whole community."[32] In working to develop a vision of business management for Catholic workers, we should emphasize contributive justice as much as distributive and commutative justice.

The common good is best promoted in small communities. Nevertheless, it is necessary in some industries that corporations be large. The solution to this problem is "to achieve smallness within large organization"[33] by apply-

---

31 Chesterton, *Utopia of Usurers*, in *The Collected Works of G.K. Chesterton*, V: 416.

32 U. S. Catholic Bishops, *Economic Justice for All: Pastoral Letter on Catholic Social Teaching and the U.S. Economy*, 1986, 71.

33 E. F. Schumacher, *Small Is Beautiful: Economics as if People Mattered* (New York: Harper &

ing the principle of subsidiarity, not only to the macroeconomy as a whole, but also within each business corporation. Tobias Lanz writes: "It must be stressed that the application of subsidiarity is far from being an idealistic endeavor. On the contrary: it is a realistic attempt to return prudence and sanity to economic life."[34]

Conclusion

In a 1936 Catholic Worker article, Dorothy Day cites approvingly a line from Leo XIII's encyclical *Rerum Novarum*: "Labor is an honorable employment."[35] That is certainly true, but it is also true that management is an honorable profession. Unfortunately, our capitalist economic system tells managers that their purpose is to organize their firms in such a way that long-term shareholder value is maximized. One of the consequences of this erroneous theory is that workers are often not treated with dignity. The proper approach to rectifying this is not to dismiss managers as irredeemably vicious, but to show them what it would mean to become virtuous managers. The Catholic Worker movement has treated business from the perspective of the worker. But what we still need is for business also to be understood correctly from the perspective of managers as both they and workers seek virtue.

David W. Lutz received an MBA and a Ph.D. in Philosophy from the University of Notre Dame. After a decade of teaching philosophy and management in Nigeria, Uganda and Kenya, he is currently Associate Professor of Philosophy and Chair of the Liberal Studies Program at Holy Cross College, Notre Dame, Indiana. He is the author of "Ex Corde Ecclesiae and Business Education," *Faith and Reason*; "Rival Philosophical Foundations of the Good Company," *Oikonomia: Journal of Ethics and Social Sciences*; and "African Ubuntu Philosophy and Global Management," *Journal of Business Ethics*.

Row, 1989), 259.

34 Tobias J. Lanz, "Economics Begins at Home," in *Beyond Capitalism & Socialism: A New Statement of an Old Ideal*, ed. Lanz (Norfolk, VA: IHS Press, 2008), 165.

35 Leo XIII, Encyclical Letter *Rerum Novarum*, May 15, 1891, 20; as cited by Dorothy Day, "C.W. States Stand on Strikes," *The Catholic Worker* (July 1936).

Distributism and the Catholic Worker Movement

John McCormick

The Catholic Worker movement is known for its criticism of the capitalist system and the social ills that stem from it. But what are the alternatives? Both Dorothy Day and Peter Maurin advocated distributism, an approach also first championed by several English writers, among them, G. K. Chesterton, Hillaire Belloc, and Vincent McNabb. Distributism originates in social encyclicals beginning with Leo XIII's *Rerum novarum* and serves as a critique of both capitalism and socialism while addressing issues of labor, solidarity, wages, ownership, and the limits of technology. It argues that a just social order necessitates not the abolition of private property, but rather widespread ownership of productive property. In other words, it favors economic decentralization, where economic power is distributed rather than concentrated.

Economic decentralization would be one result of a society of owners, where workers own their businesses, either through the cultivation of land or through ownership of the tools of production. While many Catholic Workers as well as Distributists operated within an agrarian vision, distributist theory is not limited to an agrarian approach. In her column, Dorothy Day noted:

> All workers do not have to be farmers. There are many occu-
> pations on the land. A community needs libraries, bookbind-
> ers, engravers, letterers, craftsmen of all kinds. A community
> needs bread, and bakeries, and carpenters and cabinet makers,
> and silversmiths, and laundries, and blacksmith shops. Teach-
> ers are needed and doctors are needed, and nurses. There are
> many small towns and villages that need apostles. Where the
> men who will, like Moses, so have compassion on the slavery

of their brothers that they will lead them out of the land of bondage, literally. First by word and then by deed. There are not only the Pharaohs to be considered but the Bishops.[1]

For Dorothy Day, Peter Maurin, and many other Catholic Workers it was this approach that best served the dignity of the human person. In her June 1948 column "All the Way to Heaven is Heaven," Day notes:

> THE AIM OF DISTRIBUTISM IS FAMILY OWNERSHIP OF LAND, WORKSHOPS, STORES, TRANSPORT, TRADES, PROFESSIONS, AND SO ON.
>
> Family ownership in the means of production so widely distributed as to be the mark of the economic life of the community—this is the Distributist's desire. It is also the world's desire. ... The vast majority of men who argue against Distributism do so not on the grounds that it is undesirable but on the grounds that it is impossible. We say that it must be attempted, and we must continue to emphasize the results of not attempting it.[2]

Navigating between Big Business and Big Government

One strength of distributism is that it helps to safely navigate between the twin dangers of big business and big government, both of which tend to concentrate power. In 1937, Arthur J. Penty, on behalf of the Distributist League, published *Distributism: A Manifesto* as a means of setting out the basic creed, or statement of beliefs, of the distributists which also served as a kind of response to the *Communist Manifesto*.

Penty presents the socialist vision as accepting "the industrial system as a foundation upon which to build a perfect society"[3] and only requires the shifting of ownership of the industrial factory systems from the private sphere to

---

1   Dorothy Day, "The Church and Work," *The Catholic Worker*, September 1946. Available here: http://dorothyday.catholicworker.org/articles/154.html.

2   Dorothy Day, "All the Way to Heaven is Heaven," *The Catholic Worker*, June 1948.Capitalization in the original. Available here: http://www.catholicworker.org/dorothyday/articles/159.html.

3   Arthur J. Penty, "Distributism: A Manifesto," in *Distributist Perspectives*, vol. 1, ed. John Sharpe (Norfolk, Virginia: HIS Press, 2004), 86.

the collective. Distributists, on the other hand, reject the industrial system as "unstable" and "refuse to accept it as a foundation upon which to build, because they believe that large scale industry may be as great a tyranny under public as under private ownership."[4]

According to Penty, distributists argue that "without private property there can be no economic freedom, initiative, or sense of personal responsibility."[5] These values are also at the heart of the Catholic Worker personalism as well as in keeping with the principle of subsidiarity. The danger of nationalized property is persons find themselves at the mercy of the state.

The socialists argued that private ownership of property was the cause of numerous social evils, and while the distributists agreed on the reality of the social evils, they argued it was not private property as such that was the cause, but the maldistribution of property which resulted in laws that favored large ownership at the expense of small ownership. What was necessary was a redistribution of property.

In his *What's Wrong With the World*, G. K. Chesterton says of property:

> Property is merely the art of the democracy. It means that every man should have something that he can shape in his own image, as he is shaped in the image of heaven. But because he is not God, but only a graven image of God, his self-expression must deal with limits; properly with limits that are strict and even small. I am well aware that the word "property" has been defined in our time by the corruption of the great capitalists. One would think, to hear people talk, that the Rothschilds and the Rockefellers were on the side of property. But obviously they are the enemies of property; because they are enemies of their own limitations. They do not want their own land; but other people's. When they remove their neighbor's landmark, they also remove their own. A man who loves a little triangular field ought to love it because it is triangular; anyone who destroys the shape, by giving him more land, is a thief who has stolen a triangle. A man with the true poetry of possession wishes to see the wall where his garden meets Smith's garden; the hedge where his farm touches Brown's. He cannot see the

4   Ibid., 87.
5   Penty, "Distributism: A Manifesto," 87.

shape of his own land unless he sees the edges of his neighbor's. It is the negation of property that the Duke of Sutherland should have all the farms in one estate; just as it would be the negation of marriage if he had all our wives in one harem. [6]

The Dignity of the Worker

I would now like to examine more fully the dignity of the worker. For Distributists and Catholic Workers alike, the problem of monopoly capitalism is that a few own the capital and the masses do the monotonous jobs as simple cogs or wage slaves. This deprives the worker of their fundamental dignity.

But the term capitalism can be used in varied ways. Chesterton is careful to say what he means by capitalism. It is "that economic condition in which there is a class of capitalists, roughly recognizable and relatively small, in whose possession so much of the capital is concentrated as to necessitate a very large majority of citizens serving those capitalists for a wage."[7] In other words, he is not against free enterprise or market economies, but the condition whereby the majority of people only receive wages and do not have access to capital.

Pope John Paul II also addressed this. In *Centesimus Annus* (1991) he asks:

> Returning now to the initial question: can it perhaps be said that, after the failure of Communism, capitalism is the victorious social system, and that capitalism should be the goal of the countries now making efforts to rebuild their economy and society? Is this the model which ought to be proposed to the countries of the Third World which are searching for the path to true economic and civil progress?
>
> The answer is obviously complex. If by "capitalism" is meant an economic system which recognizes the fundamental and positive role of business, the market, private property and the resulting responsibility for the means of production, as well as free human creativity in the economic sector, then the answer is certainly in the affirmative, even though it would perhaps be more appropriate to speak of a "business econ-

---

6   G. K. Chesterton, *What's Wrong With the World*, Part 1, VI The Enemies of Property. Accessed May 12, 2015. http://www.gutenberg.org/files/1717/1717-h/1717-h.htm#link2H_4_0007.

7   G. K. Chesterton, *The Outline of Sanity* (Norfolk, Virginia: HIS Press, 2001), 26–27.

omy," "market economy" or simply "free economy." But if by "capitalism" is meant a system in which freedom in the economic sector is not circumscribed within a strong juridical framework which places it at the service of human freedom in its totality, and which sees it as a particular aspect of that freedom, the core of which is ethical and religious, then the reply is certainly negative. [8]

For John Paul, human freedom and creativity are essential to a healthy economic system.

Catholic Worker Brian Terrell, in the preface to *Holy Work*, also develops the importance of creativity in our work:

> The Second Vatican Council reminds us that through labor humanity is made a partner in God's continuing creative work and that our labor should be a gift, a contribution to the common good. Many of our jobs, unfortunately, fall far from this ideal. Much of what we do is for pay alone, and many jobs are neither creative nor constructive and do little good for our neighbors. Too often, what passes for work is actually destructive, if not deadly, toward God's creation. Too often, our work dehumanizes us and impoverishes or even kills the ones God calls us to serve. Not every job done is a gift to God and neighbor. Not every job is "holy work." [9]

Pope John Paul II, in his 1981 encyclical *On Human Labor*, noted that work is a transitive activity that begins in the human subject and is directed toward an external object. Human beings take up the resources of the earth and through conscious activity direct them towards the ends and purposes of human beings. Thus work has both an objective and a subjective dimension. The objective dimension is the work considered in itself, but it is the subjective dimension that has priority. He notes: "The basis for determining the value of human work is not primarily the kind of work being done but the fact that the one who is doing

---

8   Pope John Paul II. *Centesimus Annus* [Encyclical Letter], section 42, accessed May 12, 2015, http://w2.vatican.va/content/john-paul-ii/en/encyclicals/documents/hf_jp-ii_enc_01051991_centesimus-annus.html.

9   Brian Terrell, "Preface to the 2003 edition" of Rembert Sorg, O.S.B., *Holy Work: Towards a Benedictine Theology of Manual Labor* (Santa Ana, California: Source Books, 2003), x.

it is a person. The sources of dignity and work are to be sought primarily in the subjective dimension, not the objective one." [10]

If we are to understand the significance of work, we must understand how work is an expression of human self-realization. Peter Maurin use to speak of the importance of seeing one's work as a gift to be given. Work performed as a gift is creative and central to Christian humanism. It allows ones work to be seen as a vocation and not merely a job. Maurin once said: "But they say there is no work to do. There is plenty of work to do, but no wages. But people do not need to work for wages. They can offer their service as a gift." [11]

John Paul's *On Human Labor* also develops the threefold moral significance of work. The U.S. Bishops, in their 1986 pastoral letter "Economic Justice for All," articulate it this way:

> All work has a threefold moral significance. First, it is a princi-
> pal way that people exercise the distinctive human capacity for
> self-expression and self-realization. Second, it is the ordinary
> way for human beings to fulfill their material needs. Finally,
> work enables people to contribute to the well-being of the
> larger community. Work is not only for oneself. It is for one's
> family, for the nation, and indeed for the benefit of the entire
> human family. [12]

It is this threefold moral significance that the Catholic Worker movement implicitly understood in its advocacy for the dignity of workers, their rights to organize, and to fair wages.

Pope John Paul's reflection on the dignity of the work continues through the examination of the conflict between labor and capital in the present phase of history. In this section he notes the principle of the priority of labor over capital, and that in the process of production labor is always a primary efficient cause, while capital, the whole collection of the means of production, remains a mere instrument or instrumental cause. [13] A labor system can be right and mor-

---

10 Pope John Paul II. *Laborem Exercens* no. 6.

11 Peter Maurin, "The Case for Utopia," *Easy Essays* (Chicago: Franciscan Herald Press, 1984), 39.

12 *Economic Justice for All: Pastoral letter on Catholic Social Teaching and the U.S. Economy.* 10th Anniversary Edition, (Washington, D.C.: United States Catholic Conference, 1997), sec. 97. The bishops' document references *Laborem Exercens* 6 and 10.

13 John Paul II, *Laborem Exercens*, 12.

ally legitimate if in its very basis it overcomes the opposition between labor and capital.[14]

It is easy to see how, as in distributist approaches, when workers own the capital with which they work, this division does not exist. This makes sense when we recognize that all capital first originates in labor, which has taken up the gifts of creation and transforms them by virtue of labor into the means of meeting human need.

John Paul states:

> [P]roperty is acquired first of all through work in order that it may serve work. This concerns in a special way the owner-ship of the means of production. Isolating these means as a separate property in order to set it up in the form of "capital" in opposition to "labor"—and even to practice exploitation of labor—is contrary to the very nature of these means and their possession. They cannot be *possessed against labor*, they cannot even be *possessed for possession's sake*, because the only legitimate title to their possession —whether in the form of private ownership or in the form of public or collective ownership—is *that they should serve labor*, and thus, by serving labor, that they should make possible the achievement of the first principle of this order, namely, the universal destination of goods and the right to common use of them.[15]

In capitalist approaches to work the danger is that the worker might feel and be treated as a mere production instrument rather than a true subject of work with an initiative of one's own.[16] But in the current state of affairs, John Paul insists on recognizing the four traditional rights of labor: The right to suitable employment for all who are capable of it.[17] Just remuneration for work done.[18] Third, that the labor process "be organized and adapted in such a way as to re-spect the requirements of the person and his or her forms of life, above all in the life of the home."[19] Lastly, the right of workers to form unions in order to de-

14   Ibid., 13.
15   Ibid., 14.
16   Ibid., 15.
17   Ibid., 18.
18   Ibid., 19.
19   Ibid

fend their vital interests, particularly the above mentioned rights. [20]

In a June 1948 column, Dorothy decried the conditions that were affecting the workers in California:

> On the other hand, there are such stories as that in the last issue of *Commonweal* about the de Gorgio strike in the long central valley of California, of 58,000 acres owned by one family, of 2,000 employees, of horrible living conditions, poor wages, forced idleness "times of repose" between crops, when machines are cared for but not men, women and children. "The Grapes of Wrath" pattern is here, is becoming an accepted pattern. Assembly line production in the factory, and mass production on the land are part of a social order accepted by the great mass of our Catholics, priests and people. Even when they admit it is bad, they say, "What can we do?" And the result is palliatives, taking care of the wrecks of the social order, rather than changing it so that there would not be quite so many broken homes, orphaned children, delinquents, industrial accidents, so much destitution in general.
>
> Palliatives, when what we need is a revolution, beginning now. Each one of us can help start it. It is no use talking about how bored we are with the word. Let us not be escapists but admit that it is upon us. We are going to have it imposed upon us, or we are going to make our own. [21]

Dorothy believed in revolution. She believed a new society could be built within the shell of the old. Distributist thinking was part of this revolution because she believed it promoted and protected the dignity of the worker. Her view here was not a naïve nostalgia for a bygone era but one marked by a realism that was up to the challenge, even if it was "little by little." I will end with her defense of distributism in her essay "Distributism is not Dead:"

> The very fact that people are always burying distributism is evidence of the fact that it is not dead as a solution. John Stanley buried it last year in the *Commonweal* and *Social Justice* of the

---

20   Ibid., 20.
21   Dorothy Day, "All the Way to Heaven is Heaven."

Central Verein in St. Louis some months ago buried it. But it is an issue that won't be buried, because distributism is a system conformable to the needs of man and his nature....

"There are certain writers to whom humanity owes much, whose talent is yet of so shy or retrospective a type that we do well to link it with certain quaint places, or certain perishing associations." And [Chesterton] went on to say that were Dickens living today, he would not be harking back to the past, but dealing with things just as he found them. So that he, Chesterton, was being particularly Dickensian by enjoying his surroundings as they were, and beginning from there.

It is the same with Distributism. It needs to be constantly rewritten, re-assessed, restated, with the wisdom and clear-sightedness of a Chesterton who by his paradoxes, made us see our lives and our problems in the light of Faith, who can help us today to make a synthesis of Cult, Culture and Cultivation.

In spite of the nuclear age we are living in, we can plant our gardens even if they are only window boxes, we can awaken ourselves to God's good earth and in little ways start going out on pilgrimage, to the suburbs, to the country, and when we get the grace, we may so put off the old man, and put on Christ, that we will begin to do without all that the City of man offers us, and build up the farming commune, the Village, the "city" of God, wherein justice dwelleth. [22]

John McCormick is an Associate Professor of Theology and Director of the Gerber Institute for Catholic Studies at Newman University in Wichita, Kansas.

22 Dorothy Day, "Distributism is not Dead." *The Catholic Worker*, July–August, 1956. Accessed May 12, 2015. http://dorothyday.catholicworker.org/articles/244.html.

An Economics Neither Right Nor Left: Why Dorothy Day Was a Distributist

Michael Griffin

Among twentieth-century responses to the growth of industrial capitalism, the name of E. F. Schumacher is best known for his call for a more local, inter-dependent and person-centered economics in his classic book, *Small is Beautiful*. But Schumacher also provided a more seminal sort of wisdom—one also very relevant to our current state of world financial crisis—in a famous joke he used to tell:

> A doctor, architect, and economist are sitting around talking about whose profession is the oldest. The doctor says, "Medicine came first, because God *surgically operated* on Adam to remove the rib and make Eve." The architect responds, "No, even before that, God *designed and built* the world out of chaos." "But who," the economist interjected proudly, "do you suppose *made the chaos?!*"[1]

One of those who loves Schumacher's joke is Kirkpatrick Sale, a scholar-activist who is one of many proponents of a small, Catholic economic school of thought that has come to be known as distributism. In this paper I will explore many facets of distributism, and its connection to the Catholic Social Tradition, but it seems helpful at the outset to note how, according to Sale, this movement is actually quite popular on the margins of our present economy, in ecclesial as well as secular circles. Even if the name distributism is not always used, the following practices are related to it:

---

1   Kirkpatrick Sale, in *Beyond Capitalism and Socialism*, ed. Tobias J. Lanz (Norfolk, Virginia: Light in the Darkness, 2008), xi.

> Farmers' markets, community-supported agriculture, organic farming, home gardens, local- and slow-food movements, alternative currencies, alternative medicine, alternative energy, simple living, worker co-operatives, houses of hospitality, thrift stores, pay-what-you-can coffee shops, neighborhood potluck gatherings. [2]

I mention this list for two reasons. First, I wish to show that the economic theory of distributism that I am exploring is neither esoteric, nor abstract, nor confined only to the realm of Catholics longing for a return to medieval Christendom (all of which are common assumptions about distributism). Secondly, I want to make the point that these very achievable practices—*who has not been to a potluck in the past year?*—do not need to be mere activities on the sidelines. Rather, they can be reminders of a way of doing economics, a way of understanding the purpose of human life that stands in stark contrast to prevailing models today. In this essay, I will describe what distributism is and show how it cannot be seen as a form of capitalism or socialism. And I will defend the idea that distributism, as a distinct economic school, is the best option for Catholics to choose in working towards a more just economy. Not only will I show the roots of distributism in CST but I also will illustrate its connection to one of the great icons of the Church's social witness, Dorothy Day.

Part I: The Distributist Alternative Defined

In a paragraph that has received relatively little attention, *Gaudium et Spes* calls for a quite revolutionary economic adjustment: appropriating unused land in poverty-stricken communities and providing a path to ownership of it for persons to engage in productive activity. Under the section title "Ownership, Private Property, Large Estates," the council fathers suggest that "estates insufficiently cultivated must even be divided up and given to those who will be able to make them productive" (#71). The paragraph continues with an emphasis on how to include the poor in becoming productive owners of the land, especially through "educational facilities and proper cooperative organizations."

The promotion of broad forms of ownership within communities is a consistent theme of CST, beginning with the insistence of Pope Leo XIII that "policy should induce as many people as possible to become owners" (*Rerum No-*

2   This list is based on Ibid., xi, with practices added by me.

varum, #35). The emphasis on personal ownership helps to demonstrate the way in which CST does not align with modern capitalism or state socialism, both of which have *too little ownership* in the community at large. If CST critiques the concentration of ownership both by corporations and by the state, then distributism emerges as the alternative to the various degrees of capitalism or socialism at work in dominant models. And this economic school arose in Catholic circles during the late nineteenth and early twentieth centuries—precisely the time of CST's rise and the Church's search for alternatives to the hegemonies of industrial capitalism and state socialism.

In *Rerum Novarum*, the 1891 encyclical that launched modern Catholic social teaching, Leo was clear in the value of property: "Our first and most fundamental principle, therefore, when we undertake to alleviate the condition of the masses, must be the inviolability of private property" (RN 35). The pope here is following Thomas Aquinas, who considered property necessary for human flourishing. Of course, Leo also acknowledges what Aquinas taught, namely that one's private use of their property is subordinate to the needs of others and the common good—and thus in extreme cases the poor can even make a claim in justice to the property of the rich. But in general, for Pope Leo, private property is *the* building block of social justice. *Gaudium et Spes* echoes this concept:

> Since property and other forms of private ownership of external goods contribute to the expression of the personality, and since, moreover, they furnish one an occasion to exercise his function in society and in the economy, it is very important that the access of both individuals and communities to some ownership of external goods be fostered. (71)

The emphasis on ownership and property, while not prevalent in leftist, socialist construals, was and is the starting point for distributism. Describing their efforts in the decade after *Rerum Novarum*, G. K. Chesterton wrote that he and others were trying "to preach a policy of small distributed property which has since assumed the awkward but accurate name of Distributism."[3] Historian Dermot Quinn says of these early efforts:

> Distributism is less an economic theory than a moral anthropology. It is concerned above all with the creative subjectivity

---

3   G. K. Chesterton, quoted in Race Mathews, *Jobs of Our Own: Alternatives to the Market and the State* (Irving, Texas: Distributist Review Press, 2009), 103.

of human persons, their openness to transforming grace, and their capacity for dignity through work and property. [4]

In other words, the problem with a system like capitalism is that it does not "fit" with who we are as persons or as a community. As we will see, the aspect in which the lack of fit is clearest is in what I would call the anonymity of capitalism. Consider, for example, this "anthropology of shopping," written by Chesterton's distributist co-conspirator Hilaire Belloc in an article titled "The Ruin of the Small Storekeeper." His analysis of the problem with how we shop might as well have been written today. He laments that

> wage-earners have no special sympathy with the small store-keeper. Some few of them may have the sense to feel rather vaguely that they are all in the same boat together against the big capitalists. But the wage earning masses will buy what they need wherever they can get it cheapest and do not trouble particularly about supporting the small dealer. ... As for the wealthier people, they find the small storekeeper inconvenient, compared with the large store. It seems to them squalid, compared with the comfort and luxury to which they are accustomed, and it is necessarily less able to provide at a moment's notice what they happen to want. [5]

The problem with this kind of shopping is not simply its "anonymity," but also that it perpetuates what Belloc *et al* saw as the most invidious problem: *the loss of control over the goods which enable our flourishing*. As Belloc put it, these goods are ultimately "under the control of men different from and much smaller in number than the mass of citizens" who buy their products. And time and again, the early distributists connect this problem to a loss of true freedom. They contend that a society may well allow practices like voting and lobbying, but without *economic control over their own lives* people are not really free. More than a century after the Chesterbelloc made this argument, we can see the same logic in the writing of contemporary American farmer and writer Wendell Berry. Berry puts it this way: "If you are dependent on people who do not know

---

4   "Distributism" in *Just Peace* I (1998) (Kansas City, Missouri, 1998), online at www.just-peace.org/distribute.htm.

5   Hillaire Belloc, *The Way Out* (Catholic Authors Press, 2006), 28.

you, who control the value of your necessities, you are not free and you are not safe."[6]

Here, then, is why distributism focuses so much on ownership and property, rather than just on higher wages. When the only economic good that persons really have is a wage, which could rise, fall or disappear, and when the goods of our lives are always owned by "someone else," the result is clearly a condition of precarity and alienation. All of this is why the goal most often associated with the early distributists was to create "a society of owners." This approach suggests that the great need is for *more* personal property, not less. Less personal property is what both capitalism and socialism provide: Socialism obviously concentrates property in the hands of the state, and capitalism as it is practiced concentrates property in the hands of elite corporate actors.

I would add to this that the way we conceive of property creates a clearly absurd situation today, namely that workers around the world who actually make consumer goods in fact own almost nothing (except some paltry wages), while those who often actually make almost nothing own almost everything. This is not property in the traditional sense. As Chesterton is said to have often quipped, "the institution of private property no more means the right to unlimited property than the institution of marriage means the right to unlimited wives!"

All of this brings us to the defining point of distributism. Indeed, the word itself provides the key: in this system, property is broadly distributed. That defining aspect, the distribution of property, is what distinguishes this system from being "capitalism with a heart" or "socialism that allows for some ownership"—both of which are often very attractive options for many Catholics today. Here is my argument: when we find Catholic capitalists, for example, who sincerely want to address modern problems like economic inequality or marginalization, what they really are talking about is pre-distribution of goods like education or values. And when left-leaning Catholics decry the same problems, what they really seek is re-distribution of goods in the economy. University of Chicago Nobel Laureate James Heckman (who is becoming increasingly popular in Catholic circles) actually shows both elements in this point in his oft-quoted maxim that "the predistribution of skills is the new redistribution of wealth." To be clear, we need both pre-distribution and re-distribution, but neither is precisely distribution, or distributism, which is in fact what we need most. And so

---

6   Wendell Berry, *Sex, Economy, Freedom and Community* (New York: Random House, 1993), 128.

I close with a further specification of what distribution means and why it is the indispensable basis for economic reform.

Distribution is not about something being "doled out." In my view, that is more akin to redistribution. Rather distribution is a structural characteristic of an enterprise by which persons claim ownership of that enterprise. For example, a business enterprise—let's say a grocery store—that exhibits the characteristic of distribution is one in which the contributions of all those involved, from workers to financers to farmers to shoppers gain a share of ownership commensurate with their work. The more common, and less clunky, term for this is a co-op. But I want to suggest that what is going on is activity marked by the characteristic of distribution. Let's even look at the Latin roots of the word. *Tribuere* means to allot or divide. Dis-, of course, means away from, out from. I would suggest that in this sense the quality of distribution means that ownership of enterprises are divided *away from* a singular locus and toward a broader community of persons. This idea has plenty of theological resonance, but for my purposes here, the claim is that this quality/characteristic is precisely indispensable for any just reform of economic structures.

Often CST focuses on the external life of a business—how it interfaces with society and even with other parts of the world—but does not necessarily probe the internal life: who controls the means of productions? Are workers given ownership? Who elects the board and sets the policies for distribution of the wealth and the "property" of the business?—all questions central to distributists. Thus, while helpful in these specific calls for businesses to act in greater charity and solidarity, there are fewer resources for the inner working of "subisdiarity" in the life of the business community. In my view, this is a lacuna that needs to be filled by CST. And by providing a stronger foundation for what subsidiarity can look like, offering some models by which the goods needed for a community's flourishing are controlled at an ever more local, personal level, CST could provide an impetus to respond to one of the most troubling aspects of globalization: the "paralysis" that almost all of us feel in trying to change our global economic life.

In her research on globalization, presented at the 2010 conference of the College Theology Society, Rebecca Todd Peters reported that in all of her interviews the most often repeated sense was one of paralysis: "I see the problems, yes, but... what can I do?" The great need today, Peters argues, is "to help people enter into action."[7] In CST, the word for this is usually participation. Another

7   CTS keynote, June 5 2010, University of Portland.

word could be contribution. But I argue that if our economic model truly does encourage participation and contribution, then the best test of their presence is the characteristic of distribution in every sense: property, management, work, and all aspects of the economic endeavor.

Part II: The Distributist Alternative Lived

As the title of this essay indicated, Dorothy Day is a key lens through which to see the distributist alternative. And while she knew of the doctrine and definitions outlined above, she also was inspired by the example of distributism. One of the greatest experiments in distributist history began in the early 1900s in Antigonish, a region in Nova Scotia, Canada. This area has produced some of the most heroic defenders of the principles underlying distributism—that people should own and work the land on which they live, that workers should own the corporate community in which they labor. One of these figures was the great Ronnie MacDonnell, a farmer with the Madonna House Lay Apostolate in Combermere, Ontario and an early Catholic Worker in the decades after Day founded the movement. MacDonnell consistently noted the existential starting point for distributism: "The resources of our world were created by God, not for the wealth of a few, but for the needs of all of his children. And co-operatives provide a good way to ensure that all share in this abundance."[8]

The pioneer of Antigonish was the legendary Father Jimmy Tompkins. Tompkins had grown up in Nova Scotia in an environment known well to many Catholic immigrant families: grinding poverty, the need for personal farming to feed the family, and a focus on education as a major priority in parish life. In fact, the Diocese of Antigonish boasted an under-funded but impressive college, the University of St. Francis Xavier, and it was there, as a faculty member, that Father Jimmy set in motion the most impressive achievement of the distributist movement to that point: the education of workers. In fact, this access to education was, for Tompkins, the key to putting economic life and power back into the hands of ordinary people. Moreover, Tompkins was motivated, it seems, by an understanding of the purpose of knowledge—even the purpose of a university—which challenged prevailing notions of his (and our) day. He would ask, "Why should the treasures of university knowledge be confined to boys and girls between the ages of 18 and 22?"[9] In a pamphlet to his colleagues titled "Knowl-

---

8   *Restoration* (May-June 2010), the journal of the Madonna House Lay Apostolate.

9   Mathews, *Jobs of Our Own*, 129.

edge for the People: A Call to St. Francis Xavier College," Tompkins wrote:

> Subjects like Literature, History, Economics and Philosophy,
> that were once studied by the privileged few, are being sought
> by a rapidly increasing number of grown-up men and women
> who in their teens were not in a position to pursue such stud-
> ies. ... Disabilities and unjust inequalities, scarcely realized in
> times past by the very victims, or if realized borne with dull
> resignation, have now come to the attention of all and they
> must be redressed. [10]

Even Tompkins could not have known how much this worker education
would redress injustice in Antigonish. After the first "People's School" com-
menced in 1921, and the more general work of "university extension" to educate
workers took hold, the result was to be the formation of worker groups and co-
ops that would improve the harsh life for the region's farmers and fishermen.

The ownership of homes was one of the biggest successes of the Antigonish Movement. In one region—inhabited largely by coal miners—a housing cooperative was set up, named Tompkinsville, in which 6,500 families were able
to afford homes because of a plan which included personal savings, the donation of the family's own labor to their home construction, the mutual commitment of neighbors to complete repairs, and low-interest government loans. This
co-op came about in the late 1930s, a kind of zenith for the Antigonish Movement. At the same time, there were 342 credit unions thriving, and the all-important study clubs numbered 2,265, or 19,600 individual members. [11] But as
the co-ops became necessarily bigger and more complex to meet new demands,
they started to operate like other businesses—and the rank and file membership
began to feel a loss of control over the mission of the co-op. In one sense, the
dilemma seems all too normal: the initial wave of enthusiasm for a new movement and social change gives way to complacency and expediency. And, it must
be admitted, the history of distributism is marked by this experience of the rise
and fall of various experiments in cooperative economics. Yet this is what makes
it all the more important to analyze places where long-term sustainability has
been achieved, and nowhere on the planet is this more clear than in Mondragon,
Spain.

Located in the Basque region, Mondragon has become the headquarters of,

10   Ibid., 130.
11   Ibid., 151.

and the name for, the largest cooperative economic initiative in human history. There is an irony here. While the original distributists like Belloc and Chesterton had a decided preference for small-scale, land-based artisanal and agricultural projects, Mondragon has become a massive, industrial corporation employing 30,000 plus in the production of, among other things, household appliances such as washers and dryers. Why, then, would scholars such as Race Mathews place it squarely within the distributist tradition—albeit with his modification that it represents *"evolved distributism?"* The answer is that for all its growth in the past 50 years, Mondragon has been able to sustain a business that is completely worker-owned and worker-governed, with the property— both land and the capital—that is gained through its activity being distributed to all who are part of the Mondragon corporation. The reason for its endurance can be traced back to its origins—like the Antigonish Movement, it began with a charismatic Catholic priest using *Rerum Novarum* to educate young workers about new possibilities for economic initiatives.

That priest was Don Jose Maria Arizmendiarrieta, and he came of age at a time of severe hardship and hunger. He was determined to forge a way forward for his people, a way for them to reap the rewards and profits that he knew business often created but seldom distributed. And to find that way, he turned not only to the social encyclicals mentioned, but to many economic and political theorists (including such diverse figures as Paolo Freire and J. K. Galbraith, Karl Marx and Jacques Maritain). But one source for Arizmendiarrieta that is quite interesting is the work of Emmanuel Mounier, the French personalist philosopher who so deeply influenced Peter Maurin and Dorothy Day. Arizmendiarrieta liked to quote Mounier in saying, "Economic renewal will be moral or it will not exist. The moral revolution will be economic or it will not take place."[12] Mounier had written in 1938 *A Personalist Manifesto,* in which he rejected Marx's approach in *The Communist Manifesto* for overthrowing capitalism (though he agreed it needed to be overthrown). According to Mounier, the great need is "to implant in the vital organs, at present diseased, of our decadent civilization the seeds and the ferment of a new civilization."[13]

Arizmendiarrieta saw that one of the diseased organs of economic society was the capitalist exploitation of work. "It is a social monstrosity that a system of social organization is tolerated in which some can take advantage of the work of others for their exclusive personal profit."[14] Here we can see the way in which

---

12 Ibid., 181.

13 Emmanuel Mounier, quoted in Mathews, *Jobs of Our Own,* 181.

14 Ibid., 179.

personalist economics resists the social detachment of owners and workers—a detachment that has proliferated in a globalized economy. The response needed to be social solidarity, which explains why he personally threw his lot in with the working class. It is not insignificant that Arizmendiarrieta knew of the example of the Worker Priests in France and Belgium during the '40s and '50s who developed the Christian Worker Movement to bring Catholic Social Teaching to those working on the factory floor. The solidarity that Arizmendiarrieta envisioned was an actual intertwining of the lives of managers and workers, one in which they shared the same social location. This was not class conflict, workers rising up to overthrow the bosses, but rather a kind of "communion." He explains:

> It is not enough that the bosses undertake and do good things. It is necessary that the workers participate in those things, so that a real communion among them exists. ... Where this fusion and spontaneous and generous collaboration has not been achieved, there is no real social life, and it will be difficult in such an environment to have fruitful co-existence. [15]

Like the other distributists, of course, Arizmendiarrieta had a plan for disseminating this vision of participatory solidarity: study circles, more than 2,000 of them when they were in full swing. But it was the decision of a small group of those who had been taught by Arizmendiarrieta, five who had gone on to university and success in business, that put Mondragon on the map. These five decided that they would try to set up their own business, built on the principles they had learned. As one put it, "This was no ambitious and well-considered project. What we needed was to start something, to wake up, and see what the outcome would be."[16] The closure of a local stove factory gave them their opening, so they set up shop, hired 24 workers, and made stoves.

Today, what started as one small factory co-operative has grown today into a huge network of interconnected cooperatives, all under one corporate entity with thousands of worker-owners. It is as if that first stove factory set in motion in Mondragon a wave of worker-run initiatives, all operated according to the principles of Arizmendiarrieta, whose memory still guides Mondragon. For example, one of the biggest consumer co-operatives to follow the stove producer

---

15   Ibid., 183.
16   Ibid., 187.

co-op was the Eroski chain of supermarkets. Eroski stores have an annual membership fee—in this sense, similar to the American store Costco—and shoppers receive not only discounts on the environmentally and labor friendly products, but they also receive educational opportunities such as seminars on health and nutrition. The workers who operate and own the Eroski stores number 12,000. The stores feature food—such as milk, meat, eggs and vegetables—grown by local agricultural co-ops. Other co-ops that have become prominent in Mondragon are the Credit Union, the social insurance company (for such things as life insurance), a training school and research and development centers. It is as if, according to Ronnie MacDonnell, "every area of life is covered through the cooperative network." [17]

Part III: Dorothy Day and the Distributist Alternative

The first section of this essay laid out a coherent vision of distributism, and the preceding section illustrated that it can be a practical, realistic alternative. Now I would like to conclude by briefly noting how—and why—this economic model has such deep resonance with Dorothy Day. Indeed, if her witness is increasingly being understood as worthy of veneration and imitation—the two aspects of a would-be saint—then we do well to ask why *she* was a distributist. The best answer to this question comes in the book by Mark and Louise Zwick, *The Catholic Worker Movement: Intellectual and Spiritual Origins*. The Zwicks note that the way Day embraced the idea of distributism as an alternative to both dominant economic systems. As she wrote in the July–August 1948 edition of *The Catholic Worker*:

> The alternatives are not capitalism or socialism. . . . We must take into consideration the nature of man and his needs, not just cash-commodities, food and clothing, but a home, a bit of land, and the tools with which to work, part ownership in workshops and stores and factories. [18]

Here we see echoes of *Rerum Novarum*, in which Pope Leo calls for an economy whereby an ordinary worker can acquire "a little property" in order to create a household to serve his family and the common good.

17 *Restoration*.
18 In Mark and Louise Zwick, *The Catholic Worker Movement: Intellectual and Spiritual Origins* (Mahwah, New Jersey: Paulist Press, 2005), 156.

The focus on the practical is also the basis for another resonance of Day with distributism—and against some other, fairly common, Catholic construals of work and economy. Perhaps surprisingly to some, Day absolutely chafed at spiritualities of work which indicated that all work can be sanctified. Even taking on priests and bishops who urged workers to offer up their toil for spiritual gain, Day asked: "can one sanctify a saloon, a house of ill fame? When one is in the occasion of sin, is it not necessary to remove oneself from it?"[19] While industrial capitalism might not seem to many a kindred field to something like prostitution, and thus there appears "no opportunity for sinning as the outsider thinks of sin," Day argued that in fact "it is far more subtle than that, it is submitting oneself to a process which degrades, dehumanizes."[20] For Day, the response of the Church should be not be to offer a spirituality which props up such systems. Indeed, she asked of priestly promoters of this approach, "are they on the side of big business" which offers at best wages and semi-decent conditions or "are they on the side of St. Thomas . . . and the popes" who believe in "property, which is proper to man?"[21]

In other words, the true Catholic response to industrial capitalism is not found within the framework of industrial capitalism, but by seeking a different framework—and for Day the better framework was distributism. Part of her attraction to distributism was its embrace of agrarianism as part of the life of ordinary persons and families. And she insisted that small-scale agrarianism was infinitely more practical than large-scale capitalism. Against typical criticisms of distributism as idealistic, Day responded that "we, who witness the thousands of refugees from our ruthless industrialism, year after year, the homeless, the hungry . . . suffer the ugly reality of industrial capitalism and its fruits."[22] In contrast, distributism is simply a more realistic system which corresponded to the nature of the human person. Distributism, as noted, does not dismiss city life, nor the need for some factories and large-scale production, but the difference emerges in the structure and ownership of those means of production. And, in a point very important to Day, distributism provides space and attention to the cultivation of some land by a broad swath of society. As the Zwicks note, "on a small or communal farm, the whole experience of work could be different from the assembly line or that of the migrant laborer, and the unemployed might find

19   Ibid., 164.
20   Ibid.
21   Ibid., 165.
22   Dorothy Day, *The Catholic Worker*, December 1948.

a new life on the land."[23]

In sum, Dorothy Day saw in distributism not a utopian dream but a practical and sustainable structure for human economy. As she put it, "Ours was a long-range program, looking for ownership by the workers of the means of production, the abolition of the assembly line, decentralized factories, the restoration of crafts and ownership of property."[24] As I have noted, Day's attraction to the distributist vision came through great figures like Chesteron and Belloc, but the Zwicks rightly focus on a figure of great import for Day, Fr. Vincent McNabb, an Irishman who joined the English Dominicans and wrote on economics in the 1920s and '30s. McNabb sums up well the economic claim at the heart of Day's anti-capitalist—and pro-localist—distributism: "the utilitarians were wrong in saying that 'things should be produced where they can most economically be produced.' The true principle is: things should be produced where they can be most economically consumed."[25]

One final aspect of this economic vision that deserves mention is the connection between distributism and education. Day learned from Peter Maurin the need for a "Green Revolution"—far different from Marx's Red Revolution—in which the land itself becomes a great school for learning the ways of nature, both human and divine nature. Eric Anglada's essay in this volume gives focused attention to this dimension of distributism, along with the "agronomic universities" that give structure to the school of the land.

As the introduction to this essay alluded, much of that vision and many distributist examples are emerging today, in Catholic and non-Catholic circles. Inside the Church, for example, more parishes have relationships with local farmers through Community Supported Agriculture (CSA) programs by which parishioners can purchase locally grown, nutritious food. Regarding co-ops, the local Catholic Worker community in South Bend has established a local grocery store in their poor neighborhood, thus providing access to good food for those who presently (as a survey indicated) shop at such places as the local gas station mini-mart. And Catholic business leaders, too, are beginning to display a greater desire for the kind of "economy of communion" mentioned by Pope Benedict in *Caritas in Veritate*. For example, John Mundell, a Catholic in Bloomington, Indiana owns a large engineering company and runs it according to the principles of Focalare, the lay movement of which he is a part. As recounted by John L. Allen, as well as Mundell himself in a lecture at Holy Cross College, that

23 Zwick, *The Catholic Worker Movement*, 166.
24 Ibid.
25 Ibid., 167.

means his business, while still for profit, operates not in a spirit of competition but cooperation with other firms, with their clients, and with the earth itself.[26] For example, Mundell's firm—which for some clients charges very little—received a multi-million-dollar contract for a large project at Ball State University to convert outdated heating sources to green, geothermal technology.

Thus this paper closes with a call to action, *distributist action.* The practices of distributism have always been best developed in dialogue with the moral voice of Church teaching on economics. And thus if we heed what that voice is saying today about the need for charity in truth to guide not only religious life *but economic life,* we will search for more opportunities to embody this vision, building on past practices in places like Antigonish and Mondragon, which empowered workers to use education and the dignity of their vocation to claim control over their economic life rather than to continue being cogs in the industrial machine. We can be nourished by the intellectual tradition of great distributists such as G. K. Chesterton and Hilaire Belloc and edified by the vision and example of Dorothy Day, who if beatified and canonized will become the most famous of all distributists. All of these voices and visions enrich our Catholic sensibilities within a global system that can easily de-sensitize us to the moral *telos* of economic life. In other words, the small but significant "school of distributism" can provide both vision and example for those of us wishing to pursue a richly Catholic economics.

Michael Griffin is associate professor and chair of the Department of Theology at Holy Cross College, Notre Dame, Indiana. He is the co-editor of *In the Company of the Poor: Conversations with Dr. Paul Farmer and Fr. Gustavo Gutierrez* (Orbis, 2013) and the author of *The Politics of Penance: Proposing an Ethic for Social Repair* (Cascade, 2015). He and his wife Catherine were both Catholic Workers—she at Casa Juan Diego in Houston, Texas, and both of them at St. Peter Claver Catholic Worker in South Bend, Indiana.

---

26   John L. Allen, *National Catholic Reporter Blog,* July 7, 2009.

Peter Maurin's Influence
on Dorothy Day and the
Catholic Worker

Catholic Worker
Or Catholic Radical?
Dorothy Day's American Idealism

Colin Miller

*Let it be conceded right away, before going any further, that I do
not pretend to understand Peter Maurin.*[1]

Dorothy Day met Peter Maurin in December 1932. He taught her "a Catholic
outline of history," the lives of the saints, the social encyclicals, and probably
whatever else he could get her to listen to.[2] When, six months later, the first
issue of the paper came out, it carried the name *The Catholic Worker*, rather than
the name Peter proposed, the *The Catholic Radical*.[3] Dorothy handed him the
paper, to which he replied disappointedly, "It's everybody's paper. Everybody's
paper is nobody's paper." It wasn't the title that he objected to; he had agreed to
that. It was the content. There followed a rather lengthy separation of the two
partners, one that happily ended in reunion, but that need not have. It is my
contention below that these different titles for the paper are emblematic of a
much deeper difference of each founder's vision for the Catholic Worker
Movement.

Dorothy credited Peter with being *the* founder of the Catholic Worker, being
her teacher, and being the holiest person she had ever met.[4] And yet, this paper

1   Dorothy Day and Francis J. Sicius, *Peter Maurin: Apostle to the World* (Maryknoll, New
    York: Orbis), 65.

2   Dorothy Day, *The Long Loneliness* (New York: Harper and Row, 1952), 172.

3   Ibid., 175.

4   Day and Sicius, *Maurin*, 45, 178. It is thus worth pointing out the oddity of Francis J. Si-
    cius's comment in the introduction to Day's biography of Peter (an otherwise laudable
    work), that "Dorothy probably gave too much credit to Maurin" (xvii). There is indeed
    this strange tendency throughout the history of scholarship on the Worker, to downplay

argues, she did not accept his teaching all the way down. Rather, I suggest, she remained of two minds in regard to Peter's program to build a new society within the shell of the old. On the one hand, she accepted Peter's three means, his critiques of capitalism and socialism, and, broadly, his theological politics. I take this politics to be excellently summarized in what today appears in the "Aims and Means."[5] On her other hand, however, she consistently used and supported means that Peter refused—those most American of political activities—strikes, unions, protests, marches, and the like. As such, Dorothy maintained a confidence in the American project that Peter did not share.

Peter's Church-Centered Politics

Peter thought the Catholic Church was the primary locus of any change that might take place in society at large. As such, his essays, exhortations, and recommendations were all meant primarily for the *Catholic Church*. It was the Church, after all, that the pope's encyclicals, or the words of Catholic scholars, priests or bishops could conceivably convince. This is the force of the call for "blowing the dynamite of the Church."[6] The Church was supposed to be a dynamic society that itself practiced the radical politics of Jesus. Peter's three-point program was designed to put into practice these "politics," and was always aimed at Catholics. His essays, even when heard by Marxists or capitalists, are aimed at *conversion*. The content, therefore, the mainstay, of the new society within the shell of the old, were houses of hospitality, roundtable discussions, and agronomic universities. These three correspond to his call to the works of mercy, indoctrination, and the green revolution, respectively.

This was his embodiment of Catholic Action, which was nothing less than the solution to the world's problems: "Catholic Action based on Catholic thought is the Catholic solution of men's economic problems."[7] Catholic Action, he thought, mainly involved the works of mercy. Most of the time in the "Easy Essays" when he is talking about Catholic Action, the works of mercy are the primary referent.[8] As such, he often used the phrase Catholic *social* action,

the importance Dorothy always insisted rightly belonged to this strange holy man at the center of the movement.

5   See, most recently, *The Catholic Worker*, May 2015.

6   Peter Maurin, *Catholic Radicalism: Phrased Essays for the Green Revolution* (New York: Catholic Worker Books, 1949).

7   Ibid., 3.

8   Ibid., 36.

to distinguish it from Catholic *political* action. We can see this difference in the following essays:

> Our Holy Father does not ask us to reconstruct the social order through Catholic political action, but through Catholic social action.... The Catholic Worker Movement fosters Catholic social action and not Catholic political action. [9]
>
> The Holy Father asks us to reconstruct the social order. The social order was constructed by the first Christians through the daily practice of the Seven Corporal and Seven Spiritual Works of Mercy. [10]

Thus we see that Peter did not think Catholics should put their hope in Washington, but in the Church:

> People go to Washington asking the Federal Government to solve their economic problems, while the Federal Government was never intended to solve men's economic problems. Catholic Action based on Catholic thought is the Catholic solution of men's economic problems. [11]

Peter thought the Church had all the answers; he was calling for it to be radical—rooted—enough to bring forth these answers for the world. Catholics would do this through *direct action*: by themselves simply starting to *be* the sort of society socialism and capitalism were failing to create. The state was an unnecessary middleman, and marches, strikes and protests were not efficient enough. That sort of action was what he called *political* action. Peter thought it indirect and inefficient. Why demand a third party provide what Catholics can simply do now?

While Peter's means were primarily his three-point program, he also anticipated that other practices would eventually arise. He called these tiny endeavors "institutions": cult, culture, and cultivation. Cult (the Mass) would eventually lead to culture (a life ordered to the Mass), and to cultivation (back to the land). These institutions formed the world that always grew up around those devoted to the Mass, and at times he names some of them:

9   Ibid., 38.
10   Ibid., 47.
11   Ibid., 44.

> Round-Table Discussions to learn from scholars how things would be if they were as they should be. Campion Propaganda Committees for the indoctrination of the man of the street. Maternity Guilds for the welfare of needy mothers bringing young children into the world. Houses of Hospitality to give to the rich the opportunity to serve the poor. Farming Communes where the scholars may become workers so the workers may be scholars. [12]
>
> I propose the formation of associations of Catholic employers as well as associations of Catholic union men. Employers and employees must be indoctrinated with the same doctrine. [13]

These tiny gatherings are the immediate embodiments he imagined springing up from the practice of charity and voluntary poverty involved in his three-point program. These were examples of culture derived from the cult. And we see in all of the forgoing Peter's intense personalism. He never goes to bureaucracies, but is always concerned with a *person*. Again, I suggest, he did this because this *direct* action was more efficient. Changing "social structures" meant nothing without a change of heart and mind (repentance). He agreed fully and consistently with his friend Jacques Maritain:

> It is not a question of changing the system, it is a question of changing the man who makes the system. It is not the temporal that creates the spiritual, it is the spiritual that creates the temporal.... There is no social revolution without a spiritual revolution. The trouble with radicals is not that they are too radical but not radical enough. External radicalism is not radical enough because it is external. Inner radicalism is true radicalism. [14]

"If you want to reach the man in the street," Peter quoted Cardinal Newman, "go to the man in the street." [15] And so he went straight there. Dorothy

---

12 Ibid., 80.

13 Ibid., 113.

14 This is Peter arranging the words of Maritain for *The Catholic Worker*, January 1935. Cited in Ellis, *Maurin*, 64.

15 Dorothy Day, *The Catholic Worker*, May 1966, 2.

herself says that "Peter always got back to the fundamental problem—the necessity of knowing something about what he called the 'art of human contacts.'"[16] "People learn the art of human contacts by living in a house of hospitality,"[17] Peter said. Even houses of hospitality were not just about providing food and shelter; they were about the revolution of the heart.

Peter had learned from Maritain that the means had to agree with the ends; that there had to be, in other words, "pure means."[18] His insistence upon social rather than political action, direct performance of Christian action rather than making indirect demands, is his way of ensuring pure means. For Peter, to use the wrong means was to ensure the wrong result.[19] To build up the new society by the means of the old was to simply ensure more of the old. He made this very clear:

> It is not true that the end justifies the means. Good ends require right means. To use wrong means to achieve good ends is to forget the means for the sake of the ends. Class struggle and proletarian dictatorship are not the means to bring about a Communist society. The means to bring about a Communist society are Christian charity and voluntary poverty. We can create a new society within the shell of the old with the philosophy of the new, which is not a new philosophy but a very old philosophy, a philosophy so old that it looks like new.[20]

16 Day and Sicius, *Maurin*, 76.

17 Ibid., 86. Dorothy says of Peter that he "was always getting back to St. Francis of Assisi, who was most truly the 'gentle personalist.' In his poverty, rich; in renouncing all, possessing all; generous, giving out of the fullness of his heart, sowing generously and reaping generously, humble and asking when in need, possessing freedom and all joy. Without doubt, Peter was a free and joyous person" (Ibid., 79).

18 See Jacques Maritain, "On the Purification of the Means," in his *Integral Humanism, Freedom in the Modern World, and A Letter on Independence*, in *The Collected Works of Jacques Maritain*, ed. Otto Bird (Notre Dame, Indiana: University of Notre Dame Press, 1996), XI: 73–100.

19 Dorothy quotes Peter: "I told them I'm the son of a peasant who could neither read nor write, so I'm precapitalistic. I don't like capitalism and I don't like socialism, which is the child of capitalism: that is father and son ... we are trying to go back to a functional society.... We personally renounce the acquisitive society altogether. *It is a question of techniques....* The original guilds had the idea. What they had was an ideology: the ideology of the gospel": Day and Sicius, *Maurin*, 105–107. Italics mine.

20 Maurin, *Catholic Radicalism*, 152–153.

Such is a sketch of Peter's church-centered means.

Dorothy's More American-Centered Politics

Dorothy was different than Peter in this regard. I do not know whether to say that she did not agree, or that she did not understand, or that she did not care, for Peter's principled subtly. At different places she gives evidence of each. She does, however, explicitly acknowledge the difference:

> Peter saw only the land movement as the cure for unemploy-
> ment and irresponsibility, and the works of mercy as the work
> at hand, ignoring the immediate needs of the workers in the
> unions, their conflicts and demands. I comforted myself by
> saying, "Men are more single-minded. They are the pure of
> heart." But I continued to think in terms of unions and strikes
> as an immediate means of bettering the social order. I could
> not blind myself to the conflict between us, the conflict that
> would continue between one or another who came to join in
> the movement later. When Peter said, "Everybody's paper
> is nobody's paper," when he protested the coverage of strike
> news, or the introduction of the personal element into the
> work by feature story. [21]

There is no doubt that Dorothy was heavily indoctrinated by Peter, that she endorsed his three pronged program, as well as most of his other general maxims. Yet, when it came to the *means*, a point so important to Peter, she crossed into what Peter would call political action. A brief look through a history of Dorothy's life, such as the chronology outlined in the front of her diaries, reveals this. [22] Besides the fact that they clearly fought about this, the above passage all by itself reveals at least two contours of Dorothy's divided mind. How so?

First, she here refers to the "immediate needs" of the workers, which called for "immediate means" of bettering the social order. From this we can gather that she thought Peter's proposal of the works of mercy and the land was *not* designed, or was poorly equipped, to meet those demands, and to immediately better the social order. But Peter would have begged to differ. The two disagreed

---

21 Day, *The Long Loneliness*, 180.
22 See "Chronology" in Robert Ellsburg, ed., *The Duty of Delight: The Diaries of Dorothy Day* (Marquette, Wisconsin: Marquette University Press, 2012).

about *means*, about what Peter called *technique*. Both, doubtless, thought their technique most direct, most efficient: Peter, with a call to leave the industrial complex all together, join the land movement, indoctrinate, and take care of each other in houses of hospitality, and Dorothy with a call to the bosses of businesses and government to make this more bearable within the industrial complex. She explicitly highlights this difference in her book on Peter:

> There were those who spoke of his anarchistic nature, because of his refusal to enter into political controversy, his refusal to use worldly means to change the social order. He did not refuse to use material means, physical means, secular means, the means that are at hand. But the means of expediency that men have turned to for so many ages, he disdains. He is no diplomat, no politician. He has so thoroughly discouraged in his followers the use of political means that he has been termed an anarchist by many. [23]

Apparently, however, he had not been able to discourage this in his best student. At the very heart of the Catholic Worker vision, therefore, stands the debate that Dorothy would see as that between the idealist and the realist, "the conflict that would continue" as she says. Peter, however, would reject the description: the ideal means were also the most realistic.

Second, in the passage above Dorothy says she saw these means as a way of bettering the social order. In contrast to Peter's approach, Dorothy proposes a call to *reform of the existing order*. The distinction is subtle but all-important. She appears to want the old shell to become new. This explains why Dorothy is much more apt than Peter to address demands for justice to non-Catholics and non-Christians. She elsewhere says that "when such simple issues as the rights of workers to organize into unions of their own choosing were at stake, it was very necessary to *get into* industrial conflicts, in front of factories and on picket lines, to emphasize what the popes have said in regard to the worker." [24] The pope's audience, for Dorothy, is not just the Church but *all*, and so the implication that all are bound to respect the pope's claims about the rights of the worker, even while rejecting his claims about the Lordship of Christ. Dorothy is thus anthropologically optimistic, for she thinks fallen men outside a state of grace, outside the Church, are likely to respond positively to the call of justice:

23 Day and Sicius, *Maurin*, 79–80.

24 Dorothy Day, *The Catholic Worker*, May 1947, 1, 3. Italics mine.

to give to each his due. This must be the case, for if she did not think this unions and strikes would not be an immediate means to bettering the social order. This implies, and Dorothy's life gives witness to, a sort of confidence in the American participatory government that Peter never appears to have shared.

Doing Theopolitics with Dorothy and Peter

There is no doubt that the history of the Catholic Worker has tended to follow Dorothy's vision. At least, a glance at most of the current literature put out by the movement's members show that this is where we are at the present. Since this is so, can we begin to give a "Day-ian" theological account of such Catholic activism? I am not aware of any place that she herself does this, and so we are forced to speculate based on other things that she says. Dorothy was not a systematizing writer, and, I would suggest, she does not appear herself to have a worked-out position on the matter, beyond some of the passages we have already seen. Her best answer, I think, must actually not be the one Dorothy implies above, that unconverted men can be expected to act with a minimum of justice. That would make the Church the policer of the world, rather than its hope of a whole new way of life.

Rather, and I think Dorothy evinces this view at times, Church participation in such political struggles must be a witness to the world—the proclamation of the gospel. It is preaching and not politics, witness not activism. This preaching is the Church holding itself out as a whole new way of life that is available to practice in its fullness right now, rather than a scolding of unbelievers for acting like pagans. The whole Catholic Worker tradition, Dorothy might say, is the unity of liturgy and sociology:

> Living the liturgical day as much as we are able, beginning with prime, using the missal, ending the day with compline and so going through the liturgical year we find that it is now not us, but Christ in us, who is working to combat injustice and oppression. We are on our way to becoming "other Christs." We cannot build up the idea of the apostolate of the laity without the foundation of the liturgy. [25]

If this is the case, then any "activism" and "political involvement" such as

25 Dorothy Day, *The Catholic Worker*, January 1936, 3.

Dorothy favored comes from wellspring of communion with Christ in the liturgy. When the Church lives this radical gospel life in the midst of this devastated world, particular parts of that whole life of the City of God will inevitably come to conflict with corresponding parts of the earthly city. It is this point of conflict, of friction, that holds the potential for Christian justice to break forth even beyond the usual walls of the City of God—those walls being baptism and the regular sacramental and liturgical life of the Church. This, I suggest, is exactly what Peter envisioned in his program: the full, sacramentally constituted mystical body touching the social order at strategic points already internal to its sacramental and apostolic practice. Cult produces culture and cultivation.

Dorothy's participation in political activism, then, cannot have as its goal the creation of a more just America. Rather, such participation must arise from the Church's insistence that it cannot cease being itself without denying its Head. When, therefore, compulsory nuclear defense drills demand the peaceable Church submit its non-violent culture to a culture of fear, violence, and death, Christians like Dorothy will be the first ones arrested and jailed for refusing to act like something they are not. When the Church's friends are treated unjustly by their employers, we may stand next to them when they go to ask for their due (justice), and give them our bed when they are forced to fire their bosses. Or when we, like Dorothy, see daily the horrors industrialism inflicts on workers, with so many coming in want of food and shelter, it is perhaps a natural thing that the Church, where no one goes without and each receives everything they need, devote a large amount of space and time to workers' conditions. These sorts of practices are all done not with the hopes of making America a more nearly just country, but rather as witness to the fact that an already just society already exists, the City of God. [26] This, I think, is how Dorothy sees herself, at least some of the time.

---

26 Something like this account must also be the proper place for the role of "rights" in the Church's social teaching. (Though whether this can be borne out exegetically in the magisterial documents remains to be seen.) "Rights," I suspect, properly understood, are a way that the Church has used to limit the claims of government, and of late, the State, on the lives of human beings. This is different than construing rights, as they usually are in America, as a positive piece of anthropology (usually, these days, corresponding to "needs"). The Church therefore insists on citizens' rights not to try to achieve a legal status for them (though that may be involved) but to claim to the governing authorities, again as one part of Her whole way of life coming into conflict with the world, "this far and no farther." Of course, it is to be expected that often those claims will not be respected, and then, rather than the banal shrill cries of injustice by an unrepentant power, the Church once again followers her Head in the way of silent martyrdom.

Conclusion

In the last analysis Dorothy and Peter's views appear to differ in a variety of ways that lead at bottom if not to significant theological differences then at least to significant differences in emphasis. Peter's audience was almost always the Church, with a call for the Church to be the Church—to blow its own dynamite. Dorothy's audience was some mixture of the Church and America. Peter's means were largely those always available to the Church, primarily but not exclusively the works of mercy, while Dorothy was much more wont to swerve towards what she openly acknowledged were for Peter purely political means.

Peter's insistence on avoiding the political means was based on an understanding of Maritain's pure means. If the means were not Church-means, the Church, God's society, would not be the result. For, Peter thought, the one led to the other. Another way of putting the matter is that this is a debate about efficiency: What is the most efficient technique to rebuild the social order? To this question Peter held out the gentle personalism of traditional Catholicism.

These differences in technique reveal different views of the way that Christian practices participate in the divine economy. So Peter no doubt denied Dorothy's charge of being an idealist, being naively pure in heart. Dorothy no doubt denied that her political means were not pure. Peter's point was always that, while Dorothy thought political means went to the source of the suffering, they did not in fact do so. Dorothy's realism, I suggest Peter might say, was itself a sort of American idealism, which was itself not direct enough. For the problem, as Dorothy well knew, but perhaps sometimes forgot, was not with the system, but that there was a system at all, rather than a person, to which men's hearts were attached.

Fr. Colin Miller (Ph.D., Duke University) is an Episcopal Priest in the Diocese of North Carolina. He a founder and priest-in-charge of the Peter Maurin Catholic Worker House in Durham, North Carolina, and Associate Rector for Urban Ministry at the Church of the Good Shepherd in downtown Raleigh, North Carolina. He and his wife, Leigh Edwards Miller, recently welcomed their first child, Edith Sarah, into the Catholic Worker world.

A Philosophy of Work

Thomas McDonough

The root of our evil is the lack of a philosophy of work.

—Peter Maurin

In one of Dorothy Day's columns in *The Catholic Worker*, she writes of two youths who have come to Maryfarm. She is more intent on describing the type: "The courts are full of just such young ones.... They're cynical, they gamble, they want to get rich quick.... They don't want a job, because they want big money." They are taught this attitude even in the Catholic schools. "But they are not taught to work—they are not taught a philosophy of work. They are not taught a philosophy of poverty which will make them use their talents rather than seek wages."[1]

Human work is the fundamental and decisive key to solving—gradually solving—the social question which is ultimately a matter of "making life more human," or in the language of Peter Maurin, making it "easier to be good." There was a time when Catholics had a hard time articulating such a philosophy of work as Dorothy and Peter found lacking. However, the Second Vatican Council set the foundations that John Paul II would use to build a theology of work. The focus of this paper is what St. John Paul II refers to as the "subjective dimension" of work: "through work the worker becomes more a human being."[2]

Scripture and the Church have always placed a value on human work from Genesis through the example of Jesus, God and man, who "devoted most of the

---

1   Dorothy Day, "Reflections on Work" (*The Catholic Worker*, November 1946, http://www. catholicworker.org/dorothyday/articles/227.html, accessed July 10, 2015).

2   Pope St. John Paul II, *Laborem Exercens*, 1981, n. 9.

years of His life on earth to manual work at the carpenter's bench" demonstrating that "the basis for determining the value of human work is not primarily the kind of work being done but the fact that the one who is doing it is a person."[3] John Paul reminds us that this gospel of work, understood by the earliest Christians, was never repudiated by the Church but the message was drowned out by the "various trends of materialistic and economistic thought."[4]

John Paul takes pains to clarify that the "objective dimension" of work, what is done, is subordinate to the "subjective dimension" of work, the intention. Likewise, the different sorts of work have greater or lesser objective value but the objective value is subordinate to the subjective value. He states that "each sort [of work] is judged above all by the measure of the dignity of the subject of work, that is to say the person, the individual who carries it out."[5]

Everyone works. The worker is the owner, the salaried employee, the wage employee, the homemaker, the government bureaucrat and the politician: each conscious of their own sinfulness and each trying to bring his/her work in line with the mind of Jesus Christ (which is to do the will and work of the Father).

Work is sharing in the activity of the Creator who has revealed himself as Father. When we work we are carrying out the family business. When we lose that intention—carrying on the family business of Creation in a spirit of service to the rest of our community, of the planet—we work only for ourselves (influence, money, fame), and our work loses its dignity. Carrying on the work of creation requires effort—study, preparation, execution—and must be done well, humanly considered.

The person, the worker, is on the front lines of social injustice and is always enjoined to use his or her conscience, formed in the mind of Christ who overturned the tables of the money changers. As the universal call to holiness becomes more ingrained in the hearts and souls of Christians and the employer and employee come to the mind of Christ, then consumption is curbed, the wages of the worker are not stolen, the worker uses his talents in the service of others, property rights are put in their proper perspective, and corruption is eradicated.

---

3   Ibid, n. 6.
4   Ibid, n. 7.
5   Ibid, n. 6.

Mr. McDonough's book about Dorothy Day's first year in New York, *An Eye for Others, Dorothy Day, Journalist: 1916–17,* will be published in January, 2016. He blogs about Dorothy Day and other topics at www.precursorsoffrancis.com.

Peter Maurin and the Church: Past, Present, and Future

Peter King

I am a follower of Peter Maurin. I have been a hospitaller of the Unity Kitchen Community of the Catholic Worker for forty-two years in Syracuse, New York. Unity Kitchen began in August 1970. Like Peter Maurin, I have lived in voluntary poverty, and believe in the futility of electoral politics and the efficacy of the politics of Jesus. The death and resurrection of Jesus was *the* big political event of all time. In what follows, I want to consider how the social Catholic consciousness of Dorothy Day would not have been possible without Maurin's enlightenment of her. He taught her the history of the Church by the lives of the saints. I will, moreover, argue that proceeding with a cause for her canonization without him is an injustice and a profound loss for the Catholic Worker and the Church.

Peter Maurin was born Pierre Joseph Aristide Maurin on May 8, 1877 and died on May 15, 1949. He began his life in France as the eldest of twenty-four children, living in the town of Oultet in the Lozère region in south-central France. His was a farming family that had lived on their land for 1,500 years. They were peasants of whom he said "they had roots." These "roots" gave Peter Maurin a Christianized agrarian worldview. Life was circumscribed by a village economy with family plots for raising food combined with communal fields, bakeries, and commons. It subsisted with some commerce from the farm and handcrafts, along with food production. Maurin used to say the communes of France needed study, but "historians stop at the Paris Commune" (1848). Peter Maurin did not find this life in the America of the early twentieth century.

When Peter Maurin was 14 years old, he was sent to be educated by the Christian Brothers of Mende. When he was old enough he entered their novitiate. As a Christian Brothers novice, Peter would come under the influence of St. Jean Baptiste de la Salle (b. April 30, 1651, d. April 7, 1719). His teaching method, called simultaneous—in that he taught classes in the vernacular re-placing individual instruction in Latin and offering an education to the common people—was revolutionary. Salle began this venture by giving away his posses-sions as well as his reputation and position, and took on the lowly task of edu-cating the poor. His Christian Brothers were poor and tireless. A new order with new methods ran into criticism and opposition. With that it flourished. By the time Maurin began teaching, the order was the primary provider of French edu-cation. But Peter Maurin was intellectually restless, and he subsequently left the Christian Brothers in 1903.

The life of Peter Maurin can be divided into three distinct "pilgrimages" of roughly 25 years, The first as we have seen, 1877–1903, was an accepted, paren-tally sanctioned route for him. The second period, 1903–1926, was an itinerant path of growth and individuation as he traveled and observed the weakening of rural life and the effect of urbanization. The final years of pilgrimage, 1926–1949, saw the mature man living out a vision of the renewal of the social order in keeping with modern papal social teaching.

Social Catholicism, drawing on the political theory of the Middle Ages and Leo XIII's encyclical *Rerum Novarum* (On the Conditions of the Working Man, 1891), saw groups within society as an organism. It was a theory that applied Catholic ideas of Christian humanism with economic thought found in the en-cyclicals, their goal being the revitalizing of society.

In his formative years as a Christian Brother (1895–1902), Maurin came under the influence of French Social Catholicism. It extended the Mystical Body teaching by analogy to social problems. Social Catholicism's analogy of society as a body—a unity comprised of many functioning parts—was called corporat-ism (in governing terms, the aim was grouping economic divisions into separate "guilds" and uniting them into voting bodies, parliament-like). Fascist Italy ac-tually attempted this in the 1920s.

For a social movement and an intentional community movement, this idea of growing organically vis-à-vis Eric Gill's small "cells of good living" is very ap-pealing. But Maurin pointed to three positions he rejected: anti-Semitism, mil-itarism, political activity whether on the right or the left. Le Sillon's democrat-ically proposed agenda for engagement in the political process was condemned by Pope Pius X in 1910 who suggested a smaller organization on a local diocesan level, which seems to be in line with Peter Maurin's idea of the Catholic Worker movement.

After six years of experimentation and study of Catholic social movements,

Peter left France, ostensibly to avoid further military service in 1909. He left his family behind, convinced that political solutions were mirages and never to be the primary effort of the Church or her members (in order to effect change in society, a social movement was needed). He emigrated to Canada in 1909. He wished to homestead, but it came to a sudden end what with the death of his partner in a hunting accident, which, combined with fierce Canadian winters, proved too much for him. He followed work opportunities down into the U.S. It was a life "on the bum" with periods of hard labor until World War I. For about five years, he worked alongside those on the low rung of the industrial ladder and mentally processed what he saw and heard. This included coming into contact with groups like "the Wobblies," the Industrial Workers of the World (IWW), who were attempting to "radicalize the labor movement." From them he borrowed the term "making a world where it is easier to be good."

He was in Chicago doing janitorial work when the Great War started. At this point the fortunes of war put French language teachers in demand (apparently, Maurin had learned English after he came to Canada). Peter started his own language school and lived somewhat prosperously during this period. A student convinced him to move east to New York State and the town of Woodstock in the Catskill Mountains region in 1925.

St. Philip Neri (d. 1595) as a young man in Rome had a conversion experience. Whatever happened, he would only answer when questioned, *"Secretum meum mihi"* (my secret is my own). Peter Maurin went through something similar; if anything, he was even more reticent. One thing was clear after 1926, he never charged for his French lessons and his students could give him whatever they wanted. "They didn't let me starve," he said. Of this period in his life, a student, Julia Leaycraft, interested in Hindu thought and Gandhi, has given an account. He was gracious and dignified in demeanor and would meet with his students in their homes. He would say that in regards to his new lifestyle, "he was crazy in his own way." She had the impression he was feeling his way, and after the French lessons would read some poems he had written down and ask for a reaction. He was giving of himself as someone who had "a heart inflamed by love." Up to that time, as he told Dorothy Day later on, he had "not been living as a Catholic should."

By 1927, thanks to a job given him by a Father Scully in the nearby town of Phoenicia, Maurin got a place to live and a little money as a caretaker for a Catholic youth camp on Mt. Tremper. So in the formative years of his programme of cult, culture, and cultivation, 1927–32, he had time to take the night boat from Kingston to New York City where he spent time studying in the public library and approaching anyone who would listen to explain his thoughts on steps to take toward social reconstruction.

His first attempts at sharing this new philosophical synthesis were to approach the secular Franciscan order (SFO), a group the popes had been encouraging in several encyclicals on St. Francis of Assisi in the 1920s to be a vanguard for what they called Catholic Action. Neither the secular Franciscan lay order nor the Knights of Columbus were too interested. They could not see the oncoming economic depression that Maurin was pointing to and that happened when the crash of the stock market on October 29, 1929 took place.

It is worth meditating on the parallel conversion and subsequent reaching for a vocation that Dorothy Day was experiencing at the same time Maurin's programme was incubating in his conversational method of clarification of thought in Union Square with all and sundry. For in 1926, Dorothy's daughter Tamar was born and baptized, and the following year she herself was baptized, losing Tamar's father in the process. He would not accept the idea of marriage, Catholic or otherwise. Then from 1927–32, she looked and prayed for some way to assist the laboring poor.

A small group of disciples surrounded Peter Maurin whenever he came into town and these people were mimeographing his "Easy Essays" and handing them to whoever stopped to hear what Peter had to say. Dorothy Day was making a living writing social commentary and analyzing the labor movement as well as reporting on strikes or direct actions that the unions organized. Neither Peter Maurin nor Dorothy Day had what they needed, namely a God-given enterprise to which they would put to use their "gifts, callings, and talents."

On December 8, 1932, Dorothy Day was praying at the National Cathedral of the Immaculate Conception in Washington, DC. She was longing for a way to use her gift as a writer for the cause of the poor resolute people she had seen covering a "Hunger March" of the unemployed organized by the communists, but she as a Catholic could no longer march with them. And Peter Maurin was looking for someone to help him start a journal that would be a forum for his programme of Catholic social thought. December 9, 1932 brought the future founders of the Catholic Worker movement together and Peter immediately began persistently inculcating into Day the Catholic Church's social vision for her, shaping for her a Catholic worldview. She would learn the history of the Church through the lives of the saints and would learn how to announce to the working man and woman the Church's social plan of renewal and reconstruction. Maurin's plan centered on cult, or the goods of the soul; culture, or the goods of the mind; and cultivation, or the goods of the body. Another way to express it is cult, i.e., the liturgy; culture, i.e., knowledge through literature, the arts, architecture; and cultivation, i.e., return to the land and a reformation of an American peasantry. To begin Catholic Action, Peter says, "we need to understand how things became as they are, in order to act now so as to change the future, or to find a path from where they are to a path where they should be."

Stanley Vishnewski's *Wings of the Dawn* gives a vibrant telling of a first meeting with Peter Maurin and the growing awareness of his high aim of calling forth a human being to an awareness of what it means to be a Christian. Consider these excerpts:

> I [Stanley] stepped aside to let Mary go ahead of me and then followed her into the kitchen. Peter Maurin was already sitting at the table. He was reading a pamphlet. Mary sat down next to him....
>
> I had not yet been introduced to Peter but he did not wait for an introduction. At that moment his face became alive and animated. He pointed his finger at me and said: "In the first centuries of Christianity the poor were fed, clothed, and sheltered at a personal sacrifice and the Pagans said about the Christians: 'See how they love each other.'"
>
> "Today," he continued, "the poor are fed, clothed and sheltered by the politicians at the expense of the taxpayers.
>
> "And because the poor are no longer fed, clothed, and sheltered at a personal sacrifice but at the expense of the taxpayers Pagans say about the Christians: "See how they pass the buck."
>
> Peter spoke in a rhythmical singsong. At that time I did not realize that he was reciting one of his own Easy Essays, but I had a feeling that he was quoting from something that had already been written. When he finished, he stared at me as if waiting for me to comment on what he had just said....
>
> Later I learned more about Peter's methods of conducting discussions. He had expected me then to make some comment on what he was saying. He had wanted me to state what was on my mind. Once I had commented on what he had just said he would then have proceeded to carry on the conversation from there.
>
> Peter would never dominate a conversation. He believed that a person had a right to finish a statement without being

interrupted. He would never answer a question directly. "I am not a question box," he would say. "I am a chatter box."

I finally asked the question that was on my mind. "What is the purpose of the Catholic Worker?"

To this day I do not know what color his eyes were but I know that he looked at me more intently than anybody had ever looked at me before. Peter leaped up from his chair. He looked down at me.

"The purpose of the Catholic Worker," he said, "is to create a society where it will be easier for men to be good. A society where each person will consider himself to be his brother's keeper. A society where each one will try to serve and to be the least. God wants us to be our brother's keeper. He wants us to feed the hungry at a personal sacrifice. He wants us to clothe the naked at a personal sacrifice. He wants us to shelter the homeless. To serve man for God's sake, that is what God wants us to do!" (33–35)

This view of universal solicitude and realities is something that would be very hard to imagine coming from Dorothy Day. As Peter Maurin said, he was interested in "the Big Idea." He was interested in principles, to a lesser extent in strategies and tactics. Dorothy, however, was a Christian, reporting on hardships due to the fallen human condition. By way of these, she worked up a ladder that led her to God. Seeing Peter Maurin as someone sent by God to answer her prayer for a vocation, she was submissive to Maurin as the founder, herself as the disciple. Both Peter Maurin and Dorothy Day were united in the pursuit of holiness, a mutuality that gave them their vocations.

Ann O'Connor writes on this vocation of Maurin to enlighten and to suffer:

Peter Maurin's *traditional Catholicism* gave him the ability to look forward by seeing backward. The memory of his deep-seated Christian principles, with his long-studied history of the Church through the lives of the saints and the papal encyclicals, made him see a vision—personalist and communitarian. This vision combined a reverence for the dignity of the person with a longing for Christian community. It anticipated and rejoiced in the doctrine of the Mystical Body of Christ—especially when Pope Pius XII, in 1943, issued the encyclical

Mystici Corporis Christi. … It was just after this that Maurin entered his crucible of silence (1945). [1]

It was, that is, just after this that Maurin entered the last few years of his life, a period marked by his near-total silence before his death on May 15, 1949. Shortly after, his body was brought to the house of hospitality in New York City, and then to Transfiguration Church for the funeral. He would be buried in St. John's Cemetery in Queens. His death was remarked upon by major periodicals all over the world—inter alia, *l'Osservatore Romano*, the *New York Times*, and *Time* magazine all carried obituaries that reiterated Maurin's philosophy.

In closing, I feel it is necessary to reflect on something Katharine Temple (d. 2002), long-time New York City Catholic Worker and contributing editor of *The Catholic Worker*, once said about Peter Maurin being a genius and asking for a fresh interpretation, along with others, notably Brian Terrell of Strangers and Guests Farm CW in Iowa, of the more comprehensive part of his vision which had been derailed by the over-emphasis on houses of hospitality in an urban setting. A case could be made that until the problems of hospitality were solved, the movement could not transition to the deeper aspects of Peter Maurin's thought. Yet how to state Peter Maurin's genius?

It is, firstly, the prophetic stance he took over against modernism, which Maurin considered an irreligious secularism combined with materialistic, mechanistic totalitarianism. Secondly Peter's prophetic vision saw ahead to the age of technology where, to use Marshall McLuhan's now famous phrase, "the medium is the message."

Peter's vision was unapologetically Catholic, a Catholicism that had nothing of the huge loss of confidence that has afflicted the Church since Vatican II. In the end, his personalist communitarian philosophy is an inclusive social strategy claiming for every person the *imago Dei*. What the Catholic Worker movement needs to do right now is to coalesce around the imperative of the image of God in each person, and call forth the Church to proclaim to the world: God is a God of life, thou shalt not kill!

Peter Damian Joseph King is a hospitaller of the Unity Kitchen Community of the Catholic Worker (UKC), which began in August 1970. Mr. King and his wife Ann O'Connor (1934–2015) co-authored the chapter "What's Catholic About

1   Unpublished writings by Ann O'Connor.

the Catholic Worker Movement?: Then and Now" in *Dorothy Day and the Catholic Worker Movement: Centenary Essays* (Milwaukee, Wisconsin: Marquette University Press, 2001), 128–43, eds. William J. Thorn, Phillip M. Runkel, and Susan Mountin. Further study of the UKC can be accessed in the *Unity Grapevine*, the newsletter of the UKC.

Romancing Lady Poverty Anew: Dorothy Day and the Franciscan Tradition

Lance Richey

A rebellious adolescence struggling against the more conventional expectations of a prosperous middle-class family. Dreams of travel and adventure in a time of war and civil strife. An idolization of romantic love as the highest good one could attain. A religious crisis severing family and social relationships. A radical conversion to the Gospel as the model for Christian existence. An unswerving loyalty to the Church which still recognized its all-too-human flaws. An embrace of poverty and non-violence as the supreme form of Christian witness in a world ruled by wealth and power. A new movement (of sometimes dubious orthodoxy) established on the margins of society to demonstrate the viability of the Gospel as a way of life for all peoples. A posthumous struggle between the Church and followers over the founder's legacy precisely because of its powerful appeal. In sum, a life utterly defined by its time and place, yet transcending both. A remarkable life. A saint's life. An imitation of Christ.

Despite being separated by gender, culture, language, and over seven centuries of historical change, the lives of Francis of Assisi and Dorothy Day have remarkable similarities. Indeed, more than anyone else in the American Catholic experience, she came closest to recapturing the allure of poverty and solidarity with the poor that has made the Poverello the most beloved of all Christian saints. Given their affinity, it is more remarkable still that Day never formed any institutional connection to the Franciscan tradition, choosing instead to become a Benedictine Oblate. Nevertheless, she always maintained a special devotion for the Poor Man of Assisi and recognized the affinity between his religious charism and her own work with the poor. To better understand their relationship, this paper will explore: 1) the history of Day's discovery of and lifelong interest in Francis; 2) the influence of Francis' love of poverty on her spirituality and practice; and 3) the Franciscan sources of the radical pacifism she adopted as a way of living out the gospel. Through the mediation of Peter Maurin, Dorothy Day found in Francis a spiritual model and mentor who shaped both her understanding of the Gospel and the tasks and structure of the Catholic Worker movement more profoundly than is often appreciated by her disciples or detractors.

1. Discovering Francis

In the summer of 1928, only months after her entry into the Church had ended a common-law marriage to Forster Batterham, Day first turned her attention to Francis through a reading of *The Little Flowers of Saint Francis*. As Brigid O'Shea Merriman writes, "the Christian classic provided Dorothy with a deeper appreciation for Francis than the synopsis she had already found in her *St. Andrew's Missal*. As with other works which she considered enriching, Dorothy reread *The Little Flowers* several times in subsequent years."[1] Indeed, over a half century later, the work recurs among the list of the books she read during the last two years of her life.[2] While not a primary or always historically reliable source of information about Francis, this work certainly gave the impressionable new Catholic a powerful portrait of what a literal embodiment of the gospel would look like, and helped lay the groundwork for the more thorough and mature encounter with Francis offered by Peter Maurin after their meeting in December 1932.

As part of his "education" of Day in the Catholic theological and social tradition, Maurin introduced her to Pius XI's 1926 encyclical on the septicentennial of Francis' death, *Rite Expiatis*. In the October 1944 *Catholic Worker*, Dorothy places this text alongside the prophets and the Fathers of the Church in importance for her development.[3] Far removed from the birdbath imagery of Francis in popular Catholicism, this encyclical

> provided Dorothy with a clear presentation of Francis' striking fidelity to Christ, remarking on him as a 'Second Christ,' a man whose spirit was identical with that of the gospel. *Rite*

---

1   Brigid O'Shea Merriman, *Searching for Christ: The Spirituality of Dorothy Day* (Notre Dame, Indiana: University of Notre Dame Press, 1994), 175.

2   Jim Forest, *All is Grace: A Biography of Dorothy Day* (Maryknoll, New York: Orbis, 2011), 294.

3   Mark and Louise Zwick, *The Catholic Worker Movement: Intellectual and Spiritual Origins* (Mahwah, New Jersey: Paulist, 2005), 122.

Expiatis painted a picture of a thirteenth century in need of Christian reform, a youthful Francis converted to embrace the gospel fully, whose natural inclination to help the needy was transformed by grace. The document [also] pointed out the saint's great love for poverty in imitation of Christ. [4]

In addition, the text discussed the Third Order which Francis founded for those in the world who wished to follow his call to sanctity, poverty, and (especially) non-violence—all three of which were to become pillars of the Catholic Worker ideal.

Maurin could hardly have chosen a better text to inspire a young convert like Day, whose social sympathies and spiritual ambitions so closely mirrored those of Francis. Pius XI described the social conditions in the thirteenth century when, neglecting the needs of the poor, many men

allowed themselves to be overcome by egotism and greed for possessions and were driven by an insatiable desire for riches. These men, regardless of the laws which had been promulgated in many places against vice, ostentatiously paraded their riches in a wild orgy of clothes, banquets, and feasts of every kind. They looked on poverty and the poor as something vile. They abhorred from the depths of their souls the lepers—leprosy was then very widespread—and neglected these outcasts completely in their segregation from society. What is worse, this greed for wealth and pleasure was not even absent...from those [clergy] who should have most scrupulously guarded themselves from such sin. The custom, too, was prevalent of monopolizing wealth and piling up large fortunes. These fortunes were often acquired in divers and sinful manners, sometimes by the violent extortion of money and other times by usury. [5]

Reading this in New York City during the depths of the Great Depression, Day could not have missed its contemporary significance, or have avoided being deeply moved by it.

4   O'Shea Merriman, *Searching for Christ*, 176.
5   *Rite Expiatis*, 8. See http://w2.vatican.va/content/pius-xi/en/encyclicals/documents/hf_p-xi_enc_30041926_rite-expiatis.html.

Day completed her knowledge of Francis over the next several years with several classic works on the saint. Foremost among these was Johannes Jörgensen's seminal biography *St. Francis of Assisi*, one of the first serious Catholic contributions to modern Franciscan scholarship. O'Shea Merriman writes that "her general knowledge of events in Francis' life, her appreciation of Francis' loving respect and compassion for the individual person, quotations from his Testament and Canticle of Brother Sun, all point to the Jörgensen biography as her major source."[6] It was hardly the sole source, though: references to Father Cuthbert's *Life of St. Francis of Assisi*, G. K. Chesterton's *St. Francis of Assisi*, and (several decades later) Leonard von Matt's *Pictorial Life of St. Francis* show her continued interest in the saint throughout her life. Moreover, her fellow Catholic Worker Stanley Vishnewski was "a Third Order Franciscan, although he does not attend the meetings, and has a large collection of books on St. Francis."[7]

Given her knowledge of Francis and her obvious sympathy with his ideals, why did Day not herself become a Third Order Franciscan, rather than (as eventually happened) a Benedictine Oblate of St. Procopius Abbey in Lisle, Illinois? According to O'Shea Merriman,

> At least two possibilities suggest themselves. While Maurin had great respect for Francis, he was more attracted to the Benedictine tradition; it is likely that his preference influenced Dorothy. Second, none of Dorothy's writings of this decade [the 1930s] reveal that she had made the acquaintance of any single Franciscan or Franciscan group of the stature of Virgil Michel and the Collegeville Abbey [with whom she had formed a friendship. Nevertheless, ...] she remained interested in the Franciscan charism to the end of her days."[8]

This influence sometimes expressed itself in surprising ways: "Once, while preparing for the opening of a retreat, she found herself randomly opening the Bible three times in conscious imitation of Francis of Assisi, a saint whom she greatly admired and whose life of voluntary poverty and peacemaking she strove to emulate."[9] And while she never pretended to a scholarly understand-

---

6   O'Shea Merriman, *Searching for Christ*, 178.

7   Day, *Loaves and Fishes* (intro. Robert Coles; Maryknoll, New York: Orbis, 2003 [orig. 1963]), 145.

8   O'Shea Merriman, *Searching for Christ*, 177.

9   Ibid., 26.

ing of the historical Francis or to an explicitly Franciscan spirituality, Day's journey in the Catholic faith was accompanied from beginning to end by the Poverello, who exercised a subtle but profound influence over her life.

2. Romancing Lady Poverty: Peter as Francis Redivivus

If Peter Maurin was the decisive influence in her life as a Catholic, the one who
first revealed to her that solidarity with the poor was an essential element of the
Christian life, it is certainly significant that Day in turn always spoke of Peter
in Franciscan terms. Her first biographer, William Miller, quotes Day as saying:
"Peter was always getting back to Saint Francis of Assisi, who was most truly the
'gentle personalist.' In his poverty, rich; in renouncing all, possessing all; generous, giving out of the fullness of his heart, sewing generously and reaping generously, humble and asking when in need, possessing freedom and all joy." [10] Indeed, the identification of Peter and Francis is sometimes even more explicit for
Day. Mel Piehl writes:

> Because he advocated and lived a life of absolute poverty and
> generosity based on Catholic ideals, Maurin expressed per-
> fectly Day's most deeply held beliefs about religion and so-
> ciety. His humble appearance and openhearted simplicity
> brought to mind the saints she knew so well from her studies
> and suggested that sainthood was a present as well as a past re-
> ality. "Peter was the poor man of his day," she said. "He was an-
> other St. Francis in modern times." [11]

(Given her esteem for Maurin, it is difficult to know who is receiving the greater
compliment from her, Peter or Francis.) In Peter, Dorothy experienced the Franciscan spirit in its purest form.

The most striking parallel between Peter and Francis was their insistence
on voluntary poverty as the foundation of the Christian life, without which the
practice of the corporal works of mercy becomes impossible. Day recalls Peter
saying that

St. Francis of Assisi thought that to choose to be poor is as

---

10 William Miller, *Dorothy Day: A Biography* (San Francisco: HarperCollins, 1984), 235.

11 Mel Piehl, *Breaking Bread: The Catholic Worker and the Origin of Catholic Radi-*

good as marrying the most beautiful girl in the world. Most of us seem to think that Lady Poverty is an ugly girl and not the beautiful girl St. Francis says she is. And because we think so, we refuse to feed the poor with our superfluous goods. Instead, we let the politicians feed the poor by going around like pickpockets robbing Peter to pay Paul. [12]

As Jim Forest describes their initial encounter in December 1932,

By the time Dorothy met him, Peter had not only returned to the Catholic faith but has acquired an ascetic attitude toward both property and money: he had nearly none of either and, like Saint Francis of Assisi, rejoiced in poverty as if it were his bride. His poverty was his freedom.... Like Francis of Assisi and many other saints, Peter had been living on less rather than more for years and found it freeing rather than limiting. [13]

Marc H. Ellis points out that Peter's imitation of Francis—and, by extension, that of Day and the Catholic Worker movement in general—was not rooted in some romantic bohemianism but rather in a prophetic critique of modern society in light of the gospel:

As a modern follower of Francis, Maurin was profoundly at odds with the times in which he lived.... As much as anything, Maurin's adoration of Franciscan poverty was designed to free him to preach the gospel and stand as a witness to a culture that prized affluence. His emphasis on faith and contemplation as the foundation for rebuilding the church in a time of crisis was basically Franciscan, as was his emphasis on obedience to the Catholic church, a theme he found crucial in Francis' ability to maintain his radicalism while avoiding sectarianism. [14]

calism in America (Tuscaloosa, Alabama: University of Alabama Press, 2008), 65–66.

12 Day, *Loaves and Fishes*, 48.

13 Forest, *All is Grace*, 106, 114.

14 Marc H. Ellis, "Peter Maurin: To Bring the Social Order to Christ," pp. 15–46 in Patrick Coy, ed., *Revolution of the Heart: Essays on the Catholic Worker* (Philadelphia, Pennsylva-

But Ellis goes even further than this. In contrast to O'Shea Merriman, who emphasizes his Benedictine tendencies, Ellis sees in Maurin little less than a reappearance of the Spiritual Franciscans of the thirteenth and fourteenth centuries in offering a radical critique of the existing social and ecclesial order:

> Like others who had sought to emulate the saint from Assisi, Maurin saw Francis's poverty as eschatological. For Maurin, Francis's vision of life, when embodied in the person and the community, broke through the constraints of history and institutional forms, radically questioning the lethargy and 'givenness' of personal and social life. Francis thus represented the transformation that Maurin sought: a return by the person and the community to a total dependence on God. For Maurin, this included freeing the Catholic church and the Franciscan orders themselves from the bureaucratization that had diluted the radical demands of Jesus. Through Francis, Maurin wanted to move to the beginning and the end: the following of Jesus Christ.[15]

Whether or not Maurin would have described his philosophy in such stark terms, Ellis does firmly grasp the radical implications for our society of Peter's "Green Revolution."

At the same time, Peter also taught Dorothy the crucial distinction (so often obscured by the Christian tradition throughout history and even still today) between

> inflicted poverty and voluntary poverty; between being the victims and the champions of poverty. I prefer to call the one kind destitution, reserving the word poverty for what St. Francis called "Lady Poverty." We know the misery being poor can cause. St. Francis was "the little poor man" and none was more joyful than he; yet Francis began with tears, in fear and trembling, hiding out in a cave from his irate father.... It was only later that he came to love Lady Poverty. Perhaps kissing the leper was the great step that freed him not only from fastidi-

nia: Temple University Press, 1988), 20, 19.

15 Ibid., 21.

ousness and a fear of disease but from attachment to worldly goods as well. [16]

Day also learned, both from Peter and from hard personal experience, not to romanticize either poverty or the sometimes theatrical spirituality of the Poor Man of Assisi. With very sound theological instincts, Day recognized that conversion is for almost everyone a process, and not an event:

> Sometimes, as in St. Francis' case, freedom from fastidiousness and detachment from worldly things, can be attained in only one step. We would like to think that this is often so. And yet the older I get the more I see that life is made up of many steps, and they are very small ones, not giant strides. I have 'kissed a leper' not once but twice—consciously—yet I cannot say I am much the better for it. [17]

It was also Peter who impressed upon her the quote from the *Little Flowers* in which she found the secret meaning of the struggles and humiliations involved in the Catholic Worker movement, such as Peter's being mistaken for a Bowery bum: "We can only read over again the story of St. Francis, 'This then is perfect joy,' which we are reprinting in the CW." [18] As early as 1940, Day employed this quote to make sense of the human suffering caused by the economic hardships of the Great Depression, when unemployed men were resented and shunned by their own families: "To be hated and scorned by one's very own— this is poverty. This is perfect joy. The man of the family, out of work thru no fault of his own, scorned, heaped with recriminations by wife, children. It is part of the world's sorrow. Again due to their hard hearts, more than to poverty." [19] Francis' saying, "This then is perfect joy," recurs throughout Day's writings across the decades. Indeed, the daily suffering she encountered seems to have been bearable at times only because of the example of St. Francis and his unyielding emphasis on poverty, both material and spiritual, as forming the heart of the Christian life.

---

16 Day, *Loaves and Fishes*, 82–83.
17 Ibid., 83.
18 Entry from March 11, 1959, in Day, *Duty of Delight*, 253.
19 Entry from July 24, 1940 in ibid., 59.

3. The Charism of Non-Violence

If Day's commitment to voluntary poverty as both a spiritual and a social practice can be traced (via Peter) to St. Francis, the Poverello's influence does not end there. As Francis saw clearly in the thirteenth century, the logical conclusion of voluntary poverty, of total reliance upon God for one's needs, is a renunciation of all forms of violence. Whether allowing himself to be beaten and cast out into the cold when mistaken as a thief (therein discovering "perfect joy"), or voluntarily facing death before the Sultan to preach the Gospel, or allowing himself to be stoned and mocked as a madman by the people of Assisi to obtain materials for rebuilding San Damiano, Francis modeled non-violence more effectively than perhaps any other saint in Christian history. In a feudal society ruled by force and permeated with violence, "Saint Francis of Assisi had embraced the pacifist way with remarkable impact; many thousands joined the lay order he founded, accepting an obligation neither to possess nor use deadly weapons."[20] But, as Day would have read in *Rite Expiatis*, even this demand for non-violence among Francis' followers was given the very un-Francis-like proviso, "except in defense of the Roman Church, of the Christian faith, and of one's own country, or with the consent of one's Minister."[21] As we shall see, Day and the Catholic Worker movement took Francis' injunction far more literally than did the universal Church. In any case, "the connection [Day] made between Francis' poverty and pacifism appeared to matter most to her: the topic runs as a thread through many of her writings."[22]

Once again, Peter here serves as a crucial intermediary between Dorothy and the Franciscan tradition. He "shared the joy and excitement of Francis in living the Gospel in poverty and freedom. Like Francis, Peter gave up any ideas of power, domination or expediency as means to accomplish his goals, but rather inspired others with the idea of their vocation."[23] Almost a quarter century before meeting Day, Maurin's pacifism may have led him to emigrate from France to Canada in 1909 to avoid conscription into the military.[24] His insis-

---

20 Forest, *All is Grace*, 153.

21 *Rite Expiatis*, 34. With less persuasiveness, O'Shea Merriman claims that the Third Order's "refusal to bear arms is generally acknowledged as being instrumental in the breakdown of the feudal system" (*Searching for Christ*, 287 n. 11).

22 Ibid., 178.

23 Zwick, *Catholic Worker Movement*, 116.

24 Dorothy Day and Francis Sicius, *Peter Maurin: Apostle to the World* (Maryknoll, New York: Orbis, 2004), 5. The reason for his emigration is disputed.

tence on non-violence resonated immediately with Day, and the topic (as well as its Franciscan roots) formed part of the Catholic Worker message from the very beginning. Even during the Spanish Civil War, when almost all those on the left rallied to the Republican side against Franco and the fascists, "Maurin did not speak out, though he made it clear that his way was the Franciscan way, a way that excluded violence."[25] Rather, in issue after issue of the *Catholic Worker*, "Dorothy took frequent notice of the Franciscan contribution to peace, most directly through references to Francis and, in the early years of the Catholic Worker, through reminders of the Secular Franciscans' contribution along the lines represented in *Rite Expiatis.*"[26]

Day's commitment to pacifism would face its supreme test after America's entry into the Second World War, and the division over it threatened the continued existence of the Catholic Worker movement during the war. Here, too, the figure of Francis is in the forefront of Day's mind as she struggled to remain faithful to the gospel of non-violence in a world totally engulfed in war. In the January 1942, one month after the Japanese attack on Pearl Harbor, the *Catholic Worker* carried on its front page an editorial entitled "Our Country Passes from Undeclared War to Declared War; We Continue Our Christian Pacifist Stand." It stated:

> We are at war, a declared war, with Japan, Germany and Italy. But still we can repeat Christ's words, each day, holding them close in our hearts, each month printing them in the paper. In times past, Europe has been a battlefield. But let us remember St. Francis, who spoke of peace and we will remind our readers of him, too, so they will not forget.[27]

If the appeal to the figure of Francis were not a sufficiently clear statement of the religious authority behind the paper's decidedly unpopular pacifist stance, the artwork accompanying the editorial removed all doubt: "In the center of the page was a graphic of St. Francis of Assisi with the words 'Peace Without Victory.'"[28]

---

25 Eileen Egan, "Dorothy Day: Pilgrim of Peace," pp. 69–114 in *Revolution of the Heart*, 77.

26 O'Shea Merriman, *Searching for Christ*, 177.

27 "Our Country Passes from Undeclared War to Declared War; We Continue Our Christian Pacifist Stand," *Catholic Worker*, January 1942, 1.

28 Egan, "Dorothy Day," 82. Dorothy Day and the Catholic Worker movement maintained their pacifist stance after the war, protesting civil defense exercises in the 1950s and the

At the same time, Day realized that even pacifism can become a weapon used to attack and discredit one's opponent, and to dehumanize them, if used improperly. Recognizing the complexity of the human situation and the supernatural demands made by the pacifist position, Day was wary of easy moralizing. Too many men in the Catholic Worker movement that she knew and respected had defected from her cause and enlisted during the war for Day to dismiss or belittle their moral struggles. That attitude, she clearly saw, is itself a form of violence. Instead, "Dorothy realized the consequences of her pacifism, and strove to exercise her understanding of the gospel tradition in such a way as not to appear to pass judgment on others. This she did in conscious imitation of Francis, as she strove to win them 'to another point of view, with love and with respect.'"[29] Even to those who could not share her pacifist convictions, Dorothy Day (like Francis on Crusade in Egypt some seven centuries earlier) offered at least a reminder of the possibility of non-violence as an alternative to those trapped in the violence of war.

Finally, like Francis before them, both Maurin and Day extended this strategy of non-violence to the Church, humbly submitting themselves to its authority and refusing to resort to attacks of any sort upon its leaders (even when they were deserving of censure by any natural standard). By doing so, Day and Maurin avoided the sectarian temptations that bedeviled Francis' thirteenth and fourteenth century followers (a pattern which the Catholic Worker movement has not been entirely spared). In her September 1964 column Day explicitly referenced Francis' submission to priests and bishops—their human failings notwithstanding—as a model for her own Catholic life. This attitude of disobedience and disrespect, she understood, was itself a form of spiritual violence against the Church. Indeed, "Day permitted no criticism of priests or bishops in her presence, immediately coming to their defense. She suppressed Peter Maurin's mild anti-clericalism from the Catholic Worker. She told Stanley Vishnewski that Catholics should emulate St. Francis of Assisi's attitude of respect and reverence toward the clergy."[30] However unpopular her pacifism may have been in mid-century American society, however unsavory her past, and however scandalous to middle-class sensibilities her political views, the Church reciprocated her loyalty precisely because of the obvious authenticity and sincerity of

Viet Nam War in the 1960s, though the immediate existential importance of these debates never matched the intensity of those conducted in the face of fascist aggression.

29 O'Shea Merriman, *Searching for Christ*, 179.

30 Nancy L. Roberts, *Dorothy Day and the Catholic Worker* (Albany, New York: SUNY Press, 1985), 105.

her convictions. Like Francis before Pope Innocent III, Dorothy Day could fundamentally challenge the American Church only because she was an unquestionably loyal child of it. Mark and Louise Zwick have argued that "this bond with the Church allowed Francis and the Catholic Workers to maintain their radicalism in following the gospel without losing perspective or seeking self-aggrandizement. Their critique of the Church and the secular world was their very lives."[31]

Conclusion

Like Francis some seven centuries before her, Dorothy Day posed a fundamental challenge to the society in which she lived, presenting an alternative vision of community in which the gospel values of poverty and non-violence would supplant the worldly ones of wealth and power. This vision, in all its essentials, was that of the Poor Man of Assisi, whose example never ceased to inform and inspire Day in her apostolate. Day once wrote of Francis, "Men are usually of their time. St. Francis is timeless."[32] The same is true of his ideals, and no one in the history of the American Church more effectively embodied them than Day. In the same way, and with much the same degrees of success and of failure, "Dorothy Day did for her era what St. Francis of Assisi did for his: recall a complacent Christianity to its radical roots."[33] As has been shown, though, in many respects Dorothy's accomplishment was only an adaptation and extension of the work Francis began seven hundred years earlier. Whether she thought of herself as a Franciscan in any formal sense, or whether the Church categorizes her as such, is largely irrelevant. O'Shea Merriman rightly concludes of Day, "From Francis, she imbibed continued lessons in poverty and peace and, inspired by his love for God and others, strove to promote justice and harmony among her contemporaries."[34] As such, Francis would certainly have seen Day as one of his own—as should we.

---

31 Zwick, *Catholic Worker Movement*, 117.

32 Day, *Duty of Delight*, 186.

33 Kenneth Woodward, *Newsweek*, quoted on the front cover of *Dorothy Day: Meditations*, selected and arranged by Stanley Vishnewski (New York: Newman Press, 1970; repr. Springfield, IL: Templegate, 1997), cited by Zwick, *Catholic Worker Movement*, 116–17.

34 O'Shea Merriman, *Searching for Christ*, 219.

Lance Richey is Professor of Theology and Dean of the School of Liberal Arts and Sciences at the University of Saint Francis in Fort Wayne, Indiana. He recently edited the seventy-fifth anniversary edition of *Dorothy Day's House of Hospitality* (Huntington, Indiana: Our Sunday Visitor, 2015).

Liberation and Gandhian Themes in Catholic Worker Thought: The Catholic Worker and Gandhianism

Daniel Marshall

In her seventies when I arrived at the Peter Maurin Farm in Tivoli, New York, Dorothy Day seemed unpretentious and approachable, if refined and shy, for someone whose life had been the stuff of romance and drama. As she told the story in several books, she'd associated, in 1917 at the age of twenty, with American literary and political radicals of her time—Eugene O'Neill, Mike Gold, John Reed, Max Eastman, Rayna Prohme, and others, all enamored with the Russian revolution then transpiring. They gathered in New York's Greenwich Village at a tavern on Sixth Avenue and West Fourth Street that they called "The Hell Hole," though a sign outside proclaimed it "The Golden Swan." Some of them sought refuge, from their unheated cold-water flats, around the corner from the "Swan" halfway down McDougal Street at the Provincetown Theater being made famous by Eugene O'Neill. Sixteen troubled and blissful years of rambling literary life later, after a beach cottage idyll, the birth of a daughter, and conversion, she came home to her brother's apartment on East 15th Street to find waiting for her a French peasant intellectual named Peter Maurin, who brought her a new, but very ancient, religious vision that changed everything in her life.

But I sensed that there was more to it than that. Where did Peter Maurin get that religious vision of radical revolutionary change? He had been a young activist himself, a dozen years and more earlier than Dorothy and her friends of 1917, just before and after the turn of the century, joining the De La Salle Brothers in Paris in 1893 and, from 1902 to 1908, the French Sillon movement that aimed to bring together religion and social vision. Before the first World War, probably because of the war, he had left France for a life of homesteading and hard labor in America and, at some point, experienced a religious re-conversion. In the wake of that re-conversion, reading papal encyclicals and other sources, he developed a vision of a Catholic social apostolate that he transmitted to Dorothy in 1932. So far the official version goes.

Behind this story I intuited but did not yet know the details of a ferment that was taking place in Europe, within and outside the Catholic Church, at the end of the nineteenth and beginning of the twentieth centuries, the period that was formative for both these mentors of mine and for their religious, aesthetic, bohemian, and movement comrades.

In those heady years of Peter's and Dorothy's youth, there were not one, but three powerful revolutions occurring. There were not only a Russian revolution, but also an Irish one and an Indian one. And Russian, Irish, and Indian radicals were finding sanctuary and rubbing shoulders with each other in back alleys, cultural haunts, and university districts of Paris and London that were alive at the same time with avant garde writers, artists, and philosophers.

To give context, during Peter Maurin's boyhood, anarchist activist and geographer Peter Kropotkin was making news organizing and being arrested in France. From 1896 and throughout Peter Maurin's young manhood, this great Russian student of human and animal societies was living near London, producing now-classic scholarly works opposing the idea that competition, hierarchy, and individualism are natural bases of society and proving instead that cooperation, mutual aid, and community are. After the Russian Revolution of 1917, just as Dorothy was beginning her apprenticeship in radical journalism, Peter Kropotkin returned from London to Russia, where he was received with great acclaim. In 1921, Emma Goldman spoke at his burial, the last great anarchist demonstration in Russia.

Both Peter Maurin and Dorothy Day were familiar, even before they met, with the anarchist movement that produced its secular "saint" in Peter Kropotkin, and both recommended him approvingly. Before Peter left Europe, he had visited Kropotkin-inspired cooperative workshops in southern France.

All through the nineteenth century, the Irish, starting with Daniel O'Connell and continuing with Charles Stuart Parnell and his sisters Anna and Fanny, had been developing what would become the repertoire of nonviolent revolution in the twentieth century, most notably "boycott" and filibuster tactics and every sort of outdoor demonstration. In the 1890s, Maud Gonne, the Dorothy Day of Ireland, was periodically traveling to Paris for respite and romance, returning to Ireland by way of London, fundraising for the poor and the imprisoned and tweaking the British aristocracy with impassioned speeches and witty nonviolent demonstrations. Throughout the period when Peter Maurin was active with the Sillon, she was raising her children in Paris. She survived her husband's death in the 1916 Rising and lived long into the era of Dorothy Day, never abandoning her work for the poor.

The Irish revolution—particularly its wit, grit, zest, passion for the poor, natural anarchism, and, in some representatives, nonviolence—was part of the context in which the Catholic Worker and its founders functioned, and many poor and intellectual Catholics whom they served, who joined them, and to whom they addressed themselves were ardent and informed Irish supporters of Irish nationalism and independence.

During the same end of century period, from 1887 to 1891, Mohandas Gandhi was studying law in London. In Henry Salt's Vegetarian Society there, he met G. K. Chesterton and George Bernard Shaw. George Bernard Shaw and Henry Salt were in touch with Peter Kropotkin; and Henry introduced Mohandas to the writings of Henry David Thoreau, who was not yet generally well known.

By 1893, as a newly-minted lawyer, Mohandas was in South Africa organizing a powerful nonviolent campaign for civil rights. In 1904, inspired by the John Ruskin essay "Unto This Last" and by Trappist monks at Mariannhill, he established the Phoenix Settlement, in which all were compensated equally. In 1909–1910, he corresponded with Leo Tolstoy, the Russian novelist, communitarian, and preacher of nonviolence. At this point, he had attained the same age and eminence as Martin Luther King when assassinated and was being urged by the Indian independence movement to go to India. From 1915 until his death in 1948, he was mostly in India, organizing Indian peasants and upper classes for independence.

In London in 1909, Mohandas Gandhi read a G. K. Chesterton article[1] that profoundly influenced him to do what he subsequently did. It was published in one or more of as many journals as there are commentators writing about the incident, most likely in G.K.C.'s regular column in *The Illustrated London News* (Brown). G. K. challenged Indian revolutionaries to look to their own rich culture for models rather than to imitate the British. The article struck Mohandas Gandhi like a blow. From it he derived the principle that no Indian revolution was worth having unless it built on and included peasant culture. It is said that during his career he visited every Indian village on foot.

---

1 Nancy C. Brown, "Gandhi Reference," *The American Chesterton Society* (blog), January 6, 2009, http://americanchestertonsociety.blogspot.com/2009/01/gandhi-reference.html.

This enlightenment also launched him on a search for scientifically sound, naturally rooted systems, often the best systems, that could be utilized by the poorest peasants to attain the basic needs of life, e.g., food, clothing, education, health, and community organization. This he called "constructive program."

Peter Maurin, writing in the Thirties, only referred to Mohandas Gandhi twice, in the context of "sit-down strikes" and "industrialism;" Peter preferred references to farming communities organized by Catholic missionaries as illustrations of the "agronomic university." But there are natural concordances between the Gandhian and Catholic Worker movements, if they only knew it.

Ammon Hennacy, who so profoundly influenced Dorothy Day and the development of Catholic Worker activism, lists twenty references to Gandhi in *The Book of Ammon,* and the conclusion of *The One-Man Revolution in America* is a discussion of the "other way" of Mohandas Gandhi. Returning from California in the 1970s, Dorothy Day remarked that her close friend Cesar Chavez had a volume of Mohandas Gandhi by his bedside.

If Peter Maurin had been able to continue thinking and writing throughout the 1940s, I was convinced that he would have integrated the Gandhian idea of constructive program into the *Easy Essays.*

Dorothy had read widely in Russian literature and, like Mohandas Gandhi, admired the nonviolent anarchism of Leo Tolstoy. Peter Maurin and Dorothy Day read and recommended the English Distributists—G. K.Chesterton, Vincent NcNabb O.P., Eric Gill, and Hilaire Belloc. They also read papal encyclicals, bishops' conferences, Catholic philosophers, and saints' lives.

The Catholic Worker was committed to nonviolence and to anarchism in the spirit of Peter Kropotkin, by which both Dorothy and Peter said that they meant "personalist communitarianism". Ammon energetically opposed anarchism to capitalism and knew all the key anarchists.

I was discovering in the CW a great movement, a great integration of secular and religious thought. Tolstoy—Kropotkin—Gandhi—English Distributists—Irish rebels—Catholic social tradition. From them, there is a straight line of inspiration to the Catholic Worker, called by scholar George Woodcock "the most impressive example of Tolstoyan influence" and "Christian anarchism" in the mid-twentieth century. [2]

2   George Woodcock, *Anarchism: A History of Libertarian Ideas and Movements* (Cleveland: World Publishing Company [Meridian Books], 1962), 234.

When I arrived at the Peter Maurin Catholic Worker farm in Tivoli, New York in 1972, the first thing that Dorothy had me do was to make discussion copies of a book about the leading Gandhian disciple and successor, Vinoba Bhave. No discussion occurred. I think that Dorothy never ceased to think of the Tivoli property as a retreat center, even after it was overwhelmed by the homeless and footloose. Besides, roundtable discussion was a fundamental feature of all Catholic Worker communities. Maybe she meant for me to organize discussion.

The book—*Gandhi to Vinoba*—was written by a European Gandhian, Giuseppe Lanza del Vasto, scion of a noble Sicilian family. As a young man, Giuseppe (Joseph) had left a relatively carefree life of wandering minstrelsy on the roads of Europe to seek in India from Mohandas Gandhi a solution to such outbursts of violence as the ones that everyone feared were about to course through Europe. His money was robbed when he landed. He had unexpected spiritual adventures and learned more about India than he expected. The great nonviolent leader named him Shantidas, "servant of peace", urging him to stay. It was a classic pilgrimage story which he recounted in *Return to the Source.*

Instead of staying, Shantidas returned hurriedly to Europe where he sang and played guitar in Parisian cafes throughout the war. After the surrender of Germany, he established craft workshops in Paris which soon scorned and abandoned him, and in 1948 he married a chanteuse and founded a rural community on a former Mussolini estate in the mountains behind Montpelier. The community had about one hundred members and was monastic in style; all members were given special names and wore a sort of habit, broadcloth on work days and wool for feasts, made by hand at the community.

In 1968, my wife Elizabeth and I first heard about Shantidas and his Community of the Ark from Joan and Kevin Ryan at a little Catholic Worker community outside Malaga, Spain. When we got to southern France, we visited Shantidas and his wife, Chanterelle in their apartment at the Ark. We were invited to help in the field, met the community doctor, saw the outdoor hand laundry tubs, heard about the school, joined morning meditation. In 1971, Shantidas and Chanterelle arrived in New Hampshire, where we then lived, for a tour. Dorothy may have known that I arranged for him to speak.

Shantidas and Chanterelle stayed in Manchester. They were human, approachable, and easy to talk with. Shantidas had a sense of humor and teased Chanterelle about a pretty girl on the street. Chanterelle was direct and warm.

At Mt. St. Mary's College in Hooksett, New Hampshire, on a tinkly cold white and black moonlit night, slippery with a layer of ice over deep snow, he and she, tall and magnificent, clad in soft white homegrown homespun, he with

179

a great white beard, stood beside each other like two figures from a Bergman film and spoke to a packed auditorium of young women and apple pickers sitting in pin-drop, awe-struck silence. He told them about nonviolence, founding the community a second time with vows and a leader, and resolving community issues by the practice of co-responsibility. Afterward, he answered daunting questions from several of the apple pickers and, with Chanterelle, sang songs of the loom, traditional music used by the women at the Ark as they spun, for the community practiced patriarchy and gender-based division of labor, as well as unanimity. He was at his best.

In New York City, Dorothy and Shantidas spoke together in a meeting. Dorothy spoke of the ways in which the Worker falls short of ideals, and Shantidas spoke of ideals; he appeared uncharacteristically somber and imposing. Neither leader was well, and the impression was that neither felt entirely comfortable.

Contact with the French Community of the Ark was one way in which the Catholic Worker dialogued with the Gandhian movement. Of course, the Worker also had close ties with the civil rights movement of Martin Luther King and the labor movement of Cesar Chavez, which were Gandhian-inspired, and with the War Resisters League and many other peace movement groups which revered Mohandas Gandhi, but the Ark most thoroughly implemented Gandhian spirituality and constructive program.

Dorothy fasted with the Ark in Rome in 1965 at the Vatican Council—she and twenty of the Ark women for ten days, and Shantidas for forty days. The Ark used fasting also for health.

Rome was not Dorothy's first fast. In 1959, likely through the influence of Ammon, Dorothy fasted for both physical and spiritual healing, she said, at a Florida "Rest Ranch" belonging to a Catholic doctor and respectful reader of the *Catholic Worker*, William Esser, who, she said, drove her to Mass every day.

Ammon fasted each year the same number of days as years that had transpired since the atomic bombing of Hiroshima and for men on death row; and he thought much of a naturopathic doctor, Herbert M. Shelton, who had a fifty-bed "Health School" in Texas, established in the nineteenth-century American medical reform tradition, where people fasted for recovery from just about any disease. William Esser was one of Herbert Shelton's colleagues.

Mohandas Gandhi also thought highly of Herbert Shelton, enough to invite him to India for five years to teach fasting in the Gandhian ashrams. Herbert Shelton agreed to two years, but the invitation did not come to fruition because of the World War and fraternal conflict in India. However, the Shelton "big" book on fasting was in all Gandhian ashrams. Herbert Shelton was the leading fasting doctor at the time. Mohandas Gandhi knew of fasting because, on one of his voyages, he had met a disciple of the American physical culturist Bernarr McFadden. From him, he heard about fasting for recovery from disease. Bernarr McFadden had been one of Herbert Shelton's guiding lights, and connections were made.

Fasting was for Mohandas Gandhi a breakthrough, a natural therapy that was a near-panacea and available to even the poorest peasant, and he became an enthusiastic advocate of fasting for almost every condition. He experimented unendingly with his own diet, and, after retiring from law practice and Congress, lived at a movement ashram and devoted 60% of his time to advising people about health. For expert assistance in health matters, he was dependent upon local naturopaths and medical doctors.

Of course, in America, fasting, like the rest of the reform medical tradition and natural healing, were attacked as "quackery" by modern "scientific" medicine funded by Rockefeller money and oriented toward pharmaceuticals, chemicals, and surgery.

The Tivoli farm was not so organized as the Ark. John Filligar was our farmer, and a few people helped him. Parties from the farm sometimes helped with harvesting at nearby orchards. I was not a strong harvester, in fact was fighting and fasting illness at the time, and so had little money. Nor did I function well in cold weather, and the Hudson Valley channeled the coldest of wintry blasts from the North Country. I noticed that other people at the farm did not have much money either, but were dependent on the kindness of strangers. Even if they were ambitious, problems of transportation and a depressed economy in the county were overwhelming.. Though functional, we lived in an abiding state of demoralization. It is easier to get into destitution than to get out of it.

"It's a school of nonviolence!" Dorothy said, hopefully.

Most of what Elizabeth and I knew about Mohandas Gandhi we had learned on New Hampshire apple-picking and pruning crews before we arrived in Tivoli.

The crews had been started by a sort of refugee from the City named Arthur Harvey. He had been active in the peace movement and was known to Dorothy and others in New York City. Disillusioned by movements, by large undertakings, and maybe by the world, Arthur had agreed to house-sit outside Raymond, New Hampshire. To support himself, he'd arranged to do agricultural work for local farmers, and a few friends came to join him. One was a Catholic Worker, Peter Lumsden, whom we visited in London, who told us about Arthur.

By the time we arrived in New Hampshire in late 1968, many young people were wandering the roads, avoiding or resisting a military draft and experimenting with more traditional ways of life. In them, and particularly in local youth, Arthur found a cause that he could support. He organized crews to harvest apples and berries and a pruning crew in winter. We arrived at the beginning.

Although Arthur himself ascribed to no philosophy, being a sort of skeptic, he seemed to admire principled anti-war people of integrity and radical simplicity. He had acquired a Gandhian book distributing business from an elderly Quaker and imported the entire range of Gandhian publications, including all the many constructive program titles on health, education, and agriculture that were little appreciated in this country and not yet available elsewhere.

Arthur used a mimeograph machine to publish a few peace movement tracts and other items of interest himself. When we arrived, he had just published a small booklet called "The Apple Picker's Manual," and, that first winter, on snowy days when we couldn't prune apple trees, he published another one called "The Use of Poor Means in Helping the Third World." It was a talk given by Pierre Parodi, the designated successor to Shantidas at the Ark and a medical doctor. Elizabeth had found it at the Ark house in Paris and translated it for me; and I edited it and typed stencils for publication. I suggested that Arthur publish it, and he said that it would be a "dog;" but it was an immediate bestseller within the peace movement, going into several editions and spreading Gandhian ideas of sound and simple living.

Arthur was very orderly and organized. Maybe he'd assimilated the business sense of his dad. He claimed to believe in little but manual work and local action and worked constantly, delighting in contradicting conventional liberal prejudices that surfaced among crew members.

"Words on paper!" he would say derisively, for he thought that college graduates were too literal.

"Farmers hate to spray," he said; "they see what spraying does, but have to do it to stay competitive."

"But I thought...!" people would say.

"Thought leads to error," Arthur would respond.

Arthur knew the Catholic Worker and respected it for integrity. Once or twice, Arthur attended Quaker meeting in Concord; it was a small meeting in a borrowed or rented space. That was about as close as he got to religion, except for a friend who was a Cistercian monk.

"I don't think that Ammon had much use for Arthur," Dorothy said, but Ammon was famously hard on young men. Arthur was, too.

New Hampshire small farming was a different world from the grape fields and vast irrigated row farming of central California and the wheat and corn fields of Nebraska. New Hampshire farmers were clients of packing houses, with little power. One day, as we picked strawberries, we were sprayed from the air. Another day, we saw members of a Spanish-speaking crew arrested in the field.

We learned about chemicals and varieties. We could recognize varieties at a glance and hear them falling when ripe, particularly if the new ripening hormone, Allar, had been applied. Late in apple picking season, we heard gunshots and looked nervously toward the edges of the orchards.

"Hunters are just quiet fellows who like to walk in the woods," Arthur said; "they all fire their guns late in the afternoon around five o'clock before going home."

The diet was vegetarian, and we paid into a fund for hiring a cook. I was already an ethical vegetarian, but unsophisticated about nutrition. I read books about a vegetarian Olympic swimmer and factory farming and began to realize how deficient my diet was. I became vegan and tried adding brewers yeast, lecithin, nuts, and whole grains.

Arthur did not ascribe to nonviolence, any more than to anything else, and indeed was not nonviolent; but, like the Tivoli farm, the Greenleaf crews, too, were lively "schools of nonviolence."

Others on the crews were interesting. From them I learned about the American Natural Hygiene Society, founded by Herbert Shelton in 1948, and the American Vegan Society, founded by H. Jay Dinshah in 1960; Jay was also an officer of the Hygiene Society. He spoke at Tivoli. The Vegan Society opposed hurting or enslaving animals for any reason. Its exemplars were Mohandas Gandhi and Albert Schweitzer.

Cesar Chavez was a member of the Natural Hygiene Society and fasted. Ammon Hennacy reported in *The Book of Ammon* that he had twice visited Herbert Shelton. He considered Herbert the expert on matters of health, and Herbert considered Ammon the expert on politics. Like Ammon, Herbert Shelton had been jailed for military draft refusal during World War I.

Reading Arthur's books and listening on the crews, I learned more about Mohandas Gandhi and Vinoba Bhave. Some members with knowledge had something to contribute, and some, like me, were eager to ply Arthur or others with questions. Arthur's connections were to American peace groups like Peacemakers, the Committee for Nonviolent Action, and the War Resisters League. Though they were Gandhian, they had not paid as much attention as the Ark to the Gandhian idea of "constructive program".

I wanted to do all this myself—to found a Catholic Worker agronomic university, to practice constructive program, and to fast, when needed, for political or health reasons. In the event, fasting became intrinsic and irreplaceable to the recovery of my own damaged health.

There was also talk on the crews of radical education—progressive schools, homeschooling, and growing without schooling, as championed by John Holt from Boston. Mohandas Gandhi had written much on education, and I found among Arthur's books a collection of essays written by the foremost Gandhian disciple Vinoba Bhave, including an essay on "Non-Compulsory Education," about the spirit in every child that hungers every day to learn what it needs, whether it goes to school or not, if it's not squelched by harshness or regimentation.

Such things—radical healthcare, radical education, and radical agriculture—tend to be pushed to the side in the United States by radical peacemakers. But I saw that radical peacemaking is meaningless and without roots unless it follows from radical engagement with the practical fundamentals of society and manual labor, against the coercion, exploitation, and propaganda exercised by wealth and power over fundamental practical matters, because without such confrontation and well-informed resistance we are not ourselves liberated from violence in our presumptions, practices, and understandings, nor are we equipped to change society with nonviolent alternatives. We cannot go one way in our hearts and another in our actions. It doesn't work. We must be one.

Americans do not generally have education, access, nor leisure to reflect in this way upon health, education, or agriculture and so are willing to delegate all three to professionals. But for us these things and self-reliance were everyday topics that excited us.

Around us we visited innovative homesteads and learned how to build and garden. Engineered houses, envelope houses, yurts, tipis, compost toilets, high-efficiency wood stoves, mulch, compost, surface cultivation, woodchuck-proof fencing. Elizabeth and I lived in community with a Quaker family. Among us and our neighbors, we were in touch with poetry, singing, and dancing.

The second or third apple season in New Hampshire a group of Young Quakers from New Swarthmoor Community in Clinton, New York came to the apple crews, singing. Sometimes in the evening they gathered around the bunkhouse stove, packed close and drawing others on the crew—the sturdy young men and plump, rosy, warmly-clad young women. The Quakers were people who had some connection to the land and a tradition of simple living, from families with similar values who could support them.

But, in the liberated '70s, marriages were coming apart around us, including young couples, those of seven or eight years and mid-life crisis couples. Expressing feelings was in vogue, and "encounter groups." Psychology was not sufficient in itself to help; the therapeutic modalities available were new and simplistic. Shantidas said that he hadn't found much use in psychology.

Many people sought peace rather in the ancient schools of zen, meditation, and yoga, as at the Community of the Ark, or of martial arts, such as taekwondo, which aimed to sublimate passion in discipline and quiet. Some began to take an interest in local gurus—Kirpal Singh and Ram Dass. Few besides us sought answers in traditional Catholicism.

I've explored world cultures and world traditions to find light wherever I could, integrating what I found with my own culture, and a picture has begun to appear.

Names change. The American Natural Hygiene Society is now the National Health Association. The American Vegan Society is still the American Vegan Society. The reform doctors of mid-century—Shelton, Esser, Scott, Burton—have been replaced by Fuhrman, Goldhamer, Campbell, Sabatino. Reform institutions of the past—Doctor Shelton's, Esser's, Scott's—have given way to True North, Ocean Jade, Dr. Cinque's. John Holt and Growing without Schooling were followed by John Taylor Gatto and an "unschooling" movement; and the Shanleys of Agape Community write about nonviolence toward children. The pioneering forays of Scott and Helen Nearing, Ruth Stout, and Bob and Marge Swann in the literature, methods, and economics of American farming have yielded to contemporary movements on behalf of vegan permaculture, surface cultivation, and animal sanctuary. Arthur Harvey probably still sells Indian editions of Mohandas Gandhi to those who ask, but now the complete works, even compiled editions, are available online.

The writings of Mohandas Gandhi and Vinoba Bhave are a rich body of philosophy that could well be on the book shelf and in the discussions of every agronomic university and, in this environmentally concerned age, help ground Catholic Worker efforts, as suffering servants, to rebuild the world in Christ, expressing nonviolent dominion over other creatures in the manner of Jesus's dominion over us. Eliminating war is an indispensable beginning; but peace is only going to be achieved at the same time as we achieve peace with all creation, with all life wherever it is, because we cannot be peaceful in one area of our lives and not in another. That also is impossible.

The Gandhian literature is not all directly translatable and applicable. It is written within the context of Hindu idiom and belief, but the Christ-light in Mohandas Gandhi is universal, a re-birth of Franciscan spirit so strange and ironic. It is in the mode of radical simplicity and voluntary poverty, recognizing our complete dependence upon God, and, in our technological age, is serving to return our wandering Church and people to worship of the one true God.

"I am the Way, the Truth, and the Life," said Jesus. "Truth is God," said Mohandas Gandhi. "*You* are the Christ, the Son of the Living God," said Peter. "The One is God," Shantidas said. Without Jesus, some come to the truth, said Thomas Aquinas, "but only with a great admixture of error." "There is that of God in every man," say the Quakers.

Despite the brilliant insights of the Gandhian synthesis and my personal affection for Shantidas and Chanterelle, I could not abide patriarchy, division of labor, or vows. There was too much uniformity for me at the Ark. Nor did I believe that the answer to the world's problems is to be found in interconfessional community. I believe that Jesus is the way, the truth, and the life that the Church and world need. And I need the Catholic Worker support of freedom in the Spirit.

The geniuses of these two great movements for peaceful resolution of human needs and service to life have a great deal to offer each other—the Catholic Worker, Christ-centered hospitality and works of mercy, at a personal sacrifice; the Gandhians, constructive program in service and witness to the dignity of the poorest. Integration of the philosophy of constructive program has potential to be extraordinarily enriching to the Catholic Worker.

Both movements need to be more personal in resisting the powers of the world—to learn to commune and confront more politely, positively, and powerfully, beginning with intimate relations. For it is by love, not by integrity, important as integrity is, that we will be known as disciples. So Jesus said.

When I was young and setting a course, I asked God to show me what people need and what they think they need and wisdom to discern the difference. This is what I've found. I offer it to you—new ideas that are really old ideas, so old that they look like new.

186

Daniel Marshall is a writer and academic librarian. He founded a Catholic Worker community in Berkeley, California and has been a member of two others—Peter Maurin Farm in Tivoli, New York and Arthur Sheehan House in Brooklyn, New York. He has been an agricultural laborer and a military and war-tax resister. He lives with his wife in Harlem, New York.

The Influence of French Thought on Dorothy Day

Jennifer Kilgore-Caradec

Peter Maurin was French, yet he wrote passionately about American problems:[1]

> People go to Washington
> asking the government
> to solve their economic problems,
> while the Federal government
> was never intended
> to solve men's economic problems.
> Thomas Jefferson says that
> the less government there is
> the better it is.
> If the less government there is,
> the better it is,
> then the best kind of government
> is self-government.
> If the best kind of government
> is self-government,
> then the best kind of organization
> is self-organization.
> When the organizers try

1   This paper is dedicated with gratitude to Michael Cameron and Lorie Simmons. During our University of Chicago days, Michael spoke often of Charles Péguy and Lorie, who had studied at Chartres, instigated stimulating discussions about French medieval art and architecture.

> to organize the unorganized,
> then the organizers
> don't organize themselves.
> And when the organizers
> don't organize themselves,
> nobody organizes himself,
> and when nobody organizes himself
> nothing is organized. [2]

The commentary that Dorothy Day makes of this passage reveals her personal knowledge of Charles Péguy's work, [3] which is characterized by many repetitions, particularly in his great poem *Eve* (1913). Of Peter she writes: "He actually spoke this way, using repetition to make his points. He phrased these points so simply that they sounded like free verse (and to this day people talk about 'Peter's verses')." [4] However, Peter Maurin had not received the same elite education that the working-class Péguy (1873–1914) had rather miraculously managed to acquire. He had not gone to Ecole Normale or followed Henri Bergson's philosophy classes. Maurin's brand of personalism was very practically based, as he constructed his own ideas from very diverse readings including, according to Nancy Roberts: Léon Bloy, Charles Péguy, Emmanuel Mounier, Jacques Maritain, and the various British agrarians: Harold Robbins, Eric Gill, Hilaire Belloc, G. K. Chesterton, and Vincent McNabb. [5] This paper asserts that Péguy's influence stands out particularly as a foundational pillar of Catholic Worker thought.

Shortly before meeting Dorothy Day, Maurin had most likely read Emmanuel Mounier's contribution to *La Pensée de Charles Péguy* (1931). [6] While preparing that volume, Mounier (1905–1950) was working towards the foundation of the Personalist Movement in France and the creation of the periodical *Esprit*

---

2 Dorothy Day, *Loaves and Fishes* (New York: Harper and Row, 1963), 5–6.

3 Several sections and especially the last three pages of this paper, were initially presented in French as "Charles Péguy et Dorothy Day" at a Péguy Centenary Conference held at Cerisy-la-Salle in July 2014, "Voix de Péguy: Quels échos aujourd'hui?" The proceedings edited by Jérôme Roger, will appear in the series Littérature Cerisy, Paris, Editions Classiques Garnier (http://www.ccic-cerisy.asso.fr/peguy14.html).

4 Day, *Loaves and Fishes*, 6.

5 Nancy L. Roberts, *Dorothy Day and the Catholic Worker* (Albany, New York: StateUniversity of New York Press, 1984), 30.

6 Mounier's contribution was reprinted in Emmanuel Mounier, *La Pensée de Charles Péguy: La vision des hommes et du monde*, ed. Nadia Yala Kisukidi and Yves Roullière (Paris : Le Felin, 2015), 43–155.

(1932–). Mounier's understanding of Péguy in 1931 should be linked with Madeleine Danielou's enthusiasm for Péguy.

Madeleine Danielou (1880–1956) was married and had six children before she founded the Saint Francis Xavier apostolic community devoted to education, becoming the director of Sainte-Marie de Neuilly school in the Parisian suburbs in 1913.[7] Danielou's motivation was to avoid a separation between Christian and intellectual values. She may have first encountered Péguy's writing while preparing for her agrégation at the Collège Sévigné, under the instruction of Mathilde Salomon, who would soon translate Israel Zangwill's *Chad Gadya* for publication in Charles Péguy's *Cahiers de la quinzaine* in 1905.[8]

In 1900, Henri Bergson was nominated to the Collège de France, during the same year that Péguy founded the *Cahiers*.[9] Bergson (1859–1941) was a prominent philosophical voice and the main philosophical influence for Charles Péguy—and also for Danielou. Péguy would become one of the main lifelong spiritual influences for Danielou, who was received first at the agrégation in 1903 and who eventually decided to name some of her community's schools after him in the 1930s.[10]

Mounier's contact with Danielou's school in Neuilly was no doubt one of the formative influences for his action and decision to start a review. While teaching there he met Robert Garric, whose ideas he did not find totally convincing.[11] Of course when one is looking for something the answer sometimes lies around the corner from the solution that is almost, but not quite, right. Mounier in the late 1920s and early 1930s kept company with Georges Izard, Louis-Emile Galey, André Déléage, Charles Mangin, and Georges Duveau (who had founded an avant-garde literary review in the early 1920s).[12] These were some of the people with whom he formulated his ideas and the desire to create a review. But it was

---

7   The best known of her children is Cardinal Jean Daniélou, he was the eldest, followed by Alain Daniélou, a specialist of Indian culture, Cathérine Danielou who married Georges Izard, François Daniélou, Louis Daniélou (he joined the Free France forces in England during World War II and died in the war), and Marie Daniélou.

8   Marie-Thérèse Abgrall, "Madeleine Daniélou et Péguy," *L'Amitié Charles Péguy* 123 (July–Sept 2008), 250–51.

9   Ibid., 251.

10 Charles-Péguy Bobigny was founded in 1936, and Charles-Péguy Paris in 1941. See Abgrall, Ibid., 253.

11 Michel Winock, *'Esprit' Des intellectuels dans la cité 1930–1950* (Paris: Seuil, 1996), 36. According to Winock, Garric wanted to promote supportive links between intellectuals and working classes, but he offered no philosophical basis for his actions.

12 Ibid., 37.

in fact Madeleine Danielou who suggested the name *Esprit* for the review that he would begin during the autumn of 1932 while he and Izard were staying with her at Font-Romeau in August when the project was taking shape. The intellectual historian Michel Winock has suggested that the collapse of Maurras's *Action Française* had made the climate ripe for Mounier to begin *Esprit*, and Mounier declared his motivation to his former teacher from Grenoble, Jacques Chevalier (who was not as enthusiastic about the project): "I feel ever more deeply the fundamental opposition existing between social and human ideals, even the spiritual morality of many Christians and the principles that they claim to adhere to." [13]

Simultaneously during this period, Mounier and Jacques Maritain (1882–1973) were also meeting regularly in Meudon on Sundays. [14] Maritain, who had been attracted to the Action Française, renewed contact with Bergson at this time, and was also seeking a new direction, desiring to follow the line of the papal encyclicals *Rerum Novarum* (Leo XIII, 1891) and *Quadragesimo Anno* (Pius XI, 1931).

In the introduction to *La pensée de Charles Péguy* (1931), Mounier noted that Péguy wrote in *De la situation faite*, "I say what I write. I write what I say." [15] Such a sentence, as Mounier understood, suggests a strong link between one's writing and one's life, between writing and commitment. That sentence alone might have been enough to interest Peter Maurin in Péguy. When people say about Dorothy Day that she has "something to offend everyone," they are simply repeating what Mounier said about Péguy in his introduction to *La Pensée de Péguy*, "There is something to bother everyone in Péguy's work (*Il y a dans l'œuvre de Péguy, de quoi mécontenter tout le monde*)."

Mounier writes of Péguy: "The passion for truth and the passion for justice were united in him in a joint fidelity which vibrates throughout his work." [16] Péguy could not stand "that others be excluded." [17] Péguy "alone among others succeeded at bringing about a team where there was a mixing of Catholics, Protestants, Jews and free-thinkers." [18] Péguy was fighting against preconceived

---

13 Ibid., 39. All translations from French to English in this paper are mine, unless otherwise noted.

14 Ibid.

15 Emmanuel Mounier, introduction, *La pensée de Charles Péguy* (Paris: Plon, 1931), iv.

16 Mounier, *La pensée de Péguy*, 14.

17 Ibid., 28.

18 Ibid., 39.

ideas *("la pensée toute faite")*,[19] and Mounier quotes from *L'Argent* (1913) where a portrait is made of the worker for whom "to work is to pray."[20] "Péguy had a mystical soul" and knew the value of silence.[21] One could say that Peter Maurin lived a bit like Péguy, according to the description that Mounier makes of him, showing a man preoccupied with the problem of evil:

> The most important focus of Péguy is the experience of the world's distress: it occupies his whole life and is at the intersection of all of his ideas. He intimately knew all its forms especially the most difficult.[22]

According to Mounier, Péguy in the *Note sur M. Bergson* denounced the evil hidden in the daily routine.[23] Mounier's personalism would also fight that evil, and Peter Maurin decided to translate his Personalist Manifesto into English (it was published in 1934 or 1935).[24] In a letter of June 1954, to Brendan O'Grady, Day affirmed that Maurin had been influenced by Péguy even down to the style of his own writing.[25] Though Dorothy Day did not know who Charles Péguy was when she first met Peter Maurin in December 1932, she was already aware of the uniqueness of Maurin's repetitive verse commentaries, as described in *Loaves and Fishes* (1963), his "easy essays" where she was able to later discern Péguy's influence.

Maurin named Péguy three times in the collection of those essays found in *Catholic Radicalism* (1949), and he is specifically mentioned in the introduction.[26] Maurin explained that Péguy was in Paris during the decade that he himself was there, but that they never met, and that Péguy had had no influence on

---

19 Ibid., 69.

20 Ibid., 79.

21 Ibid., 91–92.

22 Ibid., 167. See also Charles Péguy, *Œuvres en prose complètes*, III, ed. Robert Burac (Paris: NRF/Gallimard, 1992), 469, and Michel Raimond, "Péguy et la critique du monde moderne dans les années trente," *Cahiers de l'Association Internationale des Etudes Françaises* 49 (1997), 355–369, on-line.

23 Mounier, *La pensée de Péguy*, 127.

24 Dorothy Day, *The Duty of Delight, The Diaries of Dorothy Day*, ed. Robert Ellsberg (Milwaukee, Wisconson: Marquette University Press, 2008), i-book edition.

25 Day, *All the Way to Heaven, The Selected Letters of Dorothy Day*, ed. Robert Ellsberg (Milwaukee, Wisconsin: Marquette University Press, 2010), i-book edition.

26 Peter Maurin, *Catholic Radicalism, Phrased Essays for the Green Revolution* (New York:, Catholic Worker Books, 1949), iii.

him at that time. Maurin's variety of personalism was more practically and less intellectually enacted than Mounier's, with the phrase "Cult-Culture-Cultivation" which he endeavored to practice, encompassing the notions of worship, of enriching one's mind, and of growing food. [27] In many ways, this tri-partate formula would correspond to utopia as Péguy had formulated it in 1898 in *Marcel, Premier dialogue de la cité harmonieuse.* [28] Here is a passage that may have inspired Maurin:

> The workers in the harmonious city do not think of asking the city for what in our bourgeois society we call a wage or a salary for the work that they have done, because they are workers and not sellers, because they are citizens and not rivals of the city and because they are the co-citizens and not the rivals of their co-citizens. [29]

Maurin's insistence on clarification of thought was also a way of avoiding, as Péguy did, the preconceived or pre-cooked idea. No doubt Day, who was responsible for getting Maurin's *Easy Essays* published after his death, had absorbed these verses into her own system of thought. The way she describes Maurin's intentions suggests something of Péguy's early utopian vision:

> Alleviation of the immediate needs of the poor and indoctrination by example through voluntary poverty and the practice of the works of mercy, corporal and spiritual.
>
> Clarification of thought through the Catholic Worker, leaflets, articles, discussions and meetings.
>
> Houses of Hospitality in every poor parish to practice mutual aid, hospitality and charity, houses which would also provide workshops where the unemployed could be employed and where the unskilled could become skilled.
>
> Farming communes, or agronomic universities, which would be founded on the faith and poverty of the Irish univer-

---

27 Maurin's program generated a column in the *Catholic Worker*. See also Dorothy Day, *The Long Loneliness* (New York : Harper and Row, 1952), 221.

28 Several utopian texts were written by Péguy around the time of his first literary depiction of Joan of Arc in 1897.

29 Charles Péguy, *Œuvres en prose complètes* I, ed. Robert Burac (Paris: NRF/Gallimard, 1987), 62.

sities which housed scholars and students from all over Europe
and which in turn evangelized the world, and which in turn
in our day could become Christian communities of families
where the communal and private aspect of property could be
restored and man would receive according to his needs. [30]

Three "Easy Essays" by Maurin specifically name Péguy. In "Building
Churches," the Cathedral of Chartres shows the unity of thought in France of
the thirteenth Century, in a descriptive passage that may recall certain principles expressed by Péguy in *L'Argent* (1913), which also quotes the Benedictine
dictum "to work is to pray." Maurin emphasized that religious and economic life
should be "one":

> People who built the Cathedral of Chartres
> knew how to combine
> cult, that is to say liturgy,
> with culture, that is to say philosophy,
> and cultivation, that is to say agriculture.
> The Cathedral of Chartres is a real work of art
> because it is the real expression
> of the spirit of a united people.
> Churches that are built today
> do not express the spirit of the people.
> "When a church is built,"
> a Catholic editor said to me,
> "the only thing that has news value is:
> How much did it cost?" the
> Cathedral of Chartres was not built to increase
> the value of real estate. The Cathedral of
> Chartres was not built with money
> borrowed from money lenders. The
> Cathedral of Chartres was built by workers
> working for wages.
>
> Maurice Barres used to worry
> about the preservation of French Cathedrals, but

---

30 Day's introduction to Maurin, *Catholic Radicalism*, iv.

> Charles Péguy thought that
> the faith that builds Cathedrals
> is after all the thing that matters.
> Moscow had a thousand churches
> and people lost the faith.
> Churches ought to be built with donated money, donated
> material, donated labor.
>
> The motto of St. Benedict was
> Labore et Orare, Labor and
> Pray.
> Labor and prayer ought to be combined;
> labor ought to be a prayer.
> The liturgy of the Church is
> the prayer of the Church.
> People ought to pray with the Church
> and to work with the Church.
> The religious life of the people and the economic
> life of the people ought
> to be one. [31]

In "Carl Schmitt the Artist" Schmitt is presented in conflict with consumer society and against plutocratic democracy. Maurin sees him as similar to Péguy who is named in a final section:

> What Makes Man Human
>
> Charles Péguy used to say
> "There are two things in this world,
> politics and mysticism."
> Politics is just politics and is
> not worth bothering about
> and mysticism is mysterious
> and is worth all our striving.
> To give and not to take, that
> is what makes man human.

---

31 Maurin, *Catholic Radicalism*, 19–20.

To serve and not to rule,
that is what makes man human.
To help and not to crush,
that is what makes man human.
To nourish and not to devour,
that is what makes man human.
And if need be to die and not to live,
that is what makes man human.
Ideals and not deals,
that is what makes man human.
Creed and not greed,
that is what makes man human. [32]

In "On Personalism" Maurin emphasized the importance of all living creatures, using the examples of a horse, a tree, and a man. Humans stand out because they alone understand that they have rights and responsibilities. Philosophy and faith are different from reason, but humans discern the truth using all three faculties. The last section describes Mounier and names Péguy:

Emmanuel Mounier

Emmanuel Mounier wrote
a book entitled "A
Personalist Manifesto."
Emmanuel Mounier has
been influenced by Charles Péguy. Charles
Péguy once said: 'There
are two things in the world:
politics and mysticism.'
For Charles Péguy
as well as Mounier,
politics
is the struggle for power
while mysticism
is the realism
of the spirit.

32 Ibid., 48–49.

> For the man-of-the-street
> politics is just politics
> and mysticism
> is the right spirit.
> In his "Personalist Manifesto"
> Mounier tries to explain
> what the man-of-the-street
> calls 'the right spirit. [33]

With his own personal decision to no longer work for a salary, Maurin was intent on giving an example of non-possession within an American materialist society. Day noted that Maurin wanted a green revolution, which would be a return to the earth, and not the red revolution, which led to a renewal within industry. [34] There is no doubt that Dorothy Day understood Emmanuel Mounier's influence on Peter Maurin. In a letter she wrote August 12, 1976, she used Mounier's phrase "la révolution personnaliste et communautaire" to speak of Maurin's action, explaining that Maurin called himself a radical and that in doing so he was making an allusion to his real roots, and his desire to be poor, drawing from the example of Saint Francis of Assisi. [35] Apparently Maurin was a subscriber to *Esprit* from its inaugural issue. This is implied in Dorothy Day's letter to Father Terry (May 17, 1976). [36]

When the *Catholic Worker* began (May 1, 1933), Day had already matched her own goals to help the poor and to fight war with Maurin's preoccupations. Soon she would come to understand Péguy as he did. Péguy, like Day, was a journalist, editor, and publisher. His great project was his periodical the *Cahiers de la quinzaine*, published for the most part from his shop at 8, rue de la Sorbonne, across from the Sorbonne University. He wrote many of the articles himself, but also solicited and published articles from a remarkable variety of people. Of particular interest is the way Péguy incorporated literature into the review from the first, imitating Blaise Pascal's *Letters to a Provincial* in one of the earliest issues.

Péguy had fought anti-Semitism during the Dreyfus Affaire, and wrote about it in *Notre Jeunesse* (1910), which, like almost all of Péguy's writings after 1900 were published in the *Cahiers*. Péguy not only insists in *Notre Jeunesse* that

33 Ibid., 182.

34 Day, *Loaves and Fishes*, 7.

35 Day, *All the Way to Heaven*, ibook edition.

36 The complete letter (which names Péguy) is printed in Day, *All the Way to Heaven*, i-book edition.

he does not regret this commitment of his youth, but he paints a careful portrait of Bernard Lazare, where he demonstrates his affection for the atheist Jew that stood up publicly for Dreyfus and that he considered an important spiritual influence for himself. [37] Péguy's Christianity was influenced by Jewish thought. [38] He comically wrote: "Jews have been reading since eternity, Protestants have been reading since Calvin, and Catholics have been reading since Ferry" [39] — making an allusion to Jules Ferry whose educational reforms of 1881 and 1882 made French public school free and primary education mandatory, so that all children had the opportunity to learn how to read.

When Péguy began writing poetry in earnest, circa 1910, his poetry and his prose co-mingled in the *Cahiers*. There are the masterpieces in free verse, *The Mystery of the Charity of Joan of Arc* (1910), *The Portal of the mystery of Hope* (1911), and *The Mystery of the Saint Innocents* (1912) along with stricter verse forms found in the *Presentation of Beauce to Notre Dame de Chartres* (1913) and *Eve* (1913). During the same period some of Péguy's essential prose works such as *Notre Jeunesse* (1910), *L'Argent* (1913), and *Note sur M. Bergson* (1914) also appeared. The *Cahiers* are remarkable for the breadth of genres of texts published as well as for the range of opinions represented. They spoke out against injustices wherever they were found, and Péguy was an early defender of Armenians undergoing persecutions. The militant review published various articles that were anti-colonialist. Péguy intended it to be a kind of university for the common man, and many high school teachers in the provinces were subscribers. Today Péguy's complete works fill three volumes of prose and one volume of poetry in the prestigious Pléiade collection. Most of his writings still need to be translated into English. [40]

37 Like Péguy, Dorothy Day took a stand against anti-Semitism by co-founding the Committee of Catholics to Fight Anti-Semitism in 1939. See Jim Forest, *All Is Grace, A Biography of Dorothy Day* (Maryknoll, New York: Orbis, 2011), 156.

38 He was also friends with the poet André Spire, who had been devoted to the cause of the poor in Paris, and who later provided the venue for Ezra Pound to introduce James Joyce to Sylvia Beach (who published *Ulysses*). Perhaps Spire and Day knew about each other? Spire had gone to New York during World War II, and was teaching classes at the New School for Social Research, while several of his poems were published in *Poetry* (January 1942).

39 Péguy, *Œuvres en Prose Complètes* III, 1297.

40 Texts by Charles Péguy that Dorothy Day would most likely have read include translations by Ann and Julian Green: *Basic Verities: Prose and Poetry* (New York: Pantheon, 1943), *Men and Saints, Prose and Poetry* (New York: Pantheon, 1944), and by Julian Green, *God Speaks* (New York: Pantheon, 1945). Translated by Alexander Dru, *Temporal and Eternal* (London: Harvill, 1952). She probably also read Julian Green's translation of *The Mystery of the*

The Catholic Worker, intentionally or not, continued along some lines that were very dear to Péguy. Dorothy Day and Peter Maurin were combatting anti-Semitism in the 1930s, fighting for worker's rights, taking action against unjust exploitation, and supporting the cause of Civil Rights. There was certainly also the same educational bent: the readers needed to learn how to bring about social justice and peace in the world.

In Day's column "A Restatement of CW Aims and Ideals,"[41] she explained that the Catholic Worker movement had a philosophy of work that was based on voluntary poverty and works of charity. Voluntary poverty meant taking less so that others could have more.[42] In this column in 1940, Day quoted Péguy who felt he would need to answer God who would ask him where the others were when he reached heaven. Péguy believed that faith was not individual but corporate, and Day here was promoting that corporate vision of faith. In her autobiography she wrote about a philosophy of work that would be close to the Fathers of the Church and suggested reading a book by Chicago Benedictines: *Towards a Theology of Manual Labor.*[43] Day's closeness to the thought of Péguy and Mounier may also be seen through her choice to offer a translation of Mounier, *Be Not Afraid*, to Catholics in Cuba when she visited there under Castro's regime and during the embargo.[44]

Charles Péguy should be considered as one of the pillars of the philosophy underlying the Catholic Worker Movement. In her autobiography in 1952, Day mentions Péguy in the context of her first meetings with Maurin, explaining that he told her that he had been in Paris at the same time that Péguy was still working, but that he had never met or been influenced by him then, even if many people told him that he wrote like him.[45] Maurin's regret at not having

Charity of Joan of Arc (New York : Pantheon, 1950) and Pansy Pakenham's translation, *The Mystery of the Holy Innocents* (New York : Harper, 1956).

For those interested in Péguy, several recent translations can be recommended: by Jeffrey Wainright, *The Mystery of the Charity of Joan of Arc* (Manchester: Carcanet, 1986), by David Schindler, *The Portal of the Mystery of Hope* (Grand Rapids, Michigan: Eerdmans, 1996). Annette Aronowicz's study *Jews and Christians on Time and Eternity* (Stanford, California: Stanford University Press, 1998) gives detailed information about *Notre Jeunesse* and its translations into English.

41 The first installment was published in *CW* in January 1939, and the column continued into the mid forties.

42 Dan McKanan, *The Catholic Worker After Dorothy: Practicing the Works of Mercy* (New York, Paulist Press, 2008), 134.

43 Ibid., 135.

44 Day, *The Long Loneliness*, 202.

45 Quoted in Ibid., 177.

met Péguy is poignant and suggests the extent to which he admired him.

Dorothy Day read Péguy in translation and made allusions to his writings in her texts, very often by quoting him. Motivated by Maurin who spoke to her about Péguy, one may presume that she read all the translations of Péguy's works that she could find. Apart from the influence of Peter Maurin, Dorothy Day would have heard about Péguy from Jacques Maritain who visited the Catholic workers as early as 1934. As a friend of Péguy (a sometimes troublesome friend, but someone who knew Péguy well) he could accurately measure Péguy's influence on Maurin and Day. Yet, when Maritain arrived he had not yet met Maurin, and, as Day wrote in a letter to Brendan O'Grady in 1954, the first meeting between them was not an easy one: "I am not sure how much Maritain appreciated Peter's genius."[46] Being sensitive to their differences in education and social class, Day had made the first contact with Maritain, before his visit to the Catholic Worker house. Although Maritain and Maurin would never develop the closeness that once existed between Maritain and Péguy, he did write an amazing and very cordial letter in French to Maurin after that first visit.

Péguy is named or alluded to often in Dorothy Day's writings.[47] I believe her way of understanding Péguy evolved with time. She profoundly understood passages she had read, and from the quotations one gathers that Péguy acquired a place in her intimate thought processes. One quotation by Péguy that she noticed early on is thus repeated many times in her writings, beginning with her column for *The Catholic Worker* in January 1944: "Charles Péguy wrote, 'I am afraid to go to heaven alone. God will ask me, 'Where are the others?'"[48] On August 23, 1959, she wrote to Karl Meyer, whom she highly esteemed, "You seem to be very influenced by Péguy: 'where are the others?' God will say, and I believe that we must work for the others."[49] Finally, in her journal, February 22, 1966, she noted: "Faith is more precious than gold and is a gift. We cannot give it to others, but we can pray that God give it to others. Péguy wrote: 'when we get to heaven God will ask, 'Where are the others?'"[50]

In 1960 in her incisive biography of Thérèse of Liseux, Péguy is mentioned

---

46 Day, *All The Way to Heaven*, chapter IV, i-book edition.

47 The following works were consulted for this brief survey: *The Long Loneliness* (1952), *Therese* (1960), *Loaves and Fishes* (1963), *The Duty of Delight* (2008), and *All the Way to Heaven* (2010).

48 Quoted at: http://www.catholicworker.org/dorothyday/articles/398.html. Consulted July 14, 2015.

49 Day, *All the Way to Heaven*, i-book edition.

50 Day, *The Duty of Delight* IV, i-book edition.

twice in contexts that seem to reflect the greater importance of Péguy for Day than for Theresa. (Day probably did not know, at least she never mentioned, that both Saint Theresa as well as Charles Péguy were deeply interested in Saint Joan of Arc—and both wrote plays about her!) Péguy is first mentioned in the context of the story of the prodigal son:

> One of the reasons for stressing this struggle to attain to true love is St. Thérèse's statement that her mission was to make Love loved and to show that she was not dealing in abstractions. She never wrote anything that she had not experienced. She knew all aspects of love: love of mother, of father, and of family. Her love for her father enabled her to grow in her love for God her Father, an aspect of the God-head that has been too much neglected. God the Father! She could say with Péguy that she knew what God the Father meant. His Son told the parable of the Prodigal Son and told how the father treated that son, welcoming the sinner with fatted calf, fine garment, and a ring for the hand which had turned so often to evil. [51]

A little later, in the chapter "Night and Death" which speaks of the period when Thérèse knew she was ill, following intensive hemorrhaging (bleeding) on the eve of Good Friday, Day quotes Thérèse at length, and then states that when she was copying Thérèse's words she had perceived the same hope that Péguy expressed:

> When I copy down these written words of Therese about the blackness of her night, I realize them more clearly and see more clearly, too, her great love and great desire for all men. She prays for all men with that holy optimism of Charles Péguy in his great poem, "God Speaks," where he compares the folded hands of Jesus in the Our Father to the prow of a ship which ploughs on ahead through the waves, and in its wake draws all along after it. She too cries out for mercy for all, not just for her family for France for Christians, but for all. [52]

---

51 Dorothy Day, *Therese* [1960] (Springfield, Illinois: Templegate Publishers, 1985), 134.
52 Day, *Therese*, 159-160, quoting Julien Green's translation of Péguy, *God Speaks* (New York: Pantheon, 1945).

Loaves and Fishes (1963) recounts the history of the Catholic Workers and has an introduction by Thomas Merton who explained that every American Christian should read it, because it bursts the prominent myth of the baby boom years: that the problem of poverty has been resolved in the United States. Merton perceived, as he wrote, that for Day the problem of poverty was more than a sociological problem, it was a religious mystery.[53] Day had observed that Peter Maurin liked to say: "I will give you my opinion, and you will give me your opinion, and then we will both have more to think about,"[54] which strongly resembles a simple approximate synthetic translation of several lines of Péguy's *Pour Moi (Cahiers* 1901):

> *Quand je vois quelqu'un, je ne me dis jamais: Propagandons. Mais je cause honnêtement avec ce quelqu'un. Je lui énonce très sincèrement les faits que je connais, les idées que j'aime. Il m'énonce tout à fait sincèrement les faits qu'il connait et les idées qu'il aime et qui souvent sont fort différentes. Quand il me quitte, j'espère qu'il s'est nourri de moi, de ce que je sais et de ce que je suis. Et moi, je me suis toujours nourri de tout le monde . . . .*[55]

When I see someone, I never say to myself: propagandize. But I speak honestly avecwith the person. I tell him very sincerely about things that I know and ideas that I like. He tells me just as sincerely about things that he knows and ideas that he likes that are often very different from mine. And when he leaves, I hope that he has been nourished from me, from what I know and from who I am. As for me, I am constantly nourished by everyone I meet.

In Dorothy Day's journal, which was partially published in 2008 in *The Duty of Delight*, there are numerous allusions to Péguy. On March 4, 1945, Day spoke about her discussions with her son-in-law David Hennessy (who had married her daughter the previous year), and his discussion with Peter Maurin:

---

53 Thomas Merton, introduction to Day, *Loaves and Fishes* [1963] (Maryknoll, New York: Orbis, 1997), ix.
54 Day, *Loaves and Fishes*, 102.
55 Péguy, *Oeuvres en Prose Complètes*, I, 679.

> David and I talk history—Cobbet, Chesterton, Belloc, and Gill. Today Peter and I have been talking Bloy and Péguy. I must speak Wednesday to a high school assembly together with a Protestant and a Jew. We present 3 religions and the students we address have no faith, in the majority. Their leaders are Marx, Freud, Darwin. It is in the air they breathe.... What am I to talk of to these young high school students for 15 minutes at their nine o'clock assembly?... Shall I read them Léon Bloy on the Jew, or Péguy, or Maritain, or St. Paul?[56]

On April 24, 1961, we find her thinking about how Péguy represented the sinner:

> Péguy: "The sinner is at the very heart of Christendom. No one knows more about Christianity than the sinner. No one unless it is the saint. And in principle they are the same man."[57]

January 17, 1967, she evokes yet again Péguy's meeting with God:

> As Péguy said, when we face God he will say, "Where are the others?" Heaven is a banquet too (as well as a bridal couch) and as at Emmaus, "They knew Him in the breaking of bread." I think that even now we know Him in the breaking of bread together.[58]

February 4, 1969, her communion of saints included Péguy:

> I must ask Péguy to pray for all sinners in our midst, especially me, so wanting in charity. I must read again "God Speaks," in Eternal Verities. That wonderful poem about the Our Father.[59]

Given the multiplicity of her quotations from Péguy and her frequent references to him—and to Mounier (quoted five times in her journal), as well as Maritain (quoted seventeen times)—one can say that Dorothy Day knew Péguy

---

56 Day, *The Duty of Delight*, 2008, i-book edition.

57 Ibid.

58 Ibid.

59 Ibid.

well. Even if she had not read the complete works of Charles Péguy in French, [60] she had read a large part of the existing translations of Péguy's poetry and prose, and she had heard about Péguy directly from Maurin and Maritain.

After Maritain's first visit to Catholic Workers in the 1930s, he stayed in contact with Day until he returned to France after his wife Raïssa's death. As stated earlier, Day had also harmoniously integrated Mounier's ideas. In an interview in 1977, she noted that *The Catholic Worker* had begun at about the same time as the review *Esprit,* which was dedicated to the personalist and communitarian revolution. Mentioning the two publishing efforts in such proximity pointed at their shared ideals. In the same interview she was promoting immediate action, helping the poor oneself without waiting from others to help. For her, social reforms would come from the grass roots and rise toward political leaders, and not the contrary.

Because Dorothy Day was the editor in chief of the *Catholic Worker,* it would be useful to prolong the exploration of the influence of Péguy by any mention of him in the paper from 1933 to 1980. [61] And do today's Catholic Workers continue to refer to Péguy as much as Peter Maurin and Dorothy Day once did? Since 1980 it is not certain that most Catholic Workers see Péguy as the important figure leading to Emmanuel Mounier's personalism, and it is almost unfair to expect them to do so in an American culture where translations and studies of Péguy are rare. To my knowledge, Mounier's *La Pensée de Charles Péguy* has not yet been translated into English. Even if some biographies of Péguy exist in English, they are not recent and are no longer sold (though several, such as Villiers, can sometimes be found used). [62] In the critical writings about Day published over the last several decades the name of Péguy, when it occurs, is often found unaccented and sometimes with a note to explain who Péguy was. These are signs that knowledge of Péguy has in some cases disappeared from the general culture of Catholic Workers.

Notwithstanding, there are several examples of Catholic Workers who do mention Péguy. Jacques Travers spoke about Péguy and his importance for

---

60 Dorothy Day did not understand French. See *The Long Loneliness,* 241.

61 The French National Library (where this research was conducted) has a limited collection of the *Catholic Worker* (1962–1964). During those years, Péguy is mentioned in a reprint of Maurin's easy essay "Building Churches" (in the 31st anniversary issue). More work is needed to ascertain to what extent Péguy's influence on Day was visible in the paper.

62 Marjorie Villiers, *Charles Péguy. A Study in Integrity* (New York: Harper and Row, 1965). A philosophical study of Péguy was recently published: Glenn H. Roe, *The Passion of Charles Péguy: Literature, Modernity, and the Crisis of Historicism.* (Oxford : Oxford University Press, 2014).

the Catholic Worker movement at a meeting in Tivoli, New York in 1972.[63] In 1999, Mark and Louise Zwick wrote an article in the Houston *Catholic Worker* (July–August 1999) entitled "Emmanuel Mounier, Personalism, and the Catholic Worker Movement" which is currently available online.[64] Péguy is named six times and his importance is reasserted. In 2005, Zwick wrote a book on the spiritual and intellectual sources of the Catholic Worker Movement, highlighting the importance of Péguy and Mounier for Peter Maurin and Dorothy Day.

If Péguy had survived the first battle of the Marne and then the trenches, if he had not died in 1914 but rather had lived to a ripe old age, what would he have thought of the first issue of the *Catholic Worker* in 1933? No doubt if he had learned about it, he would have written about it. The closest we can get to guessing what he might have thought might be to look at Maritain's reaction. In a thank-you letter to Peter Maurin after his 1934 visit, Maritain wrote:

> I felt I had found at the Catholic Worker a little of the atmosphere of Péguy's shop at the rue de la Sorbonne. And so much good will, such courage, and such generosity!

> *Il me semblait avoir retrouvé au Catholic Worker un peu de l'atmosphère de la boutique de Péguy, rue de la Sorbonne. Et tant de bonne volonté, un tel courage, une telle générosité!* [65]

Annex: Letter from Jacques Maritain to Peter Maurin, 1934.

> *Cher Peter Maurin,*
> *Comment pourrais-je vous dire à quel point j'ai été touché en trouvant, lorsque je suis entré dans ma cabine, le paquet que vous y avez laissé pour moi. Je ne sais ce qu'il y a dedans (je veux laisser le plaisir de la découverte à mon épouse), mais je sais que c'est le cadeau de la charité fraternelle et de l'amitié. Voulez vous donc*

---

63 A cassette at Marquette University has preserved that talk.

64 http://cjd.org/1999/08/01/emmanuel-mounier-personalism-and-the-catholic-worker-movement. Consulted July 14, 2015.

65 This is an excerpt from a letter Jacques Maritain sent to Peter Maurin at the Catholic Worker in New York, December 7, 1934, See Annex. Maurin would soon be insisting that people read Maritain's chapter on personalist democracy in *True Humanism*. See Dorothy Day and Francis J. Sicius, *Peter Maurin, Apostle to the World* (Maryknoll, New York: Orbis, 2004), 76.

remercier, de ma part et de tout cœur, Margaret, la cuisinière du Catholic Worker, et lui dire qu'elle m'a fait grand plaisir.

Dites aussi à Dorothy Day combien j'ai été heureux de lui rendre visite, et ému de l'accueil que m'ont fait vos amis. J'aurais souhaité pouvoir dire tout ce qui était dans mon cœur,—jamais je n'ai été aussi mortifié de mon incapacité à parler couramment l'anglais. Il me semblait avoir retrouvé au Catholic Worker un peu de l'atmosphère de la boutique de Péguy, rue de la Sorbonne. Et tant de bonne volonté, un tel courage, une telle générosité! C'est ainsi qu'avec de maigres moyens et un grand amour le futur auquel nous aspirons ardemment se prépare.

Je garde l'impression de ne pas avoir été tout à fait clair à propos de l'Etat pluraliste, lorsque j'ai répondu à l'explication que vous en donnez. Je tiens à préciser qu'un tel Etat, avec sa fédération de structures juridiques diverses, ne se réduirait pas à un simple agrégat mais qu'il devrait avoir une réelle unité morale d'orientation, et il mériterait le nom de chrétien parce qu'il tiendrait, de façon positive, à travers ses différentes structures, à un idéal chrétien intégral. Au lieu d'être polarisé par une conception matérialiste du monde et de la vie, comme l'Etat capitaliste ou l'Etat communiste, il serait polarisé par la prise en considération de la dignité spirituelle de la personne humaine et sur l'amour qui lui est dû.

Merci encore à Dorothy Day, à Ade Bethune et à Margaret. Et soyez assuré de ma gratitude à votre égard, cher Peter.

Pourquoi vous êtes vous sauvé après avoir déposé le paquet à bord ? J'avais espéré vous voir à nouveau sur l'Aquitania.

Prions l'un pour l'autre.

Cordialement vôtre en Christ Jésus

Jacques Maritain [66]

Jennifer Kilgore-Caradec teaches English at the University of Caen (Normandy) and at the Catholic University of Paris. During research for her dissertation on the poetry of Sir Geoffrey Hill she became involved in the French society *Am-*

66 This Letter was published in English translation in the *Catholic Worker* 2:7 (December 1934) and is also found in Jacques and Raïssa Maritain, *Œuvres complètes* v.16 (Paris : Editions Saint-Paul, 2000), 457–9.

itié *Charles Péguy* and was elected vice president in 2012. Her first paper about Dorothy Day was delivered at the 2013 AFEA Congress in Angers. She has co-edited *La poésie de Geoffrey Hill et la Modernité* (2007), *Selected Poems from Modernism to Now* (2012), *Poetry and Religion: Figures of the Sacred* (2013), and *European Voices in the Poetry of W. B. Yeats and Geoffrey Hill* (2015). She also co-edits the online review *Arts of War and Peace*.

An Ecology of Hospitality
in Dorothy Day and the
Catholic Worker

'Yours for the Green Revolution': Dorothy Day, Peter Maurin, and Our Agrarian Moment

Eric Anglada

When I think of the kind of worker the job [of planet-saving] requires, I think of Dorothy Day....

—Wendell Berry[1]

I am afraid that nature may become ... enraged at our own waste here in our too blessed America.

—Dorothy Day[2]

At Peter Maurin Farm in the early 1960s, Dorothy Day watched as John Filiger, the long-time farmer for the Catholic Worker, impulsively hopped on his beloved tractor and plowed under all of the community's tomatoes and corn, simply because he wanted to restore some order to the fields. "It hurts me to think," Dorothy sighed in *Loaves and Fishes,* her chronicle of the first three decades of the movement, "of the green tomatoes that would have been ripening until Thanksgiving, of the late corn which could have been dried and fed to the pigs."[3] This image—at once exasperating and absurdly comical—captures the seemingly all-too-typical struggles of Catholic Worker farms over the last eight decades. It certainly accords with the judgment of most scholars of the movement, who simply write off the farms as its least important and certainly least successful aspect; one scholar goes so far as to label them "virtually unmitigated

---

1   Wendell Berry, *Sex, Economy, Freedom, and Community* (New York: Pantheon, 1992), 25.
2   Dorothy Day, *Loaves and Fishes* (New York: Harper and Row, 1963), 202.
3   Ibid, 201.

disasters."[4] But this glib characterization fails to take into account not only how integral those farming experiments were to the early Catholic Worker's vision for a new society, but also how prophetic Peter Maurin and Dorothy Day's call for a "green revolution" is to today's world. As more contemporary Catholic Workers are beginning to recognize the fullness of their vision, Day and Maurin's passion and vigor for the land is finally being born out within the twenty-first-century Catholic Worker movement.

Despite today's dominant image of her as a "city girl" strictly concerned with urban issues, Dorothy Day was an agrarian. She had a sacramental sensibility in which the supernatural and natural easily commingled. She was a lover of God's creation who believed we must all find our way to a healthier relationship with the soil. "How can we teach our children about creation and creator when there are only man-made streets about[?]," she once wrote in her journal. "How about life and death and resurrection unless they see the seed fall into the ground and die and yet bring forth fruit?"[5] Day was a dissident of the Machine Age, in revolt against the dehumanizing forces of industrialism. And decades before the emergence of the environmentalist movement, it was Day, along with Peter Maurin and few others, who called for a land- and craft-based society.

After a wayward upbringing marked by instability, dwelling largely amid urban civilization, Day eventually landed on Staten Island in the mid-1920s, buying a cottage on the beach. Walking within the fields and forest around her home, Day discovered a profound peace and happiness she had never before experienced in the city. It was there, amid the raw air of the country, where she found a strong appetite for prayer. The physical world came alive for her; it was the "very love of nature and the study of her secrets" that helped bring her to faith.[6] She learned every wildflower in the area, wrote articles on gardening for local papers, and even became an avid gardener herself.[7]

In the fall of 1925, while visiting her mother in Florida, Day wrote her partner Forster of her anxiety to get back to Staten Island to get manure on the garden and "to see the garden in its fall glory." Were strawberries to be planted in the fall or spring? she wondered. "It may be a sentimental notion," she wrote in

---

4   James T. Fisher, *The Catholic Counterculture in America 1933–1962* (Chapel Hill, North Carolina: University of North Carolina Press, 1989), 121.

5   Day, *The Duty of Delight: The Diaries of Dorothy Day* (Milwaukee, Wisconsin: Marquette University Press, 2008), 112.

6   Day, *The Long Loneliness* (New York: Harper and Row, 1952), 134.

7   Jim Forest, *All is Grace: A Biography of Dorothy Day* (Maryknoll, Wisconsin: Orbis, 2011), 144.

a postscript to her letter, "but I think it would be wonderful to live entirely off the land and not depend on wages for a livelihood."[8]

While living on Staten Island, Dorothy fell in with a bohemian crowd of writers and artists drawn to the country to pursue rural simplicity, self-suffi- ciency, and an alternative way of life. In the city, where many of them congre- gated at night, they drank and talked endlessly of their disenchantment with in- dustrial capitalism and about communism, anarchism, and distributism. Day's friends, the agrarians Allen Tate and Caroline Gordon, talked too "of the yeo- man farmer, whose simple, self-sufficient life was grounded in a sense of place and responsibility to others."[9] Years later, she admitted that much of the dis- cussion had gone over her head; ironically, though, it was Day probably more than anyone else in that circle of friends who actually ended up living out many of their inchoate yearnings. (Notably, a decade later, Day re-acquainted herself with Allen Tate outside of Memphis while on a tour of the South encouraging the organization of tenant farmers; Tate later remarked on Day's "fanatical de- votion to the land!"[10])

Nevertheless, in the winter of 1932, Day wasn't yet ready to concede the ar- gument of Peter Maurin—the disheveled peasant-philosopher she would later describe as looking "as though he were rooted to the ground, gnarled, strong, weather beaten"[11]—that all the problems of the day would be solved by a return to the land. She knew the satisfactions of life in the country, of the fresh air, of eating a vegetable she had cultivated herself, but it was still the city she knew best. It was there, after all, where the vast majority of the unemployed resided. "Heaven is portrayed as a heavenly Jerusalem," she would remind him. But Mau- rin was stubborn and persistent; he had a vision.

Peter shared manifold quips honed over months of rankling Communists on the streets of Union Square: "Raise what you eat, eat what you raise!" "There's no unemployment on the land!" "A society where it is easier to be good!" "Fire the bosses!" "Idle hands on idle lands!" But Peter had more than quips—he car- ried along with him notebooks filled with what later came to be called (by Day's brother, John) "Easy Essays." For years Maurin had traveled across the country,

---

8   Day, *All the Way to Heaven: The Selected Letters of Dorothy Day* (Milwaukee, Marquette University Press, 2010), 11, 15–16.

9   Paul Elie, *The Life You Save May Be Your Own: An American Pilgrimage* (New York: Farrar, Straus, and Giroux, 2004), 43–45.

10 Peter Huff, *Allen Tate and the Catholic Revival: Trace of the Fugitive Gods* (New York: Pau- list Press, 1996), 70.

11 Day, "Farming Commune," *Catholic Worker*, February 1944, 1.

performing menial labor, talking with professors about social change, and reading endlessly: philosophy, economics, theology, agriculture, politics. From these experiences, he forged his central intellectual synthesis, the Green Revolution:

> The only way
> to keep people
> from seeing Red
> is to make them
> see Green.
> The only way
> to prevent
> a Red Revolution
> is to promote
> a Green Revolution.
> The only way
> to keep people
> from looking up
> to Red Russia
> of the twentieth century
> is to make them look up
> to Green Ireland
> of the seventh century. [12]

Maurin believed that they were living in a true Dark Age. Modern society "is parked in a blind alley," he argued, and the only thing to do "is turn back." [13] "We are living in a time of chaos," Maurin wrote in an open letter to a Jesuit priest. "Our task must be to create order out of chaos." He signed off his letter, "Yours for the Green Revolution, Peter Maurin." [14] It was an appropriate valediction, for this revolution was indeed the central animating force of his life.

Maurin's theory of the Green Revolution was rooted in the medieval Irish who had lived a prayerful, communal life close to the earth, engaging in subsistence agriculture and hospitality to all travelers, and were devoted scholars. Likening their contemporary situation to the fall of the Roman Empire, Maurin saw the mission of the Catholic Worker as parallel to what the Irish had done in their

12 Peter Maurin, *Easy Essays* (Chicago: Franciscan Herald Press, 1977), 71.

13 *Catholic Worker*, April 1935, 8.

14 *Easy Essays*, 125–6.

own era. Indeed, the whole of the Catholic Worker program is prefigured by the Irish template:

> The social order was once reconstructed
> after the fall of the Roman Empire.
> The Irish scholars were the leaders
> in the reconstruction of the social order
> after the fall of the Roman Empire.
> Through Round-Table Discussions
> scattered all over Europe
> as far as Constantinople
> the Irish scholars
> brought thought to the people.
> Through Houses of Hospitality
> the Irish scholars
> exemplified Christian charity.
> Through Farming Communes
> the Irish scholars
> made workers out of scholars
> and scholars out of workers. [15]

It was this last point, the need for farming communes, that lay at the core of his program. Such communes, he believed, would enable people to combine manual labor with prayer and study. *This* would be the revolution that would transform society. His Easy Essay "Irish Culture," central to his thought, reads in part:

> The Irish Scholars established
> agricultural centers
> all over Europe
> where they combined
> cult—
> that is to say liturgy,
> with culture—
> that is to say literature,
> with cultivation—

15   Ibid., 58–9.

> that is to say agriculture.
> … What was done
> by Irish missionaries
> after the fall
> of the Roman Empire
> can be done today
> during and after the fall
> of modern empires. [16]

Not only did Day eventually come "to see what he was talking about," as she later admitted in her autobiography, but she eventually embraced Maurin's vision as her own. "[O]urs was a long range program," she wrote, "looking for ownership by the workers of the means of production, the abolition of the assembly line, decentralized factories, the restoration of crafts and ownership of property. This meant, of course, an accent on the agrarian and rural aspects of our economy and a changing of emphasis from city to land." [17]

For Maurin, the cause of the crisis, the specter looming over the Depression, was the ascendant urban-industrial regime that was the foundation of both capitalism and socialism. "The industrial revolution did not improve things, it made them worse," he lamented. [18] In stark contrast to Maurin's agrarianism, born out of his village upbringing, industrialism had uprooted people from their household and local economies as well as from the natural rhythms of creation. Industrial civilization—with its disastrous focus on money, continual growth, and technological "progress"—forced life ever further into that dark alley.

Day agreed with his critique. On a tour through the Northwest she noted in her diary her realization of the agricultural "wastelands" of the "industrial, factory system of farming." [19] In Texas, she observed the "unutterably desolate wastes on all sides—the endless prairies of Texas which have their own wild natural beauty until the hand of man touches them." [20] In *The Long Loneliness*, Day drew a bleak tableau of society, evoking a startling image of Charlie Chaplin's *Modern Times*: "Wheels turned and engines throbbed and the great pulse of the mechanical and physical world beat strong and steady while men's pulses sick-

---

16 Ibid., 206.
17 Day, *Long Loneliness*, 220–1.
18 *Catholic Worker*, February 1936, 1.
19 *Duty of Delight*, 53.
20 Ibid., 122.

ened and grew weaker and died. Man fed himself into the machine."[21]

Day and Maurin were not alone in their ideas. Both of them found a deep resonance in a small but lively set of decentralists, distributists, Jeffersonians, and agrarians—figures like Fr. Vincent McNabb, Eric Gill, Christopher Dawson, Herbert Agar, the Southern Agrarians, Arthur Penty, and G. K. Chesterton on both sides of the Atlantic, who shared in common a deep anxiety about society's devotion to the god of progress. Their counter-image of the "good life" carried more than a tinge of medievalism. This loose set admired the Middle Ages for its strictures against usury (a keystone of capitalism), its cooperative guilds, its fusion of the spiritual and the material, its union of beauty and function, and its vibrant rural culture enlivened by a robust peasantry. "The peasant does live, not merely a simple life, but a complete life," G. K. Chesterton wrote in *The Outline of Sanity*, a "Great Book" of Maurin's, often recommended in the pages of the paper. "It may be very simple in its completeness but the community is not complete without that completeness."[22]

Another of Maurin's "Great Books" was the 1930 collection of essays, *I'll Take My Stand*, written by "Twelve Southerners." Though they were not Catholic, the Twelve were fellow decentralists and agrarian companions articulating the same struggle in the South as Maurin had witnessed throughout the North. The book's introductory "A Statement of Principles" baldly articulates the fundamental tension within society: "Agrarian *versus* Industrial." They worried about the impacts of the machine upon the Southern way of life. "The tempo of the industrial life is fast, but that is not the worst of it; it is *accelerating*."[23]

One of the works in the collection, Andrew Nelson Lytle's "The Hind Tit," was the source of one of Maurin's most significant agrarian Easy Essays. Largely a lyrical defense of the elemental necessity of the subsistence farm, Lytle's essay laments its loss due to "industrial imperialism;" he worries that our technological inventions are spiraling out of control, leading society into "moral and spiritual suicide." He warns of false prophets offering "motor cars," "picture shows,"

---

21 *Long Loneliness*, 171.

22 G. K. Chesterton *The Outline of Sanity* (San Francisco: Ignatius), 136.

23 Twelve Southerners, *I'll Take My Stand: The South and the Agrarian Tradition* (New York: Harper, 1930), xxiv (emphasis mine). It should be noted that *I'll Take My Stand* is a text not without problems—namely, its racism. To be clear, Maurin was absolutely not a racist. His methodology was simple: keep what he agreed with and discard what he didn't. For two excellent contemporary discussions of this text, see Wendell Berry's essay "Still Standing" found in *Citizenship Papers* (Washington, DC: Shoemaker and Hoard, 2003), 153–164, and Nicols Fox's *Against the Machine: The Hidden Luddite Tradition in Literature, Art, and Individual Lives* (Washington DC: Island Press, 2002), 229–35.

and items in the "Sears-Roebuck catalogue." He observes that the necessary prophets for our times will not "come from cities, promising riches and store clothes." Rather, he continues in words that almost uncannily describe Maurin, "They have always come from the wilderness, stinking of goats and running with lice and telling of a different sort of treasure, one a corporation head would never understand."[24]

In November 1935, an Easy Essay appeared in the pages of *The Catholic Worker* under the headline, "Back to Christ—Back to the Land!":

> 1. Andrew Nelson Lytle says:
> The escape from industrialism
> is not in socialism
> or in Sovietism.

> 2. The answer lies
> in a return to a society
> where agriculture is practiced
> by most of the people.

> 3. It is in fact impossible
> for any culture
> to be sound and healthy
> without a proper regard
> for the soil,
> no matter
> how many urban dwellers
> think that their food
> comes from groceries
> and delicatessens
> or their milk from tin cans.

> 4. This ignorance
> does not release them
> from a final dependence
> upon the farm. [25]

---

24 Ibid., 206.

25 *Catholic Worker*, November 1935, 8. Lytle's original quote ends: "This ignorance does not release them from a final dependence upon the farm and that most incorrigible of be-

In the months after the release of the first issue of their paper on May Day, 1933, a fledgling band of Catholic Workers held roundtable discussions and hosted a variety of speakers. They fed the poor and formed a house of hospitality at which the down-and-out could stay overnight. After two years, though they had not yet been able to find a larger, affordable parcel in the country, the group of personalists began to implement the key to Maurin's long-range program. "The creation of a new society within the shell of the old was inaugurated in June, 1935," long-time Catholic Worker Stanley Vishnewski wrote, grandly recounting the beginning of their Garden Commune out on Staten Island. [26] That summer they raised a big garden, hosted guests, and held discussions in their enormous rented house. Still, there was a push to take the full step of purchasing a larger farm. "What we are doing," Dorothy wrote to one subscriber in the fall of 1935 by way of explaining their hopes for a farming commune, "is trying to put our ideas *immediately* into practice, that is to live them.... Four-fifths of the Catholic population are in cities. They have to get back to the land. " [27]

Finally, in 1936, the January edition of *The Catholic Worker* carried the bold headline, "To Christ—To The Land." "We are going to move out on a farm," Day wrote on the front page. "We are making this move because we do not feel that we can talk in the paper about something we are not practicing. We believe that our words will have more weight, our writings will carry more conviction, if we ourselves are engaged in making a better life on the land." [28]

And so they did. That spring, a carload of Catholic Workers set out from their house of hospitality amid the paved streets of New York City in search of fertile ground in which to plant the seeds of a new social order. They fashioned themselves the avant-garde of what Stanley Vishnewski called the "Green International." Seventy miles from the city, just outside of Easton, Pennsylvania, they found a solid prospect: a 28-acre farm overlooking the Delaware River. Thanks to a generous donation from a subscriber to the paper, these communitarians now had their final plank in Maurin's scheme—a true farming commune which they would name Maryfarm. In a fit of excitement, the driver, Big Dan Orr, threw himself into the grass and shouted ecstatically, "Back to the land!" [29]

ings, the farmer." (203–4).

26 Stanley Vishnewski, *Wings of the Dawn* (New York: Catholic Worker Press, 1984), 78. Thanks to Michael Schorsch for making his copy of this hard-to-find book available to me.

27 Day, *All the Way to Heaven*, p. 81.

28 *Dorothy Day: Selected Writings* (Maryknoll, New York: Orbis, 1992), 81

29 Day, *Loaves and Fishes*, 48.

With good soil, abundant fruits and a sizable asparagus patch, Maryfarm that spring was brimming with promise. The green revolutionaries canned vegetables and fruits, even sending some to the breadlines back in the city. They acquired chickens, pigs, and a milking cow. They held retreats. They provided a space to rest for the marginalized, including striking seamen. A year into their experiment Day boasted in the pages of the Distributist journal *Free America* that Maryfarm "has become the heart of the work."[30] She would later reflect in her autobiography, "In the cities it is as though we lived in concentration camps. Maryfarm is an oasis in the desert."[31]

In 1940, the Catholic Worker farmers more fully leaned into Maurin's trinity of "cult, culture, and cultivation," holding a summer-long folk school for ten adults from across the country. It was their most serious attempt yet at living out the Irish-tinged green revolution. Each day they would read and discuss a text, such as Christopher Dawson's *Making of Europe*, as well as spend time in the fields, for example pitching hay or picking cherries. ("Everybody says the school is going along fine, except that you have worked them to death," Day wrote to Maurin that July in the single extant letter she ever wrote to him.[32]) They were finally creating what Maurin called an "agronomic university." The experience was such a success that the following summer, CW farms outside of Minneapolis and Cleveland held similar integrated learning sessions. But the initial burst of energy for agronomic universities ebbed in large part because of the outbreak of the Second World War, as many young, healthy men went off to fight.[33]

Though Maurin's health steadily diminished in the 1940s, Day and others continued to write consistently in the paper about the developments on the land, as well as reports of other homesteaders and successful economic cooperatives. Such news encouraged others to start their own projects. Catholic Worker farms sprung up across the country, some of which lasted for decades. Certainly there were struggles, too—many that would haunt the farming projects for years to come. Alcoholism and ineptitude continually marred their noble efforts. The Workers' embrace of voluntary poverty frequently meant that they lacked for funds. The farming community held a "come one, come all" policy

---

30 *Free America*, Vol 1 #2: Feb. 1937; thanks to Allan Carlson for sending me his notes on this journal.

31 *Long Loneliness*, 263.

32 Day, *All the Way to Heaven*, 149.

33 For a fuller treatment of Peter Maurin, education, and his ideas on "agronomic universities," see my essay in *Houston Catholic Worker*, April 2011: http://cjd.org/2011/04/01/growing-roots-peter-maurin-and-the-agronomic-university/.

that was more idealistic than practical. Day once observed that the more people arrived, the less farm work got done. The overwhelming needs of the guests took precedence over the work of farming. They had become houses of hospitality on the land, rather than the vibrant "agronomic universities" for which Maurin pined. But significantly, they kept at it. In the 1970s, Dorothy still could brag that "our own commune has lasted 38 years"—and for that matter, continues to this very day. [34]

Day never relented in her opposition to urban-industrial civilization. "If the city is the occasion of sin," she wrote in a remarkable series of essays on the Church and Work in 1946–7, "should not families, men and women, begin to aim at an exodus, a new migration, a going out from Egypt with its flesh pots? ... Now is the time for the call from the cities... he who lives by the machine will fall by the machine." [35] Such prophetic sentiments have brought on harsh criticism from the likes of scholar Eugene McCarraher, who takes issue with Day's view that work could not be fulfilling outside the land and craft society. An otherwise admiring historian of the CW movement and of Day in particular, McCarraher nonetheless bristles at Day's pastoralism, and her skepticism of technological "progress." He fumes about what he calls her "loom-and-hoe-Luddism," wondering why she won't just get with the technological program. (Unsurprisingly, he lays much of the blame at the feet of one Peter Maurin.) [36]

Within the early Catholic Worker itself, Day encountered opposition. John Cort left the movement because of its increasing emphasis on the land and steady de-emphasis on issues of labor. He blasted Day for her hypocrisy in calling for a land movement while she in fact remained entrenched in the city. Chiding him as "willful and wayward son," Day responded in the pages of *The Catholic Worker*: "If he knew how many times I escape to my daughter's to garden [and] to can... and then there is the farm at Newburgh which provided a breadline of 350 with pork (six pigs), apple sauce, potatoes and tomatoes on Thanksgiving Day." [37] Day reveled in farm life, both on the Catholic Worker farm and on her daughter Tamar's homestead. She practiced crafts like sewing, knitting,

---

34 *All the Way to Heaven*, 406.

35 *Catholic Worker*, September 1946: 1, 8.

36 Eugene McCarraher, *Christian Critics: Religion and the Impasse in Modern American Social Thought* (Ithaca, New York: Cornell University, 2000), 116. Eugene McCarraher, "Into Their Labors: Work, Technology and the Sacramentalism of Dorothy Day" in *Dorothy Day and the Catholic Worker Movement: Centenary Essays*, ed. William Thorn, Philip Runkel, and Susan Mountain (Milwaukee, Wisconsin: Marquette University Press, 2001), 306–316.

37 *Catholic Worker*, December 1948, 3.

and weaving; she canned tomatoes, fed chickens and pigs, tended cows, weeded the garden, and hauled water. In the early 1940s, during a two-week class held at the Grail, a lay community of women in Ohio, Dorothy learned crafts and culinary skills. "We have learned to meditate *and* bake bread," she gushed at the holistic educational context, "pray *and* extract honey, sing *and* make butter, cheese, cider, wine, and sauerkraut." [38]

But it is true that Day herself was never able to dwell on the land as much as she wanted. "I have long since 'given up,' 'offered up,' the field, for the city slums," she wrote in her diary in 1943 on the grounds of Maryfarm. As much as Day loved farm life, she felt obliged to make sure the house of hospitality in the city remained a refuge for the poor and homeless. "So it is my vocation to agitate, to be a journalist, a pamphleteer, and now my time must be spent in these cities, these slums. But how wonderful it is to be out here in this Christian community, set up in the midst of fields, atop a hill, and to have samples of Heaven all about, not hell. I truly love sweet clover." She likened herself to Fr. Vincent McNabb, the radical agrarian of London and author of the influential text *Nazareth or Social Chaos*, who, when asked why he remained in the city, responded: "To get people out of here." [39]

At the time of Maurin's death in 1949—fittingly, on the feast of St. Isidore, patron of farmers—the farms had never realized his grand vision of re-building a new culture in the industrial ruins of the old. This was a disappointment to both Maurin and Day. But in the wake of her mentor's death, Day did not give up the Green Revolution; while over the next three decades she would continue her work for the poor and resistance to war, Day also made sure that the farms were always functioning and encouraged others to pursue the agrarian vision. In 1956, Day both wrote of farming communes being "an ideal form of institution," and continued her critique of urban civilization: "We need to overthrow ... this rotten, decadent, putrid industrial capitalist system which breeds such suffering in the whited sepulcher of New York." The following year, amid a reflection on her time in jail protesting the air raids, more than two decades after the start of their first farming venture, Day wrote, "I still think that the only solution is the land and *community*." [40]

---

38 Sarah McFarland Taylor, *Green Sisters: A Spiritual Ecology* (Cambridge, Massachusetts: Harvard University Press, 2009), 38.

39 *Duty of Delight*, 68.

40 *Dorothy Day: Selected Writings*, 280.

Our Agrarian Moment?

Sadly, in the autumn of 1980, Day, too, passed on without having seen the fruit of her relentless sowing of Maurin's vision for a green revolution. Instead, she witnessed the beginnings of what has been widely accepted as a different revolution of today: Norman Borlaug's agricultural developments, which Maurin most certainly would have considered a gross inversion of his ideas, and what journalist Richard Manning has dubbed likely "the worst thing that has ever happened to the planet."[41] Reliant upon mechanization, fossil fuels, synthetic fertilizers, and the use of vast amounts of water, this "revolution" has greatly contributed to the looming collapse of an ecological equilibrium: water depletion in the agricultural Great Plains, topsoil loss, "dead zones" and algae blooms created by agricultural run-off, loss of biodiversity, poorly-paid and frequently exploited migrant workers, a weakening of rural life, and, perhaps most significantly, climate change. Such devastating contemporary realities illustrate the remarkable insight of Day and Maurin, who continually called for a return to small scale, sustainable agriculture and the creation of cooperatives as a way to reclaim sanity and dignity in our over-industrialized world.

Thankfully, in this unique moment—what I'm calling, hopefully, "our agrarian moment"—more people are beginning to respond to our bleak ecological picture with actions that would have made those early agrarians proud: the creation of food co-ops, support of farmer's markets, participation in the local food movement, and community supported agriculture are some of the signs that society may finally be showing a "proper regard for the soil." Notably, this spirit of an alternative agriculture is steadily seeping into the Catholic Worker movement as well, even in many urban houses of hospitality. Gardens, once considered superfluous in light of the abundance of donated food, are now budding in the yards of many houses, offering an important step to reclaiming healthy food for the poor. The Cherith Brook community in Kansas City, Missouri, for example, not only provides meals for the hungry, offers free showers, and engages in ongoing nonviolent resistance to the nearby nuclear weapons manufacturer: it has also transformed the lawn into an orchard and a garden of raised beds for vegetables that they have fertilized with composted elephant manure from the local zoo.

The long-held image of the Catholic Worker as an urban soup kitchen or house of hospitality is beginning to shift, with younger workers becoming in-

---

41   Richard Manning, "The Oil We Eat," *Harper's*, February 2004, 41.

creasingly drawn to the original vision of the movement as a land-based one. Right now, about two dozen farm communities exist—including a few in far-away lands such as Mexico, New Zealand, and England. The heart of the agrarian renewal, however, is taking place in the Midwest. During last winter's farm gathering held in Luck, Wisconsin, long-time CW farmer Mike Miles exclaimed, "We finally have a Catholic Worker farm *movement!*"

Throughout the bitterly cold weekend in February, Catholic Workers shared their experiences engaging in "regenerative agriculture" and swapped details about how to maintain healthy, viable community on the land. Sixty people were in attendance, including a representative from the Sheep Ranch CW farm in extreme rural California, a community more than four decades old. Folks from the Mustard Seed Community Farm—a Catholic Worker outside Ames, Iowa, in the heart of "big ag"—discussed their work in prairie restoration and their efforts to get healthy food to pregnant at-risk women. Several from my own community, New Hope Catholic Worker Farm in eastern Iowa, a community now midway into its second decade, attended as well. For the majority of my seven years at New Hope, my wife and I have lived with three other couples and their children, the bulk of our labor going towards small-scale, organic subsistence agriculture that provides for more than half of our diet. Inspired by Maurin's experiments with the "agronomic university," we have offered numerous integrated learning seminars on topics ranging from permaculture to appropriate technology; from green burials to nonviolent communication; from the economic vision of Peter Maurin to alternative education.

Maurin's image of sustainable communities emerging out of the detritus of empire—communities dedicated to scholarship, prayer, and agriculture—is deeply resonant for our age. Peter Maurin, Dorothy Day, and a disparate set of Catholic Worker farmers who have lovingly cultivated the land for decades have laid a firm foundation upon which to expand and deepen. Catholic Workers, like never before, are talking about chickens and compost, soil and sustainability, gardening and the Green Revolution. In the midst of this crucial ecological and agrarian moment, perhaps it is time to re-imagine a twenty-first-century CW movement as a vibrant village, one where everyone is working for justice, clarifying their ideas about social action, and engaging in sacramental work, hands planted firmly in the soil.

Eric Anglada has been a Catholic Worker for 13 years. His essays have appeared in *America, National Catholic Reporter, The Catholic Worker, Geez, Catholic Agita-*

tor, and *The Merton Seasonal.* For the past seven years he has been a member of New Hope Catholic Worker Farm near Dubuque, Iowa. He and his wife, along with a few others, are hoping to start the St. Isidore Catholic Worker farm in the Driftless Region of the Midwest.

Love for the Stranger:
The Witness of the Catholic Worker
in the Twenty-First Century

Andrew Courter

In this paper[1] I will argue that it is crucial for Christians in America to learn hospitality from the witness of the Catholic Worker if they are to faithfully demonstrate the love of God to their neighbor in a world afflicted by many disasters and would-be disasters—climate change, the refugee crisis, wars and invasions and their massive displacements of peoples.[2] I will begin by arguing that American understandings of hospitality have subtly corrupted the radical nature of Christian hospitality. I will then observe the practice of hospitality in the context of the Catholic Worker and the notion of personalism and sacrifice found in the convictions of the Catholic Worker. As I have mentioned, we must first begin with the recovery of hospitality in the American context.

Recovering Hospitality in the Modern Era

In Elizabeth Newman's book *Untamed Hospitality: Welcoming God and Other Strangers*, she describes how hospitality has been distorted in our American context. She connects worship to divine hospitality, showing that God welcomes us into his community. Such hospitality cannot be understood as separate from the rest of our economic, political and public lives.[3] We have systematically

---

1 I am extremely indebted to and thankful for Dr. Kelly Johnson's helpful comments on earlier drafts of this paper.

2 For a more in-depth analysis regarding some of the crises we face, see Marilyn Weiner, Hal Weiner, and Matt Damon, *Journey to Planet Earth: Extreme Realities.* [Videorecording] Washington, DC: Screenscope, 2014; Widescreen, 2014.

3 Elizabeth Newman, *Untamed Hospitality: Welcoming God and Other Strangers* (Grand Rapids, Michigan: Brazos, 2007).

corrupted the word from its original meaning by eliminating the context and practices that made the word intelligible to begin with. Liberalism has subtly changed the Christian "we" to the American "we." What becomes lost in such a transition is the radical dependence and reliance on a narrative that embodies the fact that God has given us all the time in the world to practice hospitality faithfully.

While I am extremely thankful to Elizabeth Newman's work on recovering hospitality, I do think she misses how Christians have come to make the Christian "we" the American "we" through liberal democracy. By liberalism I am referring to the segregation of the "religious" from the public sphere to the private sphere of an individual's life and the perpetuation of the myth that we are not embodied or storied creatures and are therefore free to tell whichever version of our self as we would like.

Liberalism, as Stanley Hauerwas describes it, "involves the attempt to make political community possible between strangers. As a result, our polities are constantly tempted to fascist excesses because the state must supply the community that is missing."[4] In *After Virtue*, Alasdair MacIntyre describes the politics in Aristotle's day as centered around the notion of the *polis*.[5] The *polis* was the notion of the city-state, and what was fundamentally vital to Aristotle's *polis* was that it was necessarily based on friendship. The *polis*, as understood by Aristotle provides an articulate commentary for why our way of reasoning morally as a society has become so unintelligible. For Aristotle, the *polis* was necessarily attached to friendship, in fact, Aristotle went as far as to say friendship ought to be the foundation of a *polis*, for it was only in two friends, looking towards the same end, or *telos*, can they develop the virtues necessary to reach said agreed upon end. MacIntyre goes on to describe liberal democracy as a community of strangers; a group of individuals who hold no such common agreement on the end in which they ought to seek, and are therefore left therefore with a democratic type of procedural justice that they can at least all agree in theory is fair. For example when we consider the debates around the issues of immigrants and refugees that come into the country, some argue that we cannot take on the re-

4   Stanley Hauerwas and Charles Pinches, *Christians Among the Virtues: Theological Conversations with Ancient and Modern Ethics* (Notre Dame, Indiana: University of Notre Dame Press, 1997), fn 4, p. 186. Hauerwas goes on to note that "In effect, the only political alternative we have is friendship, particularly the friendship we call "church." The difficulty is that, given our political presuppositions that form of friendship is not recognized as political but rather is said to be part of the 'private' realm."

5   Alasdair MacIntyre, *After Virtue: A Study in Moral Theory*, 3rd ed. (Notre Dame, Indiana: University of Notre Dame Press, 2010), 146-64.

sponsibility to care for others when we cannot seem to find the resources take care of our own citizens. Others have argued that it is our responsibility as a prosperous nation to help those in need.[6]

In 2014, thousands of children were illegally crossing the U.S./Mexican border. The sheer number of children taking on this dangerous trek is significant, as it was almost a 50% percent increase from the previous year, reaching 58,000 children by October of 2014.[7] Theories of what caused the influx are speculative, ranging from drug muling to fleeing the escalating gang-related violence in their home countries. Due to the large number of children crossing the border, overcrowding in facilities in Texas led to undocumented immigrants being transported via plane and bus to different facilities to be in Southern California and Arizona, drawing large protests.

In July of 2014, the group "Christians Against Illegal Immigration" led protests of such transfers. They argued that love of the illegal neighbor is hated of the poor neighbor who is a U.S. citizen.[8] A local from Murrieta, a U.S./Mexico border town in Southern California, argued that "[w]e can't start taking care of others if we can't take care of our own."[9] Rhetoric denouncing illegal immigration as "stealing jobs and resources from U.S. citizens" is sometimes heard from Christians and non-Christians alike. Along with "Christians Against Immigration," Evangelicals for Biblical Immigration (EBI) represent a voice within

6   The USCCB made such a claim in "Strangers No Longer." Those with greater wealth have greater responsibility. This teaching, though seemingly simple, is incredibly counter-cultural. In California, some of the wealthy counties have openly rejected the water restriction, citing higher property taxes and aesthetic expectations for their property as reasons for why they should be exempt from any water restrictions during this time. One resident went as far as to suggest that "we pay significant property taxes for where we live. And, no, we're not all equal when it comes to water." See Rob Kuznia, "Rich Californians balk at limits: 'We're not all equal when it comes to water,'" in *Washington Post*, (6/13/2015), accessed on 15 June, 2015 at http://www.washingtonpost.com/national/rich-californians-youll-have-to-pry-the-hoses-from-our-cold-dead-hands/2015/06/13/fac6f998-0e39-11e5-9726-49d6fa26a8c6_story.html?hpid=z1.

7   The total number of "unaccompanied child migrants" in 2013 was roughly 38,000 children. By October of 2014, the number had already reached 58,000. See BBC News, "Why are so many children trying to cross the US border?" at BBC.com, (9/30/2014), accessed on 15 April, 2015 at http://www.bbc.com/news/world-us-canada-28203923.

8   For further details regarding Christian responses against illegal immigrants, see Gina Piccalo, "The Evangelical crusade against immigration," at Mashable.com (7/9/2014), accessed on 15 April, 2015 at http://mashable.com/2014/07/09/the-evangelical-movement-against-immigration/.

9   BBC, "Protesters block migrant buses in California," at bbc.com, (7/2/2014), accessed at http://www.bbc.com/news/world-us-canada-28121198.

American Christianity that rejects the recent proposals by the federal government to deal with immigration. EBI was formed after the formation of Evangelical Immigration Table (EIT), a pro-immigration Evangelical group, in order to represent the Evangelical position against immigration. According the EBI website, 75–80% of Evangelicals are against recent immigration policies, and the EIT did not represent the Evangelical majority. The mission of EBI centers their argument on 1 Timothy 5:8, which states: "If anyone does not provide for his own, especially for those of his household, he has denied the faith and is worse than an unbeliever."[10] In a letter to Congress in June of 2014, EBI argued that:

> Accelerated immigration in the context of a growing welfare state, such as ours, is unsustainable, unjust to citizens and un-biblical. It does not yield hospitality but hostility. What would help is a firm border, tens of millions of jobs, justice for citizens who've paid into social safety nets, the deportation of gangs and criminals, and the safe return home of children and others in this current Progressive open border import of people.[11]

The EBI advocates for laws that aim to protect the vulnerable in the United States. It therefore requires that we have strict immigration laws, and hold to them. The EBI argue that current immigration policy is a band-aid to a bigger problem. Forgiving those who have crossed the border illegally may solve the current issue of illegal immigrants, but will not solve the issues of the "growing welfare state" and will only encourage future illegal immigration.[12] This moral

10 With rising unemployment and foreclosures, EBI argues the U.S. government's first task ought to be to take care of those Americans. According to the EBI, not prioritizing assistance and jobs for U.S. citizens is both un-Biblical and un-American. For a more comprehensive view of Evangelicals against immigration, seeJames R. Edward Jr., "A Biblical Perspective on Immigration Policy" on the Center For Immigration Studies website, http://cis.org/ImmigrationBible.

11 Open letter to Congress, 2014, by the EBI can be accessed at http://evangelicalsforbiblicalimmigration.com/june-2014-letter-to-congress/.

12 To see how this tension at the very heart of this argument is one similar to the struggles many Catholic Workers have come to deal with, see Rosalie Riegle Troester, *Voices of the Catholic Worker* (Philadelphia: Temple University Press, 1993), 163–182. Such tensions center around similar questions: When do we say no to the stranger at the door? How is having a person sleep in the tub and on the floor respecting their dignity? That this tension also exists within the Catholic Worker and is addressed in such a different way may indicate the power of a narrative over such a community.

reasoning seeks to improve the well-being of the poor around them, and should not be easily dismissed. Yet what quickly becomes apparent in a liberal society is that such a society is not able to cope with the reality of strangers. Those who, we assume, can contribute to society in such a way that would not add to the already heavy "burden" that some call the poor are welcome. Strangers, those who threaten to become parasitic on an already strained system, are rejected. The rhetoric around immigration is a prime example of the type of "hospitality" produced by a liberal democracy. [13]

The Catholic Worker, however, seeks to welcome strangers. The Catholic Worker, as Dorothy Day set it up, was founded on the radical commands and stories found in Scripture. Even further, In *Voices of the Catholic Worker*, Michael Baxter recalled that "It used to drive Dorothy Day crazy when people would give the band-aid analogy [regarding her work with the poor in alleviating poverty] . Part of it may have been because many of the people who were criticizing weren't themselves doing anything concrete for the poor. But also, there is just this incredible lack of faith—no faith that handing this person a piece of bread would have any eternal meaning." [14] Dorothy Day's hospitality provides deep roots for the Catholic Worker to stand as a model against liberal notions of hospitality. It is therefore through the Catholic Worker practice of hospitality that others can begin to learn of the struggles and joys of Christian hospitality. [15] In order to begin to articulate the hospitality of the Catholic Worker, we must begin with one of the sources for Dorothy Day: Scripture.

The Necessity Exemplar: The Catholic Worker

In Luke's gospel Jesus confronts the Pharisees who had chosen the seats of honor. He tells them to sit at the lowest seat and not assume it was your seat to

---

13 This is not to say that "ancient" communities were able to address strangers rightly, as some Homeric societies did not deal well with strangers. My point is that a Christian formation has more in common with an Aristotelian society than it does a liberal society. I am not suggesting that Aristotelian societies were more Christian than liberal societies and not as flawed as our current milieu, but ultimately seek to illuminate the power of narrative on our moral formation. For more on the differences between Homeric and Aristotelian societies, see MacIntyre, *After Virtue*, 121–164.

14 Troester, *Voices*, 163.

15 This is not to suggest that the Catholic Worker has "figured out" hospitality, but rather their witness demonstrates to a Christian tradition (in the MacIntyrean sense) of hospitality that is capable of correcting the ills of American Christian hospitality. For American Christians to learn to argue as Catholic Workers do

begin with. Furthermore, "when you host a banquet, do not invite your friends but invite the poor, the crippled, the lame, and the blind. And you will be blessed, because they cannot repay you, for you will be repaid at the resurrection of the righteous" (14.13b–14). Upon hearing this one of the guests gave a blessing for those who have been saved or those who "eat the bread in the kingdom of God" (14:15). Jesus then tells a parable about how those who were invited to a great banquet rejected the invitation. The angered master then sends the slave out to bring in the poor, crippled, the blind, and the lame, countering the prideful and selfish hospitality of the Pharisees with a hospitality that welcomes the lowly and oppressed.

Matthew 25 goes even further by suggesting that it is in the poor, crippled, blind, and the lame that we may see and serve Christ among us. The Catholic Worker aims to embody this belief by opening houses of hospitality that take seriously scriptural themes of Jesus as a stranger, and the previous practices of the saints of the Church that courageously served the poor and the stranger as Christ. The theme of Jesus as a stranger not only allows us to rightly see the other before us, but conversely allows us to see our own "stranger-ness" to God. The Catholic Worker, as a community within the Catholic Church, maintains a certain *telos*, and therefore makes intelligible their works of hospitality within a particular tradition. They have, furthermore, been able to keep the Christian "we" from the liberal transition to the American "we."[16]

This does not mean that we should delay the lessons we could learn from the Catholic Worker until refugees settle in our neighborhood or arrive at our own doorstep, but to begin now to learn what it means to be hospitable, and to do so by looking towards the Catholic Worker, the community of saints, and towards the hospitality of Christ. With all of its imperfections, difficulties, and

about the goals and struggles of hospitality would be an improvement from current "debates." I am thinking particularly of the popularity of books like *When Helping Hurts* which, while not dealing specifically with the issue of hospitality but rather how to engage the poor, are consumed by consequentialist rhetoric and therefore cannot help but make the poor as an object to be made efficient rather than the person of Jesus Christ to be served. They furthermore are forced to understand stewardship as a type of business efficiency, fulfilling the "manager" type as described by Alasdair MacIntyre. See MacIntyre, *After Virtue*, 74–77.

16 To speak broadly of the Catholic Worker is difficult as the name and "model" of the Catholic Worker has never been trademarked. Subsequently, across the world groups refer to their community as a Catholic Worker community, and have only asked, by the original community in New York, to seek to represent the "aims and purposes" articulated by Dorothy Day.

trails, the model of the Catholic Worker offers medicinal qualities to the ailing Christian moral imagination.

Conclusion

I conclude with the exhortation of Pope Francis as he urges the Church towards intergenerational solidarity and solidarity with the poor that rightly transforms the "stranger" into a brother and friend.

> The feeling of asphyxiation brought on by densely populated residential areas is countered if close and warm relationships develop, if communities are created, if the limitations of the environment are compensated for in the interior of each person who feels held within a network of solidarity and belonging. In this way, any place can turn from being a hell on earth into the setting for a dignified life. The extreme poverty experienced in areas lacking harmony, open spaces or potential for integration, can lead to incidents of brutality and to exploitation by criminal organizations. In the unstable neighborhoods of mega-cities, the daily experience of overcrowding and social anonymity can create a sense of uprootedness which spawns antisocial behavior and violence. Nonetheless, I wish to insist that love always proves more powerful. Many people in these conditions are able to weave bonds of belonging and togetherness which convert overcrowding into an experience of community in which the walls of the ego are torn down and the barriers of selfishness overcome. This experience of a communitarian salvation often generates creative ideas for the improvement of a building or a neighborhood.... Others will then no longer be seen as strangers, but as part of a "we" which all of us are working to create.... The notion of the common good also extends to future generations. We can no longer speak of sustainable development apart from intergenerational solidarity. Once we start to think about the kind of world we are leaving to future generations, we look at things differently; we realize that the world is a gift which we have freely received and must share with others. Intergenerational solidarity is not optional, but rather a basic question of justice,

since the world we have received also belongs to those who will follow us. [17]

Andrew Courter is a graduate assistant at the University of Dayton. His research interests seek to explore and engage the intersection between Christian virtue ethics and Christian environmental ethics. Andrew received his undergraduate degree in cross-cultural studies at Palm Beach Atlantic University in West Palm Beach, Florida, and after graduating spent several years as a social worker in Columbus, Ohio before beginning graduate studies at the University of Dayton.

17 Pope Francis, Laudato Si': *On Care For Our Common Home*, 148–9, 151, 159.

Day and Derrida on Hospitality

Harry Murray

It would seem difficult to find two stranger "bedfellows" than Dorothy Day and Jacques Derrida. Day, as we know, was born in 1897 into a family of journalists, has been recommended for sainthood by the U.S. Catholic Bishops, and was a founder of the Catholic Worker Movement, a political activist, and a woman who spent half a century living among and serving the poor before her death in 1980. Derrida was born in 1930 in Algeria, a French Jew, a philosopher and literary critic, a founder of deconstructionism who was known for his highly complex, often undecipherable writing style; he died in 2004.

Even their writing styles are a study in contrast: Day was a journalist and teller of stories who rarely wrote systematically or concerned herself with abstractions, instead always drawing on stories and on sayings of the Catholic saints. Derrida seemed to delight in incomprehensibility, coining neologisms and phrases, rarely using stories or examples—to the extent that if you think you understand what he's saying, you immediately suspect that you've totally missed the point.

And yet, they had much in common—centering, I think, on their concern for hospitality. For Day, of course, hospitality was her life's work, a half-century of sharing her home with the homeless residents of the Lower East Side of New York City. For Derrida, the concern for hospitality came later in life, mostly during the mid to late 1990s, around fifteen years after Dorothy's death. His approach to hospitality differed from Dorothy's, first in that it was abstract and conceptual, and, second, in that, to the extent that he tried to give it practical application, it was at the national level, urging France to become more hospitable to the wave of immigrants flocking to the country. Certainly he did not embody hospitality in his personal life to the extent that Dorothy did, although he did state that he had "put [asylum seekers] up when necessary."[1]

Although Derrida's work on hospitality is largely confined to published speeches and interviews, hospitality became central to his thought. At one point, he went so far as to state: "Ethics is hospitality." This is a profound statement, akin in form to Gandhi's famous "Truth is God" (rather than "God is Truth.") To say that "Ethics is hospitality" is different from saying that hospitality is ethics. In the latter statement, hospitality can be conceived as a part of ethics, one characteristic of ethics among many. But to say that ethics is hospitality is to say that hospitality is the whole of ethics, that all ethics can be reduced to hospitality. We will return to this theme later.

I will argue that Dorothy, along with the Catholic Worker movement which she founded, represents one of the most determined efforts to engage in what Derrida termed the impossibility of "pure hospitality," that Derrida's framework for thinking about hospitality provides a useful framework for empowering contemporary Catholic Workers to reflect on their own practices of hospitality, and that the Catholic Worker experience leads to a deeper understanding of Derrida's insights on hospitality. Since this audience is rather familiar with Dorothy Day's approach to hospitality, I will focus on Derrida, interweaving Dorothy Day and the experience of Catholic Worker houses of hospitality where applicable.

Derrida on Hospitality

Derrida began to address hospitality publicly in 1996, apparently in response to two events. The first was the death of Emmanuel Levinas in 1995; the second, the rising debate over immigration in France, coupled with the passage of draconian anti-hospitality legislation. Derrida spoke at Levinas' funeral, and, a year later, gave a talk at a symposium in his honor. Levinas was an existentialist philosopher, greatly influenced by Husserl and Heidegger, who used the image of the face to represent the humanity of the other. Derrida argued that hospitality was a major, if not the major theme of Levinas' work, noting of Levinas' masterwork: "Although the word is neither frequently used nor emphasized within it, *Totality and Infinity* bequeaths to us an immense treatise *of hospitality*."[2]

Also in 1996, he was asked to address the International Parliament of Writ-

1   Jacques Derrida, "The Principle of Hospitality," in Jacques Derrida, *Paper Machine* (Stanford, California: Stanford University Press, 2005), 69.

2   Derrida, *Adieu to Emmanual Levinas* (Stanford, California: Stanford University Press, 1999), 21.

ers in Strasbourg in the wake of mass demonstrations in Paris over the imposition of the Debre immigration laws. The International Parliament of Writers responded to the situation with a call for the resurrection of Cities of Refuge, and Derrida concurred, entitling his talk "On Cosmopolitanism." Early in the talk, he invoked the notion of hospitality to call for the recreation of Cities of Refuge:

> in asking that metropolises and modest cities commit themselves in this way, in choosing for them the name of 'cities of refuge,'... we have been eager to propose simultaneously, beyond the old word, an original concept of hospitality, of the duty of hospitality, and of the right to hospitality.[3]

As Derrida developed the theme of hospitality over a series of talks and interviews, it became clear that his two major philosophical influences on this point were Levinas and Immanuel Kant.

What is Hospitality? What is Not Hospitality?

For Derrida, hospitality is nearly all-inclusive, an infinity rather than a totality. He asserts: "We do not know what hospitality is.... Hospitality is not a concept which lends itself to objective knowledge."[4] Drawing largely on the thought of Levinas, he equates hospitality with language, with ethics, with culture itself. At its most basic level, perhaps, he equates hospitality with intentionality, a move that can only be understood in the context of the phenomenological meaning of intentionality. In his farewell address for Levinas, he states this most clearly: "there is no intentionality before and without this welcoming of the face that is called hospitality."[5] He then continues: "And if hospitality does not let itself be circumscribed or derived, if it originally conveys the whole of intentional experience, then it would have no contrary: the phenomena of allergy, xenophobia, even war itself would still exhibit everything that Levinas explicitly attributes to or allies with hospitality."[6]

---

3   Derrida, *On Cosmopolitanism and Forgiveness* (New York: Routledge, 2001), 5. Cities of Refuge originally referred to cities established in ancient Israel to which those accused of killing another by accident could flee and be protected if they were pursued by a "blood avenger."

4   Derrida, "Hostipitality" in *The Derrida-Habermas Reader*, ed. Lasse Thomassen (Chicago: University of Chicago Press, 2006), 215.

5   Derrida, *Adieu to Emmanuel Levinas*, 50.

6   Ibid.

The word *intentional* is a key here. Derrida's early work was a response to Husserl, who defined intentionality as the orientation of consciousness toward an object. For Husserl, there was no consciousness except consciousness of something; hence, consciousness is always intentional, intended toward some object. One cannot be conscious except as conscious of an other.[7] Thus, consciousness itself is hospitality, a welcoming of the other into oneself.

At one point, Derrida quotes Levinas to the effect that language is hospitality, although he questions this equation of the two: "As Levinas says from another point of view, language *is* hospitality. Nevertheless, we have come to wonder whether absolute, hyperbolical, unconditional hospitality doesn't consist in suspending language."[8] Derrida also quotes Levinas to the effect that hospitality is the criterion for being human: "To shelter the other in one's own land or home, to tolerate the presence of the landless and homeless on the 'ancestral soil,' so jealously, so meanly loved—is that the criterion of humanness? Unquestionably so."[9]

One notion that Derrida contrasts with hospitality is tolerance. In an interview in New York City conducted shortly after the September 11, 2001 attacks, he stated: "Tolerance is actually the opposite of hospitality. Or at least its limit. If I think I am being hospitable because I am tolerant, it is because I wish to limit my welcome, to retain power and maintain control over the limits of my 'home,' my sovereignty."[10] In the same interview, however, he somewhat softens his critique by saying: "Tolerance is a conditional, circumspect, cautious hospitality."[11] Finally, Derrida affirms that ethics IS hospitality, and does so in several different places, first saying:

> the problem of hospitality was coextensive with the ethical
> problem. It is always about answering for a dwelling place, for
> one's identity, one's space, one's limits, for the *ethos* as abode
> ... So we should now examine the situations where not only is

7   Including of oneself as other, in keeping perhaps with the thought of George Herbert Mead, who states that I can be an object for myself, in *Mind, Self, and Society* (Chicago: University of Chicago Press, 1934).

8   Jacques Derrida and Anne Dufourmantelle, *Of Hospitality* (Stanford, California: Stanford University Press, 2000), 135. But Derrida himself also affirms that "the essence of language is friendship and hospitality" (*Adieu to Emmanuel Levinas*, 51).

9   Ibid., 73.

10   Giovanna Borradori, *Philosophy in a Time of Terror: Dialogues with Jürgen Habermas and Jacques Derrida* (Chicago: University of Chicago Press, 2003), 127–28.

11   Ibid., 128.

hospitality coextensive with ethics itself, but where it can seem that some people, as it has been said, place the law of hospitality above a "morality" or a certain "ethics." [12]

He also argues that

one cannot speak of cultivating an ethic of hospitality. Hospitality is culture itself and not simply one ethic amongst others. Insofar as it has to do with the ethos, that is, the residence, one's home, the familiar place of dwelling, inasmuch as it is a manner of being there, the manner in which we relate to ourselves and to others, to others as our own or as foreigners, ethics is hospitality; ethics is so thoroughly coextensive with the experience of hospitality. [13]

Finally he makes this comprehensive claim about hospitality: "hospitality is not simply some region of ethics ... it is ethicity itself, the whole and the principle of ethics." [14]

While Day and the Catholic Worker do not go so far as Derrida and Levinas, their notion of hospitality is not only concrete, but expansive. In an early, unsigned article in the *Catholic Worker* paper, the author (almost certainly Day) states: "Hospitality is the keynote of civilization. Its opposite is greed." [15] Day and the Worker equate hospitality with the ancient Christian notion of the Works of Mercy. Pat Farren once told me that the Catholic Worker simply is the works of mercy and that it doesn't matter if the Worker persists as a movement, because "as long as the works of mercy are being performed, the Catholic Worker will exist."

Unconditional vs. Conditional Hospitality

Derrida's most crucial move is to distinguish between pure (absolute, unconditional) hospitality and conditional hospitality.

there would be ... an insoluble antinomy, between, on the one

12   Derrida and Dufourmantelle, *Of Hospitality*, 149–51.
13   Derrida, *Cosmopolitanism and Forgiveness*, 16–17.
14   Derrida, *Adieu to Emmanuel Levinas*, 50.
15   Anonymous, "Houses of Hospitality" *The Catholic Worker*, November 1933, 5.

> hand, *The* law of unlimited hospitality (to give the new arrival all of one's home and oneself, to give him or her one's own, our own, without asking a name, or compensation, or the fulfillment of even the smallest condition), and on the other hand, the laws (in the plural), those rights and duties that are always conditioned and conditional, as they are defined by the Greco-Roman tradition, and even the Judeo-Christian one. [16]

In conditional hospitality, the guest is welcomed under certain conditions, which are defined by the host. As master of the house (or the country), the host prescribes the criteria for welcome and the duties of the guest. Perhaps only those invited by the host are allowed to enter. Or only certain types of people—e.g., certain nationalities, genders, races, ages, income levels—may be eligible to be guests. The host also may prescribe duties for the guest—to abide by the rules of the household, to limit one's stay to a visit of a certain length of time, to respect the host's property, perhaps to reciprocate the hospitality when the host comes to the guest's home. It seems safe to say that every culture prescribes some form of conditional hospitality. As Derrida notes, even the Judeo-Christian tradition speaks mainly of conditional hospitality. Kant's call for universal hospitality in his essay *To Perpetual Peace: A Philosophical Sketch* (1795) is, Derrida notes, a call for universal conditional hospitality. Although Kant, speaking of a nation's responsibility to welcome foreigners, calls for hospitality to all men because the Earth is the common property of all, it is still a conditional hospitality, for Kant places two conditions on it: first, that the guest live peaceably, abiding by the rules of the host nation and, second, that the guest has only the right to visit, not to remain. [17]

In contrast to this, but also as its foundation, Derrida advances the notion of unconditional, pure, absolute hospitality:

> unconditional hospitality implies that you don't ask the other, the newcomer, the guest, to give anything back, or even to identify himself or herself. Even if the other deprives you of your mastery or your home, you have to accept this. It is terrible to accept this, but that is the condition of unconditional hospitality: that you give up the mastery of your space, your

16 Derrida and Dufourmantelle, *Of Hospitality,* 77.

17 Immanuel Kant, *Perpetual Peace and Other Essays* (Indianapolis, Indiana: Hackett, 1983), 118–19.

home, your nation. It is unbearable. If however, there is pure
hospitality, it should be pushed to this extreme. [18]

Although pure hospitality cannot be written into law, it is the basis for all
attempts at conditional hospitality:

> this concept of pure hospitality can have no legal or political
> status. No state can write it into its laws. But without at least
> the thought of this pure and unconditional hospitality, of hos-
> pitality itself, we would have no concept of hospitality in gen-
> eral and would not even be able to determine any rules for
> conditional hospitality. [19]

One aspect of the distinction between conditional and unconditional hospitality is that the latter must be a hospitality of visitation, where guests need not
be invited, but simply appear. The hospitality of invitation, where a guest must
be invited, is always a form of conditional hospitality: "If I am unconditionally
hospitable I should welcome the visitation, not the invited guest, but the visitor.
I must be unprepared, or prepared to be unprepared, for the unexpected arrival
of *any* other." [20]

However, not all hospitality of visitation is pure hospitality, for other conditions can be imposed: conditions of citizenship, of gender, of obeying the rules,
etc. For Derrida, an important but largely unresolved issue concerns whether a
host should ask for a guest's name: "Does hospitality consist in interrogating the
new arrival? Does it begin with the question addressed to the newcomer (which
seems very human and sometimes loving, assuming that hospitality should be
linked to love...): what is your name?" [21] Later he revisits the question:

> Or else does hospitality begin with the unquestioning wel-
> come, in a double effacement, the effacement of the question
> *and* the name? Is it more just and more loving to question or
> not to question? to call by the name or without the name? Does

---

18   Derrida, "Hospitality, Responsibility, and Justice," in *Questioning Ethics: Contemporary
     Debates in Philosophy*, eds. Richard Kearney and Mark Dooley (New York: Routledge,
     1999), 70.
19   Borradori, *Philosophy*, 129.
20   Derrida, "Hospitality, Responsibility, and Justice," 70.
21   Derrida, *Of Hospitality*, 27.

one give hospitality to a subject? to an identifiable subject? to a subject identifiable by name? to a legal subject? Or is hospitality rendered, is it given to the other before they are identified, even before they are (posited or supposed to be) a subject, legal subject and subject nameable by their family name, etc. [22]

At one point, he states that this dilemma has a possible resolution:

Pure hospitality consists in welcoming the new arrival before imposing conditions on them, before knowing and asking for anything at all, be it a name or an identity "paper." But it also assumes that you address them, individually, and thus that you call them something, and grant them a proper name: "What are you called, you?" Hospitality consists in doing everything possible to address the other, to grant or ask them their name, while avoiding this question becoming a "condition," a police inquisition, a registration of information. [23]

Catholic Worker communities have often debated whether to ask guests' names. At St. Joseph's House in Rochester, the issue came up even in the soup line in the early 1980s. The daily meal is served in sittings of forty-eight people. Usually there are two or even three servings every day, depending on how many come. The first floor of the house is divided into two large rooms. One is the dining room/kitchen; the other contains chairs and a television so that people can wait for the meal in relative comfort. When I first came, we had a problem: when the meal was announced, people had to squeeze through a narrow door, and, all too frequently, stronger guests shoved ahead of older and weaker guests to get into the first serving. After much discussion, we decided to give out colored tickets (at first poker chips) on a first-come, first-served basis to designate which serving a person was in. We also decided to write down people's names as we handed out the chips in case of dispute. Within a short time, however, we eliminated the asking of names and simply handed out the tickets, a practice which persists to this day. Recording the names of meal guests simply seemed too intrusive.

Perhaps the most extreme example of hospitality without identification was the case of "Louie," who lived, first at Unity Kitchen and later at the staff house

---

22 Ibid, 29.

23 Derrida, "The Principle of Hospitality," 67.

of the Workers from the late 1970s until he died several years ago. When he died, what a few had suspected was confirmed—Louie was not his real name. After considerable effort a name and family were located prior to his burial.

Derrida's notion of no interrogation, at its most expansive, extended beyond humanity:

> Let us say yes to who or what turns up, before any determination, before any anticipation, before any identification, whether or not it has to do with a foreigner, an immigrant, an invited guest, or an unexpected visitor, whether or not the new arrival is the citizen of another country, a human, animal, or divine creature, a living or dead thing, male or female. [24]

Here, he extends hospitality beyond the human to all creatures. I am reminded of the first time I visited St. Joseph's House in New York City in the mid-1970s with a friend. When my friend tried to step on a particularly large and loathsome-looking cockroach, a young woman ran up to him and said "No, don't hurt him. They don't eat much."

Finally, Derrida acknowledges that unconditional hospitality is a risky endeavor: "For unconditional hospitality to take place you have to accept the risk of the other coming and destroying the place, initiating a revolution, stealing everything, or killing everyone." [25] As he elsewhere recognizes, however, "the visit might actually be very dangerous, and we must not ignore this fact, but would a hospitality without risk, a hospitality backed by certain assurances, a hospitality protected by an immune system against the wholly other, be true hospitality?" [26] When the risk involves not only oneself but others, the ethical dilemma becomes complex, even undecidable:

> Isn't willingness to invite even a potential murderer a form of selfish hubris, too? How can the host be sure that the only subject he endangers is him or herself? How can the risk of infinite hospitality ever be self-contained? The house whose doors I open to the potential rapist may be mine, but it may be shared by others, who might become victims without having been consulted about the desirability of infinite hospitality, which is

24 Ibid., 77. See also Derrida, "Hostipitality," 210.
25 Ibid., 71.
26 Borradori, *Philosophy,* 129.

> when the politics of hospitality ... has to ask ethical questions:
> "As for politics, it starts where I have no right to favor risky sit-
> uations, to take risks for others." [27]

Although Derrida's elaboration of the distinction between unconditional and conditional hospitality is contained in many documents, including a number of interviews, and is thus not systematic, the following table represents my effort to distinguish the two hospitalities. Note that to qualify as unconditional, hospitality must embody all of the unconditional characteristic, while only one condition is necessary to constitute conditional hospitality.

	UNCONDITIONAL HOSPITALITY	CONDITIONAL HOSPITALITY
arrival of guest	hospitality of visitation	hospitality of invitation
law	the law of hospitality	laws of hospitality
right	—	hospitality by right
questioning of guest at door	no interrogation of guest	interrogation of guest
degree of risk	very risky	limited risk
sovereignty	no sovereignty over home	sovereignty over home
tolerance	opposite of tolerance	tolerance
inclusion	inclusion	violence of exclusion
gift exchange	gift	reciprocity or exchange
responsibility	infinite	limited

Unconditional vs. Conditional Hospitality in Derrida

In her writings and in her life, Dorothy Day tried to emulate absolute hospitality decades before Derrida formulated the notion. In an early defense of the Catholic Worker practice of hospitality, she justified welcoming all, "deserving"

27 Jacques Derrida, quoted in Mireille Rosello, *Postcolonial Hospitality: The Immigrant as Guest* (Stanford, California: Stanford University Press, 2001), 13.

or "undeserving."

> Many times we have borne the charge that Houses of Hospital-
> ity, this "new wrinkle," do more harm than good. It is said that
> they perpetuate chronic laziness and drunkenness. Commu-
> nists ask us, "How can you say you're against capitalism when
> you keep it alive by feeding the poor the crumbs of the rich?"
> We are told to discriminate on the side of the "deserving poor."
> There is no record in the history of hospices and hospital-
> ity of discrimination. Those who disapprove feeding the "bur-
> dens of society" might look to the work of the nuns and priests
> laboring among the lepers. Christ exercised His good works
> among those who today would be lumped with "chronics."
> Hospitable in His heart, He took in the sinning woman and the
> thief beside Him on the Cross. [28]

Catholic Worker hospitality does come closer to Derrida's pure hospitality than do many social service efforts, which treat hospitality as an "ancillary service," an appendix to their real work of conversion or therapy. Rescue missions make hospitality conditional on attending a religious service, or, for shelter, on "taking a nosedive" and confessing Jesus as your lord and savior. Residential drug and alcohol treatment agencies make hospitality conditional on "sticking with the program." Battered women's shelters make hospitality conditional on establishing oneself as a battered woman. Many homeless shelters make hospitality conditional on producing a Social Security number. And on and on.

Dorothy justified unconditional hospitality by seeing the divine, seeing Christ in the guest:

> It is no use to say that we are born two thousand years too late
> to give room to Christ. Nor will those who live at the end of the
> world have been born too late. Christ is always with us, always
> asking for room in our hearts. But now it is with the voice of
> our contemporaries that he speaks ... It is with the feet of sol-
> diers and tramps that he walks, and with the heart of anyone
> in need that he longs for shelter. And giving shelter or food to
> anyone who asks for it, or needs it, is giving it to Christ. [29]

28 Dorothy Day, *The Catholic Worker*, May 1940, 10.
29 Dorothy Day, *The Catholic Worker*, December 1945, 2.

Derrida did not invoke Christ to justify hospitality; however, several times he invoked his own Jewish tradition, calling the guest "the Messiah:" "He awaits without knowing whom he awaits. He waits for the Messiah. He waits for anyone who might come."[30]

Sometimes, the guest even claims the status of Messiah. For over a quarter of a century, I have been running the Saturday meal at St. Joseph's House in Rochester. In the old days, I used to arrive early, before any of the guests, to get a few minutes of peace before the day began. (Nowadays, there are always guests waiting for me). One Saturday, there was one man waiting, someone I had known for a few years, and I let him in early. I regretted that decision the whole day. I had not realized how high he was, and he was a royal pain—not quite crossing the line at which I would ask him to leave, but skirting it, leaving me emotionally drained. The next Saturday, there was another man in the parking lot as I drove up. I didn't know him, and certainly didn't want to repeat last week's experience, so I drove around the block. He was still there. I drove around again, and when he was still there, I reluctantly parked and got out. He came up to me, and I introduced myself and asked what his name was. He replied, "Jesus!"

One of the most serious efforts to practice absolute hospitality comes not from the Catholic Worker, but from a shelter called The House of Mercy in Rochester, New York. The House of Mercy was established about 25 years ago by a Sister of Mercy, Sister Grace Miller.[31] It invoked the name House of Mercy in the tradition of Catherine McAuley, the Irish nun who founded the order and who opened a House of Mercy in Ireland to shelter homeless women. Today's House of Mercy goes far beyond that. It is open to all comers 24 hours a day, seven days a week. There is no formal intake procedure. I remember bringing a homeless couple there one afternoon. There was no one there who was obviously "in charge" to check them in. One of the guests just told them to find themselves a spot and settle in. Although there are a number of staff, most notably Sister Rita Lewis and C.W. Earsley, the house is often staffed by homeless residents or formerly homeless residents. The house has persisted for a quarter of a century despite many hardships, including the night in 2003 when C.W. was shot in the neck by a young man at the house. C.W. has continued to work at the house, although he had to use a wheelchair for several years and continues to need canes in order to walk. Guests can be barred for violence, although, as Sis-

---

30 Derrida, "Hostipitality," 219.

31 For an account of the early years of the House of Mercy, see Thomas O'Brien, *A Place of Mercy: Finding God on the Street* (Grand Rapids, Michigan: FaithAliveBooks, 2004).

ter Grace says, "we usually let them come back eventually." There is no set number of beds: men and women sleep on couches, chairs, and the floor. Although among some homeless persons, the House (and the neighborhood in which it is located) have a reputation for dangerousness, and although heated arguments are not infrequent, the community of guests and former guests has a spirit of solidarity that is rare in twenty-first-century America.

Jessica Wrobleski, perhaps the first writer to compare and contrast Catholic Worker and Derridean hospitalities, critiques Derrida's distinction between pure and conditional hospitality by arguing that certain limits to hospitality are intrinsic to the practice itself. Hospitality, for Wrobleski, intrinsically requires two limits: the limit of identity (the host must retain his/her identity) and the limit of security (the host and all in his/her home must be safe from harm):

> When thinking about conditional—as opposed to absolute—hospitality, it is worth keeping in mind two different ways in which conditions function. On one hand, a condition may refer to something required or demanded as an essential part of an agreement between two parties. In the case of hospitality, conditions of this sort are stipulations that limit hospitality on the basis of the identity or behavior or some other feature of the guest; for example, I may decide to welcome others *on the condition* that they speak my language or share my political views or are able to reciprocate my hospitality....
>
> On the other hand, "conditions" may entail those features of a situation that are necessary for the possibility of a certain result, apart from any decision or volition of those involved—such as when we speak of oxygen, sunlight, and water as the necessary conditions for plant growth. In the case of hospitality, the conditions of its possibility consist of the separate identities of host and guest, as well as a host's sufficient "possession" of a space for her to offer it to her guests with assurance that it is a place of relative safety. [32]

Thus, for Wrobleski: "Derrida's discussion of conditions ... equivocates between the two meanings noted above." [33] Wrobleski's critique is well developed.

32 Jessica Wrobleski, *The Limits of Hospitality* (Collegeville, Minnesota: Liturgical Press, 2012), 29.

33 Ibid., 30.

Few, if any, cultures have entailed practices of hospitality that do not, to some extent, acknowledge such limits. However, I think, her argument largely ignores Derrida's crucial assertion that hospitality is an aporia.

Hospitality as Aporia

Derrida treats [pure] hospitality as an aporia, an impossibility, a contra-diction in terms: "Hospitality is a self-contradictory concept and experi-

ence which can only self-destruct."[34] In saying this, he wasn't condemning hos-pitality, but rather elevating it. For Derrida, all ethically, humanly, important notions are aporia. Derrida's list of aporias includes hospitality, justice, the gift, responsibility, democracy to come, and forgiveness.[35]

The notion of aporia comes from Aristotle's *Physics*.[36] Vernon Cisney, in his commentary on Derrida, notes that aporia

> is a Greek term that literally means "no way out" or "impasse."
> ... For Derrida, the aporia is essentially connected with the
> moment of 'decision.' The decision is always, essentially, fun-
> damentally "undecidable."... We characterize a moment as a
> moment of "decision" precisely because, while there may seem
> to be, as we say, "pros and cons" that pull us into opposing di-
> rections, there is, on either side of the decision, nothing defini-
> tive that would delineate a path for us.[37]

Derrida explains his use of aporia in ethical terms:

> How to justify the choice of *negative form (aporia)* to desig-
> nate a duty that, through the impossible or the impracticable,
> nonetheless announces itself in an affirmative fashion? Be-
> cause one must avoid good conscience at all costs. ... [G]ood
> conscience is incompatible with the absolute risk that every

34   Derrida, "Hostipitality," 211.
35   Vernon W. Cisney, *Derrida's Voice and Phenomenon* (Edinburgh: Edinburgh University Press, 2014), 224–237.
36   Derrida, *Aporias* (Stanford, California: Stanford University Press, 1993), 13.
37   Cisney, *Derrida's Voice*, 224–225.

promise, every engagement, and every responsible decision—
if there are such—must run. [38]

In short, one can never act "in good conscience," one can never feel justified
because one has "followed the rules" in a Kantian sense. A passage which clarifies this sense comes from Derrida's discussion of forgiveness as aporia: "One
never asks forgiveness except for the unforgivable. One never has to forgive the
forgivable, such is the aporia of the impossible pardon that we are meditating on
here." [39]

Thus, anytime I do forgive, what is forgiven must be the forgivable. Yet, the
concept of forgiveness applies most strongly to what is unforgiveable. There
are, then, no empirical examples of "pure" forgiveness, "pure" hospitality, etc. [40]
Applying the notion of aporia to hospitality, Derrida states:

> I am not claiming that hospitality is this double bind or this
> aporetic contradiction and that therefore wherever hospitality
> is, there is no hospitality. No, I am saying that this apparently
> aporetic paralysis on the threshold "is" what must be over-
> come.... It is necessary to do the impossible. If there is hospi-
> tality, the impossible must be done. [41]

One might say that hospitality is an aporia in two senses. First, there is the
aporia between absolute and conditional hospitality. Absolute hospitality cannot be achieved, but conditional hospitality is not really hospitality. Yet, absolute hospitality can be embodied only in the form of conditional hospitality.

---

38 Ibid., 19.
39 Derrida, "Literature in Secret," in Jacques Derrida, *The Gift of Death and Literature in Se-
    cret*, 2nd ed. (Chicago: University of Chicago Press, 2008), 127.
40 In this sense Derrida's "aporia" is similar to Max Weber's "ideal type," of which Weber
    states in his major treatise on sociological methodology: "When we do this, we construct
    the concept 'city economy' not as an average of the economic structures actually existing
    in all the cities observed but as an ideal-type. An ideal type is formed by the one-sided
    accentuation of one or more points of view and by the synthesis of a great many diffuse,
    discrete more or less present and occasionally absent concrete individual phenomena,
    which are arranged according to those one-sidedly emphasize viewpoints in a unified
    analytical construct." Max Weber, *The Methodology of the Social Sciences* (New York: The
    Free Press, 1949), 90. Weber's notion of an ideal type, does not, however, require the cen-
    trality of self-contradiction that constitutes aporia.
41 Derrida, "Hostipitality", 225.

> Paradox, aporia: these two hospitalities are at once heteroge-
> neous and indissociable. Heterogeneous because we can move
> from one to the other only by means of an absolute leap....
> But—and here is the indissociability—I cannot open the door,
> I cannot expose myself to the coming of the other and offer
> him or her anything whatsovever without making this hospi-
> tality effective, without, in some concrete way, giving some-
> thing determinate. This determination will thus have to re-in-
> scribe the unconditional into certain conditions. Otherwise, it
> gives nothing. [42]

Richard McSorley, a priest associated with the Catholic Worker in Washington, D.C., expressed this aporia well:

> It's almost an in-built conflict in the Catholic Worker about
> how many [guests] you take into a house. One theory is that
> when a stranger comes to the door, it's Christ and you let him
> in. And the other theory is that if you're going to let Christ in,
> you don't want to have Christ sleep under the sink, and you
> don't want Christ to crowd out all the other Christs that are al-
> ready in there. [43]

Sometimes, this conflict breaks Catholic Worker communities apart. In the late 1970s, I spent two years at Unity Kitchen in Syracuse, New York. When I arrived in 1977, it was close to the pole of absolute hospitality: we served two meals a day to anyone who came and provided shelter to men from 8 PM to 7 AM every evening. There were 34 beds, but when the beds were full (which was practically every night), men slept on chairs. When the chairs were full, they slept on the floor between the beds. There were nights when practically every floor space was full. We had two rules—no fighting and no drinking—and did bar people for breaking those rules. However, there was no restriction on coming in drunk or high, and, if someone brought in a bottle of wine and gave it to us, we kept it in the refrigerator and returned it when they left in the morning. Conditions were, however, "primitive." One guest, when someone suggested he should be grateful for our help, screamed back: "Grateful? You should PAY me to come

---

42 Borradori, *Philosophy*, 129–30.

43 Rosalie Riegle Troester, ed. *Voices From the Catholic Worker* (Philadelphia: Temple University Press, 1993), 164.

into this dump!" Bob Tavani, a long time Catholic Worker who visited us during this period recounted to Rosalie Riegle:

> I remember Dorothy talking to those people in Syracuse when they were giving unlimited hospitality. They were young people who were overgenerous, who didn't know how to set boundaries, and got themselves exhausted. The place was just a wreck. Like a city shelter. Dorothy said, "Do your share and do it well. And then agitate the rest of the community to do their share." [44]

I was there at the time and can say that Dorothy did not visit us during my two year tenure and I never heard any story about her having told us that previously, although she did speak generally about the need to be small and personalist (in contrast to her statements about being open to anyone). In any event, some within the community pressured for more limited hospitality ("to grow smaller to serve the hidden Christ"). Henry Nicollela, one of the strongest practitioners of pure hospitality I have ever known, left for the Chicago Catholic Worker in 1978. Although Ron Jaworski and I pressed to continue unlimited hospitality for another year, the shelter was closed after Ron injured his back moving a refrigerator up two flights of stairs for two of our guests (only to discover that they had a perfectly working refrigerator already there). Restrictions on the meal soon followed, and Ron and I left the Kitchen. Eventually, it became a community that served a meal to 24 invited guests twice a week. [45]

The aporia of hospitality is also revealed at the door:

> for there to be hospitality, there must be a door. But if there is a door, there is no longer hospitality. There is no hospitable house. There is no house without doors and windows. But as soon as there are a door and windows, it means that someone has the key to them and consequently controls the conditions of hospitality. There must be a threshold. But if there is a threshold, there is no longer hospitality. This is the difference, the gap, between the hospitality of invitation and the hospitality of visitation. In visitation there is no door. Anyone can

---

44 Ibid., 164–65.

45 See Harry Murray, *Do Not Neglect Hospitality: the Catholic Worker and the Homeless* (Philadelphia: Temple University Press, 1990), 9–14, for a more complete account.

come at any time and can come in without needing a key for the door. [46]

Dorothy Day experienced the aporia at the door in very concrete ways, as illustrated by two diary entries from 1950:

> Then at 1 AM man and women [sic] came bringing a drunken woman in and I was very harsh in not taking her in. As Tom said, before dawn came, I had denied our Lord in her. I felt very guilty—more for my manner than for doing it, as we could not have all the other women in the house disturbed.

The second entry was recorded during a retreat being held at the Worker:

> Just now a knock came at the door and a young man wanted to spend the night. I told him to go eat but that we could not put him up. Always this impulse to say no. Yet each such encounter is an opportunity to see Christ in the other. Our brother. So I left the conference and told him to stay.... All the kindness we might do, but don't. [47]

Day's diary reflections reveal that for her, as for Derrida, hospitality is an aporia that does not allow for "good conscience." She makes decisions to limit hospitality, but is constantly, painfully, aware that in doing so, she is falling short of the ideal of pure hospitality. This struggle is a recurring theme in her writings, but particularly in her diaries.

Other examples of the aporia of the door abound in the Catholic Worker. At Unity Kitchen, we had a former mental patient who was one of our "auxiliary staff," as we called them then, living in the house and doing a lot of the cleanup work for a number of months. The Kitchen served two meals a day—lunch and dinner—and was open from 8 PM to 7 AM for shelter. We told Mike he had to resign as "auxiliary staff" one day after he let a very dangerous guest known as The Captain into the building when the house was closed and none of the "real" Workers were present. Another "auxiliary staff" person wrestled The Captain out of the building, ripping the metal front door off its hinges in the process.

---

46   Robert Ellsberg, ed., *The Duty of Delight: The Diaries of Dorothy Day* (Milwaukee, Wisconsin: Marquette University Press, 2008), 126–27.

47   Ibid., 137.

For about twenty four hours we were without a door, existing very uncomfortably in a state of pure hospitality, unable to close the door on anyone. We decided that Mike was too unpredictable to stay in the house when we weren't there and asked him to leave and return as a "normal" guest. In talking with Mike afterwards, it became obvious that he was consciously enacting pure hospitality. He firmly believed that the Kitchen was for everyone and that anyone, anytime, should be let in the door. Mike's hospitality was too pure for our Catholic Worker house.

The second, and more profound sense, in which hospitality is an aporia is that absolute hospitality is itself an aporia. If the host receives the guest into his/her home unconditionally, without reservation, then the host is no longer the "master of the house" and cannot, therefore, give hospitality. This aporia reveals a basic truth—that the host is not master of "his" home, that the host does not own or control his home; rather, the host is a guest of the Earth, a mere visitor at this location on the planet.

> [T]he *hôte* who receives (the host), the one who welcomes the
> invited or received *hôte* (the guest), the welcoming *hôte* who
> considers himself the owner of the place, is in truth a *hôte* re-
> ceived in his own home. He receives the hospitality that he
> offers in his own home; he receives it from his own home—
> which, in the end, does not belong to him. The *hôte* as host is
> a guest. [48]

In pure hospitality, then, the host must risk his/her own identity as host. Derrida applied this notion to the dilemma of immigration, arguing that a nation (France) must welcome immigrants hospitably even at the risk of losing its national identity.

Catholic Worker communities have taken this risk as well. Two examples of pure hospitality to the point of losing sovereignty come from central Massachusetts. One was the House of Ammon, started in 1971 in the town of Hubbardston by Father Bernie Gilgun. Prior to starting the house, he wrote to Dorothy Day: "As you know several of us have been talking, more dreaming, about a Catholic Worker House here that would accept ABSOLUTELY the whole platform without any hedging.... Naturally, the house of hospitality will be just that. The sky and the cops will be the limit." [49] A 1972 letter stated: "Both the deserving and

---

48 Derrida, *Adieu to Emmanuel Levinas*, 41.

49 Quoted in Murray, *Do Not Neglect Hospitality*, 163.

the undeserving poor ... are received as Christ. Thank God we don't have the problems of the Social Workers trying to decide which are which. All are welcome here."[50]

I never saw the House, since it had burned to the ground a few years before I went to the Mustard Seed in Worcester; however, it was frequently a topic of discussion there. At one discussion, the founder reminisced: "At the Mustard Seed, it's always been someone being asked to leave, meetings, someone forced out. It was never like that at Hubbardston. No one was ever turned away. The doors were open 24 hours a day. They just arrived and if they liked it they stayed." A former worker at the House interjected: "Yeah, if they didn't get the shit kicked out of them." One worker recalled: "We never had locks on our doors, until the motorcycle gang moved in. Then they put locks on their doors." Another recalled: "What we didn't realize at first was that someone was making the rules—it just wasn't us. People would get thrown out of the house by the strongest people there. We just moved the streets inside. It took me ten years to realize that."[51] Father Gilgun recalled of the fire which ended the house, in which one young guest lost his life:

> Dorothy so often says "Our faith and love has been tried by fire." Ours was tried by fire in more ways than you can imagine. ... We were burnt out. And something had to give. And then there was this dramatic sign from God that our work was over. And that we would be able to go on with the same work but more relaxed. ... Not so radical. Not so radical in the no rules.[52]

The other example was the Mustard Seed, where I lived one summer in the early 1980s, prior to the fire which destroyed that building. I arrived in the wake of a bitter struggle in which the "college Joes," the ideologically committed Workers, had been forced out, and the Seed was being run by a group of persons who had originally come to the house as homeless guests. In many ways, it was a perfect example of absolute hospitality—the guests had replaced the hosts. Not only was there a change in personnel—it eventually became apparent, even to me, that certain aspects of Catholic Worker philosophy were no lon-

---

50   Ibid., 166.
51   Ibid., 166–67.
52   Ibid., 167–68.

ger being adhered to under the new management, in particular the principle of nonviolence. [53]

Hospitality, Hostility and Love

Perhaps the most important area of disagreement between Day and Derrida lies in their views of the relationship between hospitality and two emotions: hostility and love. For Derrida hostility presupposes hospitality:

> War or allergy, the inhospitable rejection, is still derived from hospitality. Hostility manifests hospitality; it remains in spite of itself a phenomenon of hospitality with the frightful consequence that war might always be interpreted as the continuation of peace by other means, or at least the non-interruption of peace or hospitality. [54]

His use of the term allergy provides, I think, the clue to what he is saying. In order to develop an allergic reaction, the body must first absorb or "host" the offending agent. The negative reaction can only come about after the hospitality. Similarly, to make war, one must first absorb the enemy, at least enough to decide to commence hostilities.

For Derrida, hostility and hospitality are also linked linguistically. In a number of Indo-European languages, there is a connection among the terms host, guest, and enemy. Emile Benveniste, upon whose linguistic analysis Derrida drew, states: "To explain the connection between 'guest' and 'enemy' it is usually supposed that both derived their meaning from 'stranger,' a sense which is still attested in Latin. The notion 'favourable stranger' developed to 'guest;' that of 'hostile stranger' to 'enemy.'" [55]

Derrida even coins the neologism "hostipality" as the title of one of his key essays, an essay which concludes by referring to "the troubling analogy in their common origin between *hostis* as host and *hostis* as enemy, between hospitality and hostility." [56] And yes, as usual, Derrida's identification of hospitality and

---

53 Ibid., 192.

54 Derrida, *Adieu to Emmanuel Levinas*, 95. See also, Ibid., 50.

55 Emile Benveniste, *Indo-European Language and Society* (Coral Gardens, Florida: University of Miami, 1973), 75. Derrida appears to rely on this theory, even though Benveniste appears to reject it later in his chapter on hospitality.

56 Derrida, "Hostipitality," 226.

hostility itself constitutes an aporia, as he noted earlier in "Hostipitality" while commenting on Kant: "Already hospitality is opposed to what is nothing other than opposition itself, namely, hostility." [57]

For decades, Catholic Workers have referred to their houses of hospitality as "houses of hostility," and I think every Worker would acknowledge that hostility, and sometimes outright violence, frequently arises in the process of hospitality. In her diaries, Dorothy used the word "hospitality" rather infrequently. Intriguingly, one of the few times it is mentioned seems to be when she meant to say hostility: "It is summer time and I do not mind asking people to leave us. Some go without being asked. Mutual suspicion leads to an atmosphere of silence and hospitality [sic? Hostility?], some of which of course is directed to me. Where is our vaunted hospitality?" [58]

Although Day may appreciate the irony of Derrida's reflections on hospitality and hostility, she consistently affirmed the connection between hospitality and nonviolence, and attempted to run her houses of hospitality nonviolently. She famously contrasted the works of mercy with the works of war. The kind of "hospitality" out of which Derrida claims war arises is, for Day, no hospitality at all—simply a knowledge of the other that treats the other purely instrumentally. Day would be more likely to agree with the assessment of the New Testament Letter of James (4:1,2) that the cause of war is greed, which she (as cited earlier in this paper) identified as the opposite of hospitality.

Derrida complicates the discussion by occasionally referring to the connection of hospitality, not only to hostility, but also to the notion of hostage. In some rather cryptic passages, he notes that in hospitality both host and guest become hostage to one another: "The host thus becomes a retained hostage, a detained addressee, responsible for and victim of the gift that Oedipus, a bit like Christ, makes of his dying person or his dwelling-demanding, his dwelling-dying: this is my body, keep it in memory of me." [59] Here, Derrida is referring to a situation, as in *Oedipus at Colonus*, in which the guest dies in a foreign land, in the host's home, thus leaving the host with responsibility for the guest's body and, perhaps, burial. Later, Derrida makes the hostage situation mutual: "The guest becomes the host's host.... These substitutions make everyone into everyone else's hostage. Such are the laws of hospitality." [60]

Derrida rarely invoked the word love in his discussions, and when he did,

---

57 Idid., 210.
58 June 9, 1969 entry.
59 Derrida, *Adieu to Emmanuel Levinas*, 107.
60 Ibid., 125.

he expressed some ambiguity. I have located three relevant short passages: "Does hospitality consist in interrogating the new arrival? Does it begin with the question addressed to the newcomer (which seems very human and some-times loving, assuming that hospitality should be linked to love...): what is your name?"[61] Derrida's ambivalence about the relationship between hospitality and love stems perhaps from his reliance on Levinas, who stated at one point that hospitality "is not accomplished as love."[62] This ambivalence is supported by the study of hospitality cross-culturally, since many traditions of hospitality are not associated with love. Elsewhere, Derrida poses a series of questions which, while retaining the ambivalence, appear to suggest a stronger relationship be-tween hospitality and love: "*Who* loves the stranger. Who loves the *stranger?* Whom else is there *to love?*"[63] Finally, Derrida implies that the very idea of love arises out of hospitality: "Without this thought of pure hospitality... [w]e would not even have the idea of love."[64]

For Dorothy Day, hospitality and love are inseparable. Two of her most oft-cited sayings are: "The only solution is love" and "Love is the measure." She often quoted a saint to the effect that "it is only through our love that the poor will forgive us for our gift of bread."

For Derrida, then hospitality, hostility, and love constitute part of the apo-ria of hospitality. For Day, there is no aporia here. Hospitality is fundamentally opposed to hostility. Hospitalty flows from, and engenders, love. Perhaps the difference stems from Dorothy's extensive experience with lived hospitality, perhaps it stems from her faith, or perhaps it stems from Derrida's focus on the linguistic connections between hospitality and hostility.

Conclusions and Implications

It might not be far-fetched to say that Jacques Derrida has been hospitable to the spirit of Dorothy Day. Followers of both Derrida and Day can benefit by explor-ing the work of the other.

For followers of Jacques Derrida, the Catholic Worker provides an empirical example of concrete efforts to explore the aporia of hospitality. Pure hospitality may be an impossibility, but it is an ideal worth striving toward. As G. K. Ches-

---

61 Derrida, *Cosmopolitanism and Forgiveness*, 27.
62 Emmanuel Levinas, *Totality and Infinity* (Pittsburgh, Pennsylvania: Duquesne University Press, 1969), 254.
63 Derrida, *Adieu to Emmanuel Levinas*, 105.
64 Borradori, *Philosophy*, 129.

terton said of the Sermon on the Mount: "It has not been tried and found wanting; it has been found difficult and left untried."

For followers of Dorothy Day, Derrida's conceptualization of hospitality (both as aporia and as a contrast between conditional and unconditional hospitality) may be a fruitful framework for reflecting on the very real problems of hospitality presented at the doors of Catholic Worker houses: what is at stake when one is confronted by a guest who is drunk, high, or violent, and what is at stake when one must make that (undecidable) decision about whether to continue to provide personalist hospitality to a guest or to urge that s/he get some form of professional therapy. [65]

Christians would do well to take seriously Derrida's assertion that "ethics IS hospitality." Jesus' depiction of the Last Judgment (Matthew 25) and Isaiah's description of the fast the Lord desires (Isaiah 58) can be summed up in the sentence "ethics IS hospitality." Christians can also benefit from serious reflection on Derrida's assertion that all that is ethically worthwhile is aporia, contradiction, an impasse rather than a matter of following rules. The Sermon on the Mount is aporia, impossible to fulfill to the letter. Yet the demands of Jesus must be taken seriously. It is Jesus' offer of forgiveness that empowers us to try, and usually fail, to achieve the Sermon on the Mount. Jesus demands the impossible but offers forgiveness. For Dorothy Day, and for many Catholic Workers, there is no good conscience involved in hospitality. Hospitality involves putting oneself into situations where there may be no "good" answer, where all decisions involve guilt, involve complicity at some level. My own feeble attempts at hospitality have, if nothing else, led to deep insights into my own moral failings.

Hospitality also has theological implications. The common images invoked for God are images of power and control: King, Doctor, Lord, Architect. But the image of God invoked in hospitality is usually that of the guest, the stranger, the powerless one. The image of God as guest provides a crucial corrective to the other, power-laden images so often invoked in Christian theology. We find God in the poor, in the vulnerable. God is the One who appears to us in need, Who demands a response.

Christologically, hospitality provides powerful insight into the Incarnation and the Redemption. The Incarnation is the story of God becoming human, walking among us, often "with no place to lay His head." Although Jesus both gave and received hospitality during His life, ultimately humans refused Him hospitality, executing Him on the cross. Here, the story of Jesus diverges from

65   See Murray, chapter seven for a more thorough discussion of this issue.

most myths about gods appearing as human, because Jesus does not punish His executioners but forgives them. God forgives our lack of hospitality, and this forgiveness offers salvation to all.

A comparison of Day and Derrida reveals that serious thinkers can come to amazingly similar conclusions by very different routes. Derrida, I think, would approve of Day's question: "Where is our vaunted hospitality?" Day would, I think, acknowledge that "We don't know what hospitality is." We know Him in the breaking of the bread.

Harry Murray, Ph.D., is professor of sociology and coordinator of the Peace and Justice Major at Nazareth College. He has been associated with the Catholic Worker movement since the mid-1970s and is the author of *Do Not Neglect Hospitality: The Catholic Worker and the Homeless*. He has coordinated the Saturday meal program at St. Joseph's House of Hospitality in Rochester, New York for over twenty-five years. He has also attempted to balance his career in academia with periodic civil disobedience, most recently at the Reaper drone control center at Hancock Air National Guard Base in upstate New York. He lives with his wife in Rochester and has two grown children.

Ecumenism, Conversion, and the Catholic Worker: Dorothy Day's Appeal to Evangelicals

Richard P. Becker

Above all, it is necessary to recognize the unity that already exists.

—John Paul II

The Ecumenical Project

There's a 7-Eleven near where I teach—Bethel College in Mishawaka—and I often go there for an afternoon caffeine boost. I could walk, but if I'm pressed for time (or it's winter), I'll jump in the car for a quick trip, fill up my travel mug, and head back to the office.

To an outside observer, there is nothing noteworthy here. However, my java jaunts have real legal ramifications, for the 7-Eleven is on the South Bend side of that street, and my college is on the Mishawaka side. In practical terms, it's an amorphous, virtually invisible border. But if I got in an accident coming or going? Legal boundaries—possibly even measured in feet and inches—would have real-world significance: Is the accident under the jurisdiction of South Bend or Mishawaka courts? How will one jurisdiction handle liability claims versus the other?

That's one picture of boundaries and superficial fluidity; here's another. When I was a kid, my family visited the Four Corners Monument. It's the spot where four southwestern states meet up at one single point: Arizona, New Mexico, Colorado, and Utah. I remember having a blast with my brother running around the concrete slab that marks out the borders leading up to the common point, announcing as we tore around which state we were occupying at any given moment. The legal division between those four states is normally very clear when it counts in, e.g., litigation or criminal prosecution. But for a kid at that particular spot in the middle of the Navajo desert the legal borders are purely a source of amusement, even joy. While marking out true divisions, the Four Corners Monument serves to draw together rather than divide.

Both these images of fluid boundaries capture different approaches to ecumenism, but I much prefer the second. Before I explain why, let me take a moment to define "ecumenism." Though once common, today it is not a word that is routinely invoked or well understood. It's based on a Greek word that loosely translates as "the whole world," and it refers to anything that touches on matters common to the "whole world" of the church.

Ecumenism is a family get-together that can and should involve all the clan's disparate branches—reconciled and unreconciled. It includes Catholics, Orthodox, and Protestants of all types—everyone who calls Jesus Lord, believes in the good news of salvation from sin, and lives today in the hope of heaven tomorrow. There are disagreements, to be sure, but today we hold those disagreements amicably in a way that allows for rich relationships alongside respect for differences. We come to enjoy each other's traditions, quirks, and peculiarities; we laugh with and even at each other—in the same way cousins laugh at each other when they get together for the holidays. Better yet, think of Bilbo's birthday party in *The Fellowship of the Ring*.[1] There's competition, grievance, and dispute between various branches of the Hobbit family tree, and these are not rationalized or ignored. Still, at least for that moment, everybody is overlooking the differences and getting along, which fosters mutual good will upon which real unity can be built.

This was the vision of ecumenism promoted at the Second Vatican Council, and it was one of the Council's aims. In the Decree on Ecumenism, the Council stated that the "restoration of unity among all Christians is one of the principal concerns of the Second Vatican Council."[2] Why was it such a priority? The perhaps too easy answer is because unity was of course mandated by Christ himself in the oft-cited passage from John 17, "that they all may be one." Indeed, he commanded us to "love one another" first, and then sent us the Holy Spirit to make it possible.[3] "There is one body and one Spirit," St. Paul wrote the Ephesians, "just as you were called to the one hope of your calling; one Lord, one faith, one Baptism."[4]

---

1   J.R.R. Tolkien, *Fellowship of the Ring* (New York: Ballantine, 1955).
2   Vatican II, *Unitatis Redintegratio*, §1.
3   John 15:17.
4   Eph. 4:4–5.

Thus, unity was a priority for Jesus and the early Church, and so it's naturally a priority for us. And while nothing can disrupt the invisible unity of the Body of Christ, there's no question that wide and innumerable divisions have effectively dismantled the visible integrity of that Body.[5] We have our work cut out for us!

Yet a word of caution is in order: Authentic unity cannot be accomplished at all costs. "This Sacred Council exhorts the faithful to refrain from superficiality and imprudent zeal," the Council Fathers insisted, "which can hinder real progress toward unity."[6] St. John Paul II addressed this same idea very tactfully, yet clearly:

> Good will is needed in order to realize how various interpretations and ways of practicing the faith can come together and complement each other. There is also the need to determine where genuine divisions start, the point beyond which the faith is compromised.[7]

That brings us back to those anecdotes I related above—the 7-Eleven coffee run and the Monument: Both involve real divisions despite practical permeability, but only the second image—messing around at Four Corners—involves clearly demarcated boundaries. That's preferred, because the goal of ecumenism—at least from a Catholic perspective—is the real and thorough structural reunion of all Christians, not a mere superficial, subjective one. And overcoming division, no matter how it is accomplished, necessitates both an a priori acknowledgement that divisions exist as well as a thorough grasp of their precise location.

How do we do this? Generally the most successful ecumenical efforts include at least these three dimensions:

1. *Common ground:* This involves seeking unity where possible; understanding and good will when it isn't. Of special importance are those formal gatherings, usually conducted by those with authority in their respective traditions.

2. *Common prayer:* The Catechism refers to shared prayer as the "soul of the whole ecumenical movement."[8] This can certainly include liturgical prayer, but

---

5   Cf. *Lumen Gentium*, §8.

6   *Unitatis Redintegratio*, §24.

7   John Paul II, *Crossing the Threshold of Hope* (New York: Knopf, 1994), 147.

8   *Catechism of the Catholic Church*, §821.

not, unfortunately, intercommunion.[9] This painful sacramental separation motivates us to work all the more diligently toward real reunion.

3. *Common cause:* "Cooperation among Christians vividly expresses that bond which already unites them," the Council Fathers wrote, "and it sets in clearer relief the features of Christ the Servant."[10] In my book, this is the best kind of ecumenism—the most organic and natural, and certainly the most visible in terms of witness. It happens when Christians of all stripes come together to defend the unborn, the death row inmate, and the marginalized of every kind; when we work for peace and an end to all violence and bloodshed and war; when we strive together for justice and reconciliation in every corner of our society and world.

The Catholic Worker and Ecumenism

So what does all of this have to do with Dorothy Day and the Catholic Worker (CW)? Plenty, although you wouldn't know it once you look into it. The CW movement has a long history of welcoming everyone willing to work together for the direct relief of the poor and for a more just, peaceful world. Surprisingly, however, relatively little attention has been paid to the CW's ecumenical heritage. When I contacted Phillip Runkel, Marquette's archivist of the Catholic Worker movement, for help with this presentation, I was surprised by his response. "We don't have much on this topic," he wrote back, adding, "which intrigues me as a Protestant 'fellow traveler.'"[11]

So, here's a contribution to expanding that area of inquiry, although it is extremely limited in scope. Since I can't cover the whole gamut of Christian experience in the time I have, my focus will be on Protestantism, and specifically Protestants engaged with Catholic Catholic Workers.[12] There are CW's run by Protestants, but I'll not be addressing those here.

I'd like to further narrow my scope by focusing specifically on Evangelical Protestants—basically that brand of conservative Christianity that occupies the fuzzy space between outright Fundamentalism on the one hand and more progressive forms of traditional mainline Protestantism on the other. I grew up Evangelical, studied theology at an Evangelical college, and even spent a sum-

---

9   Cf. Colin B. Donovan, "Communion of Non-Catholics or Intercommunion," EWTN.com.

10   *Unitatis Redintegratio,* §12.

11   Phillip Runkel, email message to author, April 19, 2015.

12   Cf. Bill Tammeus, "Presbyterian-run Catholic Worker house does things backward—like Jesus," *National Catholic Reporter,* February 20, 2013.

mer in the Philippines as a short-term Evangelical missionary. And yet, after all that, I was … uneasy. Something was missing. Here's how Dorothy Day helped fill the gap.

Some thirty years ago, I stood on the porch of the St. Francis CW in Chicago and screwed up my courage to knock. It was the culmination of a host of influences and serendipitous encounters, and I had a strong feeling that it was a moment charged with life-changing potential. "This is it," I thought to myself after knocking—no answer. "Maybe here I'll find Jesus." I knocked again.

"At the time, I was a wet-behind-the-ears, suburban-raised, angst-ridden, and disillusioned Evangelical trying to rediscover Jesus in the inner city," I've written elsewhere. "The 'L' train deposited me at Wilson and Broadway, and Jesus wasn't there to greet me—a disappointment, but not really a surprise."[13] So, I headed over to the CW, still fully expecting to find him.

And find him I certainly did, in the guise of Rosalie. After I gave up on knocking and rang the bell, the door flew open and I was face to face with a raging storm. Foul oaths and language I wouldn't expect from a woman that could've been my grandmother were mixed with invective regarding my stupidity and impudence. The whole effect was paralyzing, and I didn't know what to do—so Rosie took the lead. "Don't just stand there," she screeched. "It's freezing out!" I entered and was transformed.

Actually, my life had already veered off in a wildly unexpected direction well before that encounter with Rosie, and it was the direct result of ecumenical contact. To begin with, I was raised in the Calvinist tradition, but I was immersed in Wesleyan theology at college. The fine distinctions between those and other Protestant theological frameworks troubled me: Which one was right? Moreover, I was also bothered by what I perceived to be a divorce between the Jesus of the gospels—the one who spent so much time healing the sick, feeding the hungry, and confronting social evil—and the lived Christianity I encountered in the churches, no matter what denomination. Shane Claiborne, some twenty years later, captured what I felt in his book Irresistible Revolution. "I wasn't exactly sure what a fully devoted Christian looked like," he wrote, "or if the world had even seen one in the last few centuries."[14]

Ecumenism seemed to offer some kind of relief on both fronts. I was attracted to the inclusiveness of the National Council of Churches and the World Council of Churches, and I admired their commitment to spreading the gospel

13 Richard Becker, "Love Lessons in Uptown," *Catholic Exchange*, March 20, 2014.

14 Shane Claibourne, *Irresistible Revolution* (Grand Rapids, Michigan: Zondervan, 2006), 71.

by addressing all kinds of human need, not just spiritual. I attended worship services at every conceivable denominational variant—Episcopalian liturgy and kneeling one week; Quaker Friends Meeting and silence (and awkwardness) the next. In Eugene, Oregon, I even found my way to an ecumenical reading group that included Catholics and Protestants, conservatives and liberals, academics and clock-punchers—about as diverse a group of Christians that I've ever encountered. We took turns picking out what the group would read every month, and when it came to the Catholic couple in the group—former Catholic Workers themselves—they insisted we read Dorothy Day's *The Long Loneliness*.[15]

That was a bit of a departure, for the group usually stuck to more formal theological writing, and Day's book, an autobiography, didn't quite fit. Nevertheless, the couple insisted. I wish I could remember their names, because their insistence changed the course of my life.

I read through Dorothy's autobiography like a starving man tucking into a feast, and I well remember sitting in the Fishbowl at the University of Oregon when I turned the last page. "I'll never be the same," I said out loud, and I was right. Dorothy was a Catholic, to be sure, yet she nonetheless seemed to have a real relationship with Jesus—she was that real Christian I was looking for. Still, it was a weird combination—Catholic and Christian—but not worth sorting out at the moment. Claiborne seems to have had a similar reaction when he encountered Dorothy, calling her a "sassy contemporary radical ... who converted to Christianity."[16] Of course, that's not exactly true, given Dorothy's baptism and confirmation in the Episcopal Church as a young girl, but Shane's point is clear: Dorothy's conversion to Catholicism resulted in a radical conversion of her person, both inside and out.

Ecumenically speaking, then, Dorothy was a Catholic whose life witness made her appealing well beyond her own community of faith. "She is most certainly a figure of the Church, but she belongs to the whole Christian church, and not simply its Roman Catholic portion," Mel Piehl has argued. "We still have not resolved all the serious differences among the great traditions of Christianity, but figures like Dorothy Day may be one way to bridge the gap."[17]

For me, it's certainly the case that it wasn't her Catholicism but Dorothy

---

15 Dorothy Day, *The Long Loneliness* (New York: Harper and Row, 1952).

16 Claibourne, *Irresistible Revolution*, 72.

17 Mel Piehl, "Protestant Responses to Dorothy Day and the Catholic Worker," pp. 515–530 in *Dorothy Day and the Catholic Worker Movement: Centenary Essays*, eds. William Thorn, Phillip Runkel, and Susan Mountin (Milwaukee, Wisconsin: Marquette University Press, 2001), 530.

herself that attracted and inspired—and my experience was certainly not a unique one. In the ten years I've been teaching at Bethel College, an Evangelical institution, I've seen my own experience replicated again and again, especially in terms of the impact of simply reading that one book. "Little did I know when I casually picked up *The Long Loneliness* how instrumental it would be," wrote Sarah, one of my former students. "I was captivated. I saw the heart of a woman so saturated in the cause of Christ that nothing could stop her, and her mission changed my heart." [18]

My heart was also changed and that's how I ended up in Chicago getting bawled out by a slightly unhinged Rosalie. Eventually, I got to know the St. Francis House community, and I even moved in for a while. At this point, I was still mainly interested in the Worker side of the CW equation and how those seemingly ordinary people were able to live such extraordinary lives of Christian charity and service—despite the human error and frailty that naturally accompanies such communal experiments.

It's also noteworthy that my ability to enter into things at St. Francis CW despite my being a Protestant didn't seem all that strange. After all, I wasn't the only non-Catholic involved, although I was certainly in the minority. Kassie Temple, of New York City's Maryhouse, reported a similar experience:

> I'm not Roman Catholic. People ask me why I have come to a Roman Catholic place. There are a number of answers to that. But one is I really didn't know of any other place that was doing the combination of immediate works of mercy and thought, and realizing that this was something that needed to be thought about in the light of traditional Christianity. [19]

Apparently, this is how it was from the movement's earliest days, and it put the CW on the ecclesial cutting edge. "There was not much talk of ecumenism in those days in the Holy Roman Catholic Church," wrote Dorothy, crediting Ammon Hennacy, in part, for increasing the early movement's "ecumenical spirit." [20] Here's how she characterized the Hennacy connection:

---

18 Sarah Scarborough, email message to author, April 22, 2015.

19 Kassie Temple, oral history recorded February 10, 1988 (Dorothy Day-Catholic Worker Collection, Series 9-4, Box 8, Folder 1).

20 Dorothy Day, "Ammon Hennacy: 'Non-Church' Christian," *The Catholic Worker* (February 1970, 2.8).

His association with us began in the city of Milwaukee where he was living at that time and where we had a house of hospitality. Communists, socialists, anarchists, and an assortment of unbelievers and Protestants, of who knew what denomination, used to come to our Friday night meetings. The discussions were lively [and] mostly on social questions.

Hennacy himself eventually converted to Catholicism (with Dorothy as his godmother), but he was part of the movement long before that. [21]

Much like those Friday night meetings in Milwaukee, the meetings in NYC were similarly ecumenical and reflected the soul of the movement—something Dorothy explicitly affirms in *Loaves and Fishes*:

The talks on liturgy and worship and scripture fell under the head of "cult." But, since the meetings included those of other faiths, they were also ecumenical. They were, in fact, the beginning of our work for peace among religious groups. We could all meet together, Peter pointed out, in our search for the common good. [22]

In this one brief passage, Dorothy touches on all three essentials of ecumenism—"Our work for peace among religious groups," seeking common ground; exploring "liturgy and scripture" and the experience of "cult" (in the old sense of the word), and so prayer in common; and meeting together, per Peter Maurin's insight—"in our search for the common good"—furthered the cause of incarnating love through the works of mercy. [23]

These are the contours of the CW tradition that make it such a superb ecumenical laboratory, especially for Evangelicals, for unlike formal encounters, Dorothy's followers carry on the mission side by side, regardless of faith background. When you're cooking soup or passing out blankets, you don't worry much about the denomination of those around you. It matters, but only in

---

21 Dorothy Day, "The Conversion of Ammon Hennacy," *The Catholic Worker* (January 1953), 2.

22 Dorothy Day, *Loaves and Fishes* (New York: Harper and Row, 1963), 32.

23 Cf. "The Aims and Means of the Catholic Worker," *The Catholic Worker*, May 2014: "We recall the words of our founders, Dorothy Day who said, 'God meant things to be much easier than we have made them,' and Peter Maurin who wanted to build a society 'where it is easier for people to be good.'"

terms of being a dimension of those others' personalities and histories. Being on different denominational teams does not affect how you ladle out soup. Proselytizing just doesn't happen at the CW for there are no concerns in the moment about getting everybody into the same church club—no getting people over to one side of the street or the other in other words. Another Bethel student who got involved in the South Bend CW, Susie, had this to say about her experience:

> Meeting those at the Worker was the first "Catholic" environment (and people) I'd ever been around or spent time with. I was filled with misconceptions, so I had many questions. Everyone treated me with patience, and encouraged me to ask more questions. [24]

What counts at the CW is encounter with Jesus, in the guests primarily, but in each other as well. "Previous to the Catholic Worker, I always had a sense of being 'different,' an 'outsider,'" Susie wrote, "but at the CW, I had 'found my people.' I fit in and felt alive. We shared a passion—Jesus and his command to love without measure."

In time, it became clear to me—as well as to those two students I've mentioned—that the Catholic side of the CW equation wasn't simply an afterthought. We found that the extraordinary way of life engendered there was facilitated, fed, and fostered by the life of grace that Christ affords us through his Church, the Sacraments, and the communion of saints. Eventually, I became a Catholic—but not because of any pressure from my CW friends. If anything, I felt the exact opposite, and I actually had trouble finding support for my decision to convert. "Why would you want to do that?" I often heard, and one acquaintance even forcefully argued with me that I shouldn't join the Church. "There's no need," he pressed. "You're already in!"

And in a sense, of course, that was true—both literally and figuratively. As a baptized, believing Christian, I was "in" the church, small "c," and I was also "in" the CW as a contributing member of the community. Not every Evangelical who comes in contact with Dorothy becomes a Catholic—at least if my experience with Bethel College students and the South Bend CW is illustrative in any way.

We all know the closing pages of *The Long Loneliness*—Dorothy's lyrical postscript that summarizes the CW's beginnings and ethos: "We were just sit-

---

24 Susie Yoder, email message to author, April 19, 2015.

ting there talking"—so evocative for those of us who've lived it. [25] Less remembered, perhaps, are the closing lines of Dorothy's follow-up biography of the CW in its earliest years, *Loaves and Fishes*. It's an ecumenical anecdote, and one that serves as a fitting tribute to Dorothy's lifelong appeal to all Christians to embrace radical discipleship as well as a model for how that looks—a model that we can all follow, regardless of church affiliation.

> Marie, who is a Protestant, knows that work is also prayer. During the day she has walked the city streets, gathering up all the newspapers from the refuse baskets on the corners to bring us—that is her contribution to the work of the paper. Now the singing is over. Marie picks up her broom and begins to sweep. Readying the room for tomorrow is her last act of today. She is always the last to leave. When her work is done, she pauses near the door, and then, with a little look-around of satisfaction, departs. [26]

Rick Becker, RN, MA, MS, is a convert to Catholicism by way of G. K. Chesterton and the Catholic Worker movement. He has a particular interest in ecumenism, which is reflected in his educational background and current employment. Rick and his wife, Nancy, serve as Co-Directors of Religious Education at St. Matthew Cathedral in South Bend, Indiana. In addition, Rick teaches in the nursing program at Bethel College, Mishawaka, Indiana, an evangelical institution affiliated with the Missionary Church. The father of seven, Rick resides with his family in South Bend, Indiana.

25   Day, *Long Loneliness*, 285.
26   Day, *Loaves and Fishes*, 215.

Strange Bedfellows:
The Catholic Worker Movement
and Psychiatry

Clifford Arnold

In 1972, Dorothy Day wrote the following in her diary: "Insanity is a problem in our era. In the thirties, depression and drink; in the forties, war...; in the fifties, fear, cold war; in the sixties, drugs (and violence); in the seventies, 'insanity.' One can call it many names, alienation, withdrawal, depression, nervous breakdown—we have them all, together with the troubles of the past decades."[1] Insanity is a problem in our era too, especially among the homeless folks that were Dorothy's great concern. One could even say that the focus of the Catholic Worker has shifted away from workers and towards the mentally ill, since these are now the folks in most need of hospitality. Currently, around a quarter of America's homeless adults staying in shelters struggle with severe mental illness, and when one includes substance abuse problems and other forms of mental illness, the proportion comes to about half of the population in homeless shelters;[2] this does not even include people living outside of any shelter, many of whom are among the most mentally ill people of all. It seems, therefore, that anyone who wants to make a sincere attempt, like Dorothy, at loving the poor by practicing the works of mercy should begin by confronting the problem of mental illness.

A thorough confrontation would take far more time and attention than the format of this conference allows. This paper is but a small and woefully incomprehensive attempt to point out a few aspects of mental illness in our country, and to briefly explore of how we might address the challenges of mental ill-

---

1   Robert Ellsberg, ed. *The Duty of Delight: The Diaries of Dorothy Day* (Milwaukee, Wisconsin: Marquette University Press, 2008), 513.

2   National Alliance on Mental Illness, "Mental Illness Facts and Numbers," http://www.nami.org/factsheets/mentalillness_factsheet.pdf, (May 14, 2015).

ness from within the Catholic Worker tradition. The paper begins by assuming a lofty historical perspective regarding some of the major problems of mental healthcare in our time, and then comes in for a landing by situating itself within the more personal, but somehow all-embracing, concerns and potentialities of our Little Way in the Worker movement. The paper wraps up in an even more intimate manner, with my recounting a specific friendship between me and a fellow guest at the South Bend Catholic Worker house, where I have enjoyed the privilege of living for four years.

"All budgets have been cut for hospital care..."

Just a month before she wrote the passage quoted at the beginning of this paper, Dorothy wrote the following in her diary: "All budgets have been cut for hospital care, custodial care, and the streets are alive with not just drunks and drug addicts but with these saddest of all victims of our war economy, the 'insane.' The *disturbed* seems so inadequate an expression. The plain, stark unequivocal word *insane* seems fitting. Jesus said, 'The poor you have with you always.'"[3] The year was 1972, and the process that came to be known as "deinstitutionalization" was in full swing. Deinstitutionalization has been defined as the process of moving severely mentally ill people out of large state mental institutions and then closing part or all of those institutions.[4] The main significance of the process is that inpatient psychiatric beds have virtually disappeared in the United States, leading to a wholesale transformation of the way that our society treats the mentally ill. Here are some numbers to fill out a picture: In 1955, the number of mentally ill people who resided in state psychiatric facilities totaled 560,000; today, the number is 45,000.[5] Adjusting for the fact that the population of the US has doubled since 1955, these numbers represent an astounding 95% decline in the portion of people that are cared for by state psychiatric hospitals.[6]

Here's another way to think of the impact: adjusted for population growth, there are about 800,000 people, roughly the population of Baltimore or San Francisco, living outside of dedicated care facilities who would have been hos-

---

3   Ellsberg, *The Duty of Delight*, 511.

4   E. M. Torrey, *Out of the Shadows* (New York: John Wiley & Sons, 1997), 8.

5   E. Torrey et al., *No Room at the Inn: Trends and Consequences of Closing Public Psychiatric Hospitals* (Arlington, Virginia: Treatment Advocacy Center; 2012).

6   D. A. Sisti et al., "Improving Long-term Psychiatric Care: Bring Back the Asylum," *Journal of the American Medical Association* 313 (2015): 243–244.

pitalized fifty years ago.[7] These numbers suggest that the process of deinstitutionalization has had an enormous impact on the folks who struggle with mental illness, and as a result, on society in general. The following is a list of the main conditions that people were compelled to deal on their own initiative after the support of dedicated inpatient facilities was withdrawn: around 60% of patients were burdened with schizophrenia; around 15% with bipolar disorder; 15% with various other brain diseases, such as epilepsy, stroke, Alzheimer's, and brain damage; and 10% with other afflictions such as autism or addictions.[8] If the picture seems familiar to you from your experience in your houses of hospitality and drop-in centers, now you know why!

At this point, many of you might be asking, "What could have happened to make the entire country decide in so short a time to do away with such an important and influential institution?" Answering this question will, in due time, help us to imagine the role of the Catholic Worker movement in addressing the problems that have followed deinstitutionalization, problems that Dorothy lamented in the 1970s, and that we still see all around us today. We will now briefly consider three causes that historians have discerned to explain why deinstitutionalization happened, and why it has remained the default option until now. One historical argument is that technological advances in psychopharmacology were the main precipitating factor for deinstitutionalization. Indeed, the first effective antipsychotic, called chlorpromazine, was discovered in 1952, and the first treatment for bipolar disorder, Lithium, was discovered in 1949;[9] these discoveries came just before deinstitutionalization started in earnest, around 1955. The advent of a pharmacological mode of addressing certain psychotic and mood disorders led many psychiatrists to believe that patients could be managed effectively outside of mental hospitals, and, as a result, inpatient facilities started to dismiss numerous patients. One can see this as a shift away from an emphasis on external circumstances like physical environment and structured daily routines, and towards manipulating people's internal body chemistries instead. Even the use of the term "mental illness" suggests this approach, rooted as it is in the analogy from the various non-psychiatric branches of medicine; the mind can be seen in terms of the brain, an organ like any other, which can become physiologically "ill" in the same way that a kidney or an intestine can become ill, and that can be treated with drugs to correct it. So the con-

---

7   Torrey, *Out of the Shadows*, 9.

8   Ibid., 10.

9   E. Shorter, *A History of Psychiatry: from the Era of the Asylum to the Age of Prozac* (New York: John Wiley & Sons, 1997), 249–256.

ceit goes, and so the historical argument goes too, namely that the advent of this new way of managing people by managing their brain chemistries obviated the necessity of brick and mortar institutions.

When one looks more closely at the rate of deinstitutionalization, however, one finds that drugs don't tell the entire story. If one looks at the numbers, one finds that the rate of deinstitutionalization is indeed precipitous in the decade following the introduction of chlorpromazine (the mid-'50s to mid-'60s), but not nearly as steep as the rate after 1965. In numerical terms, the psychiatric inpatient population decreased by about 50,000 people from 1955–1965, whereas from 1965–1975, in the same amount of time, the number dropped by an astounding 300,000; the rate of exit increased by a factor of six. One might ask: What happened in 1965 that can explain such a rapid decline in the mental hospital patient population? The answer, by the lights of some historians, is that 1965 saw the creation of the Medicare and Medicaid programs by the federal government. Significantly for our deliberation, these federal programs funded extensive *outpatient* mental health programs, and left it to each state to fund its own *inpatient* psychiatric beds. When the individual states saw that so much federal money was going into outpatient mental health care (upwards of 60 billion dollars in today's money!), these states discerned, quite conveniently, that inpatient hospital care was unnecessary for people with severe mental illness. By removing mentally ill patients from psychiatric hospitals, a state could make hundreds of millions of dollars appear on its budget with the flick of a gubernatorial pen. The states could console themselves with the idea that the patients would now be adequately cared for by federally-funded outpatient initiatives. We can now see why Dorothy observed in her 1972 diary entry, quoted above, that "All budgets have been cut for hospital care, custodial care, and the streets are alive with . . . the 'insane.'"[10] She was writing about deinstitutionalization when it was proceeding full-swing.

A third cause that historians have articulated to explain why deinstitutionalization happened is ideological in nature. Essentially, some of the same philosophies that animated the Civil Rights movement lent powerful impetus to efforts against mental health institutions. Writers like Thomas Szasz, R. D. Laing, and Michel Foucault formed a sometimes vociferous anti-psychiatry movement dedicated to abolishing compulsory residence in mental hospitals, among other modes of perceived oppression. Jimmy Carter's Presidential Commission on Mental Health evinced the political spirit of the time in the following statement

---

10   Ellsberg, *The Duty of Delight*, 511.

of its objective: to maintain "the greatest degree of freedom, self-determination, autonomy, dignity, and integrity of body, mind and spirit for the individual while he or she participates in treatment or receives services."[11] Eventually, a series of influential court decisions came down in the 1970s that codified this political spirit into laws that gave mentally ill patients the right to refuse medication and the right to leave inpatient mental hospitals whenever they so desired. These philosophical and legislative developments precipitated the rapid exit that Dorothy observed from her vantage point on the streets.

It turns out that the majority of people who were released from mental hospitals in the process of deinstitutionalization found adequate care in settings like families, group homes, and independent rooms in highly supervised apartments, all relying on increasingly effective medication regimes, federal monetary support, and some level of expert psychiatric care. Happily, many of them reported high levels of satisfaction, and certain studies have estimated that around 60% of people released from institutional settings could be well-cared-for in the community.[12] For many people, deinstitutionalization can be considered a success in that they were granted a much higher degree of freedom while still being able to maintain their mental health. However, for a significant minority of released patients, deinstitutionalization turned out to be an unmitigated disaster. When these people failed to settle into healthy arrangements in the community, and without mental hospitals to accommodate them, they ended up living on the streets or in jail. Commenting on the language of President Carter's commission, quoted above, author E. Fuller Torrey writes, "For a substantial minority . . . , deinstitutionalization has been a psychiatric Titanic. Their lives are virtually devoid of 'dignity' or 'integrity of mind, body, and spirit.' 'Self-determination' often means merely that a person has a choice of soup kitchens. The 'least restrictive setting' frequently turns out to be a cardboard box, a jail cell, or a terror-filled existence plagued by both real and imaginary enemies."[13] It is this latter group that forms the object of concern for most of us here today, dedicated as we are to trying to alleviate their suffering through the works of mercy.

As Torrey explains, it is not surprising that so many people with mental illness end up homeless when one considers the options available to them. When someone has a severe mental illness and, as a result, lacks enough insight to vol-

11 Quoted in Torrey, *Out of the Shadows*, 8.

12 Torrey, *Out of the Shadows*, 87, quoting R. L. Okin, "The Case for Deinstitutionalization," *Harvard Mental Health Letter*, 4 (1987), 5–7.

13 Torrey, *Out of the Shadows*, 8.

untarily follow treatment programs, the options for care in America are often truly deplorable: either the streets or prison. Despite the obvious fact that prison is an unsuitable place for people with severe mental illness, almost 15% of state prison inmates have a psychotic disorder. [14] The story is all-too-common: someone who is already living in a chaotic street environment experiences a psychotic episode wherein he poses a nuisance or a threat to others. He is held accountable to penal standards that are unjust given his irrationality, and goes to prison where he again suffers under rules and punishments that only make sense when applied to someone who is capable of rational understanding and compliance. Furthermore, he suffers extensive abuse by fellow inmates as a result of his vulnerable mental state. Upon release from an unjust and totally ineffective prison term, this person returns directly to a situation of homelessness where he eventually neglects his medication regimen because his thoughts and lifestyle are totally disorganized, and he quickly suffers another psychotic episode. Recent studies confirm that prisoners with serious mental illness are two to three times more likely to be re-incarcerated than prisoners without serious mental illness. [15] In a word, thousands of extremely vulnerable people are stuck in a revolving-door scenario, yo-yoing between homelessness and a jail cell with no effective system in place to either stabilize them once they get out of prison, or to divert them as they are moving towards incarceration. Even for the mentally ill folks who manage to stay out of jail, the options are often bleak, incapable as they are to care for themselves.

"The only solution is love…"

What should we do in the face of such a sorry state of affairs? Some find it tempting to make the following argument: since getting rid of the institutions got us into this mess, then the way out of it is to bring the institutions back. Last January, for example, a group of high-profile medical ethicists wrote an article in the *Journal of the American Medical Association* entitled "Improving Long-Term Psychiatric Care: Bring Back the Asylum." [16] They used a historical argument with similar content as the one elaborated above to demonstrate society's responsibility to bring back inpatient mental hospitals; their message is as fol-

---

14 D. J. James et al, "Mental Health Problems of Prison and Jail Inmates" (Washington, D.C.: US Dept of Justice, Office of Justice Programs, Bureau of Justice Statistics), 2006.

15 J. Baillargeon et al, "Psychiatric Disorders and Repeat Incarcerations: the Revolving Prison Door," *American Journal of Psychiatry* 166 (2009): 103–09.

16 D. A. Sisti, "Long-term Psychiatric Care," 244.

lows: what we lost by deinstitutionalization, we can regain by some manner of reinstitutionalization. I think that they are correct to an extent. For certain people who lack insight into their mental condition and into their need for treatment, and who pose a threat to themselves or to others, coercive treatment in a mental hospital seems to be the only imaginable alternative to jail.

I think, however, that their solution falls short in that it lacks the Catholic Worker sensibility that, as Dorothy wrote at the end of her autobiography, *The Long Loneliness*, "the only solution is love and that love comes with community."[17] These words would surely sound soft and sentimental to the ears of academic ethicists dealing in the brass tacks of national policy with billion-dollar ramifications, but I would still submit, no less confidently, that Dorothy's witness here is utterly important. Mental institutions without compassion are little better than jails. Indeed, the emergence of shocking reports of abuse at mental hospitals provided a powerful and salutary impetus in the process of deinstitutionalization.[18] Furthermore, I can attest from personal experience as a case worker in the mental health system in the past, and as a medical student in psychiatric clinics and on psychiatric wards, that there are few environments as cold and uncompassionate as some mental health facilities. The ethicists to whom I refer above, like most people who operate within institutions, seem to be limited to institutional answers to human questions. I propose that we dare to consider the problems of insanity from the radically sane and radically un-institutional vantage point of the Catholic Worker movement.

The Catholic Worker solution, of course, is simply to invite the people in. One of my friends, who is a clinical psychologist and a professor at Notre Dame, called South Bend's Catholic Worker house the best inpatient mental health facility in town. He thinks that the Worker does an excellent job at accommodating the needs of the mentally ill folks who show up on its doorstep. I agree with him, but with qualifications.

First, my agreement. It is true that the mentally ill guests in our house could not get better treatment elsewhere. This is true for one reason only: the members of the Catholic Worker staff in South Bend are some of the most generous, loving, and faith-filled people that I have ever met; mentally ill folks demand a lot of patience and compassion, and the Catholic Worker staff can provide both of these things in a peerless fashion. No amount of state funding can effect that kind of result if caregivers are not animated by Christ's love as Dorothy was, and as so many of the folks that are part of the Catholic Worker movement are. Such

17 Dorothy Day, *The Long Loneliness* (New York: HarperOne, 2009), 286.

18 D. A. Sisti, "Long-term Psychiatric Care," 243.

difficult work can only remain joyful and sustainable if it is animated by the Christian hope that God can bring healing and good from lives broken by mental illness, and if the work is informed by the faith that Christ and His love are somehow present amidst the suffering.

I would qualify my enthusiastic agreement with my professor friend in the following ways: First, the Catholic Worker communities can only accommodate mentally ill people who exhibit a relatively high degree of functionality. The houses are, understandably, not equipped to accommodate folks with serious, fulminant psychiatric symptoms, like frank psychosis and suicidal depression. Such care requires physical structures and specific skill sets that are not reasonable to expect in the typical Catholic Worker setup, that are indeed the proper domain of institutional settings. Second, the staff of Catholic Worker houses often fail to recognize and address the mental health problems of the folks with the milder forms of mental illness who can reasonably be treated in the setting of a Catholic Worker house. In other words, I think that there are many current guests who would benefit from a higher degree of mental health competency on the part of Catholic Worker staff members. The introduction of effective medications and other forms of treatment in the last century were indeed legitimate advances in the care of people with serious mental illness; it behooves us to facilitate our guests' benefitting by them.

I envision the following way forward for the Catholic Worker, and maybe for mental health generally: First and foremost, the Catholic Worker movement should continue to strengthen its commitment to remain in Christ, as Bishop Rhoades said last evening, [19] by staying close to the sacraments, and by attempting again and again to lay down our lives for our friends, especially among the poor. With this foundation underneath us, the Worker could then extend its ability to help the mentally ill homeless by developing various skills necessary for their care. For example, one of my South Bend Catholic Worker friends is studying to become a psychiatric nurse, and I am studying to become a physician, and perhaps a psychiatrist. The idea here is to unite faith with skills, radical Christian hopefulness with excellent professional capacities. I can see our efforts proceeding along two routes, perhaps simultaneously. Each route addresses one of the reservations that I elaborated above about the Worker's ability to accommodate folks with mental illness. On the one hand, my friend and I will probably find our way into some sort of institutional work. To some extent, as I mentioned above, my medical colleagues in the *JAMA* are correct in calling for

---

19   See Bishop Rhoades' homily in this volume, pp. 9–11.

more and better institutions; for some people afflicted with severe mental ill-ness, there really is no imaginable alternative besides jail. But, as I also mention above, institutions without Christ's mercy and love are little better than jails. Whereas it is perhaps necessary that institutional settings exist, it is also neces-sary that they be staffed by folks who are being formed by the Sacraments and by communities, like the Catholic Worker, that facilitate faith and hope in the face of terrible suffering. My hope is that my friend and I, along with many oth-ers, will be able to engage in institutional work while also remaining rooted in and sustained by the Church.

On the other hand, I also hope that my friend and I can assist in the work of hospitality in the setting of Catholic Worker houses. As I mentioned above, it seems appropriate that folks who can be accommodated appropriately at Houses of Hospitality should benefit from recent advances in psychiatric care. Some level of competency on behalf of the staff would, therefore, be fitting. My hope for my friend and myself is that we will be able to give Catholic Worker House staff people a better sense of how to understand and approach the vari-ous forms of mental illness that are amenable to accommodation in the setting of our houses.

In a word, the answer to the problem of mental illness in America has to in-volve both the indwelling of God's love through the Holy Spirit *and* the psychiat-ric competencies necessary to care for people. Without Christ's animating love, mental hospitals will often be cold and hollow places, and without psychiatric knowledge, Catholic Worker houses will be unprepared and unsuitable for the large portion of homeless people who struggle with mental illness. The answer, it seems to me, is to unite basic Catholic Worker principles of faithfulness and devotion to Christ and the works of mercy on the one hand with solid psychiat-ric knowledge and skillfulness on the other.

There was much truth undergirding the move towards deinstitutionaliza-tion; certain medical advances have indeed made it possible to care for more people outside of institutions, and there is much to say for legislation that max-imizes people's freedom from unnecessary confinement. Torrey's critique of deinstitutionalization is correct, though, in that for a significant minority of people, the remaining post-institutional options are sorely inadequate. For many of these people, whose options in the absence of dedicated institutions are limited to life on the streets or life in a jail cell, the Catholic Worker move-ment provides a bright and shining alternative. Not only can Houses of Hospi-tality provide a secure and structured environment, much like the institutions previously provided, they can also offer mercy and community, goods without which mere freedom is not actually free since it cannot pursue the good of love, namely that pursuit in which true freedom lies. Unfortunately, though, for people whose conditions are unmanageable in a Catholic Worker setting, dedicated psychiatric institutions are perhaps necessary. In both instances, Catholic Workers with increased levels of psychiatric competency can be of great assistance, on the one hand, by allowing Catholic Worker houses to better serve their guests with the aid of accurate knowledge of psychiatric conditions and treatment options, and on the other hand, by bringing faith and hope into the difficult setting of the institution.

"Strange bedfellows"

Allow me to briefly share an exemplary situation in which more psychiatric expertise would expand the possibility of accommodating a House of Hospitality guest with mental illness. The fellow who has lived in the room next to mine at the Catholic Worker House in South Bend for the last two years or so suffers from bouts of paranoid schizophrenia. For weeks at a time, he experiences bizarre delusions and fits of profound anger related to his mistaken beliefs. His delusions are sometimes persecutory, meaning that he falsely assumes that various people are out to get him. More often, though, these delusions involve irrational ideas of reference, or, in other words, he thinks that certain phenomena have strong personal significance, whereas they are, in reality, totally unrelated to him. For example, he sometimes spends a large portion of his week at the local library studying movies, and eventually convincing himself that he appears in them. If I had more psychiatric expertise, I might be able to help my friend come to terms with his condition, and maybe even help him commit to therapeutic measures, which he seems sorely to need. On the one hand, my Catholic Worker status would allow my friend to trust me in a way that he wouldn't trust another psychiatrist, because I have lived with him for years and because we are friends. On the other hand, my psychiatric expertise would allow me to understand better what he is experiencing, and to help him find ways of working through some difficult problems in his life.

I chose the title "Strange Bedfellows" for this paper because I think the Catholic Worker movement and institutional psychiatry an odd couple indeed. They reside uneasily within my own personal history, to be sure. Some of my medical colleagues have found it exceedingly strange that I live at a Worker house, and it is quite unusual for a Catholic Worker to become a physician. There are certain basic attitudes in both ways that seem to resist each other; the following juxtapositional descriptions of Medicine and the Worker come to mind: bureaucratic versus personalist, institutional versus prophetic, analytical versus holistic, and professional versus volunteer. At the same time, I think that these are desperate times, and no sincere and reasonable proposition, however improbable, should be ignored.

The term "strange bedfellows" is especially apt for this situation, given its original context in Shakespeare. The phrase is from Act II of *The Tempest*. In the play, a court jester named Trinculo seeks shelter from a raging storm under the cloak of a strange islander named Caliban, who lies on the ground feigning death because he mistakes Trinculo for one of the evil spirits that constantly drive him to madness. When he discovers his position, Trinculo quips, "... misery acquaints a man with strange bed-fellows."[20] One thought that comes to my mind upon reading this scene is a comparison between Trinculo's situation and the remarkable state of affairs which found me sleeping for a few years on the other side of the wall from a sometimes raving sufferer of delusions and madness. The miseries of mental illness and the long loneliness drove us to live in the shelter of each other's company, and to seek some sort of community, which, as Dorothy says, is the only solution to life's biggest problems.

A second meaning from the play is as follows: the miserable storm of mental illness has driven the odd company of the Catholic Worker movement and psychiatry together under the same cloak of my personal history; perhaps, then, given the fact that I have found them strangely complementary to each other, it is feasible that these strange bed-fellows could profitably engage in a wider project of offering medically skilled hospitality to people who are homeless and mentally ill and need the care the most. Such an unusual meeting would hopefully presage a departure from the false dichotomy of institutional versus communal concerns, of professional versus personal ways of encountering and helping people. Such a move towards holism seems appropriate in the context of mental illness since it affects people's lives in a more comprehensive manner than any other kind of illness. By addressing mental illness with both psychiatry and the Catholic Worker traditions in mind, we can hopefully address the anguish of mental suffering with Christ's grace and peace in the context of friendship and hospitality, or in the words of Dorothy, with the love that comes with community.

20 Shakespeare, *The Tempest*, Act II, Scene II.

Clifford Arnold lived at South Bend's Catholic Worker House of Hospitality for four years, which he thinks should qualify him for a degree. He has completed far less formative programs in the Great Books (B.A.) and in the History and Philosophy of Science (M.A.) at Notre Dame, and is currently a third-year medical student at Indiana University.

Dorothy Day's
Far-Flung Friendships

Voices from the Early Years: The Friendship between Dorothy Day and Joe and Alice Zarrella of Tell City, Indiana

Rosalie G. Riegle

In the early years of the Catholic Worker, life at the house of hospitality on Mott Street was not for the faint-hearted. Money was tight, water was cold, heat was minimal, soup lines were long, and bedbugs were rampant. There was much interest in the work, though, fueled by the growing circulation of the newspaper and Dorothy's travels across the country. She was often on the road, speaking at colleges and churches, at convents and to new Catholic Worker communities, telling people that lay men and women were called to be living with and serving the poor. She was also trying to raise money to send back to New York.

While she was away, young Joe Zarrella was often in charge, along with his good friend Gerry Griffin. Joe had come to the Worker on May Day of 1935. In a serendipitous move, he left work early that day and came upon Catholic Workers selling the newspaper in Union Square. As he told me when I first interviewed him in 1989, "That was the beginning—when the bug bit me and I was captured. And it was exciting! Never a dull moment. [He pauses and then repeats] "Always, always exciting."[1]

Joe stayed on Mott Street for five years, most of the time managing the house of hospitality, with short forays to the farm in Easton. When he would open the mail on Monday mornings, there would always be a dollar from a Mary Alice Lautner of Tell City, Indiana. One day, wearing a wide-brimmed hat, Alice herself showed up at the Worker, personally invited by Dorothy during her visits to St. Meinrad's Abbey, which is twenty-five miles from Tell City. In 1942, Joe and Alice were married, one of the first of the legendary CW weddings. They eventually moved back to Tell City where they raised their family,

1 Rosalie Riegle Troester, ed., *Voices from the Catholic Worker* (Pittsburgh, Pennsylvania: Temple University Press, 1993), 6.

and Joe unionized the factory Alice's father had managed. Both lived a long and active life in service to family, church, and community, with Joe dying in 2006 and Alice a year later.

Towards the end of the first interview with me, Joe repeats the two phrases, "never a dull moment" and "always, always exciting." And Alice comments sardonically, "I think you said that."[2] Her sense of humor gives a glimpse into their lively relationship. For instance, in introducing an anecdote, Joe said, "And I don't tell this story publicly, but ..." and Alice interrupted him with, "You are. It's going to be on tape." Joe went ahead and told it—a story about Dorothy's reaction when a sycophantic visitor asked, "Miss Day, do you have visions?"[3]

Dorothy thought a lot of Joe Zarrella and depended on him when she was away, despite his youth. She would write what he adroitly called "commissions" in her letters to him, telling him very directly what to do in running the house, financially and otherwise. She called Joe and Gerry Griffin "my boys" and "my family" and in 1939 wrote Joe that "I can travel with a light heart because of you.[4] Joe, for his part, adored her.

> I really idolized her. Anything that she asked me to do, I did.
> And, you know, she was ... your first great influences mean so
> much. I really did do anything that she wanted. I maybe didn't
> particularly like it, but I did it. I'd try to make her life easier.
> When she'd come home, I'd meet her at the bus or at the train,
> and I'd always have her room ready and maybe some flowers
> for her.[5]

Mary Alice said bluntly, "He was in love with her."[6] Looking back, Joe concludes that "it was a formative age in my life, and Miss Day was growing, too. We watched her grow and we grew with her because she shared the things that became important to her. So you could see her developing spiritually."[7]

Flowers, yes, at the early Worker, but also bedbugs. Joe recounts their

---

2   Ibid., 12.
3   Rosalie Riegle, *Dorothy Day: Portraits by Those Who Knew Her* (Maryknoll, New York: Orbis, 2003), 13. Joe said Dorothy's response was, "Oh, shit!"
4   Dorothy Day, letter to Joseph Zarella, December, 1939. Box 1-1. Zarrella Papers, Thomas Merton Center, Bellarmine University, Louisville, Kentucky.
5   Riegle, *Dorothy Day*, 11–12.
6   Ibid., 11.
7   Ibid., 12.

largely unsuccessful effort to get rid of the pests:

> Only Peter [Maurin] seemed to be immune. One time it was
> so bad that we took the beds up on the roof, soaked the mat-
> tresses with kerosene, and blow-torched the bed frames and
> the springs. But [the bugs] still came back. [8]

Truly, it was an exciting time, as the interviews in the early chapters of
Voices from the Catholic Worker show us. [9] But compared to documents from the
time, one can see that memories are often tinted with hope and grace, especially
if those doing the remembering have had fulfilling and faith-filled lives as the
Zarrellas did. Joe was a story-teller who wanted to both entertain and enlighten
his audience. Whether in person or on oral history tapes, his memories give a
lighter picture than some of his letters to Dorothy show. [10]

These letters give a more complex story, still exciting but more fraught with
tensions than Joe implies when he tells the stories. I was privileged to examine
some of Dorothy's letters to Joe on a short visit to the Bellarmine Archives; later
Phil Runkel of the Catholic Worker Archives at Marquette University shared
those to Dorothy from Joe and from Alice. [11]

Read closely, the letters between Dorothy and Joe and Alice flesh out and
complicate the memories recorded fifty years later in the oral history. They give
sometimes startling glimpses into the touch-and-go life of the early Workers
and, like all our utterances, glimpses of the writers' proclivities and personali-
ties. For instance, Joe always apologizes for not writing more often, and to the
end of his days, he both wrote and talked of Dorothy respectfully as "Miss Day."

In Dorothy's letters, one reads her laments that she is living and dining
luxuriously in convents while the Workers in New York are eating meatless
soup and debating whether they can afford apple butter to spread on the bread

---

8   Ibid., 8.

9   The Catholic Worker Archives in the Department of Special Collections and University
     Archives, Marquette University, Milwaukee, Wisconsin are the repository for the record-
     ings as well as verbatim and edited transcripts of the interviews for all the oral histories
     I've collected and edited.

10   In some recordings and transcripts of Joe's words deposited in the Special Collections at
     Marquette, one hears identical phrases, the mark of a seasoned storyteller.

11   A selection of Joe's letters may be found in *All the Way to Heaven: The Selected Letters of
     Dorothy Day,* ed. Robert Ellsberg (Milwaukee, Wisconsin: Marquette University Press,
     2010).

they give to the soup line. "Here I am deprived even of holy poverty." [12] In almost every letter, she reminds Joe to go to daily Mass and in some of his to her, he proudly relates that he's improving in his attention to Mass and spiritual reading.

During a 1939 Christmas visit to her mother in Florida, Dorothy rejoiced that her daughter Tamar would have a real family Christmas and says she is getting such a good rest that "when I come back you will find me a more disciplined and organized person." [13] Dorothy was always one to see her own faults and insisted that we should worry more about our own souls than those of others.

Joe remembered that,

> We were kind of protective of Miss Day and didn't always let her know everything that was going on, especially when she was away. I used to write to her: "Even though we're broke, we're getting along." I never really told her of the troubles we had. And they were many. We were constantly on the verge of being closed down because of lack of money. But Dorothy didn't know and when she came home, we didn't bother her. [14]

Yes, he would say they were getting along, but a close perusal of his letters show that he *did* often go into detail about their problems and privations. He may have felt he was protecting her and the details may have been even more harrowing than he tells in the letters, but today's readers can see that the news Joe shared might upset Dorothy.

For instance, on August 1, 1939, when Dorothy was on the West Coast, he writes that a guest at the farm in Easton had "attempted a fake suicide in the canal, which got in the local paper." [15] He apologizes for being the bearer of bad news and concludes the episode by saying he told her because he thought she should know. Although Dorothy would remonstrate with herself for being sensitive to criticism and saw it as a failing, she knew that stories like this suicide scare would harm the young movement.

A February 1940 letter from Joe talks in detail about the problems he had

---

12 Day, Letter to Zarrella, March 5, 1940, Box 1-2, Bellarmine.

13 Day, Letter to Zarrella, December 8, 1939, Box 1-1, Bellarmine.

14 Riegle Troester, 9–10.

15 Zarrella, Letter to Day, DD-CW, Series D-1, Box 23, Folder 7. Department of Special Collections and University Archives, Marquette University, Milwaukee, Wisconsin. Joe read portions of this letter to the audience at his 1985 presentation at Maryhouse in New York.

persuading the Con Ed bill collector to collect at the Worker last so Joe could fi-
nagle some money and make a deposit to cover the check and avoid having the
electricity and gas turned off. "And so at this writing, our bank account is de-
pleted with only $2.00 in the house of which $1.30 will go to flops."[16] As he explained to the audience in a 1985 talk he gave at the New York house:

> We always gave money out in the evening, whatever we had, to
> those that came to us when we were filled up and we couldn't
> give them any beds. Many times. ... we would give them our
> beds and sleep on the floor downstairs. But we still never met
> all the needs.[17]

Again, a letter of April 1, 1940, says: "There isn't a cent in the house and I
have to get money for the baker, the farm, the oil man, and rent for the craft
store by the end of the week. O boy!"[18]

Now we have to remember that Joe was only 19 when he came to the Worker,
whereas Dorothy was 48, more than twice his age when they met. Her approval
meant a lot to him and may have been an unconscious motive for some of his
descriptions of the problems he had solved. He also might have been nudging
her to try for more donations. Often she would get nothing for speaking, only
collecting names and the pittance for newspaper subscriptions, and Joe worried
constantly that they wouldn't have enough money to carry on.

After a time at the Worker, Alice had returned to Tell City to help her father in the factory, but she was anxious to get back to New York and the Worker
life and her letters show it. She wasn't as respectful to Dorothy as her soon-to-be
husband, and would use her first name in the salutation. In Alice's letters, she
didn't hesitate to tell stories that might upset Dorothy. In one of them, she told
of giving talks about the Worker to the Benedictines at Ferdinand, Indiana. One
of the chaplains, a Fr. Charles, came up to her afterwards and said he was glad
to finally hear something good about the Worker. Apparently a friend of his in
New York had told him that Dorothy was really a Communist and was using the
Catholic Worker as a "cover up." Then Alice regaled Dorothy with the myth he
repeated—that Dorothy could be seen every afternoon "walking up and down

---

16 Ibid.

17 Audio master , DD-CW, Series 9:1, Box 4, Special Collections, Marquette. Joe read portions of the February, 1940 letter at this presentation.

18 Zarrella, Letter to Day, DD-CW, Series D-1, Box 23, Folder 7, Special Collections, Marquette.

Park Avenue with two Russian wolfhounds and swathed in silver fox furs."[19] Dorothy might have laughed at the story, but it probably also stung her and reminded her of an anonymous letter from Brooklyn warning her to "come home and meet [her] fate."[20]

Although Alice was crazy to return to the Worker, she was not close to Dorothy while in New York.

> After I got there, I was not popular with Dorothy. And I . . . it didn't work out the way Miss Day thought it was going to. I did not become a satellite. You see, while Dorothy was gone, we all did this work. Then when she came back, everything had to stand still because we had to catch up with all the travels and everything. And she did not develop a very close relationship with the girls in the house other than Margie Hughes, who kind of guarded her. We loved her, and it was kind of a reverence, I guess, but it was strange. I, myself, felt a lot closer to Peter. After we were married and Dorothy would come out to the house, we became closer, though.[21]

Yes, they were closer but that didn't keep Alice from telling me rather disparagingly how Dorothy would always leave an unfinished bandage for Alice to finish and mail on to a leper colony.[22] Her attitude toward Dorothy remained more aloof than Joe's, although they asked Dorothy to be godmother to one of their daughters.

One can't conclude the story of the friendship between Dorothy Day and Joe and Alice Zarrella without mentioning three important people: Dorothy's young daughter Tamar and Steve and Mary Johnson, who lived in the front apartment of the building on Mott Street. Tamar was nine when Joe first came to the Worker and it seems he acted like a young uncle to her, especially when Dorothy was traveling. Tamar was in boarding school on Staten Island and Joe would pick her up on the weekends, bringing her little treats, and take her to the movies and other outings before returning her to school on Sunday evenings. In my first conversation with Tamar, she remembered fondly her days with Joe. Dorothy reminded Joe to take care of "my baby," saying that Tamar was "the

---

19 Lochner, Alice. Letter to Day, April 17, 1941. Ibid.
20 Day, letter to Joseph Zarella, July 14, 1938. Bellarmine.
21 Riegle Troester, 70–71.
22 Ibid.

community's child."[23] Joe took the responsibility seriously.

But it was Mary and Steve Johnson who gave Tamar the stability she didn't get from Dorothy's peripatetic existence. If Joe was her young uncle, the Johnsons were her New York grandparents. Steve Johnson worked under Bishop Fulton Sheen at the Society for the Propagation of the Faith, and Alice told me that had "independent means" and that they spent all they made on the Workers, often feeding Joe and Gerry a good Sunday dinner.[24]

As Alice describes the relationship, Mary and Dorothy were "great friends and loving enemies."[25] Mary was older than Dorothy and so felt free to tease her, using a rapier-sharp Irish wit. But when she was on the road, Dorothy would write how she missed going up with "her boys" to their apartment at the end of a long and hectic day.[26] They would relax with the Johnsons over for a coffee or a glass of wine, and it was there that Dorothy would let down her hair and tell stories about the early days and her conversion and talk about the books and ideas that influenced her. In a natural conversational way, she taught the young men what was important to her faith and as Joe says, they grew along with her.

You know, I love to tell the stories, and my book on Dorothy is full of them, but we have to be careful not to use only the parts of her which appeal to us, to make her what a member of the Haley House CW community in Boston once called informally "Dorothy as Anecdote." When we talk about her living in the same room with a woman of the streets, then in the next breath we need to talk about her being arrested with Cesar Chavez in efforts to unionize the farmworkers who sow and harvest that food. When we talk about her quoting the Dostoevsky story about "giving away an onion," we also have to talk about her strong writings against war.

In 1940, as the US was gearing up for entrance into World War II, Dorothy asked Joe to travel to Washington with her to testify for the acceptance of conscientious objector status for Roman Catholics. Despite the facts that the two of them were lay people and that the official church had only asked that clergy be exempt, they were successful, and the Catholic Worker was involved in two camps for Catholic CO's.[27] And in these early Zarrella years, the Catholic

---

23 Day, Letter to Joseph Zarella, June, 1940, Box 1-2. Bellarmine.

24 Joseph and Mary Alice Zarella: Riegle Troester transcripts, July 15, 1989, Series W-9.4, Box 9. Marquette.

25 Riegle Troester, 7.

26 Day, Letter to Joseph Zarella, Dec, 1939. Box 1-1. Bellarmine.

27 Riegle, 44. See also Gordon Zahn, *Another Part of the War: The Camp Simon Story* (Amherst, Massachusetts: University of Massachusetts Press, 1979).

Worker was very supportive of unions, even opening a soup kitchen at the docks when the seamen were on strike.

Dorothy's spirituality was all of a piece and the great struggle of her life was to join the practice of charity and the work for justice, so there was no paradox in her eyes between a traditional Catholic piety and militant nonviolent advocacy to "make a world where it's easier to be good."

What do we take away from this glimpse into the past? First, don't fret if, like Joe, some of your memories of earlier days are seen through rosy glasses. "Memory matters" and there's probably good reason for the tint. Second, if you're living comfortably in a CW house with heat and hot water, don't beat yourself over the head. (But don't, like Joe, resort to blowtorches to get rid of the reincarnated CW bedbugs—get them early, hopefully with a pro bono exterminator.) You may be living in voluntary simplicity instead of the poverty seen in the letters and oral histories of the original communities, but if you're doing it to raise families and to be sustainable for the long haul, Dorothy would bless you, I think. Thirdly, all of us, whether in Worker houses or not, need, like Joe and Alice Zarrella, to read and re-read and live in our own lives the wisdom of Dorothy's words—in her diaries, her letters, her books, and in her columns, all available in books and online. As her tombstone says, "Deo Gratias" for Dorothy Day.

Rosalie G. Riegle taught English at Saginaw Valley State University for 33 years, where she was honored with a Landee Teaching Award and a Rush Lectureship. The mother of four and grandmother of seven, she collected and edited four oral histories and co-founded two Catholic Worker houses of hospitality in Saginaw, Michigan. Her latest books are *Doing Time: Resistance, Family, and Community* (2012) and *Crossing the Line: Nonviolent Resisters Speak Out for Peace* (2013). Dr. Riegle lectures often on Dorothy Day, the Catholic Worker movement, and nonviolent direct action. She is on the National Committee of the War Resisters League.

Comrades Stumbling Along: The Friendship of Dorothy Day and Catherine de Hueck Doherty

Robert Wild

Introduction

Dorothy Day is of course well known to many of us here. But what of Catherine de Hueck Doherty?[1] Some present may not know much about Catherine, so let me begin by briefly introducing her. Then we shall focus on the remarkable similarities between these two women as seen through my analysis of their correspondence from which the title of my talk is drawn. In an undated letter Dorothy wrote to Catherine: "It is good to urge each other on to virtue, but remember, we are comrades stumbling along, not saints drifting along in ecstasies."

Catherine was a Russian émigré who opened what she called Friendship Houses in Toronto in the early 1930s to help those out of work due to the Great Depression. I knew Catherine from 1970 until her death in 1985. I never met Dorothy. The friendship between these two is one of the great untold stories of contemporary Catholic history. The causes of canonization for both are currently in progress; I am the postulator for Catherine's cause.

I believe the real person is very often revealed in her or his correspondence. When we are writing deep, personal letters to others we are not usually consciously editing anything. Thus, I will be quoting quite extensively from their letters because these are the most accurate primary sources for their relationship. I want you to hear *their own voices* instead of my commentary on their

---

1   *Comrades Stumbling Along: The Friendship of Catherine de Hueck Doherty and Dorothy Day as Revealed through Their Letters* (Staten Island, New York: Alba House, 2009). All the correspondence quoted in this article is from this book unless otherwise noted. Permission granted by Alba House for the use of this material.

friendship. Besides Catherine's letters I will also be using some of her diary entries.

But before I begin I want to clarify a certain fact. There is a general opinion that Dorothy inspired Catherine's original apostolate. This is not true. We shall see that Catherine was already involved in her apostolate several years before she heard about Dorothy through the very first issue of *The Catholic Worker* in 1933. It is *very true*, however, that Dorothy was Catherine's most life-long inspiration of any of her contemporaries.

Their First Contact

1933 was a significant year for the lay apostolate: Sheed and Ward opened their New York office; in May Dorothy and Peter Maurin published the first issue of the *The Catholic Worker*; and Catherine in Toronto was studying the papal social encyclicals and implementing them with her Houses of Friendship. As soon as Catherine had read the first issue of the *CW* she wrote Dorothy for copies. It was very moving for me the first time I read the following first exchange of letters between them.

> December 12, 1933
> Dear Miss Day,
> Your Catholic Worker came to me thru Rev. Fr. Stroeh of Toronto, where I work amongst the foreign born Canadians which is easy because I am Russian myself. There is nothing as yet that has aroused as much interest in my people as your paper. I am anxious to get it because it does so much good. It makes them realize that the Church is interested in the worker.
> Thank you for the splendid work you are doing.
> *Catherine de Hueck*

Dorothy responds the following week:

> December 19, 1933
> Dear Mrs. De Hueck:
> Your letter made us very happy and we are sending the paper as you suggested to the place you mentioned.
> The Archbishop [McNeil of Toronto] has already sent us his subscription and a very kind letter. If you can use more copies

to distribute among your friends, we will be very glad to send you a dozen.

Trusting that you will remember us in your prayers, and we need them especially for the House of Hospitality, I am, sincerely, *Dorothy Day*

Catherine and her associates used to pass *The Catholic Worker* out on street corners in Toronto and on the church steps after Mass on Sundays. The following are brief excerpts from longer letters to show their growing relationship. Catherine had sent Dorothy a description of her apostolic activities.

On March 19, 1934, Dorothy wrote:

I can't tell you how interesting I found your report. I am wondering if I cannot use parts of it. Indeed, the report as it stands could apply to New York, Chicago, or any big industrial town. If you are ever in New York, look us up. Sincerely.

And just three weeks later, April 11, 1934, Dorothy wrote:

Is there any chance of your coming to New York for a few days? Our belief is, you know, to start in little ways, and our small store is so humble that no one passing by on the street is afraid to come in. Beginnings must be made, and women being practical and never too optimistic, are the best ones to make these beginnings. Sincerely...,

On May 22, 1934, Dorothy wrote:

Thank you for your letters. They are very interesting. God bless you for your enthusiasm and for your work. We do indeed pray for your House of Friendship, and pray for us too. The main thing is never to get discouraged at the slowness of people or results. People may not be articulate, or active, but even so, we do not know ever the results, or the effect on souls. That is not for us to know. We can only go ahead and work with happiness at what God sends us to do. [And for the first time she signs:] With love, *Dorothy Day*

First Meeting

In August, 1934 Catherine attended a summer school of Catholic Action at the Catholic Summer Center in Stamford-in-the-Catskills, New York. Both Peter Maurin and Dorothy spoke there. In a post card to Catherine before the meeting (July 23) Dorothy wrote:

> I was dreading my visit to Stamford. I'm very shy about speaking, but now that you are there I look forward to it. I shall count on an extra day there to be with you. Your news is splendid—you can tell me a great deal and help me much.
>   Love, *D. Day*

In her diary for August 10, 1934, Catherine wrote: "O Jesus, I am happy today—I thank you for having allowed me to meet Dorothy Day. Bless her and keep her, and bless thy priesthood."

And after leaving this conference where they must have spent several days together talking, swapping apostolic notes, and getting to know one another, Dorothy wrote (August 14, 1934):

> Just a hasty note to thank you for your kindness and to remind you that I am offering up the mass tomorrow for you. I feel so rested and refreshed after my visit. Love, *Dorothy*

After this initial contact, Dorothy came to Toronto on several occasions. From Catherine's diary, February 12, 1935: "Dorothy Day arrived at 12:30. It was lovely to see her again. She has such a wonderful spirit."

Besides their correspondence, we are fortunate to have several early eye-witness accounts, and an important one from our good friend Stanley Vishnewski. He was one of Dorothy's earliest and most faithful followers. He had a love for both Friendship House in the '30s and '40s, and Madonna House in Combermere, Ontario after 1947. He visited Combermere several times. I had the good fortune to have met him. He published a book entitled *The Wings of the Dawn*. Chapter 11, about Friendship House, is significantly called "Sister Movement" in relationship to the Catholic Worker. In the following passage he is talking about the time after the visit of Dorothy (1935) to Toronto:

A few weeks later, the Baroness[2] came to pay us a visit. Dorothy and the Baroness sat around the round table in the privacy of the kitchen. They talked at length about the work they were both doing. The Baroness told Dorothy of the opposition that was being raised against her in Toronto. "I've been accused of being a Communist. I don't know how long I will be able to continue the work." Dorothy tried to console her by telling her of the many slanderous attacks she had suffered since starting the Catholic Worker.

The closing of Friendship House in Toronto was very devastating to Catherine. Besides the rumors of her being a Communist, the local clergy could not comprehend how a woman—and a Russian refugee at that—could be starting a quasi-religious community. And the new archbishop was not so much against Catherine as he didn't really know her. He set up a committee to investigate her situation. They decided against the continuance of her apostolate. It was during this trial, more than at any other time in their relationship, that Dorothy's friendship, support, and love was lavished upon Catherine. In one of her most significant and beautiful letters, Dorothy wrote:

> Written with a million interruptions   c. Nov. 1936
> Dear Catherine,
>
>   Got your last two letters and cannot really make head or tail of the whole thing. If they are closing Friendship House, it is really disastrous. I thought they were only taking them away from you and handing them over to an Order to run. That is bad enough of course, but it is the kind of thing which is always happening in the history of works such as ours. I'm always expecting I'll be asked to leave the work for the good of the cause, and I'm more or less prepared for it. All the kind of gossip and rumors that have gone around about you, have gone around about me too these last years. I'm supposed to be an immoral woman, with illegitimate children, a drunkard, a racketeer, running an expensive apartment on the side, with money in several banks, owning property, in the pay of Moscow, etc. etc.

---

2   This was a nickname for Catherine derived from the fact that her family were minor nobility in pre-revolutionary Russia.

I should think you would feel privileged and happy to be sharing in some of our Lord's sufferings, and above all not surprised as though it were something entirely unexpected. What in the world do you expect? The very fact that there is all this obstruction and hindrance and trouble shows the work must be succeeding beyond your wildest hopes; otherwise the devil would not be putting so many hindrances in the way and trying to break down your morale. For that is surely what is being done.

When you write in such terms as "I have fallen a hundred times to our Lord's three," I wonder at you. I wish to goodness I were up there to talk to you. You will think I am cold and unsympathetic, but really, darling, I am not at all. I have been thinking of you constantly for the past week.

What I am wondering about is why you are fleeing. I should think you would hold your head up through it all, and if you are deprived of any work to do, abandon yourself completely to divine providence, try to keep to ordinary routine as much as possible and leave things in God's hands to work out. If you are deprived completely of a means of earning a living and have no money for rent or food, I would quite simply throw myself on their charity; in your humility be a charge to them, instead of a person who has been taking a charge off the shoulders of others. But I would not flee from the scene of strife and persecution. I'd stay right there and face them out. Besides, you are making a decision right in the heat of things which is never good.

I purposely make this letter frank and sane as possible, because you are in such a state of mind. But at the same time, if you do not believe you have our love and sympathy, you are lacking in faith in us. We most truly believe though, that the devil makes all this hullabaloo just when work is accomplishing the most good, so for that you should be most happy.

Much, much love. *Dorothy*

After the decision to dissolve Friendship House, Fr. Carr, Catherine's spiritual director, suggested she go to visit Dorothy. Catherine wrote of her arrival in New York in our *History of the Apostolate:*

I was deeply moved, therefore, when she met me at Grand
Central Station and indulged in the luxury of a taxi fare from
there to Mott Street where the Catholic Worker was then located. She and Peter Maurin and all the staff brought tears
to my eyes by singing to me the Church's "Hymn of Confes-
sors"—those who have suffered greatly for the Faith but were
not martyred for it. They made my stay so pleasant, in a spiritual and friendly way that I began to take on a new life.

The next prolonged and intense period of their friendship was when,
through the efforts of Fr. Paul of Graymoor and Fr. John LaFarge, S.J., Catherine agreed to open a Friendship House in Harlem. Sometime in late January,
1938, she took a train to New York City. She spent several weeks at the Catholic
Worker before she rented an apartment at 138th Street and began her apostolate
to African Americans. Although their apostolates were distinct, there were frequent visits and relations between Catherine, Dorothy, and those who worked
with them.

Again, Stanley put it this way: "In those early days Friendship House and
the Catholic Worker were considered by many to be Sister Movements engaged
in the Apostolate. Catherine and Dorothy would meet once a week at the Child's
restaurant in the mid-town area for lunch to discuss the various problems of
their respective apostolates." Catherine wrote about one of these visits with
Dorothy in her diary of May 3, 1939:

> Went to Child's. Had a lovely visit with her. Always consider
> her wonderful, more convinced than ever that she is a saint.
> What a joy it is to be with her. She shines with an inward light
> that no one can suppress. Her difficulties are as mine—mostly
> with the human beings and their blindness and self-love—and
> their ability to put second things first.

Child's was a little bit of heaven for Catherine, one of those enchanted
places to which you always want to return with a great nostalgia. In February 10,
1942, she wrote to Dorothy:

> Dear D.D.: It is a long time since I have written to you or seen
> you. But daily, in fact, several times a day, I have talked to the
> Lord about you in my own funny way, and I have found you

and in His heart too, and I know that you have been praying for me.

Nothing has changed since the first day I have met you. You mean just as much to me now as you did then, and I need you and your wonderful example and friendship and advice now, just as much as I did then. Will you in your great charity give me a little bit of it now?

Could we meet and have lunch at Scraffts or Child's some day soon. After this Friday I shall be at my desk at F.H. Write to me or call me up and let us meet soon.

Dorothy also looked back with nostalgia at those early intimate meetings. In a letter in the early 1940s, she wrote to Catherine:

I want to be seeing you soon. Can't we run off by our selves, meet half way the way my sister and I do, so we will both be free of our respective families for a few hours? You know, I often think with joy of that first visit we had together in that nice large apartment of yours in Toronto. We really had time to talk, and space to talk in. You and I need a lot of space and when we get to heaven we'll put in our bid for mansions where we can stretch. I always think of you with love and sympathy in that one room filled with books and people, bulging with talk. Not enough room. God bless you and pray for me. *Dorothy*

And on the occasion of Dorothy's death, Catherine's thoughts again went to those precious intimate moments they shared together:

When I moved to Harlem, New York, Dorothy Day and I became even closer. There was only about five miles between her house and my Harlem House. So occasionally, when we both had enough money, let's say about a dollar, we would go to Child's (a popular restaurant in America at the time), where you could get three coffee refills; and we used to enjoy each cup and just talk. Talk about God. Talk about the apostolate. Talk about all the things that were dear to our hearts.

But—between you and me—we were both very lonely because, believe it or not, there was just the two of us in all of

Canada and America, and we did feel lonely and no question about it. Periodically we would have a good cry in our coffee cups. We really cried, I mean honest, big tears. We would sit there, and the waitress would look at us. Dorothy and I would hold hands, and we would cry. We had had it! But we would always rally; and I think rallying is a sign of perseverance. [3]

As you know Dorothy entitled her autobiography, *The Long Loneliness*. And, at the heart of Catherine's spirituality was her desire to assuage the loneliness of Christ. I think one of their strong bonds was their loneliness, caused by their being pioneers in an area of Catholic life that was little understood or appreciated, even in the Church. They met in the loneliness of Christ.

What follows is the most beautiful and touching letter Catherine ever wrote to Dorothy. It wasn't easy to influence Catherine! But I would say that Dorothy was Catherine's greatest example and inspiration for her apostolate. And the following letter confirms this for me. In 1945 Catherine is living in Chicago with her new husband, Eddie Doherty. She was not sure of her next step, so it is a time of reflection on the past in order to get some insights for the future.

November 26, 1945

Dear DD,

It has been now over a month that a great desire to write to you has come to my heart. I have been making, as you know, "pilgrimages" into my distant and not so distant yesterdays, stopping now here, now there, to render thanks to the Lord of Life, for this special grace or that, for this wonderful gift or sorrow, and for that infinite moment of joy. Short as my life is, as any human life is, there are, strange to say, many a shrine in it before which, as is the custom of my people, I can bow low from the waist, touching the earth with my hands, and singing alleluias in my heart for each.

For in the clarity of the past, the terrible awesome clarity that is shed on the past, I should say, all things have indeed woven themselves into a rosary of all three mysteries, the sorrowful, the glorious, the joyful, and together they seem now to

---

3   *Restoration*, February 1981.

become the steps that will maybe lead my poor soul, my sinful soul, to the Lord of Mercy.

Amongst the memories of my yesterdays is a shrine that I reached into today, at which, in a manner of speaking, I still worship. Long ago and far away I arose in search of the Lord, for there was a mighty hunger in my soul for him. Only I was confused by the many roads and cross roads that stretched out before me in a maze that bewildered me. When suddenly, out of nowhere, you came, and hand in hand we walked together. You knew the way out of the maze, you most certainly did.

And as we were walking along the road one eventide—or was it many?—a Stranger joined us, a strange Stranger who spoke beautifully and convincingly about the Lord. We went to sup with him, and in the breaking of the bread we knew him as Christ the Lord. At times it seems to me that the road was just your soul, and at other times it comes to me that it was your words that brought the Stranger to our side. He materialized, as it were, out of them, at least for me. He spoke, if I remember correctly, across the divide of years with your voice. One thing I know is that we both "knew him at the breaking of the bread." Was it in the little strange Church full of Italians where we both went to Communion, and after which we had that enormous breakfast in some beanery on Canal St., during which it seemed the Lord was still with us?

I have never forgotten these far away days, DD, when you and I and a few others, started on the lonely hard road of the Lay Apostolate. We were very young then, and so full of zeal and hunger and love. Praise be to the Lord that none of these virtues have left us—except "youth." But as I make my strange pilgrimages into my yesterdays, both distant and near, I find myself sorrowful, that you and I do not exchange the speech of men, while we are still in the land of men. For a friendship like ours, me-thinks, is a great and holy gift of God. And though you and I know that we are very close in prayer and meet daily at his Table, nevertheless, I think we should renew that inner closeness, and express it again, as it were, in the halting simple words of human love and understanding.

Dorothy's Continued Interest in Catherine's Apostolate

In February–March, 1961, Dorothy spent several weeks at our house in Balmor-hea, Texas. She wrote to Catherine during her visit:

> Dearest Catherine, enjoying your hospitality this last week, and hope I can stay until Monday, almost another week. It has been a taste of heaven being here, a real oasis, not only on this particular physical journey, but on my journey through life. It has been a retreat, in a way, and I am grateful for it, and grateful for you and all you mean to me and to so many people.
>
> Reading Restoration for so long, and getting Stanley's awed reports each time he has made a visit, I have of course kept up with the growth of your Secular Institute.[4] And now that I have seen it truly in action, with priest and team, I can appreciate better the truly magnificent work you have done.

Catherine responds (March 6, 1961):

> I was so happy to get your long letter. You and I don`t correspond often. Perhaps there is no need to write for people who really love one another as deeply as we do in the Lord. But I confess that my heart rejoiceth when I get a letter from you. For I never forget that we were "pioneers together," and that you stood by me like the rock of Gibraltar when I needed you. God bless you.

Another example of Dorothy's continued interest in Catherine's apostolate and, you might say, their mutual influence on one another, was Dorothy's interest in Catherine's classic book *Poustinia*. It came out in early 1975, and in the *Worker* for May, 1975, Dorothy wrote:

> Marge [Hughes] is packing up to go to West Virginia, but finding a place to plant the garden in the little yard of one of the two small houses which we have named St. John of the Cross, and St. Teresa of Avila. They are the nearest thing we have for

---

4   At the time Madonna House was not a Secular Institute but was seeking such status.

our young volunteers to use a *Poustinia*, which Catherine de Hueck Doherty of Combermere, Canada, has introduced us to through her book by that name, published by Ave Maria Press. Most of the winter I have lived in one and Marge Hughes in the other with her son John.

Dorothy wrote a blurb for the cover of Catherine's book *Poustinia*: "Catherine de Hueck Doherty has the gift of a great and joyous faith and of making life an adventure, a pilgrimage. Her book shows us a new way of growing in the spiritual life. I'm delighted!"

Dorothy's last note to Catherine came on January 31, 1978:

> Dearest Catherine:
> I am swamped with visitors and can't concentrate to write. We have a full house here at all times. Yet I would shrink at the idea of a "poustinia." How contrary we humans are! I send my love. I have a little box of polished stones (from Minnesota) and always think of your dear husband when I met him in Arizona. [Where we had another house.] Excuse this scrawl. Much love to you, in our dear Love, *Dorothy*

The Last Visit

In November, 1978, Catherine went with one of our Madonna House priests, Fr. Emile Briere, to visit Dorothy for the last time. She was living at Mary House on 55 E. 3rd St. A few days before their visit Dorothy had celebrated her 81st birthday. Here are some of Catherine's most beautiful reflections about Dorothy recorded after this meeting.

> Well, this was quite a red letter day as far as I was concerned. It was the fact that I met Dorothy Day. She had her 81st birthday. She looks so thin, so thin. Life is sort of ebbing out of her. Only her eyes are still sparkly. For me this was a red-letter day. To me there was really nobody there, only Dorothy. I looked at her, and I sort of took her in with my whole heart, my mind, my eyes, my body, my everything. And I said to myself, "Catherine, you are meeting a saint. Don't you ever forget it, the saint of New York."

But I must admit that, as far as one thing is concerned, I sat in front of a saint. And I looked at this saint and I know what a saint is like. Dorothy is saint. So I felt good about that part of it, but I must admit that I felt sad, sad, sad that I don't measure up to any of what she does. But then, maybe the Lord will have mercy on my soul.

Catherine's Reflections in Restoration upon Dorothy's Death

Dorothy's death, five years before Catherine's, provoked the latter to reminisce upon the former in the newspaper of Madonna House:

> One day, in front of our door on Portland Street in Toronto, stood a Red Cross ambulance. Out of the ambulance came Dorothy Day and quite a few of the Catholic Workers. They had acquired an ambulance cheap and forgot to remove the Red Cross sign. Eventually they did paint over it, but it startled us the first day.
>
> Yes, we were friends, Dorothy and I. I rejoice that she is with God, for if anybody has had a glorious welcome in heaven, Dorothy Day is one. I am sure that the Trinity and Our Lady, the saints—all of them, and the angels—were there to greet her.
>
> Everything I read about her after her death stressed that she was a pacifist, that she was a social action person, and that she was outstanding in protecting the rights of the workers, and so on. I saw in her an unbounded charity that had no limits, unless it was the sky. I saw her go to jail if she felt jail was the right place to right an injustice. I saw her believing, believing with her whole heart, that everyone that came to the Catholic Worker was Christ, and that here there were no exception. That is the Dorothy Day I know. What I remember is pure sanctity.
>
> Of course, I leave it to the Church to decide. But I am a woman, and when I have known a person since 1933–34 and up to this day, I know that what I saw is the gospel lived out without compromise. If that isn't sanctity, then I don't know what is.

Final Thoughts

In my capacity as postulator of Catherine's cause, I continue to delve more deeply into their relationship, and in doing so I am struck by the fact that if Catherine and Dorothy hadn't been so united in Christ in the lay apostolic movement, and in zeal for the kingdom of God, most probably their differences of character, background, and approach to life would not have drawn them together in any kind of friendship. Their friendship is a profound example of how Christ can draw and bind together, in love, people of very diverse temperaments and backgrounds, and unite them by the power of his Holy Spirit.

The friendships of the saints during their lifetimes is also a special work of the Holy Spirit. Such relationships show us how to help one another along the path of holiness. Are we not all called to help one another become saints? The friendship of Catherine and Dorothy was deep, holy, and lasting, and can inspire us to cultivate similar friendships in our own lives.

These two great women were raised up by the Holy Spirit at the same historical moment in the Church of North America. They were almost mirror images of one another. Their apostolates covered roughly the same historical period, from 1930–1980, they were both totally loyal Catholics, serving the poor, conditioned by the great depression, women of prayer, dedicated to the Church, founders of movements that continue to this day.

As the two outstanding pioneers in the Catholic lay movement, they are increasingly being recognized side by side in the history books: "Two women who manifested strong leadership and Christian compassion after the Great War were Catherine de Hueck in Canada and Dorothy Day in the United States. Both were charismatic women exercising the ministry of the church."[5]

Richard John Neuhaus, of blessed memory, links their names and apostolates in this way: "Both Dorothy and Catherine understood that orthodox Christianity is ever so much more radical than the radicalisms that the world regularly throws up to challenge or recruit Christian faith; and they understood that the way of high adventure is not to trim the Church's teaching but to penetrate ever more deeply into living the mystery of Christ."[6]

---

5 Terence J. Fay, S.J., *A History of Canadian Catholics* (Montreal and Kingston: McGill-Queen's University Press, 2002), 212.

6 *First Things*, December, 2000.

Fr. Bob Wild was ordained in the Diocese of Buffalo, New York in 1967, and since 1971 has been a member of the Madonna House community founded by Catherine de Hueck Doherty. She died in 1985 so he knew her personally since his joining the community. He has edited a number of her books and has written several himself on her spirituality. In 1990 he was appointed postulator for her cause. Presently he is one of the Guest Masters at the Madonna House retreat center for clergy, where he continues to write, do spiritual direction, and continue his research on Catherine's life. One of his main apostolic activities is giving retreats for priests in both Canada and the US.

Hollywood's Underbelly: Friendship House and the Catholic Worker as Catholic Critique of Unfettered Capitalism

Leigh Miller

In the early twentieth century, two young Catholic women opened store-fronts as houses of hospitality in some of the poorest neighborhoods of the United States and Canada. One, the Catholic Worker house, was opened by Dorothy Day in New York in 1933. The other, Friendship House, was opened in the early 1930s by Catherine de Hueck (later to become Catherine De Hueck Doherty) in Toronto, with a second opening in Harlem in 1938. Upon Doherty's reading of the Catholic Worker paper, she and Day became correspondents and friends. The almost simultaneous appearance of such similar movements—lay-led Catholic houses of hospitality in the poorest urban neighborhoods—inde-pendently and at the same time is remarkable. Though the women's personali-ties and charisms differentiated the houses in many respects, the commonalities of the apostolates of these two contemporaries are striking. Indeed, their shared vocation to live among and in solidarity with the poor in light of Catholic Social Teachings shows that the establishment of Doherty and Day's houses of hospi-tality was no coincidence at all. As I will argue in this paper, the writings of Day and Doherty—as well as those of their contemporaries and sometime coworkers Thomas Merton and Peter Maurin—reveal that Catholic houses of hospitality represent the active Catholic response to poverty in its fullest form.

Catholic Social Teaching, inaugurated by Pope Leo XIII's *Rerum Novarum* in 1893, names a collection of Catholic magisterial teachings attempting to re-spond to the social and political upheavals across Europe and North America caused by industrialized capitalism in the late-nineteenth and early-twenti-

313

eth centuries. Day and Doherty interpreted Catholic Social Teaching as rejecting both communism and capitalism as solutions to the problems of widespread urban poverty. Moreover, for Day and Doherty, their opposition was not primarily based on the inability of either system to provide adequate material prosperity (though both failed to do so), but on the vices bred by the dependence of both capitalism and communism on the over-systemization inherent in industrialism and large government. Christianity, in following Christ, is not against poverty *in and of itself.* In fact, the Church (and therefore Day and Doherty) were for poverty, properly understood. What they were against is any destitution unworthy of human beings, the social isolation bred by an obsessive search for material prosperity, and the vices that these tend to engender in desperate people.

It is notable that Day and Doherty chose not to embrace mainstream charitable or philanthropic attempts to assist the poor in becoming successful within the capitalist system, precisely because they believed this approach was good neither for the poor nor for themselves. The path proposed by hospitality houses rejects all attempts to make the poor successful, and thus rich. Rather than trying to achieve comfort and power for the urban poor through the systemic—and thus depersonalized—means employed by both communism and capitalism, hospitality houses depend upon personal relationships with the poor directed toward the common good, and embrace the Christian demand for personal holiness and sacrifice. To deal with poverty otherwise, or to think primarily that poverty in itself is something to be "dealt with" or "solved" in the first place, would seem to involve a perversion of Catholic teaching and its call to personal holiness.

At first glance, Day and Doherty seemed perfect candidates for the Communist movements of their day. The Communists, as both Day and Merton saw, appeared to be the only group identifying with "the transient and unemployed throughout the country,"[1] often by "performing some of the works of mercy that Christians should be expected to do."[2] In the process, the Communists gained a sizable following among the urban poor where Day and Doherty's houses of hospitality were located.[3] As they looked for a way to (in Day's words) "win justice for the poor,"[4] both Doherty and Day frequently found themselves accused of belonging to (or at least sympathizing with) the Communists, who

1   Dorothy Day, *House of Hospitality* (Huntington, Indiana: Our Sunday Visitor, 2015), 60.
2   Thomas Merton, *The Seven Storey Mountain* (Orlando, Florida: Harcourt Brace, 1998), 324.
3   Ibid., 374.
4   Ibid., 373.

also saw the "rotten, decadent, putrid industrial capitalist system" as responsible for the proliferation of a poor urban underclass.[5]

Yet, neither Doherty nor Day could align themselves with the Communists, however natural a partnership may have seemed from the outside. Both had, from different ways, emerged from Communist worlds. Dorothy had briefly been a Communist herself during college, and later commented: "If I could have felt that communism was the answer to my desire for a cause, a motive, a way to walk in, I would have remained as I was."[6] Doherty had been a bourgeois during the Communist revolution in Russia; she was exiled as a young woman after seeing the Soviet revolutionaries kill much of her family.[7] But as Catholics, Day and Doherty knew Communist ideology to be incompatible with their faith, summed up by the fact that "the Communist revolution aims, among other things, at wiping out the church."[8] However attractive its work made it to the poor, both women were repelled by the Communist demand for violent revolution, which reduced the poor to parts of the unidentifiable "mass" rather than recognizing them as brothers and sisters for whom Christ died. In response to this, Day and Doherty saw their mission among the poor to include—through their schools or round-table discussions or pamphleteering—introducing man "to the encyclical and [trying] to take away the stones he held in his hands, given him by the followers of anti-Christ," the Communists.[9]

Both women recognized that an essential part of their witness was to embody an alternative to Communism. Indeed, the popular appeal of Communism often served as a motivator for their own efforts. Reflecting on Doherty's Friendship House in Harlem, Thomas Merton wrote "that Communism would make very little progress in the world, or none at all, if Catholics really lived up to their obligations...: that is, if they really loved one another, and saw Christ in one another, and lived as saints, and did something to win justice for the poor."[10] Day saw how the Communists' commitment to "their world mission

---

5   Dorothy Day, "On Pilgrimage—September 1956," *The Catholic Worker*, September 1956, 6–7, http://www.catholicworker.org/dorothyday/articles/710.html (accessed July 26, 2015). As cited in Brian Terrell, "Dorothy Day's 'Filthy, Rotten System' Likely Wasn't Hers at All," *National Catholic Reporter*, April 16, 2012, http://ncronline.org/news/people/dorothy-days-filthy-rotten-system-likely-wasnt-hers-all (accessed July 25, 2015).

6   Dorothy Day, *The Long Loneliness* (New York: Harper and Row, 1952), 141.

7   Madonna House Apostolate, "Her Life," Catherine Doherty, www.catherinedoherty.org/life/ (accessed July 26, 2015).

8   Merton, *Seven Storey Mountain*, 373.

9   Catherine de Hueck Doherty, *Friendship House* (New York: Sheed and Ward, 1946), 28.

10   Merton, *Seven Storey Mountain*, 373.

[despite] any hardship that is entailed" served as a challenge to "arouse Catholics to such zeal" for the poor.[11] In Doherty's words, "Friendship House and the Catholic Worker... exist primarily to awaken people—Roman Catholics at that—to their obligations, by assuming, in a spectacular manner, the corporal and spiritual works of mercy; and using all the means of propaganda papers, lecture platforms, writing, and above all, living, to bring forth these forgotten fundamental truths."[12] One of the fundamental truths that the modern world has forgotten, Day argued, is that men have a "sense of their own dignity, that dignity which they possess because Christ shared their humanity, their unemployment, their dire need."[13] This recognition of personal dignity can only be accomplished by performing the works of mercy, since it is only through personal, sacrificial relationships (rather than the depersonalized systemic revolutions) that man comes to understand the truth about Christ's sacrificial love.

Catholic houses of hospitality obviously could not support Communism, but neither could they accept the capitalist society of the United States. The noblest goal of the capitalist society is to make the poor rich; Day and Doherty wanted rich and poor alike to become holy. It is often overlooked that the establishment of houses of hospitality, with their focus on personal relationships at a personal sacrifice, indicates that a Catholic response to the poor was not to be found in tweaking the foundations of a capitalist economy. Such an approach would simply mean adapting the poor to be more successful at accumulating wealth, with the dream, perhaps, of making the whole system more amenable to such accumulation for all who followed into its principles.

Along with the Communists, Day and Doherty knew the urban poverty they encountered to be a *necessary* part, indeed the underbelly of, an unfettered, industrialized capitalism. Putting hope in the ability of the capitalist system eventually to eliminate a poor working class deprived of the means of self-sustenance ignored the basic foundations of pure capitalism itself. Both women, like Merton after them, understood the poverty of their day to be a mirror of the sins and ills inherent in the capitalist system, a stance that often had both women accused of being Communists themselves. The creation of hospitality houses where people could learn an alternative way of living with one another was their

11 Day, *Long Loneliness*, 212.

12 "Catherine de Hueck to Thomas Merton, October 14, 1941," in Thomas Merton and Catherine de Hueck Doherty, *Compassionate Fire: The Letters of Thomas Merton and Catherine de Hueck Doherty*, ed. Robert A. Wild (Notre Dame, Indiana: Ave Maria, 2009), 10.

13 Dorothy Day, "Houses of Hospitality," in *Dorothy Day: Writings from Commonweal*, ed. Patrick Jordan (Collegeville, Minnesota: Liturgical Press, 2002), 59–60.

primary response to systematic social ills. Both communism and capitalism created moral and material destitution amongst its followers that could be upended only first by changing people rather than systems.[14]

The first aspect of capitalism—recognized by Day and Doherty to be inseparable from urban poverty—is in its creation of and dependence on an economically dependent, low-income, wage-earning class. By the time she wrote *The Long Loneliness*, Day knew of Hilaire Belloc (1870–1953) and his writing on "the Servile State," or "the Welfare State," as Peter Maurin referred to it.[15] Belloc describes in his book *The Servile State* the distinction between the poor (particularly the rural poor) before the advent of industrialism, who have a lack of liquid funds but have ownership of the means of production, and those with whom Day and Doherty worked, who were deprived of the means of production and thus reduced to a sort of wage slavery.[16] The nature of a capitalist system requires a class of people who own the capital and another class whose role in the system is simply to operate the capital at wages determined by the owners. Without access to the means, and often even the skills, to provide for one's own basic needs, the poorest class was at the mercy of those able to provide money in return for whatever labor was available, creating what Belloc could call wage slaves.[17]

The distinction between owners and wage-earners is exacerbated even more by the goals encouraged by capitalism. Unfettered capitalism, by encouraging a capital-owning class, assumes that a man will come to interpret his "riches as his own property" rather than as "the common good."[18] In this case, it is not only unsurprising, but—as Catholics will continue to argue even today with Pope Francis—perhaps unavoidable that the owners of capital will make attempts to pay laborers at *the lowest price* they can in order to achieve the highest profit. No other goal is encouraged by capitalism than the continued acquisition of goods and wealth. With the advent of industrialism in particular, man was increasingly able to be replaced either by machines or by more desperate men willing to work an "unskilled" position for less money. It was particularly in the poor neighborhoods of New York that the destitution of those who had no goods and

---

14   Dorothy Day and Francis J. Sicius, *Peter Maurin: Apostle to the World* (New York: Orbis, 2004), 106.

15   Day, *Long Loneliness*, 222.

16   Hilaire Belloc, *The Servile State* (New York: Henry Holt and Co., 1946), 14.

17   Ibid., 88.

18   Dorothy Day, "Distributism Versus Capitalism," *The Catholic Worker*, October 1954, 1, 6, http://www.catholicworker.org/dorothyday/articles/175.html (accessed July 26, 2015).

could often sell not even their labor was a condition encouraged by, and even required by, industrial growth and competition. In Day's words, while "wheels turned and engines throbbed and the great pulse of the mechanical and physical world beat strong" it was "men's pulses [that] sickened and grew weaker and died. Man fed himself into the machine."[19]

Those reduced to this form of industrial poverty could only dream of a life in the upper class of the capitalist system. But even if the achievement of such material comfort were available to all, the central problem of the capitalist system—at least from a Catholic point of view—would remain. What Day and Doherty found was that industrial capitalism's unavoidable emphasis on personal ownership, acquisition of goods, and competition for low prices required and fomented a set of concomitant vices. Those who found themselves "successful" in the capitalist system inevitably had to embrace another set of values, placing the good of personal acquisition, and thus the good of their own comfort, above all other goods. If one's material comfort were not first and foremost, the aim of growing business, making a profit and thus expanding capital became nonsensical. Thus, hand in hand with the personal acquisition of capital that capitalism encouraged, were the concomitant vices these goals required. Moreover, the vices encouraged by unfettered capitalism were found not only amongst the bourgeois and upwardly mobile, but were woven into the moral fabric of society such that the values (or, rather, vices) of capitalism were taught to the poor themselves.

One of the most powerful descriptions of the urban poverty in which Day and Doherty lived was given by their mutual friend, Thomas Merton. Writing as an outsider, Merton condenses into a few pages a searing theological assessment of life in Harlem. His description of Harlem in the 1930s still describes the poorest parts of many cities in the United States today. Merton identifies in Harlem, almost entirely populated by blacks at the time, the reduction of the poor to Belloc's wage slavery, describing it as a place where people "are herded together like cattle, most of them with nothing to eat and nothing to do."[20] At a time when racial prejudice is at its most obvious, the residents seem to be "bound inward by an iron ring of frustration: the prejudice that hems them in with its four insurmountable walls."[21] He observes the open practice of lust in Harlem's brothels, rampant prostitution, and the drunkenness and dope-rings that riddle the

---

19   Day, *Long Loneliness*, 171.

20   Merton, *Seven Storey Mountain*, 378.

21   Ibid., 378.

place. [22] Such observations mirror Day's own description of the vices she saw endemic amongst the poor, who became "drunken, drug-ridden, vicious and obscene in many cases" as they found themselves unable to cope with the suffering of the poverty forced upon them in another way. [23]

Since Doherty's Friendship House frequently worked with the children of the neighborhood, the children's experiences captured both her own and Merton's attention. Merton describes the children in Harlem, the "Magnifying Mirror" [24] of the place, to be "crowded together like sardines in the rooms of tenements full of vice, where evil takes place hourly and inescapably before their eyes, so that there is not an excess of passion, not a perversion of natural appetite with which they are not familiar before the age of six or seven." [25] The main activity of the children, who almost never know a "clean, wholesome home," is "to survive amidst the filth and immorality of Harlem... [where] evil is their constant companion." [26] It is no wonder, then, that children who know all of these horrors by age seven grow up to be "devoured, in [the] dark furnace [of] Harlem, by marihuana, by gin, by insanity, hysteria, syphilis." [27]

These descriptions are not merely sensationalist or, worse, classist or racist in their portrayal of poor urban neighborhoods like Harlem. Rather than intending to disparage Harlem, they offered it as a more obvious manifestation of the vices passed down from the "whited sepulcher of New York." [28] In particular, Merton considers Harlem an indictment of the rich downtown that is the only thing the industrialized capitalist city "offers in the way of an ideal" to the poor of Harlem. [29] In describing Harlem, Merton realizes the

> terrifying paradox of the whole thing: Harlem itself, and every individual Negro in it, is a living condemnation of our so-called 'culture.' Harlem is there by way in divine indictment against New York City and the people who live downtown and

22 Ibid., 378–9.

23 Day, "Houses of Hospitality," 60.

24 Merton, Seven *Storey Mountain*, 379.

25 "Thomas Merton to Catherine de Hueck, December 6, 1941," in Merton and Doherty, *Compassionate Fire*, 6.

26 Ibid., 6–7.

27 Merton, *Seven Storey Mountain*, 378.

28 Day, "On Pilgrimage—September 1956," 7. As cited in Terrell, "Dorothy Day's 'Filthy, Rotten System' Likely Wasn't Hers at All."

29 Merton, *Seven Storey Mountain*, 378.

make their money downtown. The brothels of Harlem ... and all the rest are a mirror of the polite divorces and the manifold cultured adulteries of Park Avenue: they are God's commentary on the whole of our society.[30]

Indeed, Merton continues, Harlem, full as it is with obvious vice and suffering, "is, in a sense, what God thinks of Hollywood," precisely because "Hollywood is all Harlem has, in its despair, to grasp at, by way of a surrogate for heaven"[31] The capitalist system not only assumes a materially poor underclass, to be used or discarded according to the demands of the economy, but by offering the prosperity of the capital-holding class as the only alternative, inevitably incentivizes the poor to disregard the virtues that capitalism itself sees as irrelevant or disposable.

Because capitalism foments both poverty and vice, aiming to make the poor man rich in such a world is an untenable option for the Catholic. To possess whatever it is that "passes for culture in the world of the white people" as the only alternative to the poverty of Harlem is hardly more than a "dubious privilege"; to aspire to the world of the white people is a "sorry task" as it is only the same, though more secretive and hidden, of a life as that which "is preached from the housetops of Harlem."[32] Among the gods of the modern man, Doherty writes, "the first child of the bourgeois spirit" is man himself, and thus his own "COMFORT."[33] This bourgeois spirit (the term is taken from the Russian philosopher Nicholas Berdyaev) has left both the Harlems and the Hollywoods of the world as a "'man-made hell' ... a surrealistic desert in which modern man lives in company of dead, twisted trees of his sick imagination."[34] The only difference between the rich and the poor in such a world is that the one with money may find an escape "from his misery [... in] tranquilizers and endless sessions ... with psychiatrists," while the poor find his escapes in illegal outlets. Merton attests that "the white man's culture," then "is not worth the jetsam in the Harlem River,"[35] while Doherty goes so far as to say that, because of its deceptive appearance, the alternative of bourgeois modern urban or suburban life was actu-

---

30 Ibid., 379.
31 Ibid.
32 Ibid., 378–9.
33 "de Hueck to Merton, October 15," in Merton and Doherty, *Compassionate Fire*, 16.
34 "Catherine de Hueck Doherty to Thomas Merton, March 17, 1962," in Merton and Doherty, *Compassionate Fire*, 60.
35 Merton, *Seven Storey Mountain*, 379.

ally "more tragic, more hellish" than the slums which they encountered in their work.[36]

Upon reflection, this indictment of modern culture by those who found the opening of hospitality houses as the most appropriate Catholic charity for the poor man should not be surprising. In fact, by electing to establish houses of hospitality rather than create agencies or programs for upward mobility in the system that exists, Day and Doherty already indicated a Christian hope in the conversion of hearts, rather than a hope in powers and principalities. In fact, given the state's involvement in the capitalistic culture, the giving of the poor man over to the care of the state was, at best, a "dubious hospitality."[37] The state is ill equipped to do any good other than, at best, sustaining the physical lives of its constituents and, more likely, accommodating the poor in ways only that fit its own system, with no concern for the other, more important parts of the human being. This meant the state was only able to offer a version of flourishing—i.e., material comfort—that was already revealed "in all its horror … as it is seen in the eyes of God" in the slums the poor were seeking to escape.[38]

Seeing traditional philanthropy's utter inability to address the vices bred by industrialized capitalism, Day indicts public welfare: in its "care for the poor, [it does] nothing to give man the power to control his baser nature," thereby keeping man in the same hole of spiritual misery and brokenness.[39] Thus, in standing against Communism, Catherine and Dorothy's apostolates found themselves required to stand equally against the unfettered capitalism that fueled much of the urban poverty that then birthed Communism (capitalism's "son," according to Peter Maurin).[40] Given the state's complicity in the goals of capitalism, both Day and Doherty found in the living out of the Christian works of mercy an answer to the poverty and misery they encountered daily.[41] The alternative to industrial capitalism and its communist offspring, both of which seek only material rather than spiritual prosperity, was the Sermon on the Mount,

---

36 "de Hueck Doherty to Merton, March 17," in Merton and Doherty, *Compassionate Fire*, 60.

37 Day, "Houses of Hospitality," 59.

38 Merton, *Seven Storey Mountain*, 379.

39 Day, "Houses of Hospitality," 60.

40 "I don't like capitalism and I don't like socialism, which is the child of capitalism: that is father and son … we are trying to go back to a functional society … We personally renounce the acquisitive society altogether. It is a question of techniques.," in Day and Sicius, *Peter Maurin: Apostle to the World*, 105–107.

41 Day, *Long Loneliness*, 141.

which "answered all the questions as to how to love God and one's brother." [42]

While Catholic Social Teaching addressed, in broad strokes, the problems in the modern social order, Day considered a personal commitment to sanctity and the works of mercy as the "spiritual weapons at their disposal" against the sin and poverty encountered in the world around her. [43] Even though Day (against the advice of Peter Maurin) and the subsequent Catholic Worker movement have become known for its activism and involvement in traditional political struggles, for Day no activism was possible or remotely effective without love at a personal sacrifice. That most of her time and energy were expended in the decidedly small daily tasks of running of Catholic Worker Houses, rather than participating in more celebrated causes and protests, demonstrates its centrality. Doherty was even more explicit: though other means would be at their disposal, the members of her houses "were never to forget their primary duty was personal sanctification, and that the heresy of good works should at all times be watched for." [44] In other words, "pure political action, without any charity behind it" would make no important or lasting improvements on American lives. [45] Change for the poor, Merton attested, would come not primarily through traditional "political action," as the Communists mistakenly chose to think, but first through personal holiness, sacrifice and charity. [46]

The commitment to personal love as the means of Catholic Action can be found in both Day and Doherty's struggle to win Catholics entrenched in the bourgeois capitalist culture to the life they saw to embody the Catholic social teachings. [47] Writing to Merton, Doherty emphasized that the popular idea of Catholic Action, involvement in traditional politics, need first be replaced by the acknowledgement that reform "starts with YOURSELF. You have only one person to REFORM, and that is *you*." [48] Such a methodology, relying not on "frail human methods, not on theatricals, or meetings, or speeches, or conferences, but on God, Christ, and the Holy Ghost" required the much more difficult work of personal sacrifice and suffering. [49] Seeking to put "charity behind" politi-

---

42   Ibid.

43   Ibid., 212.

44   Doherty, *Friendship House*, 6.

45   "Thomas Merton to Catherine de Hueck, October 6, 1941," in Merton and Doherty, *Compassionate Fire*, 3.

46   Ibid.

47   Ibid.

48   "de Hueck to Merton, October 14," in Merton and Doherty, *Compassionate Fire*, 9.

49   Merton, *Seven Storey Mountain*, 381.

cal action necessitates fomenting charity, that is, to feed the poor first, not by the easier means of law, but "at the cost of our own appetites, and with our own hands, and for the love of God." [50] Without such personal sacrifice, never would the poor regain a sense of the human dignity they possess in Christ, a knowledge that their lives were worth the sacrificial love of another human life. Yet Doherty and Day found that the attempt, not to make the poor rich, but "to make 'the rich poor and the poor holy... [was] a revolution obnoxious" not only "to the pagan man," but often to Catholics themselves. [51]

As Day and Doherty found, many American Catholics had often also become enamored with the principal of material comfort as the highest good that, if not poor themselves, asking for a sacrifice of personal comfort for the sake of the poor was often unpopular. Day lamented how difficult it was to induce Catholics "to accept voluntary poverty as a principle," not first to help the poor—though it would do that as well—but "so that they would not fear the risk of losing... life itself." [52] Doherty, later in the Madonna House, commented that all the young visitors there were "frightened of pain," and so, then, "frightened of meeting [a Crucified God]." [53] The call to enact personal charity at a personal sacrifice, to extricate both the rich and the poor from the perverted goods of industrial capitalism, was a hard demand for those who knew no other good.

Doherty believed the only way to "purify the Church," to offer the Church to the poor as a stronger and better alternative to Communism, was "the martyrdom of the West." [54] If Catholics would be committed to "going out and being a saint," [55] then perhaps, Merton thought, "we may wake up one morning and find that the whole is leavened." [56] The work of personal holiness, the hard work of loving, not man in the abstract, but our neighbor, is the first and ultimate call of Christ on our hearts. To believe, with Merton, that revolution will come only from the work of conversion is to believe in the work of the Holy Ghost in ourselves. Then, if Day was right that "the final word" about *The Catholic Worker* "is love," it will, indeed, be "a harsh and dreadful thing [so that] our very faith in

50 "Merton to de Hueck, October 6," in Merton and Doherty, *Compassionate Fire*, 3–4.

51 Dorothy Day, "Beyond Politics," *The Catholic Worker*, November 1949, 1, 2, 4, www.catholicworker.org/dorothday/articles/166.html (accessed July 26, 2015).

52 Day, *Long Loneliness*, 212.

53 "Doherty to Merton, March 17," in Merton and Doherty, *Compassionate Fire*, 61.

54 "Catherine de Hueck Doherty to Thomas Merton, October 11, 1962," in Merton and Doherty, *Compassionate Fire*, 70.

55 "Merton to de Hueck, October 6," in Merton and Doherty, *Compassionate Fire*, 3.

56 Merton, *Seven Storey Mountain*, 382.

love has been tried through fire," but it will be the only way by which Catholic charity can authentically live.[57] The revolution of love comes not by a personally detached faith in a disembodied system, but by the hard work of personal love.

The emergence of the Friendship House and the Catholic Worker around the same time can be no coincidence. Instead, their appearances as places giving space for personal love and sacrifice to be mutually enacted were the work of the faithful Catholics not trying to change or tweak fundamentally corrupt systems from the outside, but rather to change the people who make up those systems. Industrialized capitalism and its communist child seek only the material welfare of people and thus cannot help but create people to seek first the things of this world, rather than the things of heaven. To create a society, as Maurin says, in which it is easier to be good is to create a society of people who seek first the things of God, not by outward coercion but by a conversion of the heart. Catholic Workers have often been accused of being idealistic, and there is something to that charge. We have to live with one another, and most of us love God far less than we ought, if we do at all. Nevertheless, the hospitality house stands as a prophetic witness about where our hopes as Christians should lie, and to where our energies should first be directed.

Leigh Miller works at home taking care of her daughter, Edith, and helping her husband maintain a house of hospitality in Durham, North Carolina. She lived in Christian community for six years before getting married and spent five of those years involved in the Community of the Franciscan Way, an Episcopal Catholic Worker, that was located in Durham. Leigh holds an MTS from Duke Divinity School and does occasional freelance theological writing.

---

57 Day, *Long Loneliness*, 285.

Dorothy Day and Pittsburgh's Catholic Radical Alliance

Paul Dvorchak

Among Roman Catholics of a certain age, the life of Dorothy Day is well known. One mission of the Catholic Worker that Day founded was St. Joseph's House of Hospitality, a home for homeless men in New York City. Within three years of the start of St. Joseph's House an organization in Pittsburgh called the Catholic Radical Alliance (CRA) began its own House of Hospitality of the same name as that in New York. This paper will explore and examine Dorothy Day's influence, inspiration, and active involvement in the creation of the Catholic Radical Alliance and Pittsburgh's St. Joseph's House of Hospitality.

Even before the beginning of the Pittsburgh house, Dorothy Day visited Pittsburgh to investigate the different issues facing Catholic workers who were employed in the Pittsburgh region's steel mills and coal mines. In the mid 1930s, the rights of workers was the issue that was predominant in many American minds, especially Catholics. The Communist Party of the United States posed a real threat to the Church in America as the great majority of Catholics, especially in the industrial Northeast, belonged to the working class. During the Great Depression, 32 percent of Pittsburgh's workers were unemployed. 60 of 200 organizers of Pittsburgh's Steel Workers Organizing Committee (SWOC) were Communists. [1]

Dorothy Day visited Pittsburgh in the summer of 1936 and recorded her visit in her column in the *Catholic Worker* newspaper. Day visited with Catholic union leaders such as John Brophy, Philip Murray, and Pat Fagan, all involved in organizing steelworkers and coal miners. She also met with Father Adalbert Kazincy, who spoke at an open air meeting at St. Michael's Church in Braddock,

---

1   Kenneth J. Heineman, "A Catholic New Deal: Religion and Labor in 1930s Pittsburgh," *The Pennsylvania Magazine of History and Biography* 118 (1994): 370.

Pennsylvania. Day quoted Father Kazincy: "Remember you have an immortal soul, he told them. Remember your dignity as men. Don't let the Carnegie Steel Company crush you. For the sake of your wives and children and homes, you need the union. . . . I favor a yearly wage. I favor security so that they will not live in fear."[2]

These early visits of Dorothy Day to Pittsburgh confirm the labor related emphasis of the Worker movement in Pittsburgh and the subsequent prominence placed on workers' rights by the CRA. Pittsburgh's CRA looked to Day and the Catholic Worker for inspiration and as role models. One of the founders of the CRA, Fr. Charles Owen Rice (1908–2005) had begun a youth group as an assistant pastor at St. Agnes Church in the Oakland neighborhood of Pittsburgh. In a 1935 letter to Dorothy Day from Rice, he enclosed one dollar and asked her to send twenty copies of the "last worker." He told Day that he had a club for Catholic high school students in the public school. "I want to wake them up. Some stirrings of life are noticeable already."[3]

One of the young men who belonged to Rice's club and a parishioner of St. Agnes was Alan Kistler who later became the director of services for the AFL-CIO.[4] Kistler played an important role in the development of Pittsburgh's house of hospitality and the CRA. The St. Agnes youth group formed the nucleus of the lay membership of what was to become the CRA.

Father Rice—along with Father Carl Hensler[5] and Monsignor George Barry O'Toole[6]—co-founded the CRA in June of 1937. The Alliance (or CRA) supported the unionization of workers at the H. J. Heinz Company and the Loose

---

2 "To The Point" *The Pittsburgh Catholic* (August 13, 1936): 8. See Dorothy Day. "Experiences of C.W. Editor in Steel Towns with C.I.O.," *The Catholic Worker*, August 1936, 1, 2. at: http://www.catholicworker.org/dorothyday/Reprint2.cfm?TextID=302.

3 Letter of Charles Owen Rice to Dorothy Day, (October 10, 1935), Dorothy Day-Catholic Worker Collection, Marquette University Archives, Milwaukee, Wisconsin (hereinafter cited as "DD-CWC").

4 The role of Alan Kistler (1921–2008) in the labor movement was best summarized in the May 13, 2008 statement issued by AFL-CIO President John Sweeney on the death of Kistler. The statement appears at http://www.aflcio.org/Press-Room/Press-Releases/Statement-by-AFL-CIO-President-John-Sweeney-on-Dea2.

5 Carl Peter Hensler (1898–1984) was a priest of the Diocese of Pittsburgh. Educated in Rome, he was a pupil of minimum wage proponent Msgr. John A. Ryan.

6 George Barry O'Toole (1886–1944) was a native of Toledo, who received doctorates in philosophy and theology from Urban University in Rome. He was the first rector of the Catholic University of Peking in China. He was the sole cleric to testify before a Senate hearing in 1940 in opposition to the pending military conscription act.

Wiles Biscuit Company in Pittsburgh. In addition to its union activities, the CRA would also establish St. Joseph House of Hospitality.

The CRA was officially announced in *The Pittsburgh Catholic* in two install-ments on June 3rd and June 10th, 1937. Both editions featured the organization at the top of the front page in a bold subtitle *Catholic Radical Alliance*, with no byline.[7] The article began by explaining that the organization planned to get a Catholic Worker group started in Pittsburgh as the city was in the heart of man-ufacturing and mining. It gave a short history how Day and Maurin began the Catholic Worker in New York.

> The ideal behind the "Catholic Worker" might best be termed simply living Christianity. They started out with the inten-tion of bringing Catholic teaching to the workers and the poor; with the idea of bringing charity of Christ to all; with the idea not merely of patching up a Godless, tottering society but of reconstructing it on Catholic principles. They wanted to start building a Christian social order.... It was a tremendous, am-bitious program. Only either madmen or good Catholics could have conceived it. [8]

In a column adjoining this is another typed in larger bold letters: **To Sup-port Heinz Strikers.** In this article it was reported that the CRA would support the Canning & Pickle Workers Union, A.F. of L. in its demand to be recognized as the bargaining agent for Heinz employees. Beginning that very morning, mem-bers of the Alliance would join the picket line outside the Heinz plant on the North Side.

Inspired by Dorothy Day and the Catholic Worker, Pittsburgh's Catholic Radical Alliance opened St. Joseph's House of Hospitality at 901 Wylie Avenue on July 20, 1937.

A typewritten, unsigned document exists in St. Joseph House of Hospital-ity archives titled "Brief History of St. Joseph's House of Hospitality, Pittsburgh, Pa." The document speaks of the opening of the house.

---

7   "Catholic Radical Alliance," *The Pittsburgh Catholic* (June 3, 1937): 1; "Catholic Radical Alliance," *The Pittsburgh Catholic* (June 10, 1937):1. See K.K. McNulty, *Is It I, The Witness of Monsignor Charles Owen Rice,* (Pittsburgh: D.A.R.T. Corporation, 1988). In the latter work, Rice stated that he began to write for *The Pittsburgh Catholic* on the CRA and that both he and Alan Kistler wrote all the CRA columns.

8   "Catholic Radical Alliance," *The Pittsburgh Catholic* (June 3, 1937): 1.

The policy of the House was established on the basis of the prototype in New York, that is to say, to furnish food, shelter and clothing free of charge without questioning, keeping of statistics or case-records—in short, without red-tape of any sort. ... The House in Pittsburgh opened on July 20, 1937 in a vacant butcher shop on Wylie Avenue, located in the slums of the town. From the beginning we served to the limit of our capacity, some 200 meals per day and floor space at night for as many men as could be accommodated in the two rooms, while hundreds had to be turned away every day for lack of facilities.[9]

Dorothy Day visited Pittsburgh shortly after Pittsburgh's House of Hospitality opened. The August 19, 1937 edition of *The Pittsburgh Catholic* reported that Day was in Pittsburgh for two days on her way from New York to Cleveland. She talked to the Catholic Radical Alliance and she gave them ideas on establishing a House of Hospitality. The article also reported on members of the Alliance visiting the Catholic Worker in New York. [10]

The next issue of *The Pittsburgh Catholic* provided more detail on Day's visit. Local members of the Alliance wanted a member from the Catholic Worker from New York to come to Pittsburgh to help organize their House of Hospitality. Day discouraged that idea, saying the Pittsburgh House should be run by locals. The advice was to start small, even if only in a store front. [11] The same article mentioned a more detailed visit of those from Pittsburgh to the New York House on Mott Street and a farming commune in Easton, Pennsylvania.

The same edition of *The Pittsburgh Catholic* had an adjoining column titled "Dorothy Day's Talk On Communism." Day spoke to the Alliance on August 18 and discussed the differences between Communism and Christianity. She said that "Communism may be regarded as a perverted kind of Christianity, a heresy.... We, on the other hand are very prone to neglect the communal aspect of our religion. We deny the Mystical Body of Christ in many ways. How many of us look upon the Negro as our brother in Christ?" She ended the talk speaking

---

9   "Brief History of St. Joseph's House of Hospitality, Pittsburgh, Pa." Typewritten on St. Joseph's letterhead with the address 61 Tannehill Street, Pittsburgh 19, Pennsylvania. Located at St. Joseph House of Hospitality Archives, 1635 Bedford Ave., Pittsburgh Pennsylvania 15219 (hereinafter cited as "SJHHA").

10   "Catholic Radical Alliance," *The Pittsburgh Catholic* (August 19, 1937): 1.

11   "Catholic Radical Alliance," *The Pittsburgh Catholic* (August 26, 1937): 1, 16.

about the importance of ideas and the importance of spreading ideas. "Revolutions begin in the printing press." [12] Of this last idea, the members of the Catholic Radical Alliance took Day's teaching to heart as all subsequent editions of the Pittsburgh Catholic, for at least the next year and a half, had articles written by a member of the CRA.

There were differences between the New York and Pittsburgh Catholic Worker organizations. Alan Kistler said that the New York Catholic Worker became strongly pacifistic while the Pittsburgh group tended more toward labor issues. For instance, Fr. Rice started labor schools. The schools taught labor history and tactics and the Church's teachings about those issues. Kistler mentioned that the labor schools had access to published literature from the National Catholic Welfare Council (NCWC). The NCWC published pamphlets on unions, guilds, cooperatives, women at work and the family, plus the papal encyclicals and study guides. [13]

The large number of unemployed and homeless men in Pittsburgh forced St. Joseph House of Hospitality to move to a larger facility. But the move was not without controversy. *The Pittsburgh Catholic* of March 31, 1938 had an article titled: "House of Hospitality Moves to Tannehill St. But Not to Stay There." The author stated that St. Joseph House of Hospitality moved its meager belongings to the old St. Rita's home, but they did not intend to stay there as the place was too large and if the "group were to stay in it, and expand, the result would be institutionalization. The Catholic Worker ideal, which is the one followed by the C.R.A., calls not for a centralized, large House of Hospitality but for a number of smaller ones. ... In a big building the personal touch is lost."[14] The building at 61 Tannehill Street was long and narrow with 52 large rooms, ten bathrooms, 2 kitchens and a chapel.[15] "Here we served from 800 to 1000 meals per day and accommodated from 600 to 700 men at night. There were beds available for about 350 men on the basis of first come, first served, the overflow slept as best as they could on the floor in the Halls and on the stair-cases." [16] St. Joseph House of Hospitality remained at this address for thirty-six years, until 1974 at which time, it moved to its present location at 1635 Bedford Avenue.

On May 25, 1938, almost two months after the move to Tannehill St., Dor-

---

12 Ibid. 16.

13 Interview of the author with Alan and Marie Kistler (July 30, 1991), SJHHA.

14 "House of Hospitality Moves to Tannehill St. But Not to Stay There," *The Pittsburgh Catholic* (March 31, 1938): 1.

15 James W. Garvey, *50th Anniversary St. Joseph's House of Hospitality 1937–1987*, SJHHA.

16 "Brief History of St. Joseph's House of Hospitality, Pittsburgh, Pa.," SJHHA.

othy Day paid a surprise visit to Pittsburgh, leaving the next day. At first she didn't like the large size for fear of institutionalization but she changed her mind and said she would ask other bishops to turn over vacant property to serve the poor.[17] Day reported her visit in the *Catholic Worker* newspaper.

> In Pittsburgh a tremendous building has been turned over to the Catholic Radical Alliance and so far only one end of one floor has been cleaned up for use. The Akron group, mostly rubber workers, drove me to Pittsburgh and when we arrived in town there was no food in the house, just the soup stewing on the stove in huge milk cans for the next day. We sent out for baked beans and bologna and sliced up onions to top off the meal. [18]

Dorothy Day was back in Pittsburgh on July 2nd and recorded the visit in this lengthy entry in her journal.

> Got in last night by bus.... The halls of St. Joseph's house smell of cats. They have cleaned up one wing and about thirty men are being housed and fed three meals a day, and about 500 their lunch of stew. A man donates $100 worth of meat a month which is a godsend and they get vegetables from the produce market. Someone gave a truck. They are all drinking sassafras tea since one of the merchants at the market gave them a big basket of the root bark for brewing. I had some for supper last night and it was good.... And I wished the princes of the church were living voluntarily down in a place like this where the food is scarce and often bad. Today for instance for breakfast was coffee so weak that the skim milk, slightly soured, took from it any color it had.... For lunch a very greasy lamb stew, plain lettuce, and boiled parsnips. No one ate any parsnips but the stew was cleaned up.... But there is nothing in the house for the coming week to make soup out of. The cellar is full of baskets of radishes, parsnips, and woody turnips, slimy lettuce, and spinach. The place is full of flies as a result of

17 "Catholic Radical Alliance," *The Pittsburgh Catholic* (June 2, 1938): 1.
18 Dorothy Day, *Catholic Worker*, (June 1938):1, 2.

the decaying vegetables and the cellar is half flooded with water which makes it worse. . . . Tomorrow the soup line will get a concoction of turnips and parsnips and lamb fat. . . . I shall concentrate on the food problem and drag in the lay apostolate on that basis. It is an insult to St. Joseph, our provider, to serve such meals. . . . Fr. Rice was just in—he has been ill and is still weak, but feeling better after his retreat. The trouble is the lay people have left the work to him, thinking three priests are at the head of this Alliance. It should be the work of the laity. Most of the money comes from young curates who can ill afford to help. [19]

It is hard to overstate the importance that Dorothy Day had for Pittsburgh's Catholic Radical Alliance. In the June 23, 1938 edition of *The Pittsburgh Catholic*, the Catholic Radical Alliance column announced that Dorothy Day would be coming to Pittsburgh the first two weeks of July for a vacation with her daughter. [20] Dorothy Day was thus something of a celebrity to Pittsburgh Catholics. Her July 1938 visit was billed as a vacation for her, but she had many speaking engagements as well. She spent her time during this Pittsburgh visit speaking to study clubs on the Catholic Social Movement. She spoke to the St. Vincent De-Paul Society at St. Mary of Mercy; to the Pittsburgh Council of Catholic Women; to the study club called the *Sheep and Goats* at Sacred Heart in Shadyside; and to the local branch of the Catholic Daughters of America. She spoke at St. Lawrence O'Toole and to St. William's in East Pittsburgh; she also spoke to the Catholic Forum and to Holy Innocents Parish. [21] The next week's edition of the newspaper recapped Day's two-week visit to Pittsburgh and mentioned that she also spoke to about 400 people at Duquesne College of the Holy Ghost and to a similar group at Seton Hill College. She then left Pittsburgh for Philadelphia. [22]

On January 23, 1939, Father Rice wrote to Dorothy Day. The letter reads as a confession or as one admitting failure to a mentor.

> Somehow or other your Pittsburgh branch does not satisfy me, it does not jell. I earnestly believe it is my fault. At times I am

---

19 Robert Ellsberg, ed. *The Duty of Delight: The Diaries of Dorothy Day* (Milwaukee, Wisconsin: Marquette University Press, 2008), 28–30.

20 "Catholic Radical Alliance," *The Pittsburgh Catholic* (June 23, 1938): 16.

21 "Catholic Radical Alliance," *The Pittsburgh Catholic* (July 7, 1938): 1, 16.

22 "Visit Completed By Dorothy Day," *The Pittsburgh Catholic* (July 14, 1938): 1.

quite convinced that it would go far, far better without me. I am lazy, I don't endoctrinate [sic] enough, I often dont [sic] keep close tab enough.... However in spite of all I could do we were degenerating in the direction of a very efficient "Catholic" flop house.... There is something wrong with the movement here as it has operated under my direction. I run a very efficient flop-house, I feed the men well, they respect me and, God help us, think me a very holy and worthy man. I get my name and picture in the papers, I talk on the radio. We hold meetings we have all manner of meetings and committees, but we are not Catholic Workers."

The last paragraph asked Dorothy Day to send or lend a young man from New York, "who has the true spirit." [23] Now that the CRA and St. Joseph's House of Hospitality were operating out of the larger Tannehill Street building, it is easy to see how difficult it must have been to maintain the idealism that existed at the smaller Wylie Avenue address.

Dorothy Day next visited March 23rd, 1939. She was in Pittsburgh long enough to address the regular meeting of the CRA. She remarked how much the place has improved since her last visit. Her talk was a review of Catholic Worker principles but she emphasized the "little way" for spiritual perfection and human progress. She talked of the importance of study and preparation "because the idea of revolution, even a Catholic and bloodless one" needed that. She said that the New York Catholic Worker often had to trust in Providence when things looked bad. They were usually in debt but something always turned up. Her visit was reported in the *Catholic Radical Alliance* column of *The Pittsburgh Catholic*. In the same column, under the heading "Liturgical Movement," the author stated,

A neglected phase of the Catholic Social movement will be emphasized at tonight's meeting. A paper on the liturgy in general will be read, to acquaint the people with the prayers and functions of the Church which are characteristic of the universal worship in the Mass and the Office. Other meetings will treat of more specific liturgical matters, and will tie up the

23   Letter of Charles Owen Rice to Dorothy Day (January 23, 1939), DD-CWC.

ideas of the liturgy with the movement of social justice. [24]

This meeting was a preview for the colloquium to be held at St. Joseph's in early April.

On April 10, 11 and 12, members of the Catholic Worker Movement from across North America held a "Colloquium on Social Catholicism" at St. Joseph's House of Hospitality in Pittsburgh. Representatives from different Catholic Worker houses from the United States and Canada came to Pittsburgh to discuss the following topics: liturgy, Catholic sociology, voluntary poverty, anti-Semitism, peace, agrarianism, and labor. Those who did attend were active in both the Liturgical Movement and the Catholic social movement. Mass was held and Compline was sung each afternoon. [25]

The connection between the liturgical movement and Catholic social activism, which culminated with the Second Vatican Council, is surprising in that not only were these issues being discussed in the late 1930s but that these clergy were actually celebrating innovative liturgies. There was a conscious connection between those dedicated to living out the radical Gospel and the study and reform of the Roman Catholic Liturgy. This issue, the relationship between the Catholic experience of Liturgy and Catholic concern for social problems and solutions, needs further study and research.

In a later Catholic Radical Alliance column in *The Pittsburgh Catholic* under the simple subtitle *Liturgy,* the author relates that a discussion took place at a CRA meeting on August 3, 1939 at which a critical study of the canon of the Roman Mass was undertaken. One part of the discussion was on the placement and the efficiency of the *epiklesis* in the canon. These discussions show that the young men and women who volunteered and staffed St. Joseph's had more on their mind than feeding and housing the poor. [26]

There was dissension within St. Joseph's House of Hospitality. An unsigned letter exists in Marquette's archives addressed to "Bill" on St. Joseph's letterhead from Tannehill Street.

> Seems a young revolution has started here among the younger
> cw-minded people. ... There are certain evils and injustices
> that are unavoidable in a place so big. ... The works of mercy

24 "Catholic Radical Alliance," *The Pittsburgh Catholic* (March 30, 1939): 1, 16.
25 "Catholic Worker Colloquium Held," *The Pittsburgh Catholic* (April 13, 1939): 1, 8.
26 "Catholic Radical Alliance," *The Pittsburgh Catholic* (August 17, 1939): 13.

are pushed away by keys, stewards, rules, time limit, etc. The zeal of the people who were on Wylie is gone. Fr. Rice and Fr. Lappan agree its wrong.... This is a big chariot upon which one can ride to self-glorification—it's a temple to materialism and profit and efficiency at the sacrifice of everything we believe in.... There's a lot of enthusiasm on the part of 6 or 8 youngsters....I would like to get some opinion from N.Y. When you pass this on to D.D. tell her she didn't see the third floor when she was here. I think the expansion of the third floor is what caused most of the upsetting or rather aggravated a bum situation that was lacking c.w. principles. [27]

The letter is dated April 15, 1939, three days after the colloquium.

The Second World War exacerbated the tensions that already existed within St. Joseph's over the issues of pacifism and conscientious objection. These tensions not only existed within Pittsburgh's CRA and St. Joseph's House of Hospitality, but within the Catholic Worker movement on a national level.

Four priests who were associated with Pittsburgh were influential or participated in Dorothy Day's attitude toward war. One of the co-founders of the Catholic Radical Alliance, Msgr. George Barry O'Toole, accompanied Day to Washington D.C. in their mutual efforts to oppose the compulsory Selective Training and Service Act of 1940. [28] Day spoke in front of the Senate Military Affairs Committee on the Catholic Worker's opposition to the draft. [29]

Another Pittsburgh priest who had an influence on Day's pacifism was Fr. John J. Hugo. Hugo's influence on Day's spirituality is immense and well known. The Selective Service Act did become law in October 1940, and Day and the Catholic Worker position only became more resolved. Hugo wrote a note to Day: "No doubt [pacifism] is all clear to you; but then you have not tried to work it out doctrinally. If you knew no theology, it would probably be simpler to make a solution. Yet the decision must be based on doctrine. Pacifism must proceed from truth, or it cannot exist at all." [30] According to William Miller, the pacifism of Day and the Catholic Worker stemmed from reasons of history and

---

27 Letter (unsigned) addressed to Bill at the New York Catholic Worker (April 15, 1939), DD-CWC.

28 Public Law 783, 76th Congress, approved September 16, 1940.

29 William D. Miller, *A Harsh and Dreadful Love: Dorothy Day and the Catholic Worker Movement* (New York: Liveright, 1973), 163.

30 Ibid,.166.

the suspicion of capitalist war mongering and profiteering. Hugo suggested that a Catholic opposition to war should be based on Scripture and the teachings of the Church.

Some Catholic Worker houses stopped selling the New York *Catholic Worker* newspaper because of Day's strict pacifism. Day wrote an article suggesting that those houses no longer belonged to the movement. Her statement was directed at St. Francis House in Seattle. Fr. H. A. Reinhold of the Seattle House sent a letter of protest to Day. He thought it wrong for the whole movement to be centered on this one issue and that she should not adopt a dictator's method toward dissension.[31]

Fr. Hans Ansgar Reinhold (1897–1968) is the third priest mentioned with a Pittsburgh connection. He is best known as the co-founder of *Orate Fratres* (later *Worship)* with Fr. Virgil Michel, OSB. Both of these priests were influential in the liturgical movement that culminated with the reforms of Vatican II. Reinhold, a native of Germany, served on the front lines of World War I. After the war, he spent a year with the Benedictines at the Abbey of Maria Laach, considered the birthplace of liturgical renewal in Europe. After Hitler came to power, Reinhold hoped to publicize the idea that the Nazis were persecuting both Jews and Christians. He believed there was little difference between the Nazis and Bolsheviks. His bishop, Wilhelm Berning, disagreed with Reinhold, and labeled Reinhold a Bolshevik. Reinhold opposed the signing of the Concordat between Berlin and the Vatican in July of 1933. A year later, Reinhold was arrested by the Gestapo, but released. In the spring of 1935, he fled to England for fear of being rearrested by the Gestapo. But his bishop sent word that he was not a true refugee and that he was officially on leave without permission. He came to the United States in 1936, but had a difficult time acting as a priest because American bishops believed Reinhold's German bishop. It was Dorothy Day who prompted Reinhold to come to the U.S. and for a time helped find a place for him to live in the Diocese of Brooklyn. Reinhold eventually found his way to the Benedictines of St. John's in Collegeville and then to Seattle.[32]

It was Fr. Reinhold who influenced Fr. Charles Owen Rice to abandon the pacifism of Dorothy Day and back Roosevelt's war effort. Rice admitted Reinhold's influence on his rejection of pacifism in a later *Pittsburgh Catholic* col-

---

31 Ibid.,169.

32 Jay P. Corrin, "H.A. Reinhold: Liturgical Pioneer and Anti-Fascist," *The Catholic Historical Review* 82 (1996): 436-458. See also H.A. Reinhold, *The Autobiography of Father Reinhold* (New York: Herder and Herder, 1968); Julia A. Upton, *Worship in Spirit and Truth: The Life and Legacy of H.A. Reinhold* (Collegeville, Minnesota: Liturgical Press, 2009).

umn.[33] In June of 1940, Dorothy Day wrote a circular letter to all Catholic Worker houses that asserted that pacifism *was* a central doctrine to the Catholic Worker movement. This was the letter that Fr. Reinhold was responding to. Fr. Rice also wrote to Day on August 13, 1940. He said he was glad to get the letter, but

> You will probably be shocked, though, to findout [sic] that I feel differently from you in the matter of Conscription and other military matters. I am afraid I have become a "war monger." I turned over your letter to Allan [sic] Kistler; he has been our active "Peace Man," locally, but Allan [sic] and the others did nothing about it because they are not conscientious objectors. I hope you do not feel that we have all "let your [sic] down" but we have to "call them as we see them.[34]

Dorothy Day visited St. Joseph's House in Pittsburgh for a short visit in the latter part of November 1940. She spoke to a "fairly large group" on the counsels of perfection.[35] She believed that these counsels of voluntary poverty, chastity, and complete obedience applied to lay people as well as professed religious.[36] Day's first retreat with Fr. John Hugo was not until July of 1941, but it was evident that she was already thinking in the strict spiritual terms that Hugo preached.

On June 12–14, 1941, Dorothy Day visited both St. Joseph House and the newly formed St. Francis House in Pittsburgh. She reported her stay in the *Catholic Worker.* She said that St. Joseph's was the only house in the movement that had a priest in charge. She recounted how hard the house had it in the beginning, retelling the story about having parsnip soup and sassafras tea for a week. But now because of Fr. Rice's begging, the men are served three good meals daily. She conveyed a good impression of the spirit of the house in that there was efficiency and informality because the place was staffed mostly by those who came there in need. There was daily Mass, Benediction, and rosary.

---

33 Charles Owen Rice, "Dorothy Day and World War II Pacifism." *The Pittsburgh Catholic* (Nov. 7, 1997): 5.

34 Letter of Charles Owen Rice to Dorothy Day (August 13, 1940), DD-CWC.

35 Alan Kistler, "St. Joseph's House of Hospitality" *The Pittsburgh Catholic* (November 28, 1940): 8.

36 Dan McKanan, *The Catholic Worker after Dorothy: Practicing the Works of Mercy in a New Generation* (Collegeville, Minnesota: Liturgical Press, 2008), 49.

St. Joseph's also served as a community center with meetings and neighborhood children taken on picnics.

Day also mentioned that Rice was very involved in union activities and that she spent some time with Amy Balinger, the head of the laundry workers' union which had 1,400 members, 75% of them Catholic and 80% women. She hoped that New York would do something with their laundry workers. She also criticized the union movement's class war attitude and that "we must have Christians before we have good union men."[37]

Dorothy Day's influence was significant and substantial to the beginning of St. Joseph House of Hospitality in Pittsburgh. She and the movement she started provided both inspiration and practical advice on the establishment of a radical Catholic Christian witness to the social problems that existed in Pittsburgh in the waning years of the Great Depression and the years at the beginning of World War II. These extraordinary times also produced an extraordinary response from the lay people and clergy who tried to live out their faith according to Dorothy Day's radical Catholic Christian vision.

Paul Dvorchak is a graduate of the University of Pittsburgh, with a MA.T. from that University and a M.A. from Duquesne University. He served as Assistant Director of St. Joseph House of Hospitality in Pittsburgh 1987–2001 and as Director 2001–2012, retiring in 2012.

37 Dorothy Day, "Day After Day—July/August 1941," *The Catholic Worker* (July/August 1941): 1, 3, appearing at:. http://www.catholicworker.org/dorothyday/Reprint2.cfm?-TextID=373.

Dorothy Day Gives Manuscripts, Records, Correspondence to Library

Marquette Tribune, 9 January 1965

Dorothy Day, co-founder of the Catholic Worker movement and newspaper has presented her own papers and those of the movement to the Marquette University Memorial library, it was announced recently.

Fifty cartons of manuscripts, correspondence and Hospitality House records have been received, including the papers of the late Peter Maurin, Miss Day's co-founder. Marquette will also have a complete microfilm of the newspaper, the Catholic Worker, which was begun in 1932, and now has a circulation of 70,000.

The papers trace the movement from its beginning in the early thirties to the present. Its aim, according to Miss Day, is to "create the kind of social order where it is easier for men to be good."

Earlier Marquette announced the acquisition of the McCarthy papers, and the papers of the Catholic Association for International Peace.

Miller to Do History

William Miller, associate history professor, who has Miss Day's permission to examine the papers for

UNPACKING AND SORTING material donated by Dorothy Day, co-founder of the Catholic Worker movement and newspaper, are (from left) Robert Miller, librarian, Fr. Thomas O. Hanley, SJ, and William B. Ready, director of libraries. Miss Day donated 50 cartons of manuscripts to Marquette.

Fr. Thomas O. Hanley, SJ, director of the American Historical Collection and Studies at Marquette, said that the Catholic Worker papers are significant in the social

verted to Catholicism. Her interest in the worker and the poor was a carry-over from earlier days when she had been active in Socialist and

Archival and
Historical Challenges
in Dorothy Day Scholarship

The Cause and the 'Chives:
Curatorial Reflections

Phillip M. Runkel

Marquette University began its archival relationship with the Catholic Worker movement in March of 1962, following the receipt of six boxes of Dorothy Day's papers and records of the New York Catholic Worker community. This extraordinary acquisition was largely due to the initiative and collecting acumen of the director of libraries, William Ready. He had first contacted Day five years before (around the time that he was extending a similar invitation to J. R. R. Tolkien). However, she had already forged close ties to faculty members and alumni at Marquette in the decades since her first visit in the spring of 1935. With the CW movement less than two years old, journalism senior Nina Polcyn prevailed upon her dean, Jeremiah O'Sullivan, to invite Day to campus. In his thank you letter, written soon afterwards, he revealed the deep impression she had made on him and others in attendance. He concluded, "In all my life I have not come in contact with any person, with the exception of my father, who has meant so much in helping me formulate my ideas and determining the course of my thought and action."[1] Supported by O'Sullivan, Polcyn and other alumni of the journalism college founded Holy Family Catholic Worker House in downtown Milwaukee in 1937.

Today the Dorothy Day-Catholic Worker Collection comprises more than 300 boxes, including the personal papers of Dorothy Day, Peter Maurin, and others involved in the movement; records of past and present Catholic Worker communities; photographs; audio and video recordings; and a wide variety of publications. It has been housed on the third floor of Raynor Library since the building's completion in 2003. Before then, archivists and collections were con-

---

1   Jeremiah O'Sullivan to Dorothy Day, May 20, 1935, Dorothy Day-Catholic Worker Collection, Series D-5. Box 5, Folder 1, Marquette University Archives.

signed to the basement of the original Memorial Library. This didn't appear to deter researchers, however. The DD-CW Collection had emerged as a "draw" by the early 1980s, thanks in large part to the efforts of historian and pioneering Catholic Worker scholar William Miller, who organized events to celebrate Day's eightieth birthday and commemorate the first anniversary of her death. In 1997, Marquette hosted a major conference of scholars and Catholic Workers to observe the centenary of Day's birth.

Most records are open to research use. The twenty-five-year seals Day placed on her diaries and family correspondence were lifted on November 29th, 2005. We marked this occasion with a premiere screening of the first full-length documentary on her life, by Claudia Larson. We then turned our attention to the publication of her diaries and selected letters by the Marquette University Press, securing the services of Robert Ellsberg as editor. Our most recent project was the cataloging and digitization of over 700 audio recordings related to the CW, including Dorothy Day's talks, Friday night meetings at the New York CW, and oral history interviews. We anticipate launching another digital records project in the near future.

In March of 2000 the Vatican approved the opening of Dorothy Day's cause, entitling her to be called a "Servant of God." The present stage, the "diocesan phase," entails:

1. Gathering together Day's published and unpublished writings.

2. Taking testimony from eyewitnesses—people who knew DD—concerning her exercise of the heroic virtues.

We provided 4,000 photocopies in 1984 to an MU graduate student employed by the Claretian order, which had begun to promote her canonization the year before. It is unclear if this will need to be replicated for the Dorothy Day Guild. Hundreds of oral history transcripts are on file here. Some of these may be consulted as well, particularly those of people who are deceased.

This "packaging" of Dorothy Day by the institutional church concerns many of her friends and followers. They fear that Day's piety and remorse over her early abortion will be emphasized to fashion her into "The Pro-Life Saint," at the expense of her legacy of social radicalism. Eventually, CW houses would be taken over by Catholic Social Services, and the remaining anarchist/pacifist disciples of Day would have to regroup under a new name.

The case for calling Dorothy Day a saint has been persuasively argued, though. In his address at our Centenary Conference, Jim Forest declared that she would "be the patron saint not only of homeless people and those who try to care for them but also of people who lose their temper." He noted that "the record of who she was, what she was like and what she did is too complete and accessible for her to be hidden in wedding cake icing."[2] Of course I hope he is right, though I've attempted to maintain my official neutrality in this debate.

My bonafides in this regard were called into question, however, by a small but persistent group of anti-canonization campaigners following the bishops' vote in November 2012 to move the cause forward. If some Catholic Workers feel the process isn't worthy of Day, as Kenneth Woodward noted in his authoritative work, *Making Saints*,[3] these opponents find her unworthy of the process, harking back to much earlier diatribes that appeared in *Our Sunday Visitor* and *The Wanderer* and the hecklers who called her Moscow Mary. Letters from the 1960s retained by Day and now in the CW Archives attest to the suspicions some readers of *The Catholic Worker* newspaper harbored in the Cold War era. The vast majority of subscribers did not share these sentiments, of course.

The anti-sainthood bloggers' bible is *The Catholic Worker Movement (1933–1980): A Critical Analysis*, authored by the English ultra-traditionalist Catholic writer Carol Byrne and published in 2010. It appears to have been based to a considerable extent on Day's FBI file, though she also cites many of her writings. In a commentary posted on Tradition in Action's website on 26 November 2012, titled "Irregularities in Dorothy Day's Cause of Canonization," Dr. Byrne conveniently provided a bullet-point list of eight major "impediments," including "persistent disobedience" to the church hierarchy, "active support" for communists and their organizations, and "condoning violent revolution against the government."

Byrne and others of her persuasion raised several of these points in comments on articles published online at this time. In response to negative evaluations by commenters on an article on the *National Catholic Register*'s site ("Bishops to Consider Sainthood Cause of Dorothy Day," 13 November 2012), I posted the following:

> As custodian of Dorothy Day's papers for the past 50 years, the
> Marquette University Archives seeks to preserve all significant
> documentation of her actions and beliefs. Inquiries and vis-
> its are welcomed. It should be noted that Dorothy Day corre-

2   Jim Forest, "Dorothy Day: Saint and Troublemaker," in *Dorothy Day and the Catholic Worker Movement: Centenary Essays*, eds. William J. Thorn, Phillip M. Runkel, and Susan Mountin (Milwaukee, Wisconsin: Marquette University Press, 2001), 577.

3   Kenneth L. Woodward, *Making Saints: How the Catholic Church Determines Who Becomes a Saint, Who Doesn't, and Why* (New York: Simon and Schuster, 1990), 32.

sponded with thousands of people. A few were Communists. But the vast majority were not—Mother Teresa, for example. [13 November 2012]

In response, minbee66 (publisher of the principle anti-canonization blog, *Dorothy Day Another Way*) stated that "Dorothy Day's Communist correspondents and friends were people she was much more intimate with and interacted with more frequently than Mother Teresa," citing Elizabeth Gurley Flynn and Anna Louise Strong as examples (19 November 2012).

Vic Biorseth, proprietor of the *Thinking Catholic Strategic Center* website (now renamed the *Embattled Catholic American Thinker*) weighed in on Christmas Eve with a column lauding Carol Byrne as "a great illuminator of our day," who had exposed that "monster" Dorothy Day as not only a traitor to her country [but] a traitor to her Church." He had a ready rebuttal when I invited readers to visit the Archives and make up their own minds: "If you want to know the truth about a Marxist, don't ask the Marxist. If you want to know the truth about a Marxist revolutionary organization, don't go to the organization's propaganda. You're looking for truth in all the wrong places."

At least one politician joined the anti-canonization campaign at this time. In a letter dated 7 January 2013 and published online by Tradition in Action, state senator Richard Black of Virginia wrote Pope Benedict to forcefully express his revulsion at the bishops' support for Day's cause, terming her a woman of "loathsome character," one "whose views supported the violent extermination of Christians throughout the world." In response I sent him the following email on January 18:

> Dear Senator Black:
>
> People are welcome to consult Dorothy Day's papers in the Marquette University Archives and judge for themselves how "loathsome" she was. I've looked at thousands of letters to and from Day and her associates, as well as her diaries and manuscripts, in the course of processing her papers, and come to a very different conclusion. (I can assure you that no unflattering documents have been expunged from the record during the 35 years I have served as curator of the Dorothy Day-Catholic Worker Collection.) The FBI agents who compiled her dossier were relying on informants, who have been known to have had axes to grind or to have been just plain mistaken. While

some of her occasional references to Communist dictators may have been insufficiently critical, I am aware of no credible evidence that she supported their regimes, or remained a Marxist after her conversion in 1927. Dorothy Day was a pacifist, unalterably opposed to the "violent extermination" of anyone.

The senator didn't reply.

The next month, February 2013, Cliff Kincaid, director of the Accuracy in Media Center for Investigative Journalism, posted two pieces on his site *Religious Left Exposed*: "Carol Byrne Sets the Record Straight about Dorothy Day," and "Pope's Possible Successor Promotes Marxist for Sainthood" (referring to Cardinal Timothy Dolan). In response, I ventured to "attest to the integrity of the scholars who have written on the movement," observing that they had frequently based their works on extensive research in the Marquette University Archives. To Byrne, who replied on Kincaid's behalf ("Exchange over Dorothy Day's Marxist Views," 28 February 2013), this suggested that I did not "think it worthwhile to consider any other view of Dorothy Day than those put forward by a minuscule band of her supporters who have done research in the Marquette Archives." She characterized these students of the movement as "a special interest group who had already nailed their colors to the Catholic Worker flag."

At the time she wrote this, more than 40 academic scholars unaffiliated with the Catholic Worker had produced books and unpublished dissertations on Day and the CW. Of these, roughly half based their studies on research in the Dorothy Day-Catholic Worker Collection. I wouldn't consider any to be outright hagiographers, and some were sharply critical in their approach. However, earning Dr. Byrne's seal of approval seems a daunting task indeed.

After several months of furious blogging on this issue, things have quieted down a bit, but the afore-mentioned minbee66 still frequently updates her site. Her post "How Objective Are Day's Potentially Confusing Advocates?" finds all the major writers on Day hopelessly biased, with the exception, of course, of Carol Byrne. While singling out former Catholic Workers, such as Robert Ellsberg and Jim Forest, she also dismisses scholars Mel Piehl and Nancy Roberts, noting that they "endorsed many of Day's beliefs." I don't escape unscathed either, being accused among other things of "circular reasoning" in "testifying to the sincerity and accuracy of CW's attempts to interpret or disown some of Day's well-known statements, perhaps in an attempt to create a softer, gentler Dorothy Day."

In the end, all we in the Archives can do is to try our best to preserve and help disseminate the documentary evidence of the "real" Dorothy Day for interpretation by her advocates, opponents, and those falling somewhere in between. I'd like to continue to play a part in this for as long as I can. I can't wait to see how it all turns out!

Phil Runkel has served as an archivist at Marquette University since 1977. He is primarily responsible for Raynor Memorial Library's Catholic social action holdings, including the Dorothy Day-Catholic Worker Collection.

Dorothy Day,
the Filthy Rotten System,
and the Catholic Church

Brian Terrell

By the time I arrived at the Catholic Worker in New York in 1975, a poster featuring Bob Finch's photo of Catholic Worker movement's cofounder Dorothy Day was already ubiquitous. It could be found, and it still can be today, tacked on the walls of soup kitchens, hospitality houses, and farming communes or mounted and framed in rectories and academics' studies.

Dorothy, already in her seventies, is portrayed sitting serenely, almost regally, on a camp stool framed by guns and clubs hanging on the belts of two cops ready to take her into custody. The text under the photo, "Our problems stem from our acceptance of this filthy, rotten system," attributed to Dorothy Day, is widely quoted by scholars, journalists, and Catholic Workers even more since her death in 1980. It is rare to find a reference to Dorothy and the movement she cofounded that does not include it, and it is offered by some as a distillation of her prodigious body of writing into a few pithy words.

This is Dorothy Day's most famous quote. The problem is that she probably never said it.

I was unaware of any controversy about this until I read a letter in the summer 2008 issue of *The Roundtable*, a journal published by the St. Louis Catholic Worker community. Bill Barrett, an old friend and my contemporary at the New York CW, commented on the fact that the "filthy rotten system" line was mentioned four times in a previous issue. "Dorothy hated to hear that quoted back to her," he wrote and insisted that Dorothy would not even allow the poster in question in the house.

Dorothy's ill ease with this quote and the poster was news to me and so I made an informal poll of a few others who knew and worked with Dorothy. Some shared Bill's memory and told me that these words were so uncharacteristically uncouth that she could not have uttered them. Others were equally confident that this condemnation of the "filthy, rotten system" was so typically characteristic of Dorothy's speech and thought that they did not question its authenticity.

My efforts to find the origins of this quote were inconclusive. The archivist for the CW papers at Marquette University, Phil Runkel, could find no reference to the quote earlier than the poster itself, which was first published by *WIN Magazine* in 1973.

One of Dorothy's biographers, Jim Forest, did a search in Dorothy's writings of the word, "rotten" and found this in a column of Dorothy's from 1956: "We need to change the system. We need to overthrow, not the government, as the authorities are always accusing the Communists of conspiring to teach to do, but this rotten, decadent, putrid industrial capitalist system which breeds such suffering in the whited sepulcher of New York."

Former managing editor of The Catholic Worker Tom Cornell offered a promising lead. "My clear recollection is that (Dorothy) said these words in an interview in the offices of the National Catholic Reporter in Kansas City, that she did not expect to be quoted, and that when she saw the words in print she was offended to be quoted using language which she considered vulgar and crude." While not quite convinced, this was enough to sate my curiosity about the matter and I dropped the question for a few years.

But it did not go away. As if doubts cast on the authenticity of Dorothy's reputed denunciation of this filthy rotten system had breathed new life into it, scholars, journalists and Catholic Workers alike kept using the quote more than ever before. In the blossoming of the Occupy Wall Street movement in 2011, the analysis that "our problems stem from our acceptance of this filthy, rotten system" had definitely found resonance. Hand lettered placards attributing this scathing critique to Dorothy Day popped up at Occupy encampments all over the United States and abroad.

This resurgence rekindled my interest in the origins of the quote. If my previous queries were motivated by little more than idle curiosity, seeing it taken up by a new, young and dynamic uprising gave the question more significance for me. I came really to want the quote to be Dorothy's. Thus I renewed my search of its genesis and forwarded Tom's recollection of an interview with Dorothy at the National Catholic Reporter to Joshua MeElwee, a friend on the staff of the paper.

Delving into the paper's "morgue," Joshua found the interview Tom remembered in the NCR's February 18, 1970, issue. A discussion between Dorothy and well known NCR writer, Gary MacEoin, their conversation was presented as a Lenten reflection under a headline reading "Money and the Middle-Class Christian." The editors put a large box in the body of this article with a sub-headline proclaiming in large, bold type: "Dorothy Day: Our problems stem from the acceptance of this lousy, rotten system."

Here, I am convinced, is the "smoking gun!"

Except for the substitution of the word "filthy" for "lousy," this saying struck a chord and for good or for bad, whether she liked it or not, these words became Dorothy's in the public mind. There is a problem, though; in that these words attributed to Dorothy are a paraphrase at best, an editor's characterization of Dorothy's words and not her own. However stirring or true to Dorothy this adage might or might not be, it is not hers. Taken out of the context of the interview, "Dorothy Day: Our problems stem from the acceptance of this lousy, rotten system" is misleading and it distorts the intention Dorothy expressed to Gary MacEoin.

In this Lenten reflection, Dorothy mourns the condition of the Catholic Church: "I feel that over and over again in history the church has become so corrupt it just cries out to heaven for vengeance," she said. "The crisis is something terrific," Dorothy went on, citing the reduced numbers of vocations. But closed church buildings and abandoned ministries are a "purification" of sorts, she insisted, as if the Lord is taking into hand "what we don't do ... ourselves."

"You think it has a great deal to do with property?" Dorothy was asked. "I think it's a result of the corruption in the institutional church," she answered, "through money and through their acceptance of the lousy, rotten system."

Clearly, in this interview Dorothy expressed her conviction that it is the church's "acceptance of the lousy, rotten system," its accumulation of wealth, its blessing of usury and industrial capitalism and the wars that support it, from which the church's problems stem. She was speaking specifically here of the church, not of society at large. It can be said, and she said as much in her 1956 column Jim Forest cited, that the same goes for the latter, but this was not what she was trying to say in Kansas City in Lent, 1970.

Perhaps it was a lack of clarity created by this editors' short-cut that was at the heart of Dorothy's reported irritation over the NCR and the poster that it apparently spawned. If in her own column in the paper for which she was editor and publisher Dorothy did not demur from excoriating "this rotten, decadent, putrid industrial capitalist system," it is unlikely that she would take offense at having similarly abrasive words attributed to her by the editors of the NCR or *WIN Magazine*.

Another possible basis for her irritation is that, given her ambivalence about the popular culture of the 70s, it may have simply mortified her to be immortalized as a pop icon on a poster. "Don't call me a rock star, I won't be dismissed so easily," to paraphrase another legendary Dorothy quote, the origins of which are equally elusive.

The results of my quest were published, appropriately, in the *National Catholic Reporter*, April 16, 2012, "Who Says it's a Filthy, Rotten System? Tracing Dorothy Day's Most Famous Quote." This article raised vigorous discussion on the paper's on-line comment section, and in personal messages to me in other venues.

Some offered the sheer volume of occasions where this quote has been published as evidence of its authenticity, as though saying something enough times makes it true. I was given several references to sources of the quote that my correspondents regarded as irrefutable evidence that the quote did originate with Dorothy, but none of these dated before *WIN Magazine* published the poster in 1973.

One source that was brought to my attention by several critics, friendly and otherwise, was Daniela Gioseffi's book, *Women on War: An International Anthology of Writings from Antiquity to the Present.* I was already aware of this work and it is a fine and useful collection. This book was published in 1988, eight years after Dorothy's death, however, and fifteen years after the poster in question first appeared. A footnote to the quote attributed to Dorothy cites it simply, "from a public speech" without any suggestion of where or when this public speech occurred or who first recorded it.

While *Women on War* is one of hundreds of publications where the quote appeared in the years after Dorothy's death, for some reason it acquired a place of authority in the minds of some, definitively settling for all time the question of the origins of "our problems stem from our acceptance of this filthy, rotten system." Catholic Worker archivist Phil Runkel asked Daniela Gioseffi for her source of the quote, and she replied in an April 2, 2012, email, "I don't recall the source." She did admit, "I got it somewhere, from *WIN* or *The Catholic Worker*." In other words, while it is not possible that *Women on War* is the source of the quote on *WIN*'s 1973 poster, it is altogether likely that the poster is the source for the quote in *Women on War*, published in 1988.

For some readers, even though in my article I suggested that "we need to overthrow this rotten, decadent, putrid industrial capitalist system" works better than the quote on the poster and that it "can be more easily defended as authentically Dorothy's," thought that my point was that I do not believe that the system is filthy or rotten at all, or that I believe that Dorothy did not think so. The question for some is not whether Dorothy actually said this or nor, but whether she should have said it and for what motive would one even ask the question in the first place. "I find nothing wrong with that statement. I hope you don't either," Daniela Gioseffi said in her email to Phil Runkel.

A prolific blogger named Minbee66, "How Objective Are Day's 'Potentially Confusing' Advocates?" interpreted what I wrote as an attempt to disassociate Dorothy from her critique of capitalism and included my article as one of "CW's attempts to interpret or disown some of Day's well-known statements, perhaps in an attempt to create a 'softer, gentler' Dorothy Day."

Far from promoting a "softer, gentler" Dorothy, my research and article exposes her harsher, more stringent assessment of the Catholic Church than many of her admirers will own. The organizers of this conference classified this paper in the category "Dorothy Day and the Radical Critique of American Society." It might more properly belong listed under "Dorothy Day and the Radical Critique of the Catholic Church," but, somehow, there is no such category at this conference.

The origins of Dorothy Day's most famous quote are important and should be remembered for the fact that they show how the quote has been distorted over the years by the loss of a crucial detail—that these harsh words were directed at the church that she loved with all her heart, even as it was so often a scandal to her. "I feel that over and over again in history the church has become so corrupt it just cries out to heaven for vengeance," is the proper context for her observations about "this filthy rotten system," and the poster misses the mark.

Often Dorothy quoted the theologian Romano Guardini, "the church is the Cross on which Christ is always crucified. One cannot separate Christ from his bloody, painful church. One must live in a state of permanent dissatisfaction with the church." Rereading, meditating upon this over the years, I am growing in appreciation that for Dorothy, as for Father Guardini, living in a state of permanent dissatisfaction with the church is not only a possibility for some but an imperative for all. If we are not at times scandalized by Christ's bloody, painful church, nor angered by its sins and injustices, as Dorothy was, then there is something wrong with us. If we are not sometimes like her offended by its corruption, we do not truly love the church as Christ made visible as she did. One of Dorothy's many gifts to the church is how she showed that it is possible for a conscious and compassionate person to remain in the Catholic Church, simultaneously loving and criticizing it—indeed, criticizing it because loving it!

Brian Terrell has been with the Catholic Worker movement since he dropped out of college in 1975 to join the community in New York City. He was an associate editor of *The Catholic Worker* and continues to write for that paper. He presently lives on a Catholic Worker Farm in Maloy, Iowa, and is a co-coordinator for Voices for Creative Nonviolence.

Dorothy Day:
Scholarship and Inspiration for
Contemporary Students

Susan M. Mountin

1997 was the year of the Dorothy Day Centenary Conference at Marquette University during which I developed an interdisciplinary course on Dorothy Day and the Catholic Worker Movement. The course mysteriously hovered between the College of Journalism and the College of Arts and Sciences in the theology and history departments. Students taking the course were able to apply for credit in any of those disciplines. In fact the placement and ownership of the course that first offering was so mysterious that somehow I was not paid to teach it because no one department would take responsibility for it or figure out how to share the expense and we had a few dozen students registered for it. In the spirit of Dorothy Day and Peter Maurin's call to voluntary poverty I adopted their model, sallied forth, and have been ever grateful for the opportunity to teach a course for nearly two decades which so captures the religious imagination and interest of students. But like many teachers I have honed the course and the process over the years, constantly reflecting on what and how to engage students in this important study whose results I now share with readers.

The following year the course landed permanently in Theology. Yet as a former Catholic journalist and as someone who began studying the Catholic Worker, I continued to teach the course from the perspective of many disciplines. There is history in the story and loads of it: the immigration movement in the United States; the Depression, the labor movement, a series of wars which provided fodder for the peace movement; the racial justice movement. The story is marked by hunger and homelessness, unemployment, racial and gender concerns, to name a few. For the journalist there is a treasure trove of analysis: advocacy journalism, personalist journalism, starting a newspaper, the plain and clear writing of Dorothy, Catholic Worker art and illustrations.

But the foundation is and always remains theological: Jesus in words and deeds, the teachings of the church, sacramentality, voluntary poverty, prayer, devotion to the saints, the spiritual and corporal works of mercy, Catholic Social Teaching, peace and conversion. The Catholic Worker story, the Dorothy Day and Peter Maurin story, is not only multi-disciplinary but it also provides intriguing windows for students to learn, research, study, and write about a time and a story that is countercultural, historical, and eerily prophetic. Seeing students as scholars of this captivating story and finding ways to facilitate and accompany them in the learning process is extremely gratifying. The topics readily allow for what AAC&U (the American Association of Colleges and Universities) has named as a "high impact practice" with a service/community based learning experience (it is required for the course) as the service becomes "a text" for the students who spend 15–18 hours in the course of the semester in placements that readily connect with course topics: shelters, meal programs, Milwaukee's own Casa Maria Catholic Worker House, adult immigrant tutoring programs, the city and county jails are just a few. Regular inclusion of discussions and short writing assignments based on their service integrates the service learning with the rest of the course.

Most important it gives the next generation a model of Catholic living sorely needed today. A favorite oft repeated comment from students is "why has no one told us about these radical teachings of the Catholic Church? They are so cool." or "I left the church in high school but I am coming back because of this class." At least two students were inspired by Dorothy's conversion and eventually landed in the campus ministry RCIA program.

I do say to them clearly at the start of the course that the course is not about their conversion. It is not about them agreeing with or believing everything they will read and study. But it is about wrestling with the ideas, beliefs, and values found in the commitments of Dorothy Day, Peter Maurin, and Catholic teachings about social justice. It is also about curiosity and discovery since they as researchers have the chance to dig into, read, and dialogue with primary sources. For many of the students sadly much of their education has been found in text books and secondary sources. But Marquette is blessed with a huge Catholic Worker archive collection including personal papers from Dorothy, Peter, and other workers, and so our students benefit from actually physically reading letters and documents typed and/or written by Dorothy, which is a moving experience once they learn the basics of her life. Nearly twenty years after the centenary conference, the gift of technology (largely and vociferously debated at the Centenary conference as a way to promulgate and spread ideas of the Worker) now makes many sources easily available on-line with a few strokes of the keyboard.

It is that scholarship I address today. How does a teacher get students excited about learning about something from a previous century occurring likely even before the birth of their grandparents? The methodology that works amazingly well is based on the experience of a student from about fifteen years ago who unwittingly taught me how to transform the course for optimum student interest. This student was active in hunger and homelessness volunteer work on campus especially in Midnight Run, a lunchtime meal program (originally run from 10 PM to midnight) out of a van offered by students daily for the unemployed, homeless, and underemployed guests and neighbors who frequent our downtown urban campus She had her backpack stolen from the van while she was serving up soup. The experience raised all kinds of questions about "the deserving poor and about feeling violated and at risk in caring for the poor."

After a long discussion fraught with tears, this 19-year-old questioned whether she could continue serving. Sometimes as a teacher one is blessed with moments of inspired grace. I suggested she take her questions to the archives and Dorothy Day's writings and actions, knowing full well that Dorothy wrestled with some of the same questions. She not only did that but ended up writing an invented dialogue (a short play) between herself and Dorothy and on the day of her class presentation she had (with permission) engaged a friend and theatre student to come dressed in Dorothy-like clothing with her hair in braids pinned in a crown around her head to play the part of Dorothy. Seated at a table with cup of tea in hand, the student interviewed "Dorothy" asking dozens of questions about her fortitude and endurance in serving the poor for so long. The presentation was so strong that for the next several years the two students regularly presented their vignette to students working on hunger and homelessness issues through Campus Ministry and other campus venues.

I now begin every first class by passing out index cards. On one side I ask each student to write what it means to them to "put on Christ." I acknowledge to them that in the class are believers and non-believers, Christians and others of a variety of religious practices. I have had Muslims, Hindus, Sikhs, as well as agnostics and atheists take the class. With the pervasiveness of Christianity in U.S. culture I ask each of them to articulate what that might mean "to put on Christ" regardless of their own vantage point. On the other side of the index card I ask them to write a short paragraph about a social justice concern in the world today, here and now, that they are most concerned about and what about that issue they are most curious about in the form of a question or questions.

Questions about war and peace, the economy, race, AIDS, gender, ecclesiology, spirituality, faith and doubts, poverty, protests, health care, immigration, the elderly, the homeless who wander our campus inevitably are raised.

These questions become the starting point of a private tutoring conversation when I meet with them individually outside the classroom (the class is usually 30–40 students) to help them prepare for the research they will engage in as they read pages of *The Catholic Worker* newspaper, Dorothy's columns and books, and other sources. From that conversation they hone in on significant research questions they then take to their archival and library research. The assignment is relatively plagiarism-proof because they must articulate their own personal questions and then proceed. A month later they have written a paper and present their questions and their discovery to the class in short presentations.

One class is actually held at the archives (to take the scariness out of it insofar as some of our students have never crossed the threshold of the library much less the archives!) and Marquette's expert archivist Phil Runkel explains the history of the collection. He also gives an overview of what is there and how to request the documents, and we teach them basic etiquette and practices required in the archives. I make a point of telling the students that if they want to impress their other faculty members and improve their grades overall on papers, checking the archival collection on a wide range of topics is not a bad way to go when appropriate. At the same time I challenge them to read more deeply and broadly and find something I did not know about the CW story. They rise to the occasion and I am amazed at how willing they are to read far beyond the required texts. Phil puts out copies of the *Worker* for them to read over the decades. Much of the collection is now digitized and more and more resources are available on line every month although I want them to touch the actual editions since we have access to them.

Every student is required to read the inaugural May 1, 1933 edition (also now on line) and then groups are assigned to read issues from particular decades, drawing comparisons between Catholic Worker foci and topics and what they know of history. Most of them get pretty excited as they see convergence, but they also come to realize that the worker movement and the ideas of Peter and Dorothy are countercultural and challenge convention. They also discover a history of the Catholic Church and theology and practices that often surprises them. Students often proclaim they "did not know research could be so much fun!"

The service-learning component also challenged and changes students.

When students react to the "required" nature of the service learning I point out that the service becomes a living textbook providing experiential knowledge and a kind of sensate knowledge not easily acquired solely from reading. From the beginning I teach them Ignatian means of paying attention to the experience, using their senses. Their first short assignment after visiting their service learning site is to write what they see, smell, hear, taste, and feel. Imagine students who grew up in a comfortable suburb. Walking into a men's shelter in the city housing 80 men a night, they will write about the smell of urine, alcohol, dirt, sweat, stale coffee, etc. They will see disheveled and tired men. They will feel a blast of heat, hear showers in the distance, and see men shuffling in the upstairs dorm. Repeating the exercise toward the end of the semester their observational powers focus on individuals they have met and the stories of the people they have heard often with poignant chronicles of bad choices or luck. They write about what they have learned from these seemingly destitute individuals and how they see friendships they have made with people they used to hold in contempt.

Their experience and the experiences of Dorothy and the Catholic Workers converge. At the same time they begin to understand Dorothy's comment from Archbishop Helder Camera often attributed to her: "If you feed people you are a saint, if you ask why they are hungry you are a communist." (It is uncertain as to the origin of that comment since both get credit for it.) They start to ask, "why are people hungry in this city in the neighborhood and in the world?"

Rigorous scholarship of Catholic Social Teaching accompanies the service learning and the students read *Rerum Novarum, Centesimus Annus, A Place at the Table*, as well as other Bishops' letters on immigration and hunger and poverty. These pronouncements are often a surprise to all the students who usually have not been privy to the breadth and depth of the church's teaching about contemporary issues. In another paper they integrate their service experience and particularly what they are learning about the populations they are serving with with the teachings of the church. That is powerful medicine for young people who thought the church was irrelevant.

Tapping into the depth of the Catholic Worker story and the spirituality of Dorothy Day—particularly in the curious juxtaposition of her deep piety with her commitment to justice—opens a world of inquiry for 18–22 year olds. Ideally this story makes them more curious, helps them to connect other aspects of their college curriculum with theology, and spurs them to listen and learn in a different way. It is grace in action.

Susan M. Mountin directs Manresa for Faculty at Marquette University, an initiative designed to focus on exploring and deepening the role of faculty in a Jesuit Catholic institution. As of January 2015 she also directs a Lilly Endowment Inc. funded program "Pastoral Leadership in a Cultural Context" for early career ecumenical Christian pastors, She has been a Catholic newspaper and magazine editor, free-lance writer, and campus minister. She was formerly associate editor at the *Milwaukee Catholic Herald* and *U.S. Catholic.* She served in Campus Ministry at Marquette for 25 years and for eight additional years directed another Lilly funded initiative in the Manresa Project: A Program for the Theological Exploration of Vocation. She teaches courses on *Dorothy Day and the Catholic Worker Movement, Ignatian Spirituality, Social Justice/Social Activism, and Christian Discipleship* and often directs Ignatian-styled retreats for church groups and parish councils.

The Personalism
of Dorothy Day and the
Catholic Worker

Dorothy Day's Synthesis
of Love of God
and Love of Neighbor

Ben Wilson

A number of months ago at the St. Peter Claver Catholic Worker in South Bend, Indiana, a lively dinnertime conversation unfolded about what Dorothy Day meant when she said, "you love God as much as the one you love the least."[1] Each of us around the table ventured some earnest thoughts on the matter. Characteristically, one of the older wisdom figures of the community, whose words are as few as they are profound, remained quiet. Eager to hear his insights on the topic, I asked this good soul as directly as possible: "what do you think about the love of God and the love of neighbor?" He paused for a moment, and then announced, "Well, I'm for it!"

While Dorothy Day was scarcely a person of few words, my community member's quip strikes me as altogether Dorothy-like. Dorothy was unmistakably *for* it. The desire to love God and love her neighbors, both near and far, animated her entire life's work. And she was for *it*. Without either commitment disappearing into the other, Dorothy reached such a unity between love of God and love of neighbor that she too might have said she was for "it" rather than for "these two things."

The compatibility between love of God and love of neighbor might appear obvious. After all, Jesus sums up the entire law and the prophets on these two commandments.[2] Theologians ranging from St. Augustine to Karl Rahner treat the topic extensively.[3] Benedict XVI devoted his encyclical *Deus Caritas Est* to

1 Dorothy Day, *On Pilgrimage* (Grand Rapids, Michigan: Eerdmans, 1999), 166, cited on http://www.catholicworker.org/dorothyday/daytext.cfm?TextID=486.

2 See Matthew 22:27.

3 For studies of these thinkers, see Sr. Pascale-Dominique Nau, OP, "Love of God and Love of Neighbor in the writings of Saint Augustine," *Dominican Monastic Search* 16 (1997):

describing the "unbreakable bond" between the two.[4] For Dorothy, however, the pairing of love of God and love of neighbor seemed highly unlikely for much of her early years given her simultaneous idealism and realism, religiosity and radicalism. As a young woman, Dorothy in alternating fashion believed—or perhaps it would be more accurate to say "feared"—that she had to renounce either human affection in order to be truly about God, or reject God if she were to be fully on the side of the poor. Dorothy's conversion hinged on finding a "third way" uniting these two loves. On the precipice of deciding whether or not to enter the Catholic Church, Dorothy exclaimed: "How I longed to make a synthesis reconciling body and soul, this world and the next."[5]

In this paper, I will retrace several of Dorothy's many steps to arriving at this "synthesis" that enabled her to call her busy, crowded, noisy life among the poor a "contemplative vocation" in which she daily received Christ in the Eucharist as well as in the guests at the Catholic Worker.[6] As this conference is dedicated to looking at Dorothy's ongoing significance for the Church in the twenty-first century, I will then draw out several implications of Dorothy's synthesis for our own time marked by a trend towards the privatization of faith and the secularization of work for justice.

Regarding terminology, I frame the question as the relationship between "love of God" and "love of neighbor" to reflect Dorothy's customary way of writing about this topic which she drew from Jesus's own words in the synoptic gospels.[7] In our own time, we might question the adequacy of the term "neighbor" to circumscribe our obligations towards others in a world characterized by simultaneous globalization and segregation. Does the language of loving one's neighbor implicitly endorse a narrow enclave mentality? I propose that "neigh-

---

9–16; Karl Rahner, *Theological Investigations Volume 4*, trans. Karl-H. Kruger and Boniface Kruger (Baltimore: Helicon/London: Darton, Longmann and Todd, 1969): 247; and Karl Rahner, "The Unity of the Love of God and Love of Neighbour," *Theology Digest* 15 (1967): 88, cited by Gerald J. Beyer, "Rahner on the Radical Unity of Love of God and Neighbour," *Irish Theological Quarterly* 68 (2003): 251–280.

4   http://w2.vatican.va/content/benedict-xvi/en/encyclicals/documents/hf_ben-xvi_enc_20051225_deus-caritas-est.html, §16.

5   Dorothy Day, *The Long Loneliness* (New York: Harper and Row, 1952), 172.

6   Jim Forest, *Love is the Measure: A Biography of Dorothy Day*, (Maryknoll, New York: Orbis, 2000), 125.

7   See Matthew 22:27, Mark 12:30, and Luke 10:27. The theme of love of God and love of neighbor—and this particular phrasing—remained Dorothy's central focus throughout her life, as she alludes to when she writes: "It is an opportunity to show what we mean what we write when we repeat over and over that we are put her on this earth to love God an our neighbor" (Forest, *Love is the Measure*, 99).

bor" as a theological and geographical concept carries a radical injunction that is both definite and universal. Jesus recounts the parable of the Good Samaritan in response to the question "Who is my neighbor?" in order to dismantle any exceptions to the category that we might propose.[8] "Neighbor," in Dorothy's parlance, likewise signifies an all-inclusive category. No class of people so occupied Dorothy's heart and imagination, though, quite like the poor. Dorothy did not content herself with an abstracted sense of kinship with her global neighbors. She deliberately chose to make her home among the poor and to form actual neighborly relationships among them. Embodying the evangelical thrust of the Sermon on the Mount, Dorothy took the concept of neighborly concern to the point of inviting the poorest of her neighbors to live under her own roof in Catholic Worker Houses of Hospitality. Following Dorothy, this paper presupposes that "neighbor" admits no exceptions while carrying a firm preferential option for the poor.

Dorothy's Pilgrimage: Forging a Path Uniting Love of God and Love of Neighbor

Taking as her own the self-description of a character in Fyodor Dostoyevsky's *The Possessed*, Dorothy states at the outset of her autobiography: "All my life I have been haunted by God."[9] Dorothy recalls as a child being "filled with a natural striving, a thrilling recognition of the possibilities of spiritual adventure."[10] In the midst of a non-practicing Christian family, Dorothy grew increasingly devout, which led her to become, as she later described, "alternately lonely and smug."[11] In her high school journal, she confessed her struggle to "overcome all physical sensation and be purely spiritual" since, as she saw it at the time, "the only love is of God and is spiritual without taint of earthliness."[12] For the young Dorothy, her life was oriented entirely to love of God, and to achieve this she felt she must shun the world around her. One's neighbor appeared to her to be a stumbling block on the road to God.[13]

---

8   See Luke 10:29.

9   Day, *The Long Loneliness*, 10.

10 Forest, *Love is the Measure*, 9.

11 Ibid., 5.

12 Ibid., 12.

13 These pious aspirations of a young Dorothy reveal something of her characteristic single-heartedness. Reading her early journals in the context of her entire life shows these lines to be early seeds that grew into the durable brand of love that Dorothy tirelessly pro-

Dorothy's lonely religious fervor soon shifted into an insatiable appetite to experience the world and find community. [14] Of her time in college, she wrote: "My freedom intoxicated me. I felt it was worth going hungry for." [15] While hungry for experience, Dorothy was far from being self-absorbed. Walking through the slums of Chicago awoke in Dorothy a profound sense of purpose and solidarity. She noted, "from then on my life was to be linked to theirs, their interests were to be mine: I had received a call, a vocation, a direction in my life." [16] In this newfound calling, Dorothy found kindred spirits among the followers of Karl Marx whose anthem "workers of the world unite," as she writes, "seemed to me a most stirring battle cry... a clarion call that made me feel one with the masses." [17]

Within just a few short years of declaring in her journal her desire for a pure love of God untainted by the things of the world, an increasingly socially conscious Dorothy strained with equal intensity to put behind her anything that prevented her from being one with her impoverished neighbors. Scandalized by what she perceived as the Church's lack of concern for justice for the poor, Dorothy adopted the Marxist view of religion as an "opiate" that she did not need. [18] In Dorothy's passion to live with and for the poor, she sought to cast faith behind her, thinking, "religion would only impede my work." [19] Love of God and love of neighbor again seemed incompatible to Dorothy, but now she opted to privilege love of neighbor.

moted and embodied. Her adolescent eagerness to "overcome all physical sensation" matured into her adult capacity to endure hunger strikes, imprisonment, extensive travels and correspondence, and of course, the lifelong daily sacrifices of living for and among the poor.

14 In her autobiography, Dorothy relates how no one particular course of study during her time at the University of Illinois held her interest. Rather, "it was experience in general that I wanted." (Day, *The Long Loneliness*, 45). Jim Forest describes Dorothy's lifestyle during her first job, saying: "If the first month's diet was meager, Dorothy's work provided well for her huge appetite for experience" (Forest, *Love is the Measure*, 21).

15 Day, *The Long Loneliness*, 49.

16 Forest, *Love is the Measure*, 13.

17 Dorothy Day, *Selected Writings*, ed. Robert Ellsberg (Maryknoll, New York: Orbis, 1993), 14. Jim Forest echoes Dorothy's sense of solidarity, saying: "She found her burden of loneliness was eased when she walked through the slums." Forest, *Love is the Measure*, 17.

18 Dorothy describes in her autobiography her disappointment at "the scandal of businesslike priests, of collective wealth, the lack of a sense of responsibility for the poor, the worker, the Negro, the Mexican, the Filipino, and even the oppression of these.... 'Am I my brother's keeper?' they seemed to say in respect to the social order. There was plenty of charity but too little justice" (Day, *The Long Loneliness*, 171).

19 Forest, *Love is the Measure*, 15.

Her first stint in jail for civil disobedience occasioned a still-nascent convergence of Dorothy's two loves. In witnessing from the inside, as it were, the suffering of fellow inmates, Dorothy felt a rush of visceral connection with all who suffer. She observed: "I was the mother whose child had been raped and slain. I was the mother who had born the monster who had done it. I was even that monster, feeling in my own breast every abomination." [20] While in jail, she sank into a deep depression. She asked for a Bible and found in the Psalms a renewed source of joy that they had first brought her as a child. [21] This up-close and personal view of the plight of her neighbors led Dorothy to turn to God to find comfort.

Although her thoughts returned to God in this time of bleakness, Dorothy emphatically pointed out that it was not need or despair that pushed her to God, but rather, a surplus of love that drew her back. [22] After her release from jail, Dorothy continued her work with radical newspapers, but she no longer suppressed her religious instincts. Dorothy even credited her association with communists, despite their explicit hostility to religion, as having helped cultivate in her a desire for the type of public and universal action she was attracted to in the Catholic liturgy. [23] From her friend Eugene O'Neill, Dorothy first heard Francis Thompson's evocative poem "The Hound of Heaven," which tells of the soul's fortunate inability to escape God's dogged pursuit. While still far from becoming Catholic, Dorothy began dropping into Catholic churches at irregular hours to pray. After a desperate affair with Lionel Moise, which led to her having an abortion, and then a short-lived marriage to a wealthy older man, Dorothy entered into a long-term relationship with Forster Batterham. Although he believed in neither God nor marriage, Dorothy regarded their love as having directly fostered her own conversion. In her autobiography, Dorothy recounts:

---

20 Ibid., 28.

21 Ibid., 29.

22 Jim Forest cites Dorothy as saying of this time: "I am praying because I am happy, not because I am unhappy" (Forest, *Love is the Measure: A Biography of Dorothy Day*, 45–6).

23 In *The Long Loneliness*, Dorothy explains: "My very experience as a radical, my whole make-up, led me to want to associate myself with others, with the masses, in loving and praising God" (Day, *The Long Loneliness*, 159). While Dorothy attributes ways in which communism helped form her for faith, she also identifies its inability to satisfy her deepest desires: "If I could have felt that communism was the answer to my desire for a cause, a motive, a way to walk in, I would have remained as I was. But I felt that only faith in Christ could give the answer. The Sermon on the Mount answered all the questions as to how to love God and one's brother" (Day, *The Long Loneliness*, 141, cited in Mark and Louise Zwick, *The Catholic Worker Movement: Intellectual and Spiritual Origins*, (New York: Paulist Press, 2015), 9.

"I have always felt that it was life with him that brought me natural happiness, that brought me to God."[24] Dorothy's loneliness subsided during these rich years with Forster and she experienced the joy of new life when she discovered she was pregnant after thinking herself infertile after her abortion. Holding her newborn daughter Tamar in her arms, Dorothy felt: "No human creature could receive or contain so vast a flood of love and joy as I often felt after the birth of my child. With this came the need to worship, to adore."[25] Human love enabled Dorothy to recognize and respond with love to God who she sensed had long been pursuing her.

As is well-known, precisely as Dorothy made these initial perceptions of the close unity between love of God and love of neighbor, she and Forster simultaneously began a painful separation which she continued to mourn for years.[26]

24 See, for instance, Dorothy's comment "I could not see that love between man and woman was incompatible with love of God" (Day, *The Long Loneliness*, 153). Shortly thereafter she continues, "It was because through a whole love, both physical and spiritual, I came to know God" (Day, *The Long Loneliness*, 160). Dorothy drew upon the tradition of St. Augustine in forging the synthesis of love of God and love of neighbor. She writes: "My conversion began many years ago, at a time when the material world around me began to speak in my heart of the love of God. There is a beautiful passage in St. Augustine, whose *Confessions* I read at this time. 'What is it I love when I love Thee,' it begins, and goes on to list all the material beauty and enjoyment to be found in the life of the senses. The sea, which surrounded us, rather, it was a bay leading out to sea, provided food, fish and shellfish in abundance, even the sea weeds, which a Japanese friend told me were part of the food of her people. Our garden grew vegetables; the fields berries, the trees fruits. Everything spoke to me of a Creator who satisfied all our hungers. It was also the physical aspect of the Church which attracted me. Bread and wine, water (all water is made holy since Christ was baptized in the Jordan), incense, the sound of waves and wind, all nature cried out to me." (Dorothy Day, "Bread for the Hungry," *The Catholic Worker*, September 1976, 1, 5. *The Catholic Worker Movement*. http://www.catholicworker.org/dorothyday/Reprint2.cfm?TextID=258.)

25 Day, *The Long Loneliness*, 159.

26 While she began to perceive the spiritual connections between love of God and love of neighbor, and she gave thanks for the concrete ways in which human love helped lead her to God, Dorothy also recognized that disordered human attachments can be stumbling blocks on the road to God. She writes that "it got to the point where it was the simple question of whether I chose God or man." (Day, *The Long Loneliness*, 160.) Shortly after her separation from Forster, Dorothy confesses in a letter to him her sense of the primacy of the spiritual life, but also the intensity of her physical longings: "It is terribly hard to even mention my religious feelings to you because I am sure you do not think I am sincere. But it is not a sudden thing, but a thing which has been growing in me for years. I had impulses toward religion again and again and now when I try to order my life according to it in order to attain some sort of peace and happiness it is very hard but I must do it. Because even though it is hard, it gives me far more happiness to do it, even though it means my combating my physical feelings toward you." (Robert Ellsberg, "Dearest For-

Whereas Dorothy previously criticized the Catholic Church for not doing more to go to the aid of the poor, she began to notice that many of the poor were themselves drawn to the Church. Dorothy came to see the Church as being the Church *of* the poor even as she longed for it to become a Church *for* the poor. [27]

Compelled by the faith she saw in those who flocked to the Church, Dorothy persevered in breaking from Forster to become Catholic and have Tamar baptized. Even so, Dorothy knew nothing of the Church's modern social teaching. [28] Thus, she did not yet see in the Church a model of a united love of God and neighbor; rather, Dorothy loved the Church for being "Christ made visible" while she lamented her temporary social inactivity as a neophyte Catholic because she did not yet see how to integrate faith and social action. [29] As Jim Forest notes in his biography of Dorothy, in her early years as a Catholic, "she had no deep friendships with Catholics and no real welcome from radicals. She had a religious faith and a social conscience but no community." [30] Dorothy had to wait to meet Peter Maurin to be given a vision for the sort of synthesis between love of God and love of neighbor that she had so long desired.

The Catholic Worker movement was born of the union of love of God and love of neighbor, as Peter envisioned it and Dorothy embodied it. In the words of Dorothy, Peter exhorted her and anyone who would listen to "stretch out their arms to their brothers, because he knew that the surest way to find God, to find the good, was through one's brothers." [31] In the very first issue of the *Catholic Worker* newspaper, Dorothy wasted no time sharing the good news of this synthesis and one gets the sense that Dorothy is almost reassuring herself of the veracity of what she had long hoped might be true. She writes:

> [*The Catholic Worker*] is printed to call their attention to the
> fact that the Catholic Church has a social program—to let
> them know that there are men of God who are working not

ster," *America* (November 15, 2010): http://americamagazine.org/issue/755/ideas/dearest-forster.)

27 As she explains in her autobiography, the sense of solidarity with ordinary people of faith throughout the centuries drew Dorothy to the Church more than any rational apology for the Church: "Without even looking into the claims of the Catholic Church, I was willing to admit that for me she was the one true Church" (Day, *The Long Loneliness*, 159).

28 Ibid., 172.

29 Watching a street demonstration from her apartment window shortly after becoming Catholic, Dorothy lamented not being able to join the demonstrators.

30 Forest, *Love is the Measure*, 55.

31 Day, *The Long Loneliness*, 195

> only for their spiritual, but for their material welfare. ... Is it
> not possible to be radical and not atheist? Is it not possible to
> protest, to expose, to complain, to point out abuses and de-
> mand reforms without desiring the overthrow of religion? [32]

In keeping with Peter's Easy Essay "Blowing the Dynamite," Dorothy wanted others to know what she had come to believe: that Christianity needed to be actually done, not done away with, in order to bring about radical social change. [33]

It is overly facile to say Peter solely provided ideas and Dorothy simply carried them out, but Dorothy certainly concretized the movement's ethos of love. She perennially called to mind the words of the elder Zosima in *The Brothers Karamazov* that love in reality is a harsh and dreadful thing compared to love in dreams. [34] Love of God, if untethered from our relationships with others, seemed to Dorothy to become either anemic or gravely distorted. Dorothy had withdrawn from the Christian faith of her childhood because, judging by its adherents, it "had no vitality. It had nothing to do with everyday life; it was a matter of Sunday praying. Christ no longer walked the streets of this world." [35] On the other hand, Dorothy grieved "how mixed up religion can become" when the faithful lose sight of the neighbor and instead perceive a stranger, a foreigner, an enemy, as she felt was the case when priests were called upon to bless bombs before war. [36] In Dorothy's synthesis, our love of neighbor serves to demonstrate, purify, and make real the love we profess towards God: "This work came about because we started writing of the love we should have for each other, in order to show our love of God. It's the only way we can know we love God." [37] Dorothy thus deeply internalized the logic of 1 John 4: "Beloved, let us love one another,

---

32 Dorothy Day, "To Our Readers," *The Catholic Worker* (May 1933), 4, http://www.catholicworker.org/dorothyday/Reprint2.cfm?TextID=12.

33 Peter Maurin, *Easy Essays* (Eugene, Oregon: Wipf and Stock, 2003), 3. Dorothy's insight into Christianity as both radical and necessary stems in part from Fr. Hugo's frequent citation of G. K. Chesterton, as Jim Forest explains: "At the 'famous' retreat with Fr. Hugo, Dorothy would have often heard him quote G. K. Chesterton's observation: 'Christianity has not been tried and found wanting. It has been found difficult and left untried. Even watered down, Christianity is still hot enough to boil the modern world to rags'" (Forest, *Love is the Measure*, 83).

34 Fyodor Dostoyevsky, *The Brothers Karamazov*, http://www.ccel.org/d/dostoevsky/karamozov/htm/book02/chapter04.html.

35 Dorothy Day, "The Long Way Home," in *Selected Writings* ed. Robert Ellsberg (Maryknoll, New York: Orbis, 1993), 15.

36 Forest, *Love is the Measure*, 96.

37 Dorothy Day, "Fall Appeal, 1977," in *Selected Writings*, 359.

because love is of God; everyone who loves is begotten by God and knows God. Whoever is without love does not know God, for God is love." [38] Love of God requires love of neighbor.

Ultimately, Dorothy regarded love of neighbor, and the love of the poor in particular, as fundamentally oriented to love of God. She described her approach to loving other people as "practicing the presence of God." [39] Committed to the literalism of Matthew 25, Dorothy urged her readers to care for the poor not because they remind us of Christ, but because "they *are* Christ, asking us to find room for Him, exactly as He did at the first Christmas." [40]

Because of the divine image in which one's neighbor is made, one can love God in and through one's neighbor, but Dorothy always retained an abiding sense of God's primacy and transcendence. For Dorothy, the intersection as well as distinction between love of God and the love of neighbor resides in the relationship between Creator and creatures. All created beings possess intrinsic worth, but always in reference to their Creator who bestows this worth upon them. Dorothy railed against any reduction of other people into mere means towards our own ends, but she was likewise concerned with the temptation to cling to human love as an end in itself apart from God. Shortly after naming her relationship with Forster as having helped lead her to God, Dorothy adds the qualification: "In the eyes of God, any turning toward creatures to the exclusion of Him is adultery and so it is termed over and over again in Scripture." [41] Significantly, Dorothy names this as adultery whereas we might expect to hear her call it idolatry. Her choice of the word "adultery" makes vivid her conviction that the soul's primary relationship is with God, which in turn bears fruit in our loving relationships with others.

Thus for Dorothy, love of God motivated, fed, and sustained love of neighbor. In Dorothy's journals, she recounts striving to "do everything with love, for the love of God." [42] A 1940 issue of *The Catholic Worker* makes certain the movement's priorities:

---

38 Scripture texts in this work are taken from the New American Bible, revised edition © 2010, 1991, 1986, 1970 Confraternity of Christian Doctrine, Washington, D.C. and are used by permission of the copyright owner. All Rights Reserved. No part of the New American Bible may be reproduced in any form without permission in writing from the copyright owner.

39 Day, *Selected Writings*, 92.

40 Day, "Room For Christ," in *Selected Writings*, 97.

41 Day, *The Long Loneliness*, 171.

42 Day, *Selected Writings*, 213.

> This work of ours toward a new heaven and a new earth shows a correlation between the material and the spiritual, and of course, recognizing the primacy of the spiritual. Food for the body is not enough. There must be food for the soul. Hence the leaders of the work, as and many as we can induce to join us, must go daily to Mass, to receive food for the soul. [43]

For Dorothy, the "work" of the Catholic Worker was first the "work" of the liturgy, which in turn feeds the corporal and spiritual works of mercy. Dorothy was glad to show visitors how the Catholic Worker fed the hungry and gave shelter to the homeless, but as she said, "If an outsider who comes to visit us doesn't pay attention to our praying and what that means, then he'll miss the whole point." [44] Put most succinctly, the synthesis Dorothy achieved is this: love of neighbor grounds and makes real one's love of God, and love of God provides the ultimate source and horizon of one's love of neighbor. [45]

The Contemporary Significance of Dorothy's Synthesis: Formation for Faith and Action

So, what does Dorothy's example mean for us? Was her synthesis simply resolving an only apparent contradiction that she eventually learned to see beyond? I suggest that for as long as campus ministry and social justice clubs signify different "camps" on college campuses, for as long as faith is seen as a wholly pri-

---

43 Day, "Aims and Purposes," in *Selected Writings*, 91. For Dorothy, loving one's neighbor as Christ requires the eyes of faith, similar to the faith by which one acknowledges the Blessed Sacrament as the Body of Christ. She writes, "[Many people ask]: 'How can you see Christ in people?' And we only say: It is an act of faith, constantly repeated. It is an act of love, resulting from an act of faith. It is an act of hope, that we can awaken these same acts in their hearts, too, with the help of God, and the Works of Mercy. . . . The mystery of the poor is this: That they are Jesus, and what you do for them you do for Him. It is the only way we have of knowing and believing in our love" (Day, "The Mystery of the Poor," in *Selected Writings*, 329).

44 Jim Forest recounts Dorothy's anguish at subsequent generations of Catholic Workers divorcing faith from action, privileging action as she had once done. He recounts: "A major area of distress for her in the 1970s was what seemed to her the erosion occurring in the spiritual life of her fellow Catholics, including those in the Catholic Worker movement. More than ever Catholics seemed attentive to social issues she had been raising for forty years, but they were increasingly neglectful of the disciplines of Church life that were fundamental to her" (Forest, *Love is the Measure*, 130).

45 As summed up by Mark and Louise Zwick, the Catholic Worker "does not accept a dualism between work for justice and charity, between public and private life, between theol-

vate affair and community service is pursued as a résumé-builder or public relations boost, for as long as there is distance between the faith we profess and the faith we practice, we stand in need of Dorothy's prophetic insistence upon the radical nature of the Christian faith. Drawing most immediately from my context working with Notre Dame's Summer Service Learning Program, a three-credit theology course that includes an eight-week service immersion in communities of need throughout the country, I will conclude by offering four insights from Dorothy's life that can foster our own forging a union between love of God and love of neighbor.

First, Dorothy's long journey to arriving at her ultimate "sythensis" serves as a reminder to truly reverence the ways God may be acting in our own or other people's lives, even if one does not acknowledge God's presence at a particular time. Even when attempting to separate herself from God, Dorothy sensed that the "Hound of Heaven" relentlessly pursued her. In retrospect, Dorothy could identify how her very human experiences with Forster of enjoying nature, finding companionship, and experiencing natural happiness helped lead her to God. Dorothy's long journey to discovering the love of God reminds us to take seriously our experiences and relationships as potentially revelatory of God's presence. When conversing with others who do not explicitly name love of God as a motivating factor in their lives, we would do well to recall how Dorothy's journey provides testimony to the fact that "love of God" refers first and foremost to God's love of us. [46] Our own love of God is a response, sometimes much delayed, to God's own unflagging care for us.

Second, while Dorothy's path to God reiterates the importance of human relationships, Dorothy's asceticism beckons our hearts ultimately towards God's love, which alone corresponds to the depth of our hunger for and capacity to love. If placing any creature before God amounts in Dorothy's view to adultery, then a love that is faithful, true, and generative is one that loves God before all, in all, and above all. By fostering in ourselves and in others this type of love, we

---

ogy and social theory or economics, between cross and resurrection, between spirituality and religion, between body and soul—they are all inextricably interwoven in the best of Catholic tradition" (Mark and Louise Zwick, *The Catholic Worker Movement: Intellectual and Spiritual Origins* [New York: Paulist Press, 2015], 295).

46 Dorothy points to the book of Hosea as a prime example of God's love of humanity. She writes: "In the book of Hosea in the Old Testament, the picture of God's love is the picture of the prophet loving his harlot wife, and supporting not only her but her lovers. What foolish, what unjudging love! And the picture of God's love in the New Testament is of Christ, our Brother, dying for us on the Cross, for us who are ungrateful, undeserving. Let us love God, since He first loved us" (Day, *Selected Writings*, 359).

come to love others not less but more since it frees others from the burden of being everything to us.

Third, Dorothy's incarnational spirituality serves as a timely corrective to our own increasingly virtual age in which technology exerts considerable influence in the domain of friendship. "Following" someone or "liking" a person's comments or "friending" a new acquaintance all signify ways of connecting with others, but at a very definite remove from the other. While we, or our students, or others we work with, might support worthy causes using social media, there is no replacement for actual contact with people in need. Invoking Dorothy as a proto-proponent of experiential service learning, we can draw upon her incarnational spirituality and praxis to help ground our contemporary ways of talking and thinking about relationships. This active work requires commensurate time for prayer, theological reflection, and discussion, as Dorothy so frequently did, in order for the seeds of active love to take root in our lives. By engaging in and reflecting upon concrete practices of love of neighbor, we will come to perceive with greater clarity who our neighbors really are and what our relationship is to them. And, if we take Jesus at his word that what we do to the least of his brothers and sisters we do to him, our very image of God stands to be expanded, challenged, and continually re-enfleshed.

Finally, Dorothy's unceasing effort to ever more faithfully love God and neighbor reminds us that becoming truly loving requires a lifelong journey. In her book on St. Thérèse the Little Flower, Dorothy readily acknowledges: "We want to grow in love but we do not know how. Love is a science, a knowledge, and we lack it."[47] As an internationally recognized speaker and figure, Dorothy easily might have focused on her successes when promoting her work and the movement. Instead, she frequently called to mind a phrase she had learned on retreat with Fr. Hugo: "You love God as much as the one you love the least."[48] As is characteristic of many saints, Dorothy remained utterly convinced of God's enduring presence in those around her as well as of her own failings to reciprocate and channel God's love.[49] Dorothy's example challenges us, and in turn those we work with, to resist the allure of self-congratulation, regardless of how

---

47 Day, "Therese," in *Selected Writings*, 189.

48 Forest, *Love is the Measure*, 134.

49 The content of Fr. Hugo's retreat—as well as Dorothy's frequent attendance at it—reiterated for her the constant need and ability to go deeper. She comments, "I have made this retreat eight times, and always there is something new, always there is something to learn about how to progress in the love of God and one's neighbor" (Day, "On Pilgrimage," in *Selected Writings*, 220). She continues in this same entry, "My whole life, so far, my whole experience has been that our failure has been not to love enough."

demanding or fruitful our work is. With Dorothy, we can echo what she felt even at the end of her extraordinary life: we have "scarcely begun." [50]

Ben Wilson serves as an assistant director of the Summer Service Learning Program (SSLP) and co-director of the Social Enterprise and Microfinance Internship (SEMI) at the University of Notre Dame's Center for Social Concerns. Ben earned a Bachelor of Arts in philosophy and a Master of Divinity, both from Notre Dame. His prior professional experience includes teaching high school scripture and philosophy as well as fundraising at United Way of Central Alabama. He and his wife Mary Ann and their two children are members of the St. Peter Claver Catholic Worker extended community in South Bend.

---

50 Forest, *Love is the Measure*, 134.

The Value of Persons and the Social Activism of Dorothy Day: A Causal Link

Rob Arner

A disregard for the personhood of an individual or group is widely recognized as manifesting itself in degrading treatment or violence toward vulnerable individuals or groups. While not necessarily always the root cause, dehumanizing language is ubiquitously present as an exacerbating factor in cases of violence and oppression as perpetrators seek to cognitively rationalize or justify the maltreatment of others.[1] This well-attested link between debasing terminology and oppressive treatment provides the jumping off-point for this paper, which seeks to explore through the writings of Dorothy Day, an avowed personalist, the converse connection: how a high estimation of the value of people might lead to benevolent treatment and advocacy on their behalf.[2] This research will 1) survey and categorize the different ways Day spoke about the value of persons, 2) explore the shape of her activism on behalf of the poor and other vulnerable groups, and 3) point out the existing connections between how she spoke about the value of people, and how she lived those convictions in her career as a Catholic Worker.

Day's Rhetoric of Personal Esteem

My examination of Day's body of writing reveals four distinct categories of personal esteem that Day employed to express her convictions that human persons

1 Sociologist William Brennan maintains that "name-calling" of the very type that begins in childhood school-yard bullying, is "invariably" an essential component of any widespread oppression, discrimination, enslavement, or annihilation. See *Dehumanizing the Vulnerable: When Word Games Take Lives* (Chicago: Loyola University Press, 1995), 3.

2 This paper is condensed from the author's 2013 dissertation completed for Lutheran

are extremely valuable: 1) an incarnational spirituality that sees Christ in others; 2) personal dignity by virtue of certain endowments from God; 3) the interconnectedness of all humanity, especially as focused through the doctrine of the Mystical Body of Christ; and 4) the belief that *all* persons are called to be saints and are therefore valuable because of their divine election. These categories can each be observed at every stage of Day's public activism as a Catholic Worker, demonstrating the influence of her radical social formation as well as the personalism of Peter Maurin and Emmanuel Mounier.

The first major category Day used to express her esteem for human personhood was borrowed directly from the gospels. The apocalyptic parable of the Last Judgment in Matthew 25:31–46, in which the Son of Man commends those who served him in the human needs of "the least of these" while condemning those who failed to do so, served as an overall interpretive framework for Day's spiritual life. It was a central text to which she referred again and again, not only for its injunctions to perform the works of mercy, but for its surprising theo-anthropological revelation that an action done for the benefit of poor, suffering, or imprisoned persons is an action done to Christ himself. Day took this to mean that, in some mysterious way she could not fully comprehend, the persons whom she saw before her *were* Christ, a conviction which compelled her to love them as she would love Christ himself in whatever ways she could. "Dorothy's spirituality was truly immanent and incarnational," Jim Forest recollects, "a love of God as seen in creation, especially in those the world has forgotten." [3] For the object of Christian worship to be manifestly present (although hidden) in finite persons, this demanded nothing but the highest respect and esteem from Day who loved Christ dearly—as much in the sacrament of the Eucharist as in the "human sacrament" of those whom she loved. [4]

Day elaborated on this theme in her diary. She does not mean that we should overlook their human flaws or evil actions. Rather, she seeks to correct a tendency to define others by their sins, to focus on another's flaws rather than our own. In doing so, she brings her attitude more into conformity with the Sermon on the Mount.

Theological Seminary at Philadelphia, *Personalism and Human Dignity in the Struggle for Justice in 20ᵗʰ Century America: Dorothy Day, Martin Luther King, Jr., and Cardinal Joseph Bernardin.*

3   Jim Forest, quoted in Rosalie Riegle, *Dorothy Day: Portraits of Those Who Knew Her* (Maryknoll, New York: Orbis, 2003), 71.

4   Brigid O'Shea Merriman, *Searching for Christ: The Spirituality of Dorothy Day* (Notre Dame, Indiana: University of Notre Dame Press, 1994), 224.

This blindness of love, this folly of love—this seeing Christ in others, everywhere and not seeing the ugly, the obvious, the dirty, the sinful—this means we do not see the faults of others—only our own. We see only Christ in them. We have eyes only for our beloved, ears for His voice....What mother ever considers the ugliness of cleaning up after her baby, or sick child or sick husband? These things are not mentioned by critics. But to the saints everyone is child and lover.[5]

Day strove to avoid letting her biases and prejudices affect what she felt was God's call to see Christ equally and universally in all persons. This even-handedness is reflected in a diary entry written on her 1962 journalistic pilgrimage to communist Cuba, which was still fresh from Fidel Castro's successful revolution three years earlier: "I am talking to myself as I write this, and my first thought is—I go to see Christ in my brother the Cuban, and that means Christ in the revolution[ary], [and] Christ in the counter-revolutionary. But to both sides, being violently partisan, such an attitude will be considered reasonable by neither."[6]

A second way Day's words reflected her esteem for people was through her writing about human dignity in ways that always connected a person's value to certain endowments from a person's relationship with God. Human dignity was thus not intrinsic in the person in abstraction from God, but could only be understood in the context of the Creator blessing and calling the human person "very good" (Gen. 1).

Day used the "image of God," the classic biblical theme of human dignity drawn from the first creation story in Genesis, as a way of expressing the value of human persons by highlighting the resemblance and special affinity between them and the divine Person. While on pilgrimage in India, she commented on the violence and unrest that was so common there, pointing out that it was an affront to God as well as a violation of human value: "The violence here, from refugees from Pakistan, from students, is a crying out for recognition of the poor man, as men, as people, God's children, made in His image, whom He loved so much He gave His only begotten son to redeem them, to share their sufferings, their humanity."[7] Day was keenly aware of the power of this concept to

---

5   Diary entry dated February 1944, in Dorothy Day, *The Duty of Delight: The Diaries of Dorothy Day*, Robert Ellsberg, ed. (Milwaukee, Wisconsin: Marquette University Press, 2008), 73–74.

6   2 September 1962 diary entry, in *The Duty of Delight*, 328–329.

7   Diary entry dated 4 September 1970, in *The Duty of Delight*, 485.

transform and ennoble the lives of persons who had been told that or treated as if they were worthless, calling upon the *imago Dei* to instill in the downtrodden a sense of their own value and dignity.

In a "Letter to the Unemployed," published in *The Catholic Worker* while the Depression raged, Day wrote to encourage the down-and-out whose spirits had been crushed by brutal poverty and the exploitive capitalist system, urging them to keep their faith in God and in themselves. Take note at the way Day weaves together different ways of speaking of human dignity besides the *imago Dei* to combine their potency in this passage:

> It is a battle to hang on to religion when discouragement sets in. It is a battle to remember that we are made in the image and likeness of God when employers, treating you with less consideration than animals, turn you indifferently away. It is a fierce battle to maintain one's pride and dignity, to remember that we are brothers of Christ, who ennobled our human nature by sharing it.... To those who are without hope, I remind you of Christ, your brother. Religion, thought in terms of our brotherhood through Christ, is not the opiate of the people. It is a battle "mighty to God unto the pulling down of fortifications." Do not let either capitalist or Communist kill this noble instinct in you. [8]

By drawing attention to the human person as reflecting God's sacred image, Day underlined the invaluable dignity each person possesses by virtue of his or her likeness to the Creator.

Day also viewed human dignity through the lens of the incarnation. For her, one of the most important effects of Christ taking on human flesh was the transformation of human nature. Christ, she believed, made human nature infinitely more valuable when he assumed it himself: "Human nature being what it is, I can only believe that men are capable of much goodness, through Christ who took upon Himself our human nature and exalted it." [9] In this way, she came to possess a positive anthropology, unwilling to consider human sinfulness apart from the incarnation that occurred to redeem humanity of it. This led her to the conviction that human beings are essentially good, but not in a naive, Pollyannaish way. In her life caring for the poor of the Bowery, she had seen some of the

8   Day, *By Little and By Little*, Robert Ellsberg, ed. (New York: Knopf, 1983), 82–84.
9   Day, *From Union Square to Rome* (Maryknoll, New York: Orbis, 2006), 153.

worst that human persons are capable of. Rather, her conviction of humanity's goodness stemmed from the value that God placed upon us, the fact that human persons are so valuable to God that he became incarnate and died on the cross for us. [10] Of the poverty-stricken, alcohol-abusing homeless men of the Bowery, she wrote, "Certainly... [they] are the lost sheep. They are our brothers in Jesus; he died for each of them. What respect we should feel for them!" [11] The fact that Christ valued each person enough that he died for everyone, without exception, transformed Day's social conscience and implored her to offer the same evaluation of their worth and dignity.

Likewise, following the heuristic apocalypticism of her Christian faith, Day sought to cut through the outer appearances to see these "ambassadors of God" not as the world regarded them, but through the eyes of Christ. She deeply yearned for the eyes of faith, as her notes from one retreat make clear: "When will I learn to love all, men and women, with an intense awareness of their beauty, their virtues, strengths, to see them as Christ sees them?" [12] Seeing others as Christ sees them has the potential to impact one's own self-image as well. One time on a visit to England, Day ate lunch with a Catholic member of the House of Lords. She took some House of Lords stationary and began to write to a young man she said was very depressed. "You see what this paper is," she wrote, "These are all high and dignified people. Remember that you are the brother of Jesus and the son of a King. Never forget that." [13] This seeing others with the eyes of faith was an essential component of Day's activism, and motivated her even when times became difficult or the work became wearying and burdensome. Sometime in 1940, she wrote a letter to a Catholic Worker house that had become discouraged and tired of the daily grind of performing the works of mercy:

10 In 1953, Day wrote to Cardinal Francis Spellman, Archbishop of New York and the most powerful Catholic prelate in the United States at the time, urging him to use his influence with the President to spare Ethel and Julius Rosenberg, admitted Communists who had been convicted of spying for the Soviet Union and passing on nuclear secrets, from the death penalty. "We are so careless of life these days, so profligate of this humanity of ours, that Christ paid so much for," she wrote. "He showed how He loved traitors. By taking on their human nature and dying for them. He has bought the Rosenbergs with a great price. How much we should love them. Please, dear Father of us all in this area, erring and faithful alike, please make this hard gesture of love" (10 June 1953 letter to Cardinal Spellman, in Day, *All the Way to Heaven*, Robert Ellsberg, ed. [Milwaukee, Wisconsin: Marquette University Press, 2010], 214–215).

11 *By Little and By Little*, 112.

12 Day, quoted in William Miller, *All is Grace* (Garden City, New York: Doubleday, 1987), 97.

13 Eileen Egan, quoted in Riegle, *Portraits*, 38.

You can look at all the men at all the houses and see them as pretty rotten. That, of course, is the way we should see things; to see men as but dust; from the human point of view that is perfectly true ... But from the standpoint of the supernatural they are a little less than the angels and if we could only keep that attitude toward them! When we are in love with people we see all the best that there is in them and understand very clearly their failures and their lapses. [14]

The third way that Day's esteem for personhood manifested itself in her writing was her stress on the interrelatedness of all humanity. Persons are valuable, she reasoned, both because we matter to others and because a joy experienced by or a pain inflicted on one person directly or indirectly has an impact on everyone else. Reflecting on a phrase from the preamble to the constitution of the Industrial Workers of the World, Day molded her convictions about just how and to whom we are related as a human community. Instead of the IWW's understanding of labor unions in solidarity with one another against the bourgeois class, Day held that *all*, worker and employer alike, are held together by an indissoluble bond in Christ. As she explained in a letter late in her life, "I can only believe 'an injury to one is an injury to all,' the slogan of the IWW, in the sense that we are all one in Christ Jesus, members of one another." [15] The universality of this connection became a defining principle in Day's moral vision, teaching her yet another way that human persons are valuable and deserve respect and protection, from the greatest to the least. This sense of interconnectedness with the entire human community was not well-understood by everyone, as a story Day tells in her diary makes clear:

Once when I went to see a woman we were caring for in the mental ward, the doctor asked me what was my interest in her. Was I a relative? I said, not wishing to enter into a discussion of our work—"She is my sister, isn't she, since all men are brothers." He looked at me keenly and said, "You know, religious mania is one of the worst forms." [16]

14 Undated 1940 letter to the Buffalo Catholic Worker community, in *All the Way to Heaven*, 121–123.

15 21 January 1972 letter, in *All the Way to Heaven*, 388.

16 Diary entry dated July 1963, in *The Duty of Delight*, 341–342.

The sense of universal interconnectivity, when apprehended and understood most directly through the doctrine of the Mystical Body of Christ,[17] thus drives the person to seek out mutual relationships, and to form community life around the guiding principle of love.

Day respected no socially imposed boundaries. This connection she felt to others, understood through the universalizing doctrine of the Mystical Body, transcended racial, national, even religious confines. Writing at a time when Jim Crow segregation laws were enforced in many parts of the country, the Catholic Worker was deliberate from its outset in including racial minorities in every aspect of the work. Well before the widespread civil rights activism of the 1950s and '60s, Day was consistently attentive to questions of race, advocating not only for equal treatment under law, but for a radical embrace of people of all races on the basis of the interconnectivity of all humanity before God. In 1942, Day wrote to President Roosevelt, urging him to intervene on behalf of a black death row inmate who Day felt had not gotten a fair trial because of his race. "We beg you to intervene for Odell Waller, whose mother appeared at that meeting the other night," Day wrote, "and by your clemency to show that there is a recognition in this country that we are together sons of God and brothers in Christ, and we are aiming indeed toward a Christian democracy. We pray for you daily in these terrible times."[18] The practical effect of this keen sense of interrelatedness is that no one is a stranger, no one is "the other," no one is rightly the object of our scorn or mistreatment. No one is an enemy.

The final major category into which Day's rhetoric of personal esteem took form was the idea of sainthood. She spoke of holiness or sanctity as the universal vocation of all; God calls all persons in whom Christ dwells to be saints. In this way, Day dignified the vocation of each person in a teleological sense. Day's concept of sainthood, like the other categories of personal esteem she employs, cannot be understood apart from God and his purposeful making of a very good personal creation for a destiny of holiness. As Day put it in her diary, human

17 Day once remarked that the Mystical Body of Christ is "the doctrine which is behind all our efforts" (Miller, *All Is Grace*, 150). This metaphor, which Paul describes at length in 1 Corinthians 12, was not limited for Day to those who followed Christ overtly. A quotation she frequently cited, which she attributed to St. Augustine, says that "All [persons] are members or potential members of the Body of Christ." By leaving the "potential" open there, Day sought to allow room for God, for whom, as she frequently noted, there is no time, to make the decisions about who was "in" or "out." The human imperative, then, if one is determined to leave the judging to God, was to treat all persons impartially, as if they were members of the Mystical Body of Christ, and therefore worthy of the highest esteem.

18 23 June 1942 letter to President Franklin Roosevelt, in *All the Way to Heaven*, 138.

persons are made with one purpose: identification with Christ. [19]

For Day, becoming a saint was not an amorphous ideal; it was given specific shape by Jesus Christ whose practice of the works of mercy and challenging of the unjust social order demonstrated what holiness meant. It was this life, exemplified by Christ and enabled by God's grace, that Day felt was the universal vocation of all, even if not all lived into that calling. It was the saints, rather than chiefly the institutional hierarchy, that kept the Church going throughout history.

She believed that *all* persons, and especially those who are "in Christ," are called to a life of heroic virtue and sanctity. There was no greater purpose in life than this: "Instead of fearing death, which changes nothing, we should fear life. This is because those who wish to enter heaven must be saints. Sanctity must be achieved in our lifetime. We are here for no other reason. We are not changed in Purgatory. We are cleansed.... If we wish the joy of Heaven, we must cultivate a taste for it here." [20] This vocation dignified the human person in the sight of God. To be holy is to fulfill the unique purpose God has planned for each one of us, no matter how small it may be.

The Shape of Her Activism

Having explored Day's rhetoric of personal esteem, it is time to turn to an examination of her social activism to discover how it was shaped by her profound convictions about human value. The first and most important part of Day's activism was her practice of the works of mercy. For Day, the works of mercy were not only a way to meet the immediate needs of a person in distress, but also a symbolic protest against the unjust social order which necessitated such interventions be necessary in the first place. Day calls their performance "a real action as well as a symbolic action" that keeps us walking "in the steps of Jesus when He fed the multitude on the hills, and when He prepared the fire and the fish on the shore. He told us to do it. He did it Himself." [21] And she links the works of mercy

---

19 Diary entry dated 26 June 1945, in *The Duty of Delight*, 92. Merriman's excellent explanation of Day's single-minded pursuit of holiness is worth noting: "Stated abstractly, Dorothy's purpose was the attainment of sanctity. Stated in the concrete reality which was Dorothy's life, the attainment—which was also gift—was growth in love for Christ. Over and over, Dorothy had expressed her spirituality in terms of love for God and love for her neighbor. The meeting place for both was her ardent love for Christ: Christ as God made human and Christ within every human being" (*Searching for Christ*, 166).

20 Day, in Miller, *All is Grace*, 75–76.

21 *By Little and By Little*, 341.

with God's revelation about human value—all people are valuable and deserve our help and protection, therefore there are none who are "unworthy" of our aid: "God's will is that all men be saved. *All men.* All the unworthy poor, the drunks, the drug-ridden, the poor mentally afflicted creatures who are in and out of our C.W. houses all day. And yet Jesus told us what we were to do—feed the hungry, clothe the naked, shelter the homeless, 'worthy or unworthy.'" [22] At Day's houses of hospitality, the guests got the best food, drink, shelter, clothes, and companionship that could be provided. Because of their value as persons, they deserved nothing less. In loving and serving the poor, Day quickly came to recognize that it could be a very thankless job. But she considered it her duty to provide them with the basics needed for physical life in order that their spiritual life might flourish as well and their full dignity and potential be realized. The performance of the works of mercy was Day's way of taking on to herself the burden of care for others. It was service to the poor, "at a personal sacrifice," as Peter Maurin often said. This was Day's way of joining with Jesus in the work of the cross.

As central as the works of mercy were to Day, she realized that charity is not enough if the fundamental problems that caused the need for charity in the first place are still present. Part of Day's vision of human dignity, the dignity of work, meant that the goal was to help the poor not just to scrape by on charitable handouts, but to move to a position of self-sufficiency where they could make a living by their own labor if at all possible. So a significant part of the works of mercy involved not only getting a person back on his or her own two feet, but also fighting for the kind of social change necessary for this to happen. For Day, justice must go hand in hand with mercy; a holistic Christian witness is incomplete without total dedication to both. Persons are too valuable to be allowed to starve or to have their dignity diminished by existing on perpetual charity. Her personalist brand of justice is aimed, ultimately, at making the works of mercy obsolete and unnecessary.

A second prominent channel of Day's social advocacy was her antiwar, antiviolence activism. Throughout her career, even in the face of stiff resistance by other Catholic Workers, Day remained a staunch pacifist, as morally opposed to the deliberate destruction of the human persons as she was opposed to the gnawing destruction and degradation of the person brought about by poverty. She counseled young men to resist the draft, and promoted imprisonment or voluntary service as alternatives for conscientious objectors. The infinite value

---

22   Ibid., 351 (emphasis original).

of the person, Day believed, means that something eternal and irreplaceable is lost when a person is killed through neglect or belligerence, and she took a solid stand for her entire life against all killing of human persons.

Daniel Berrigan recalls reading about this stance shortly after coming out of prison for his burning of the draft cards during Vietnam, and being captivated by its beauty and simplicity: "What held me in thrall was an absolutely stunning consistency. *No* to all killing. Invasions, incursions, excusing causes, call of the blood, summons to the bloody flag, casuistic body counts, just wars, necessary wars, religious wars, needful wars, holy wars—into the fury of the murderous crosswinds went her simple word: *no.*"[23] The essence of her opposition to war was the common-sense observation that war is the opposite of the works of mercy. Making no equivocation where her efforts lay, in reflecting on all the tensions, problems, and controversies within Church and society, she felt that there was no higher priority than the promotion of nonviolence.[24]

Day's most important early writing on pacifism and war came in 1936 at the outset of the Spanish revolution. Day responded to that crisis with an article in the paper entitled "On the Use of Force" in the November 1936 issue in which, after explaining nonviolence in the Scriptures with Christ and the apostles as exemplars, she lamented that "now the whole world is turning to 'force' to conquer. Fascist and Communist alike believe that only by the shedding of blood can they achieve victory." But Day distinguished the Catholic attitude toward bloodshed through her interpretation of the gospel teaching in the beginning of the article, concluding "But their teaching, their hard saying, is that they must be willing to shed every drop of their own blood, and not take the blood of their brothers. They are willing to die for their faith, believing that the blood of the martyrs is the seed of the Church."[25] Day's pacifism was nearly unheard of among Catholics at the time. "It was an unusual and even daring act to assert that one was at the same time a practicing Catholic and an absolute pacifist."[26] As a result of this stance, subscriptions to *The Catholic Worker* dropped by more than one third.

Her stance against war was rooted not in a sense of moral purity or

---

23 Berrigan, "Introduction," in Day, *The Long Loneliness* (San Francisco: Harper and Row, 1981), xix–xx (emphasis original).

24 "To me nonviolence is the all-important problem or virtue to be nourished and studied and cultivated" (diary entry [no date], in *The Duty of Delight*, 463).

25 *By Little and By Little*, 77–78.

26 Eileen Egan, "Dorothy Day, Pilgrim of Peace" in *A Revolution of the Heart: Essays on the Catholic Worker*, Patrick G Coy, ed. (Philadelphia, Pennsylvania: Temple University Press, 1980), 69-114, cite pp. 71–72.

self-righteousness, but in a deep concern for the lives of the persons shattered or lost in war. Each life, whether those of the people designated "the enemy" or those of one's own country, is precious in the sight of God.

> We must love our enemy, not because we fear war but because God loves him. Mike Wallace asked me that question: Does God love murderers, does He love a Hitler, a Stalin? I could only say, "God loves all men, and all men are brothers."
>
> There is so little time on a broadcast, in an interview, so little time to answer or to think. I could have said, "Christ loved those who crucified Him. St. Stephen loved those who stoned him to death. St. Paul was a murderer. We are all murderers." [27]

Although Day was keenly aware of her own complicity in the nation's wars, she never let this sense of collective guilt paralyze her. Instead, she sought to identify each deep level of involvement in war, both her own and that of American society, and to uproot it wherever possible. She came to loathe the subversion of Christian "sacrifice" language by the military, seeing it as blasphemous and dishonest, noting ruefully in her diary how soldiers and revolutionaries often speak of "laying down their lives" without noting its converse: "(always *that* is expressed, rather than being the instrument of taking the lives of others)." [28] Every person working to build weaponry, munitions, and supplies for the military, every time a young man cooperated with the system by registering for the draft, every time one pays income taxes (and this was the major reason Day never paid taxes in her life), one materially supports the war effort, tacitly giving assent to it regardless of one's views of the politics of the war. [29]

In her later years Day also took several concrete actions of protest to oppose war in American society. Perhaps the most well-known was her protest against New York City's civil defense laws in the 1950s in which New York and other large metropolitan areas nationwide began to hold duck-and-cover or fallout shelter drills for the expected nuclear war with the Soviet Union. She called

---

27 *By Little and By Little*, 322.

28 Diary entry dated October 1969, in *The Duty of Delight*, 465 (emphasis original).

29 As she reflected in her diary, "Wars today involve total destruction, obliteration bombing, killing of the innocent, the use of atom and hydrogen bombs. When one is drafted for such war, when one registers for a draft for such a war, when one pays income tax, 80% of which goes to support such war, or works where armaments are made for such war, one is assenting to take the steps towards this war" (diary entry dated 1 January 1954, in *The Duty of Delight*, 190–193).

them "rehearsals for death," and refused to comply. On the appointed day in 1955, rather than go with the rest of the city to the shelters as the law required, Day and some other pacifists sat on park benches to enjoy the sun instead. That year, and for the next five years until the law was repealed in 1960, the demonstrators were arrested in increasing numbers. She felt that the civil defense laws, besides lulling people into a false sense of security, accustomed people to living in fear. And the human person, according to Day, cannot flourish under such conditions.

Another important channel of Day's activism with links to her convictions about personal esteem is her consistent support for the rights of workers, labor unions, racial minorities, and other underclasses against the rich and powerful. Recognizing as she did God's special concern for the poor and working class and their value in his sight, Day committed herself to working with the budding labor movements in their struggle for fair compensation and working conditions. It was a matter of human dignity, which she was convinced is violated whenever workers are exploited and are not able to enjoy the fruits of their labor. It was a fundamental injustice that people were unable to adequately feed, clothe, and shelter themselves and their families because of dehumanizing labor conditions and entrenched, systemic injustices designed to keep the employing class wealthy at the expense of the laboring class. In this, one can clearly see the influence of Day's earlier socialist affiliation. But her predilection for workers was not only socially conditioned: it was an unshakeable religious conviction as well. To Dorothy Day, the workers were where Christ was to be found, and in aligning herself with them as she always did unless or until they were proven wrong, [30] Day was identifying herself with the Christ in them, even as she was identifying herself with Christ the Worker who had been crucified by the powerful elites of his day. While Day clearly shared many of the concerns of the Left, she faulted them for their tendency to abstract and idealize the proletariat away from the personal reality of the people it encompassed. "There is so much more to the Catholic Worker Movement than labor and capital," she wrote in response to overzealous communist hunters who scrutinized the Catholic Worker, because "it is people who are important, not the masses." [31]

One example of Day's efforts on behalf of organized labor will help illus-

---

30 See *All the Way to Heaven*, 101.

31 *The Long Loneliness*, 221. In her personal diary, Day elaborated on this fundamental point: "The masses, insensate, unthinking, moved by propaganda, by unscrupulous rulers, by Stalins and Hitlers, are quite a different thing from the people, temples of the Holy Ghost, made to the image and likeness of God" (4 March 1945, in *The Duty of Delight*, 88–89).

trate the passion with which she fought for workers' rights as well as how her social engagement in this sphere sprang directly from her convictions about personal value. In 1949, responding to abysmal pay and working conditions, New
York City gravediggers formed a fledgling union and went on strike in order to
demonstrate to the city how valuable their services were. As bodies began to go
unburied throughout the city, a sanitation crisis ensued, causing public senti-
ment to turn against the gravediggers. Francis Cardinal Spellman was no ally
of the gravediggers union. He ordered the seminarians under his jurisdiction
to fill in as gravediggers in order to help break the strike. To Day, this was not
only an example of the Church choosing the wrong side of the labor dispute, but
also an example of the powerful cardinal using his influence against the powerless whose modest demands were quite reasonable. As she later explained in
an interview with Robert Coles, it was "a Cardinal, ill-advised, [who] exercised
so overwhelming a show of force against a handful of poor working men. It was
a temptation of the devil to that most awful of wars, the war between the clergy
and the laity."[32]

Day wrote to the Cardinal, sharing her concerns, and imploring him to re-
lent in his "war" against the workers. In her letter, Day is upfront with him, sharing her conviction that what is at stake is nothing less than the workers' human
dignity. "It is not just the issue of wages and hours as I can see from the conversation which our workers have had with the men. It is a question of their dignity
as men, their dignity as workers, and the right to have a union of their own, and
a right to talk over their grievances." Then Day explains that to her, wealth and
poverty and class struggle are ancillary concerns. What she is chiefly focused on
is the respect and dignity due to the workers: "Regardless of rich and poor, the
class antagonism which exists between the well-to-do, those who live on Park
Avenue and Madison Avenue, and those who dig the graves in the cemetery, the
issue is always one of the dignity of the workers. It is a world issue."[33] The workers' dignity was under attack in what was nothing less than a "war," and Day as a
pacifist would have no part of the oppression.

Fair working conditions and wages were not the root of what she sought,
but natural corollaries of the end she pursued; even if working conditions,
wages, and hours are fair and just, if workers are treated as less than partners,
less than co-owners, something is fundamentally unjust.

---

32 Quoted in Robert Coles, Dorothy Day: *A Radical Devotion* (Reading, Massachussets: Addison-Wesley, 1987), 81

33 4 March 1949 letter to Cardinal Spellman, in *All the Way to Heaven*, 170–71.

> Let us be honest, let us say that fundamentally, the stand we
> are taking is not on the ground of wages and hours and condi-
> tions of labor, but on the fundamental truth that men should
> be treated not as chattels, but as human beings, as "temples
> of the Holy Ghost." When Christ took on our human nature,
> when He became man, He dignified and ennobled human na-
> ture. He said, "The Kingdom of Heaven is within you." When
> men are striking, they are following an impulse, often blind,
> often uninformed, but a good impulse—one could even say an
> inspiration of the Holy Spirit. They are trying to uphold their
> right to be treated not as slaves, but as men. [34]

Day's ultimate goal, then, in the realm of workers' rights was not just a con-
tinuation of the old system, slightly tweaked to accommodate for less disparity
between owners and workers. She sought an end to the present wage system altogether through decentralization, cooperation, and profound respect for the
value and importance of the person. She focused her vision on "the new social
order as it could be and would be if all men loved God and loved their brothers
because they are all sons of God! A land of peace and tranquility and joy in work
and activity. It is heaven indeed that we are contemplating." [35]

In short, for Day, her high regard for the value of persons was the most com-
pelling reason behind her social activism, no matter the issue. Day's social advocacy was driven by her nascent understanding that persons are inestimably
valuable. This explains why Day sought to "[care] for the victims of the existing
social order, trying to help create a society that didn't throw people away like
used Kleenex." [36] She fought against the exploitation of any person for any reason, from "the usury of the loan companies who suck the blood of the poor and
force them into destitution" [37] to the wars that destroy persons in both body and
soul. Day became convinced that genuine love of humankind or of "the masses"
was impossible "without first affirming the unique and eternal character of
every created person." [38] It was the sense of the person as a being of spirit as well
as body that helped Day to realize the person's true value. The incarnation of
Christ brought this lesson home to her forcefully, convincing her that "heaven

34 Day, *By Little and By Little*, 241.

35 Ibid., 87.

36 Jim Forest, *All is Grace* (Maryknoll, New York: Orbis, 2011), 257.

37 Diary entry dated 14 January 1962, in *The Duty of Delight*, 322.

38 Miller, *All is Grace*, 75.

and earth are linked together as the body and soul are linked together,"[39] and that therefore it was not enough just to feed or house the person; the person had to be cherished as well.

Undergirding all of Day's activism and her profound esteem for the human person was her Christocentrism. Christ, who had taken upon himself human flesh and human nature, ennobled the person to the highest degree. The doctrine of the Mystical Body, besides offering a theological way of speaking of the interconnectivity of all humanity, also undergirded her incarnational spirituality, which turned the person into something sacred, of infinite value. It was, she said, the foundation that undergirded the entire movement.

> It plainly and boldly suggests that the one with whom we eat in the soupline tonight is Christ himself. ... The practical effect of all this is the attempt to recognize the person of Christ in all who come, transcending traditional categories of adversary and ally. The preferred principle, therefore, is service and suffering love, modeled on the servanthood and humility of Christ himself.[40]

Dorothy Day's esteem for personhood, formed from her exposure to personalism and her Christian faith, thus proves to be the predominant cause of her remarkable career as a social justice advocate, shaping it indelibly in every respect.

Perhaps the clearest place Day demonstrated her conviction of the inestimable worth of the human person came early in Day's career as a Catholic Worker. In the January 1941 edition of *The Catholic Worker,* Day juxtaposed a report in the *New York Times* that the 1942 budget for war and military expenditures was to be $17,485,528,049, with the announcement of the birth of a baby boy named William to a homeless woman at the CW house on Mott Street. In characteristic fashion, she highlights the underappreciated value of the small things, St. Thérèse of Lisieux's "little way" over against the massiveness of the military budget reported in the *Times.* William, she says, is worth far more than that or any sum.

---

39 Day, *On Pilgrimage* (Grand Rapids, Michigan: Eerdmans, 1999), 202.

40 Angie O'Gorman and Patrick G. Coy, "Houses of Hospitality: A Pilgrimage to Nonviolence," in *A Revolution of the Heart: Essays on the Catholic Worker* (Philadelphia: Temple University Press, 1980), 247.

William, our new baby down here at Mott Street, is hereby headlined on our front page, as the biggest news of the month, the gayest news, the most beautiful news, the most tragic news, and indeed more worthy of a place in a headline than the seventeen billion, four hundred and eighty-five million, five hundred and twenty-eight thousand and forty-nine dollars headlined in *The New York Times* this morning. William himself is worth more than that sum, more indeed than all the money in the world. He is indeed but dust, the Lord knoweth it, but he is also little less than the angels. He is a creature of body and soul, a son of God and (by his baptism down at Transfiguration Church last Sunday at 2 PM.) a temple of the Holy Ghost. For his sake our Lord God came down from Heaven, was begotten by the Holy Ghost, born of the Virgin Mary, was made man, lived with us for thirty-three years, and suffered and laid down His life. For William's sake as well as for the sake of each one of us. [41]

Rob Arner, Ph.D., is adjunct professor of theology at Chestnut Hill College in Philadelphia, Pennsylvania and at Reformed Episcopal Seminary in Blue Bell, Pennsylvania. He is also the author of *Consistently Pro-Life: The Ethics of Bloodshed in Ancient Christianity* (Eugene, Oregon: Pickwick Publications, 2010) and serves on the board of Consistent Life (www.consistent-life.org). He enjoys being an at-home dad for his three children.

41 *By Little and By Little*, 157.

Day and Niebuhr on
the Great Depression

Kurt Buhring

The recent state of economic and political realities has elicited much comparison with another period in United States history, the Great Depression. The 1929 stock market crash and ensuing economic depression necessitated and fostered a host of economic, political, and cultural responses. While these have been studied and commented upon rather extensively, less has been explored in terms of theological and ethical responses. This essay will examine the religious responses of two significant Christians of the period, Dorothy Day and Reinhold Niebuhr. Some evangelical Christians saw the Great Depression as God's judgment of American sinfulness and hedonism. From this perspective, an individualistic focus on spiritual matters was called for. In contrast, other Christians believed the root of the problem would not be found in individuals, but rather in the injustices of the capitalist system itself.

Early in their lives, both Dorothy Day and Reinhold Niebuhr called for a radical restructuring of economic and political systems in response to the Great Depression. It is important to point out here that both Day and Niebuhr came to their early passion for social justice through lived experience and encounters with poverty and injustices in the world. Their views were based on observations and experiences of how real people were affected by the Depression; Day took on a life of voluntary poverty at a young age, and Niebuhr served as a pastor in Detroit with a working class congregation. Though similar in their early radical calls for social justice and strong critiques of capitalism, Day and Niebuhr would move in differing directions as the 1930s went on. Day would reconcile her yearning for justice with a fuller sense of charity and a personalist approach that emphasized care, love, and the works of mercy, not federal programs, as a solution to poverty. In distinction, Niebuhr came to accept reform rather than revolution and recognized Roosevelt's New Deal as at least moving toward a measure of justice. It is suggested here that the basis of their differing views can be found in their ideas of human nature and in their advocacy of distinct ideals. While Day crafted an ethic of care, Niebuhr called for an ethic of justice. The essay will first consider Day and Niebuhr's early positions, then explore each thinker's more mature perspectives during the Depression.

Like Niebuhr, from an early age, Day was frustrated with social injustices, such as poverty. In *The Long Loneliness*, she remembered, "I felt even at fifteen, that God meant man to be happy, that He meant to provide him with what he needed to maintain life in order to be happy, and that we did not need to have quite so much destitution and misery as I saw all around and read of in the daily press." She continued,

> I wanted life and I wanted the abundant life. I wanted it for others too. ... I wanted everyone to be kind. I wanted every home to be open to the lame, the halt and the blind. ... Only then did people really live, really love their brothers. In such love was the abundant life and I did not have the slightest idea how to find it. [1]

At the time, Day asserted, religion would not provide any satisfactory answers. In fact she referred to religion as a drug and as an impediment to her social justice yearnings. [2]

Though imperfect to her, the many leftist political movements of the time, such as socialism, appealed to Day. She believed these organizations were at least *doing* something in the face of social injustice. Further, she saw such groups as actively seeking to get at the root of injustices, rather than dealing only with the symptoms. [3] From this perspective, Day held a very low view of *mere* charity. She explained, "our hearts burned with the desire for justice and were revolted at the idea of a doled-out charity. The word charity had become something to gag over, something to shudder at." Previewing her later shift though, she added, "The true meaning of the word we did not know." [4] At this point, Day criticized the charitable efforts of the churches both because she believed them

---

1 Dorothy Day, *The Long Loneliness: The Autobiography of the Legendary Catholic Social Activist* (San Francisco: HarperOne, 2009), 38–39.

2 Ibid., 43.

3 Ibid., 45.

4 Ibid., 87.

to be ineffective and resented by the poor. [5]

However, despite the appeal of the various politically active social justice-oriented movements of the period, Day was still left yearning for something more, something greater. Eventually, she came to convert to Catholicism in December 1927. Even after her conversion though, she felt she had betrayed "the poor of the world," the masses. [6] She wrote, "I was just as much against capitalism and imperialism as ever, and here I was going over to the opposition, because of course the Church was lined up with property, with the wealthy, with the state, with capitalism." [7] So, despite her conversion, there was still something missing.

As reflected in her letters in the period between her conversion to Catholicism and her work with Peter Maurin, Day's reaction to the stock market crash and the early days of the Depression was largely concerned with her own well-being. In late 1929, Day was employed as a writer for films in California. She expressed her hope that the stock market crash would not affect the movie business the way it had impacted other businesses, though it ultimately did. [8] After California, Day moved to Mexico, then New Jersey, and, in the fall of 1931, to Florida to live with her mother. Here she wrote of her anxiety over her own financial situation. [9] Eventually, Day returned to New York in April 1932. Around this time, Day turned her attention to the plight of the poor more fully. For example, on an assignment to Washington, D.C. for *Commonweal* in the fall of 1932, she covered the "Hunger March of the Unemployed." [10] She searched for a path of action that would bring her commitment to the poor together with her nascent religious identity. She explained, "How I longed to make a synthesis reconciling body and soul, this world and the next." [11] This is where her partnership with Peter Maurin enters the picture.

Just as Day's views would develop over time, Niebuhr's thinking shows shifts and growth. Niebuhr worked as a pastor in Detroit from 1915 to 1928. While there he came to understand something of the social and economic realities working class people encountered and began to develop "a kind of preferen-

5   Ibid., 150.

6   Ibid., 144.

7   Ibid., 149.

8   Dorothy Day, *All the Way to Heaven: The Selected Letters of Dorothy Day*, ed. Robert Ellsberg (New York: Image Books, 2010), 40–44.

9   Ibid., 47–49.

10 Ibid., 60–61.

11 Day, *The Long Loneliness*, 151.

tial option for the poor."[12] Niebuhr asked, "Who is better able to understand the true character of a civilization than those who suffer most from its limitations? ... Who will have more creative vigor in destroying the old and building the new than those in whose lives hunger, vengeance and holy dreams have compounded a tempestuous passion?"[13] He took wealthy titans of industry, such as Henry Ford, to task for unjust treatment of workers.[14] In 1926, Niebuhr indicted the power and greed within American industry and called out Christian churches for focusing on personal moral issues and ignoring efforts to "establish more Christian standards in industrial enterprise."[15] In 1927, he criticized the "ethical impotence of the modern church" in "its failure to deal with the evils and ethical problems of stock manipulation."[16] Unlike liberal thinkers, Niebuhr asserted that our reason is tainted by self-interest that we refuse to recognize. At this stage of his life, Niebuhr saw this flaw especially among the higher socio-economic classes. Niebuhr's "process of change" away from liberalism was "accelerated" by the Great Depression.[17]

Though initially similar to liberal thinkers and social gospel advocates, Niebuhr came to be highly critical of such views. "In this period, liberals tended to believe in the developing goodness and rationality of people, in the growing health of democratic and economic institutions, and in the certainty of a better and better tomorrow. Thus they downplayed ... the persistence of selfishness, irrationality, and brutality."[18] Niebuhr recognized these forms of evil in the historical realities and events of his day, including especially World War I and economic, social, and political injustices.

In his well-known *Moral Man and Immoral Society*, published in 1932, Niebuhr wielded a Marxist hammer to shatter liberal views of history as ever progressing and "liberal illusions regarding the efficacy of reason and love in

12 Don Schweitzer, "The Great Depression: the Response of North American Theologians," in *The Twentieth Century: A Theological Overview*, ed. Gregory Baum (Maryknoll, New York: Orbis, 1999), 51.

13 Reinhold Niebuhr, *Moral Man and Immoral Society* (New York: Scribner's Sons, 1960), 157.

14 Reinhold Niebuhr, *Love and Justice: Selections from the Shorter Writings of Reinhold Niebuhr*, ed. D.B. Robertson (Louisville: Westminster John Knox, 1992), 98–103.

15 Reinhold Niebuhr, *Leaves from the Notebooks of a Tamed Cynic* (New York: Meridian, 1957), 115, 117.

16 Ibid., 153.

17 Arthur M. Schlesinger, Jr., *The Politics of Hope* (Boston: Houghton Mifflin, 1963), 133.

18 Langdon Gilkey, *On Niebuhr: A Theological Study* (Chicago: University of Chicago Press, 2002), 31–32.

social relations."[19] Niebuhr explained, "In every human group there is less reason to guide and to check impulse, less capacity for self-transcendence, less ability to comprehend the needs of others and therefore more unrestrained egoism than the individuals, who compose the group, reveal in their personal relationships."[20] Niebuhr went on to assert, "Teachers of morals who do not see the difference between the problem of charity within the limits of an accepted social system and the problem of justice between economic groups, holding uneven power within modern industrial society, have simply not faced the most obvious differences between the morals of groups and those of individuals."[21] For Niebuhr, the ethic of Jesus is personal, not social.[22]

Further, modern industrialization had led to "concentration of wealth in the hands of a few, the overproduction of goods, and the breakdown of the capitalist economy."[23] In 1933, Niebuhr announced that capitalism was dying and that "it ought to die because it is unable to make the wealth created by modern technology available to all who participate in the productive process on terms of justice."[24] "The sickness of capitalism, Niebuhr said, was 'organic and constitutional;' it was rooted in 'the very nature of capitalism,' in 'the private ownership of the productive processes.' There was no middle way."[25] Niebuhr explained, "under the present organization of society, the economic life of a whole nation is bound up with the private enterprises of individuals. Furthermore the unequal distribution of wealth under the present economic system concentrates wealth which cannot be invested, and produces goods which cannot be absorbed, in the nation itself."[26] Though Roosevelt's New Deal attempted to apply political power to economic inequalities, it would never be sufficient.[27] In modern industrialized society, economic powers had conquered and transcended political powers.[28] "Liberal reforms that left economic power in the hands of the wealthy

19 Schweitzer, "The Great Depression," 50.

20 Niebuhr, *Moral Man*, xi–xii.

21 Ibid., xxii.

22 Niebuhr, *Love and Justice*, 29–40.

23 Schweitzer, "The Great Depression," 50–51.

24 Niebuhr, Reinhold, "After Capitalism—What?" *The World Tomorrow* March 1 (1933): 203–205.

25 Schlesinger, *Politics*, 137-138. See also Reinhold Niebuhr, *Reflections on the End of an Era* (New York: Scribner's Sons, 1934), 24, 30, 53, 59.

26 Niebuhr, *Moral Man*, 89–90.

27 Ibid., 207.

28 Ibid., 15.

failed to address the root of the problem. The crisis could only be resolved by the socialization of industry."[29] Though it was an ideal that could never fully be achieved, Niebuhr advocated the Marxist vision of justice. "'From each according to his ability, to each according to his needs' is indeed an ideal, which is as impossible of consistent application in the complexities of society as the Christian ideal of love. But it is an ideal toward which a rational society must move."[30] Throughout the 1920s and 1930s then, Niebuhr indicted capitalism, called out the greed and self-interest of the wealthy, and advocated for a socialist restructuring of America.

Thus, early in their lives, Niebuhr and Day each asserted that only radical, systemic changes to the economic and political structures could be the effective way to address the Great Depression. Day would maintain that radical change was needed, but her focus moved from structures to people after she met Peter Maurin. She wrote of her encounter with Peter Maurin, "The Peasant of the Pavements," as a great turning point in her life.[31] Together, Day and Maurin would found the Catholic Worker Movement in 1933. In the January, 1935 *Catholic Worker* newspaper, it was explained, "When asked what is the program of the Catholic Worker by those interested in political action, legislation, lobbying, class war, we reply: It is the program set forth by Christ in the Gospels."[32] According to Day's understanding of the life of Jesus, resistance to capitalism did not entail a revolutionary overthrow of the system. Instead, the life of Jesus exemplified living with and as the poor, rather than an overt challenge to the powers that be.[33] Maurin envisioned "working from the bottom and with a few."[34] In a letter response to an angry reader, Day wrote in 1935,

> The great work which is to be done is to change public opinion, to indoctrinate, to set small groups to work here and there in different cities who will live a life of sacrifice, typifying the Catholic idea of personal responsibility. Numbers and organizations are not important. We are just beginning after all. But one person can do a tremendous amount of boring

---

29 Schweitzer, "The Great Depression," 51.

30 Niebuhr, *Moral Man*, 159–160.

31 Day, *The Long Loneliness*, 166.

32 Thomas C. Cornell, Robert Ellsberg, and Jim Forest, eds., *A Penny a Copy: Readings from The Catholic Worker* (Maryknoll, New York: Orbis, 1995), 19.

33 Day, *The Long Loneliness*, 204–205.

34 Ibid., 221.

from within, in his office, factory, neighborhood, parish, and among his daily acquaintances and associates. [35]

Day and Maurin looked to emulate the message and method of Jesus.

As a way to address some of the problems—economic *and* spiritual—of the Depression, Day and Maurin crafted their program of action. This program consisted of houses of hospitality, farming communes, or agronomic universities, round table discussions, and a newspaper that would popularize the program for, in their words, the man in the street. [36] Here the focus will be on the houses and the farms.

Day and Maurin had their differences, but these differences often complemented each other. While Day was a woman of action, Maurin "stressed the importance of theory." [37] When Day thought of the workers and poverty, she had in mind the factory workers of the cities, while Maurin envisioned agricultural work and craftsmanship, often with a rural setting in mind. [38] Such distinctions aside, both the houses of hospitality and the farms stressed community and charity—and not the *mere* charity Day had criticized earlier.

The houses of hospitality were inspired by Day's view of Jesus. The Worker saw the immediate remedy to poverty as performing the corporal and spiritual works of mercy. [39] Day and Maurin were concerned about the material well being of others, specifically the poor, the marginalized, and the outcast, because Jesus was. [40] Jesus committed his life to living among and, more importantly to Day, as the poor. She wrote, "One must live with [the destitute], share with them their suffering too. Give up one's privacy, and mental and spiritual comforts as well as physical." [41] To Day and Maurin, voluntary poverty acted as a "liberating force" that would free one to perform the works of mercy. [42] Only then can one truly give of oneself to others. June O'Connor explains, "Although she certainly believed in freedom and was jailed on behalf of it, she did not speak in terms of freedom. Rather, she acted out of a personal freedom and urged others to do the same while highlighting always that the important point was how one used

---

35 Day, *All the Way*, 103.
36 Day, *The Long Loneliness*, 172–173.
37 Ibid., 169.
38 Ibid., 175.
39 Ibid., 244.
40 Ibid., 204–205.
41 Ibid., 214.
42 Ibid., 179.

one's freedom, namely, for the neighbor, through the works of mercy."[43] Day asserted, "we must have a sense of personal responsibility to take care of our own, and our neighbor, at a personal sacrifice. ... Charity is personal. Charity is love."[44] In contrast to her earlier emphasis on an abstract notion of structural justice, she now argued, "It is the people who are important, not the masses."[45] It was the people, as individuals, unique individuals, with unique needs, who were being served. She wrote, "the desperate condition of transients, uncared for either by federal or state relief, makes this necessary."[46] The service, or care, provided by the Worker was often made necessary because of the misguided efforts of the state.

Their philosophy of anarchism, though Day preferred the term personalism, was in large part based on their notions of charity and personal responsibility. She recognized our responsibility to others, saying, "we are our brother's keeper," not the state.[47] Day was critical of what she referred to as "Holy Mother the State" taking responsibility for the poor. Feeding the hungry was a "burden imposed upon" Christians "by Christ Himself." Day extended this idea of responsibility, arguing, "not only as Catholics but as patriotic Americans who love our country, we feel the necessity of personally being responsible to do something for those who come to us."[48] Robert Coles clarifies, "for Day anarchism meant *increased* responsibility of one person to another, of the individual to the community along with a much lessened sense of obligation to or dependence on the 'distant and centralized state.'"[49] Thus, Day's anarchism was less a negative critique of government and more of an advocacy for personal expressions of care for one another.

Day and Maurin "wanted none of the state relief" of the New Deal programs such as the National Recovery Administration.[50] An important element of the Worker's critique of the state was its militarism. June O'Connor relates that Day "eschewed conventional political action because the government she observed was dominated by commercial and financial interests and deeply implicated in

43 June O'Connor, *The Moral Vision of Dorothy Day: A Feminist Perspective* (New York: Crossroad, 1991), 42.

44 Day, *The Long Loneliness*, 179.

45 Ibid., 221.

46 Day, *All the Way*, 125.

47 Day, *The Long Loneliness*, 179.

48 Day, *All the Way*, 126.

49 Robert Coles, *Dorothy Day: A Radical Devotion* (Boston: Da Capo, 1989), 96.

50 Day, *The Long Loneliness*, 180.

supporting the means of warfare."[51] In addition, the government *might* be able to address material needs, but this was not the entirety of the problem. "Men are not merely mouths to be fed and bodies to be sheltered, but are creatures of body and soul, and we maintain that it first belongs to the Church to care for them and that only in times of national emergency should the state bear so gigantic a burden as it is doing today."[52] Only a personalist response to the Depression could meet the holistic needs of those suffering.

Day and Maurin both felt that the aims of the New Deal were misguided, though Day gave more positive support to the efforts of labor unions. Day related that one of Maurin's "criticisms of labor was that it was aiding in the creation of the Welfare State, the Servile State, instead of aiming for the ownership of the means of production and acceptance of the responsibility that it entailed."[53] Likewise, Bill Kauffman explains, Day frequently argued against the New Deal saying it wrongly focused on *"Security* for the worker, not ownership."[54] However, in distinction from Maurin, Day considered unions as viable, though imperfect, means toward the eventual goals the Worker expressed. In 1936, Day wrote: *"The Catholic Worker* does not believe that unions, as they exist today in the United States, are an ideal solution for the social problem, or for any part of it. We do believe that they are the only efficient weapon which workers have to defend their rights as individuals and Christians against a system which makes the Christ-life practically impossible for large numbers of workers."[55] Again, the same year, Day explained: "When workers are striking they are following an impulse, often blind, often uninformed, but a good impulse, one could even say an inspiration of the Holy Spirit. They are trying to uphold their right to be treated not as slaves but as human beings. They are fighting for a share in the management, for their right to be considered as partners in the enterprise in which they are engaged."[56] While Peter liked to say, "Strikes don't strike me," Day still insisted that the Catholic Worker try to help fight for

---

51 O'Connor, *Moral Vision*, 81.

52 Day, *All the Way*, 126.

53 Day, *The Long Loneliness*, 222.

54 Bill Kauffman, "'The Way of Love'—Dorothy Day and the American Right," in *Dorothy Day and the Catholic Worker Movement: Centenary Essays*, eds. William Thorn, Phillip Runkel, and Susan Mountin (Milwaukee, Wisconsin: Marquette University Press, 2001), 224.

55 In David L. Gregory, "Dorothy Day and the Transformation of Work: Lessons for Labor," in *Dorothy Day and the Catholic Worker Movement: Centenary Essays*, 284.

56 In John Cort, "Dorothy Day, the Catholic Worker, and the Labor Movement," in *Dorothy Day and the Catholic Worker Movement: Centenary Essays*, 258

"better conditions and higher wages" for workers.[57] In a 1949 letter to Cardinal Spellman, Day would assert it wasn't about worker wages as much as human dignity.[58] The Catholic Worker's anarchist philosophy and advocacy of personal responsibility culminated in the long range program of agronomic universities, or farming communes.

In the farms, Maurin saw solutions to "unemployment, delinquency, destitute old age, man's rootlessness, lack of room for growing families, and hunger."[59] While Day was concerned with labor issues, Peter saw these as "patching up" the system "instead of trying to rebuild society itself," which was a goal of the farming communes.[60] In his vision, scholars and workers would learn from each other, guided by Maurin's philosophy of work as an exchange of gifts, rather than for a wage.[61] The farms emphasized a "return to the land," where there is always work. A model of self-sufficiency, and a forerunner of current small farm, localist approaches, Maurin's slogan was "Eat what you raise, raise what you eat!"[62] Also evident in this component of the program of action was an understanding of the human as communal[63] and as co-creator with God.[64] For Day, community was the "social answer to the long loneliness."[65] And, finally, love of God could be expressed primarily through love of individuals in community.[66]

As Day had moved from her younger demand for structural justice and systemic restructuring, Niebuhr also developed during the 1930s. Though originally critical of Roosevelt and the New Deal as not radically enough tempering the inherent flaws of capitalism, by 1940 he grew to appreciate the positive value of steps in the right direction.[67] A few reasons can explain Niebuhr's shift away from radical politics toward at least tepid support of the New Deal. First, Niebuhr no longer believed that socialism would be an effective political

---

57 Dorothy Day, *Loaves and Fishes: the Inspiring Story of the Catholic Worker Movement* (Maryknoll, New York: Orbis, 2003), 22, 39.

58 Gregory, "Transformation," 280.

59 Day, *Loaves*, 44.

60 Ibid., 21–22.

61 Day, *The Long Loneliness*, 178.

62 Ibid., 176, 227.

63 Ibid., 229.

64 Ibid., 227.

65 Ibid., 224.

66 Ibid., 285–286.

67 Schweitzer, "The Great Depression," 51.

force in the United States. In fact, he resigned from the Socialist party in 1940. [68] Niebuhr now more strenuously applied his examinations of the ambiguities of reason and power to the working classes. He now came to see more fully the imperfections of the proletariat. Like the wealthy, the lower socio-economic classes were corrupted by self-interest as a primary motivating force. Next, Niebuhr also became dissatisfied with bickering within labor unions, the greed and egotism of union leaders, and the ostracization of non-union workers. [69] Finally, "what was decisive" in Niebuhr's move from socialism toward Roosevelt was the increasingly dire threat of Nazism. [70] In short, "the defense of democracy was a higher priority than social revolution." [71] Whereas the Socialists were mostly isolationist, Arthur Schlesinger offers, "the canny and opportunistic political realism of Roosevelt gained new stature in Niebuhr's eyes; rather than merely an artistic juggler, Roosevelt now seemed almost to have the dimensions of a great democratic leader." [72] Roosevelt's policies offered viable, though imperfect, responses to Hitler's ambitions and actions.

Niebuhr believed that the Kingdom of God could not be achieved on earth; perfect love and perfect justice are impossibilities. However, Roosevelt's New Deal at least moved toward relative measures of justice, "imperfect harmonies of justice," which are not to be taken lightly. [73] "The task of political life is ... to balance the forces within a community so that on the one hand a relative justice and peace are possible and that on the other hand the dangers of tyranny and anarchy are avoided." [74] Thus, Niebuhr came to recognize the positive and pragmatic aspects of the New Deal.

Given this pragmatism, or Christian realism, Niebuhr likely would have seen the Catholic Worker Movement as unrealistic, though admirable, as a response to domestic poverty and irresponsible as a response to international politics. According to Niebuhr, Christian ideals provide an "absolute standard

---

68 Peter Maurin liked to quote a "French author" who claimed, "He who is not a Socialist at twenty has no heart, and he who is a Socialist at thirty has no head." Day, *Loaves*, 8.

69 Despite her support for the worker and labor unions, Day, too, found fault with aspects of union realities. David L. Gregory explains, "The Catholic Worker unsparingly criticized the aristocracy of organized labor, repudiated the influences of atheistic communism within labor, and thoroughly condemned the materialism of the capitalist ownership elites" (Gregory, "Transformation," 283).

70 Schlesinger, *Politics*, 143.

71 Schweitzer, "The Great Depression," 51.

72 Schlesinger, *Politics*, 143–144.

73 Niebuhr, *Love and Justice*, 29.

74 Gilkey, *On Niebuhr*, 48–49.

by which to criticize society," but not a foundation for a "responsible ethical stance."[75] While a Christian ideal of love may be operative among individuals, justice is the Christian ideal for larger collectives.[76] Niebuhr believed it was hard enough to approximate justice, let alone love "which demands more than justice."[77] In order to approximate justice, collectives must be coerced toward what is ethical in this sense. He asserted, "A simple Christian moralism counsels men to be unselfish. A profounder Christian faith must encourage men to create systems of justice which will save society and themselves from their own selfishness."[78] Thus, society has the need for systems of taxation and social security.[79]

Much of the difference between Dorothy Day and Reinhold Niebuhr is rooted in their different views of human nature, which are consequently manifested in differing emphases for ethics—for Day, care, for Niebuhr, justice. Though she clearly was aware of human sinfulness and depravity, Day importantly emphasized that we are capable of goodness. She admitted, "I can well recognize the fact that people remaining as they are, Peter's program is impossible. But it would become actual, given a people changed in heart and mind, so that they would observe the new commandment of love, or desired to." Continuing, Day explained, "[Peter] aroused in you a sense of your own capacities for work, for accomplishment. He made you feel that you and all men had great and generous hearts with which to love God. If you once recognized this fact in yourself you would expect and find it in others."[80] Coupled with a positive appraisal of the potential for goodness in us all, throughout her life, Day developed an ethic of care. June O'Connor asserts, "Day's appeal to others to share her vision was not cast in terms of justice and rights as much as it was cast in terms of dignity, respect, and love for the brother and sister whose keeper she believed she was."[81] In addition to differing theological anthropologies then, O'Connor's distinction between an ethic of care and an ethic of justice is a valuable way to contrast Day with Niebuhr.

In 1927, Niebuhr offered that "human nature is an intriguing amalgam of potential virtue and inchoate vice, in proportions sufficiently variable to

---

75 Schweitzer, "The Great Depression," 52.
76 Niebuhr, *Moral Man*, 3, 23.
77 Ibid., 75.
78 Niebuhr, *Love and Justice*, 28.
79 Niebuhr, *Love and Justice*, 28.
80 Day, *The Long Loneliness*, 171.
81 O'Connor, *Moral Vision*, 63.

prompt both trust and fear." [82] For Niebuhr, many Christians, especially Catholics, think of human nature too optimistically. While also avoiding the other extreme, evident within what he referred to as a Protestant "theory of total depravity," Niebuhr called for a Biblical view of humanity that would more realistically stake out a middle ground. We are sinful, full of pride and self-interest; however, we are also created in the image of God and redeemed by Jesus. [83] Niebuhr too would grant that we are capable of greatness, as a result of being redeemed in Jesus Christ. "[M]en are not completely blinded by self-interest or lost in this maze of historical relativity.... What remains with them is something higher—namely the law of love, which they dimly recognize as the law of their being, as the structure of human freedom, and which, in Christian faith, Christ clarifies and redefines." [84]

While we maintain this potential, however, we often fall short, according to Niebuhr. Niebuhr serves as a reminder of the limitations of ourselves and our world, yet also the importance of our possibilities, imperfect though they may be. "The social ideal of Jesus is as perfect and as impossible of attainment as is his personal ideal. But again it is an ideal that cannot be renounced completely." [85] It is because of our redemption in Jesus Christ that this ideal remains vitally important. In 1939, Niebuhr asserted, "Truth is always partly corrupted by power and interest. But it is in the margin of purity where truth transcends interest partially that civilization is built and men maintain a sane world, where there is some hope of adjusting interest to interest, life to life, and value to value." [86] This margin of purity where truth transcends partially may offer only a sliver of hope, but it is nevertheless the basis of Niebuhr's response to the Depression.

Day and Niebuhr held very similar views early in their lives. Both of them critiqued the injustices they saw as inherent in capitalism and worked to be in solidarity with the poor. As their thought developed, Day and Niebuhr diverged. Whereas Day shifted toward calls for a personalist ethic of care and love, based on the life of Jesus, Niebuhr came to recognize the value of reform as at least approximating an ethic of justice, even though imperfect. Though differing in their theological anthropologies and approaches to the Great Depression, both Day and Niebuhr serve as figures who personified our immense capacity to *strive* toward love and justice.

82 Niebuhr, *Love and Justice*, 241.
83 Ibid., 46–54.
84 Ibid., 53–54.
85 Ibid., 32.
86 Ibid., 80.

Kurt Buhring is Associate Professor and Chairperson of the Department of Religious Studies at Saint Mary's College, Notre Dame, Indiana. His teaching areas include social justice, interreligious dialogue, religion and science, and religion and politics. He is the author of *Conceptions of God, Freedom, and Ethics in African American and Jewish Theology.*

The Dorothy Option?
Dorothy, Benedict, and
the Future of the Church

Joshua D. Brumfield

After scandalous social events like race riots, school shootings, and banker bailouts Grandma would have been likely to quip, "the world is going to hell in a handbasket." The great philosopher Alasdair MacIntyre might agree. We are now experiencing the symptoms and fruits of life "After Virtue." MacIntyre famously concluded his opus with a call for a new "—doubtless very different—St. Benedict."[1] Journalist Rod Dreher has lately popularized this call as the "Benedict Option,"[2] which places its hope in the foundation of stable and local communities, not only to sustain authentic Christian communion but also to evangelize the world precisely through that communion.

Here I argue for something like what Mark Gordon has termed a "Dorothy Option."[3] I contend the Catholic Worker movement as envisioned by Peter Maurin and Dorothy Day provides a model for living the relation between communion and mission, a model which, deeply influenced by St. Benedict's own response to the problems of his day, might be an effective tool to challenge "this filthy rotten system," to enable the Church once again to be a dynamic social force for good in the world. To this end, I shall first outline the parallels between St. Benedict's model and Dorothy's approach. Second, I will explore how the

---

1   Alasdair MacIntyre, *After Virtue: a Study in Moral Theory* (Notre Dame, Indiana: University of Notre Dame, 2007), 263.

2   MacIntrye's call has been popularized as the "Benedict Option" by Rod Dreher in "Benedict Option: a medieval model inspires Christian communities today," *The American Conservative*, Dec. 12, 2013. Accessed at http://www.theamericanconservative.com/articles/benedict-option/.

3   Mark Gordon, "Catholic Citizenship and the 'Dorothy Option,'" *Vox Nova*, June 17, 2011. Accessed at http://vox-nova.com/2011/06/17/catholic-citizenship-and-the-dorothy-option-a-guest-post-by-mark-gordon/.

Dorothy option, like monasteries of old, can provide an appropriate and needed image for the future of the Church in its attempts to evangelize this secular age.

1. St. Benedict's Option

First, St. Benedict's response to his experience of the corruption and moral decay of Rome—his retreat to hermetic life—reveals that he saw the church as a society standing in contrast to "the world." He is a man "who, in an age of dissipation and decadence, immersed himself in the uttermost solitude. Then, after all the purification he had to undergo, he succeeded in rising again to the light. ... where he assembled the forces from which a new world was formed."[4] Thus, in response to the debauchery of Rome, he did not seek to find the movement of the Spirit active within crumbling Roman society. Rather, he withdrew to the desert turning to the Lord. The original monastic impulse was to be counter-cultural, to separate oneself from the distractions of the world in order to be single-mindedly devoted to God.

This withdrawal is not mere escape, but retreat for purification and formation. There must be time and space for the development of the common unity that makes a community. And in order for Christian communities to function as the leavening of society as did the monasteries of old, they must be constituted of persons possessing the joy, freedom, and peace of having encountered Christ. Only thus are persons or communities ennobled eloquently to bear witness to the joy of the gospel. In other words, these communities must be a space, a people, in whom others can encounter and experience their shared life as convincing and attractive. But before they can be encountered, they must actually share and possess that common unity which makes a community. If that common unity is developed, if there is the proper communal formation, the community, precisely "through their persuasive capacity and their joy" can become that urgently needed "convincing model of life."[5]

Secondly, since St. Benedict realized this need, in forming his monasteries he emphasized liturgical formation and personal conversion. The first word of Benedict's Rule is "listen;" from the start, he exhorted his monks first to be attentive to God's Word. Benedict attempted to encourage radical conversion to Christ through prayer and spiritual reading. This life of listening ordered by the

---

4 Joseph Ratzinger, *God and the World: a Conversation with Peter Seewald* (San Francisco: Ignatius, 2002), 392.

5 Joseph Ratzinger, *Without Roots: the West, Relativism, Christianity, Islam* (New York: Basic Books, 2006), 121.

divine office and centered on work, prayer, and hospitality cultivated humility, generosity, and obedience in the monks and helped them both to acquire a thoroughly biblical imagination and to develop virtuous habits grounded in service to the Lord. The monasteries themselves offered a setting where God's Word could more easily be heard and lived. This shared life organically developed into a rich biblically-based culture. Benedict thought that praising God was the best medicine for a depraved and poverty-stricken world; history seems to indicate he was correct.

Third, the radical orientation to Christ demanded by the Rule implies the aforementioned counter-cultural approach to the church's relationship to the world. It was precisely because monks lived and breathed in this liturgical milieu that they were able to bring Christ to the Western world, which happened slowly, organically, as it were. Over time monasteries became centers of learning particularly important during the Middle Ages. The primary goal was not to minister to the wider church or to evangelize, but to establish a community of Christians devoted to helping each other live out the gospel and to offering hospitality to any who needed it. Thus they laid the communal and liturgical roots for what would become Christian Europe. And they did this precisely through their hospitality, their labor, and their prayer.

Dorothy once quoted John Henry Newman's description of the patient, hope-filled, world-restoring work of Benedict and his monks:

> [Benedict] found the world, physical and social, in ruins, and his mission was to restore it in the way, not of science, but of nature, not as if setting about to do it, nor professing to do it, by any set time or by any rare specific or by any series of strokes, but so quietly, patiently, gradually, that often, till the work was done, it was not known to be doing. It was a restoration rather than a visitation, correction, or conversion. The new world which he helped to create was a growth rather than a structure. Silent men were observed about the country, or discovered in the forest, digging, clearing, and building; and other silent men, men not seen, were sitting in the cold cloister, trying their eyes, and keeping their attention on the stretch, while they painfully deciphered and copied and re-copied the manuscripts which they had saved. There was no one that 'contended or cried out,' or drew attention to what was going on; but by degrees the woody swamp became a her-

mitage, a religious house, a farm, an abbey, a village, a seminary, a school of learning, and a city. Roads and bridges connected it with other abbeys and cities, which had similarly grown up; and what the haughty Alaric or fierce Attila had broken to pieces, these patient meditative men had brought together and made to live again.[6]

It is this Benedictine model which Joseph Ratzinger had in mind when he argued that "throughout the great upheavals of history [monasticism] has continued to be the indispensable bearer not only of cultural continuity but above all of fundamental religious and moral values, the ultimate guidance of humankind. As a pre-political and supra-political force, monasticism was also the harbinger of ever welcome and necessary rebirths of culture and civilization."[7] The presence of this "force" demands authentic Christian community to possess a public character. Put another way, ecclesial communities cannot bear fruit if they are merely withdrawn minorities. After all, the Quakers and Amish, despite their fervent faith and consistent form of life, do not qualify as "fruitful" in this sense. They have not evangelized American society as any "options" for the Church of the future must do.

Alasdair MacIntyre was right. The Church and world of today are in need of a new, doubtless very different St. Benedict to model for the Church how to bring stability, unity, peace, and justice to the world—how to bring Christ to world. I think the model developed by Dorothy Day and Peter Maurin might be just what is needed today.

2. Dorothy's Benedictinism

Dorothy Day was a Benedictine Oblate.[8] Through Peter Maurin and others, she and the Catholic Worker Movement were deeply influenced by the monastic tradition. St. Benedict's example, as I have summarized it, emphasizes the

6   John Henry Newman, "Mission of St. Benedict," in *Newman Reader—Works of John Henry Newman*, (National Institute for Newman Studies, 2007). Accessed online at http://www.newmanreader.org/works /historical/volume2/benedictine/mission.html. Dorothy quotes this passage in "Monte Cassino," *The Catholic Worker*, March 1944, pages 4–5. Accessed at: http://www.catholicworker.org/dorothyday/Reprint2.cfm?TextID=943.

7   Ratzinger, *Without Roots*, 55.

8   Cf. *The Catholic Worker*, June 1943: "I was converted to being a [Benedictine] oblate by reading and re-reading the Desert Fathers." Accessed at http://dorothyday.catholicworker.org/articles/392.html.

need to 1) withdraw from society 2) so as to be liturgically formed as a community 3) for the purpose of being a concrete people in whom God can be encountered in the world. Let us now see how this might be manifest in the "Dorothy option."

First, like St. Benedict, Dorothy and the early Catholic Workers also recognized the wisdom of the monastic impulse to withdraw from the world. In February of 1944 she wrote:

> In time of chaos and persecution, men escape to the desert. One of the Fathers of the Desert, Abbot Allois, said, "A man cannot find true repose or satisfaction in this life unless he reckons that there is only God and himself in the world." That's personalism. On the other hand, "With our neighbor," St. Anthony says, "is life and death." He was another desert father, and he was a communitarian.... Then St. Benedict came along and his rule is still being used by tens of thousands of monks all over the world. This rule ... is still animating the lives of men. And it was a rule, written not for priests, but for laymen. ... [W]hy cannot it be used by the family?[9]

Dorothy recognized the need to escape to the desert, just as Jesus did before the dawn of his public ministry, to be alone with God. She recognized that this Rule, this way, is not reserved to the clergy. It can be practiced by the layman, by the family, by the farming commune or hospitality house.

Of course, the skeptic posing as a realist might ask whether an escape to the desert is likely to effect a world so saturated by media and technology, individualism and capitalism. Yet, even then, before TV was accessible and before the internet and smart phones existed, Dorothy recognized the need for consistent retreat. This is why she attended "The Retreat," given by Fr. Lacouture and others, over twenty times, arranging to have it offered at Worker houses and farms so that "the spirituality of the retreat would be rooted in all those associated with the Catholic Worker movement."[10] As Dorothy explained it, "To us the retreat was the good news. We made it as often as we could, and refreshed our-

---

9   Dorothy Day, "Farming Communes," *The Catholic Worker*, February, 1944, pages 1 and 8. Accessed at http://dorothyday.catholicworker.org/articles/149.html.

10   Mark and Louise Zwick, *The Catholic Worker Movement: Intellectual and Spiritual Origins*, (Mahwah, New Jersey: Paulist, 2005), 235.

selves with days of recollection."[11] The Retreat taught them detachment. It gave them the space, the silence, to do what St. Benedict commands in the first word of his *Rule*: Listen![12] Accordingly, like Benedict she emphasized the importance of stepping back from the world in order to serve those in it.

Second, St. Benedict instituted early forms of the Divine Office and suggested *lectio divina* to help his monks because he recognized that the Christian dynamism needed to change the world could be received only from Christ in the liturgy. Dorothy and Peter, influenced as they were by another Benedictine, Virgil Michel, also recognized the link between the liturgical life and the renewal of the world. For Michel, "The liturgy is the ordinary school of the development of the true Christian, and the very qualities and outlook it develops in him are also those that make for the best realization of a genuine Christian culture."[13] Thus it should come as no surprise that Dorothy quoted him as having concluded, "The liturgy is the indispensable basis of social regeneration."[14] Paraphrasing Augustine, one might say the eucharistic liturgy both makes the Church and demands Christians "be what they see" when they receive the Eucharist. It demands that they, that we, become His flesh for the life of the world. This is true worship. As is attested by one of his Easy Essays, Peter Maurin's view was not much different. He wrote:

> The central act of devotional life
> in the Catholic Church
> is the Holy Sacrifice of the Mass.
> The Sacrifice of the Mass
> is the unbloody repetition
> of the Sacrifice of the Cross.
> On the Cross of Calvary
> Christ gave His life to redeem the world.
> The life of Christ was a life of sacrifice.
> The life of a Christian must be
> a life of sacrifice.
> We cannot imitate the sacrifice of Christ

11 Dorothy Day, *The Long Loneliness*, (San Francisco: Harper and Row, 1997), 259 and 263.

12 St. Benedict, *Rule of Benedict*, Prologue.

13 Mark and Louise Zwick, *The Catholic Worker Movement*, 59, n. 4, quoting Virgil Michel, "Christian Culture" in *Oratre Fratres* 13 (1939), 303.

14 Dorothy Day, "Liturgy and Sociology," *The Catholic Worker*, December 1935, 4. Accessed at http://dorothyday.catholicworker.org/articles/16.html.

> on Calvary
> by trying to get all we can.
> We can only imitate the sacrifice of Christ
> on Calvary
> by trying to give all we can. [15]

This understanding of the intrinsic link between liturgy and life, Eucharist and mission, is why Dorothy admits that "the Liturgical movement has meant everything to the Catholic Worker from its very beginning. The Mass was the center of our lives." [16] And why shouldn't it be? After all, "In the Liturgy we have the means to teach Catholics, thrown apart by Individualism into snobbery, apathy, prejudice, blind unreason, that they are members of one body and that 'an injury to one is an injury to all.'" [17] Indeed the Church's response and the Catholic Worker's response to the diseases of this secular age must come from the liturgy, from Christ in the Eucharist. Like Benedict, Dorothy realized here is the dynamite of the Church, and through this liturgical formation, we receive the weapons of peace and love needed to bring about God's revolution.

Third, for Dorothy, Peter, and the early Catholic Worker Movement, making the Retreat, reciting prayers, and living a version of monastic life was all ordered towards loving God by loving neighbor, which meant changing the social order via the Works of Mercy. Believing the "central act of devotional life" to be the sacrifice of Christ which must be imitated by "giving all we can," Dorothy argued "that it is very necessary to connect the liturgical movement with the social justice movement. Each one gives vitality to the other." [18] The Retreat helped the Catholic Workers to understand the sacramental nature of their daily sacrifices. Dorothy explains, "[Lacouture's] teaching of the love of God so aroused our love in turn, that a sense of the sacramentality of life was restored for us, and a new meaning was given to our lives." [19] This sacramentality of life ought not to be interpreted as implying love in the abstract, which may lack the

---

15 Peter Maurin, quoted in Zwicks, *The Catholic Worker Movement*, 63.

16 Dorothy Day, "On Pilgrimage—March 1966," *The Catholic Worker*, March 1966, 1, 2, 6, 8. Accessed at: http://dorothyday.catholicworker.org/articles/249.html.

17 Dorothy Day, "Liturgy and Sociology," *The Catholic Worker*, December 1935, 4. Accessed online at: http://dorothyday.catholicworker.org/articles/16.html.

18 Dorothy Day to Fr. Henry Borgmann, Dec 30, 1933, The Catholic Worker Papers, W-2, Marquette University Archives. Quoted by Mark and Louise Zwick, 60.

19 Day, "Obituary for Fr. Onesimus Lacouture, SJ," *The Catholic Worker*, Dec 12, 1951. Quoted by Mark and Louise Zwick, 235.

concrete action demanded by the gospel, by any truly human encounter. After all, Dorothy would often quote from Dostoyevsky "Father Zossima's unforgettable words 'Love in practice is a harsh and dreadful thing compared to love in dreams.'" To this Dorothy asks,

> What does the modern world know of love, with its divorces, with its light touching of the surface of love? It has never reached down into the depths, to the misery and pain and glory of love which endures to death and beyond it. We have not yet begun to learn about love. Now is the time to begin, to start afresh, to use this divine weapon. [20]

Therefore, just as the common unity of Benedictine monasteries once changed the world through hospitality, so the Dorothy option can show the Church how to change the world through love in practice, harsh and dreadful as it may be.

3. The Dorothy Option in the Age of Pope Francis

In April of 2015, Pope Francis promulgated *Misericordiae Vultus*, [21] announcing the extraordinary jubilee of mercy which began on December 8th of the same year. Quoting Saint John Paul II, he explains,

> The present-day mentality, more perhaps than that of people in the past, seems opposed to a God of mercy, and ... tends to exclude from life and ... from the human heart the very idea of mercy. The word and the concept of 'mercy' seem to cause uneasiness in man, who, thanks to the enormous development of science and technology ... has become the master of the earth and has subdued and dominated it (cf. Gen. 1:28). This dominion over the earth, sometimes understood in a one-sided and superficial way, seems to have no room for mercy. [22]

---

20 Day, "Love is the Measure" *The Catholic Worker*, June 1946, 2. Accessed at http://dorothy-day.catholicworker.org/articles/425-plain.htm.

21 Pope Francis, *Misericordiae Vultus, Bull of Indiction of the Extraordinary Jubilee of Mercy,* (Rome, April 11, 2015). Accessed at http://w2.vatican.va/content/francesco/en/apost_letters/documents/papa-francesco_bolla_20150411_misericordiae-vultus.html.

22 Pope Francis, *Misericordiae Vultus*, 11, quoting John Paul II, *Dives in Misericordia*, 2.

Adding to John Paul's characterization, we must admit the world is now even more technocratic. The citizens of the U.S. and the members of the Church are even more polarized by race and by politics, by economics and ethics. In this clime how can a Dorothy option bear witness to a fulfillment of the Church's mission of mercy? Can the Dorothy option be useful here? Pope Francis seems to think so. [23]

Without in any way denigrating the great work and witness of any of the other new movements, I identify three aspects of the "Dorothy option" which respond to particular needs of the Church in America today and in the future, offering: 1) a withdrawal from technology and mainstream society; 2) transcendence of the standard polarized positions via radically Catholic positions; 3) a commitment to the Mystical Body of Christ lived in the Works of Mercy.

1) In light of the hegemony of modern media, one might reasonably describe secular society as a riptide which grabs persons and pulls them into the deep. We can't swim against the tide. The message is too ubiquitous; the tide too strong. We'd be swept away. Rather than directly opposing it, the proper response to encountering a riptide is to swim perpendicular to the tide, to withdraw from it in order to rest, to gather one's strength before continuing one's mission. This notion of withdrawal, often perceived as a weakness of the "Benedict option," is not an example of defeatism, quietism, or escapism. It is withdrawal for the purpose of mission.

Dorothy, Peter, and others who attended the retreat recognized the danger of what was then the great technological distraction of the age, the radio. Their avoidance of the radio and other technologies allowed Dorothy and Peter to give witness to the importance and the power of withdrawal for the sake of silence, and formation. Dorothy recognized

> If we do not keep indoctrinating, we lose the vision. And if we lose the vision, we become merely philanthropists, doling out palliatives. The vision is this. We are working for "a new heaven and new *earth*, wherein justice dwelleth." We are trying to say with action, "Thy will be done on *earth* as it is in heaven."

---

23   Pope Francis, "Visit to the Joint Session of the United States Congress," *Apostolic Journey of His Holiness Pope Francis to Cuba, to the United States of America, and visit to the United Nations Headquarters*, (Washington, D.C.: Vatican, September 24, 2015). Accessed online at https://w2.vatican.va/content/francesco/en/speeches/2015/september/documents/papa-francesco_20150924_usa-us-congress.html.

We are working for a Christian social order. [24]

Many are now so easily drugged into evil indifference by opiates and alcohol, but more often by soft cushions, excessive consumption, and glowing screens. Dorothy and Peter recognized the need to withdraw for continual re-formation. As Dorothy admitted,

> The problem is gigantic. Throughout the world there is homelessness, famine, fear, and war, and the threat of war. We live in a time of gigantic evil. It is hopeless to think of combating it by any means than that of sanctity. To think of overcoming such evil by material means, by alleviations, by changes in the social order only—all this is utterly hopeless. [25]

A Dorothy option can both remind us of the need for withdrawal from internet opiates and evil economics in order to be formed in the Mystical Body and at the same time call us out of our indifference to the only radical activism which can confront our world, that activism based in sanctity.

2) Dorothy's and Peter's integration of monastic and liturgical piety with personalistic radicalism allows them to transcend the many polarizations of modern society. They do not neatly fit labels or stereotypes. The now common race riots, torturous imprisonments, and capitalist cronyism make it even clearer than it was when Dorothy said: "People are just beginning to realize how deep-seated the evil is. This is why we must be Catholic Radicals, we must get down to the roots." [26] This withdrawal from the mainstream of society integrated with rootedness in the dynamism of the Gospel places Catholic workers outside the binary cultural categories and empowers them, empowers us, to bridge the gap and to be a force for unity in a splintering world. Just as their advocacy of Distributism placed them outside of both capitalism and communism, so today a "Dorothy option" can show Christians how to offer a third way to a troubled world and how to find the common unity which must be the basis of Christian community.

---

24 Dorothy Day, "Aims and Purposes," in *Modern Spiritual Masters: writings on contemplation and compassion*, ed. Robert Ellsberg, (Maryknoll, New York: Orbis, 2011), 169.

25 Dorothy Day as quoted in William D. Miller, *Dorothy Day: A Biography* (San Francisco: Harper and Row, 1982), 432.

26 Dorothy Day quoting Peter Maurin in "Peter Maurin 1877–1977," in *The Catholic Worker*, May 1977, 1, 9.

3) Perhaps the element of a Dorothy option which most sets it apart as an appropriate image for being Church in the age of Pope Francis is Dorothy's commitment to the Mystical Body of Christ lived in the Works of Mercy. These were the wick with which they aimed to blow the Church's dynamite, enabling it to again become the dominant social dynamic force. Michael Baxter explained, "The social theory to which Maurin referred in his essay was dynamic because it possessed an explosive ingredient: Jesus Christ. The image of dynamite jolts the listener/reader into imagining Christ and the Church in temporal rather than in purely spiritual terms. ... In contrast to standard Catholic social theory, [Maurin's] social theory was, in a word, ecclesial." [27] Thus this ecclesial social theory wasn't merely a theory; Peter and Dorothy shared too sacramental a view of reality to allow the words, the form, to be left unaccompanied by the requisite matter. They put this theory into action. After all, as Dorothy explained,

> We consider the spiritual and corporal Works of Mercy and the following of Christ to be the best revolutionary technique and a means for changing the social order rather than perpetuating it. Did not thousands of monasteries, with their hospitality, change the entire social patterns of their day? [28]

Pope Francis shares this view and calls the Church to respond. He admits, "Perhaps we have long since forgotten how to show and live the way of mercy ..., we must admit that the practice of mercy is waning in the wider culture. ... The time has come for the Church to take up the joyful call to mercy once more. It is time to return to the basics and to bear the weaknesses and struggles of our brothers and sisters. Mercy is the force that reawakens us to new life and instils in us the courage to look to the future with hope." [29] The world needs to see the mercy of God in the Church. The Church needs the Dorothy option to again show it how to live the way of mercy, so that, as Pope Francis adds "we may become a more effective sign of the Father's action in our lives." [30] The dynamite

---

27 Michael Baxter, "'Blowing the Dynamite of the Church': Catholic Radicalism," in *Dorothy Day and the Catholic Worker Movement: centenary essays*, ed. William Thorn, Phillip Runkel, and Susan Mountin, (Milwaukee, Wisconsin: Marquette University Press), 79–94, at 84.

28 Dorothy Day, "Catholic Worker Ideas on Hospitality," *The Catholic Worker*, May 1940, 10. Accessed at http://dorothyday.catholicworker.org/articles/358.html.

29 Pope Francis, *Misericordiae vultus*, 10.

30 Ibid., 3.

cannot be blown if the Church's message is deemed hypocritical. Therefore, Francis continues, "it is absolutely essential for the Church and for the credibility of her message that she herself live and testify to mercy. Her language and her gestures must transmit mercy, so as to touch the hearts of all people and inspire them once more to find the road that leads to the Father." [31]

In a time when the poor are so often robbed of their dignity and responsibility by an indifferent society and a patronizingly paternal state, when the homeless are kicked off the streets, and prisons overflow, pious platitudes, eloquent speeches, multitudinous marches, and political platforms will neither fix the social order nor save souls. And so a Dorothy option can remind the Church at large, with Pope Francis, that the Works of Mercy are necessary practices for our own salvation and are prerequisites for making the Church once again a socially dynamic force. After all, Dorothy believed

> There is nothing that we can do but love, and dear God— please enlarge our hearts to love each other, to love our neighbor, to love our enemy as well as our friend. ... We are supposed to love as Christ loved ... That was the New commandment. To love to the extent of laying down our lives, dying to ourselves. To accept the least place, to sit back, to ask nothing for ourselves, to serve each other, to lay down our lives for our brothers, this is the strange upside-down teaching of the Gospel. [32]

This is the strange upside-down teaching and example of the Dorothy option. This is a powerful means for starting the right kind, the Christ-kind, of revolution. This is what a Dorothy option can contribute to the Church in the age of Francis and to the Church of the future.

Joshua D. Brumfield, Ph.D. is Visiting Professor of Theology at Our Lady of Holy Cross College in New Orleans, Louisiana.

---

31 Ibid., 12.
32 Dorothy Day, "Love is the Measure," *The Catholic Worker*, June 1946, 2. Accessed at http:// dorothyday.catholicworker.org/articles/425-plain.htm.

SOLIDARITY HALL

WISDOM + COMMUNITY

The non-profit publishing organization Solidarity Hall launched in 2013 as a group blog (www.solidarityhall.org) created by a circle of friends based in Chicago, New York, Washington D.C. and abroad.

We share a communitarian vision that includes themes of localism and an interest in new economic models while also grounded in traditional wisdom of the kind found in social theorists such as G. K. Chesterton, E. F. Schumacher, Jane Jacobs, Wendell Berry, and Dorothy Day. (Thus we are neither "left" nor "right," but both "old" and "new.")

✦

Solidarity Hall Press published its first book title in 2015, *Radically Catholic in the Age of Francis: An Anthology of Visions for the Future.* This collection featured the work of a number of younger writers — mostly but not all Catholics — and offered our sense of how the work of rebuilding American society could benefit from the social vision of the new pope, itself a mix of old and new.

The section headings are Conscience, Community, City and Church, with commentary on topic ranging from the cult of the self, kinship with the poor, and a Catholic vision of the environment to an economy of inclusion, the migrant church, and reflections on the Orthodox Church in Russia.

✦

At the beginning of 2016, Solidarity Hall has published a second book, the present one, in cooperation with the organizers of the conference of the same name, held at the University of Saint Francis last May.

Also launched in January 2016: *The Dorothy Option*, a new group blog at the Patheos website, in which we bring the ideas of Dorothy Day, Peter Maurin, and other like-minded social theorists and activists into contact with the current crisis of our common life in this country.

The themes explored here by our circle of writers include radical hospitality, community renewal, the economy of sharing, and practicing non-violence. The new blog can be found at: www.patheos.com/blogs/thedorothyoption.

Made in the USA
Middletown, DE
18 February 2016